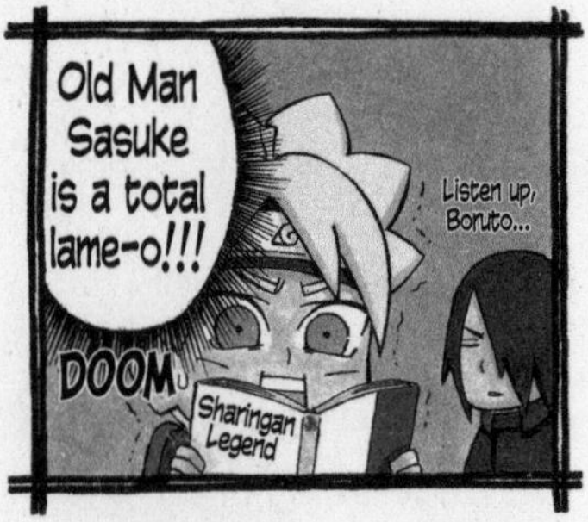
Listen up, Boruto...
Old Man Sasuke is a total lame-o!!!
DOOM
Sharingan Legend

This volume will be my last time drawing Sasuke and friends in their teen years. The thought does make me feel a little sad...but the next series will be called *Boruto: Saikyo Dash Generations*, and it will feature Boruto's generation! A much older Sasuke might appear in it too?! Look forward to it!

—Kenji Taira, 2017

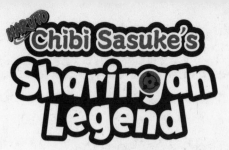

NARUTO Chibi Sasuke's Sharingan Legend

SHONEN JUMP MANGA EDITION

VOLUME 3

STORY AND ART BY KENJI TAIRA

Translation: Amanda Haley
Touch-Up Art & Lettering: Snir Aharon
Design: Yukiko Whitley
Editor: Alexis Kirsch

UCHIHA SASUKE NO SHARINGAN DEN © 2014 by Masashi Kishimoto, Kenji Taira
All rights reserved.
First published in Japan in 2014 by SHUEISHA Inc., Tokyo.
English translation rights arranged by SHUEISHA Inc.

The stories, characters and incidents mentioned in
this publication are entirely fictional.

Printed in the U.S.A.

Published by VIZ Media, LLC
P.O. Box 77010
San Francisco, CA 94107

10 9 8 7 6 5 4 3 2 1
First printing, May 2018

viz.com

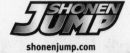
shonenjump.com

NARUTO Chibi Sasuke's
Sharingan
Legend

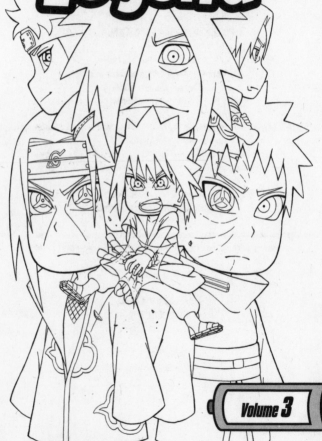

Volume 3

⬡ THE UCHIHA CLAN!!

Based on Naruto by **Masashi Kishimoto** Story and Art by **Kenji Taira**

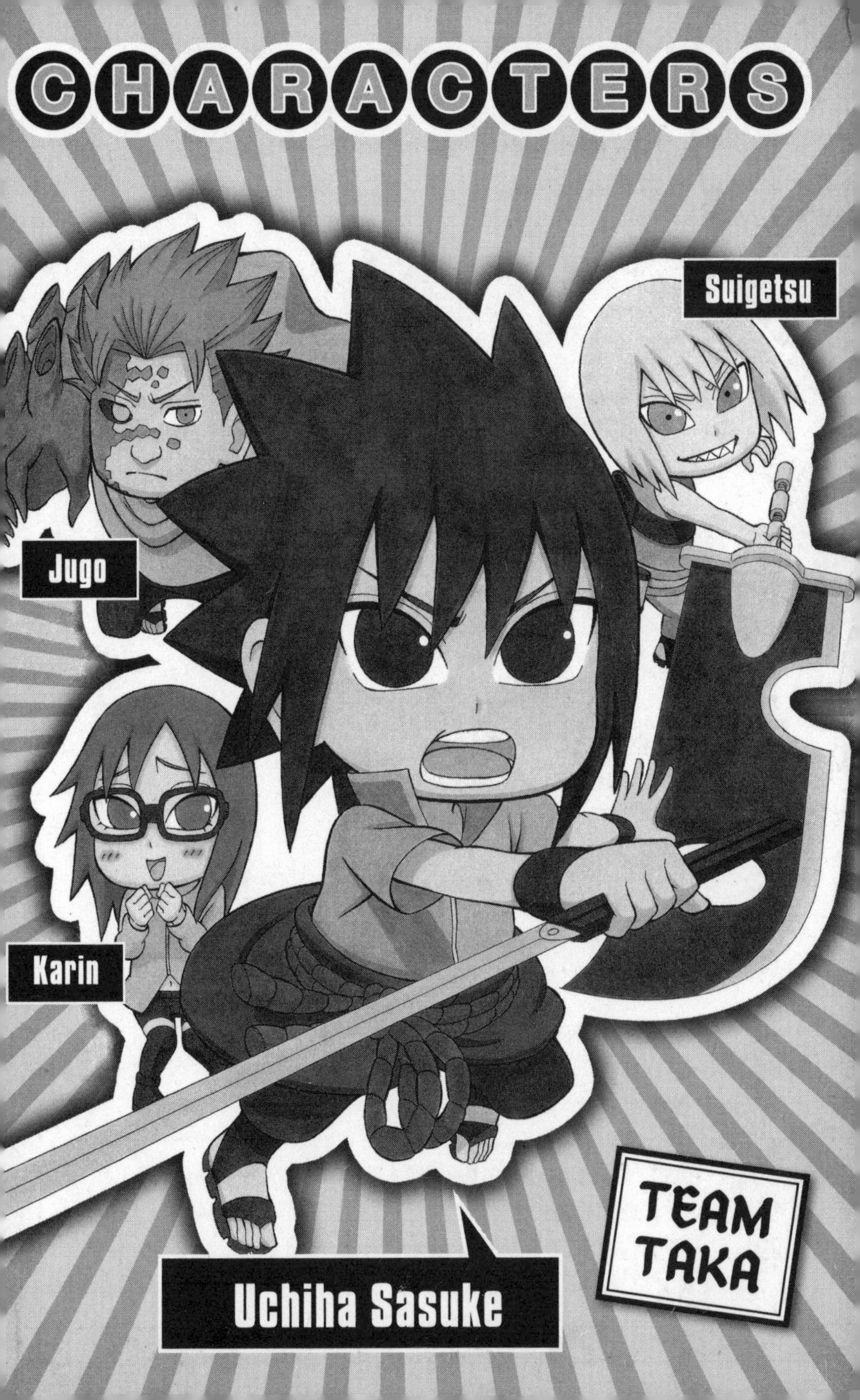
CHARACTERS
Suigetsu
Jugo
Karin
Uchiha Sasuke
TEAM TAKA

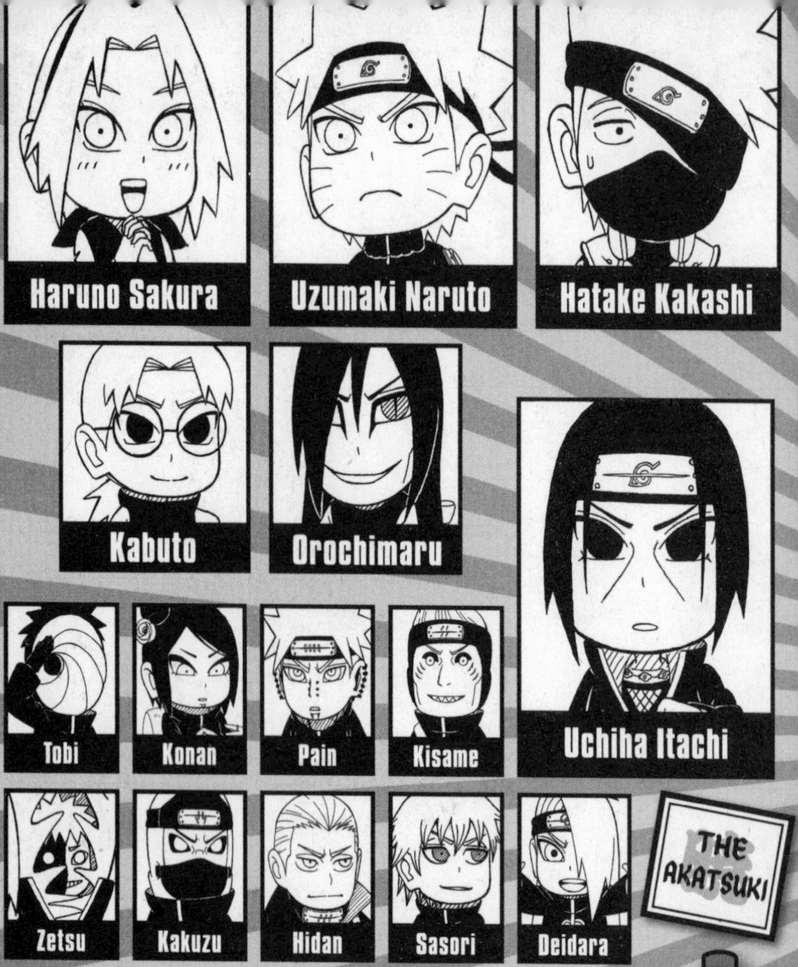
Hatake Kakashi
Uzumaki Naruto
Haruno Sakura
Uchiha Itachi
Orochimaru
Kabuto
Kisame
Pain
Konan
Tobi
THE AKATSUKI
Deidara
Sasori
Hidan
Kakuzu
Zetsu

OUR STORY

Uchiha Sasuke was once a ninja of Konohagakure Village, until he parted ways with Naruto, Sakura and the others. Now he travels as a rogue shinobi with Suigetsu, Karin and Jugo. Together, they are Team Taka. Sasuke devotes every day to the search for his big brother, Itachi. Will he ever make it to Itachi, his objective? Either way, Sasuke's long journey is bound to be eventful!

NARUTO Chibi Sasuke's
Sharingan Legend

VOL. 3
THE UCHIHA CLAN!!

CONTENTS

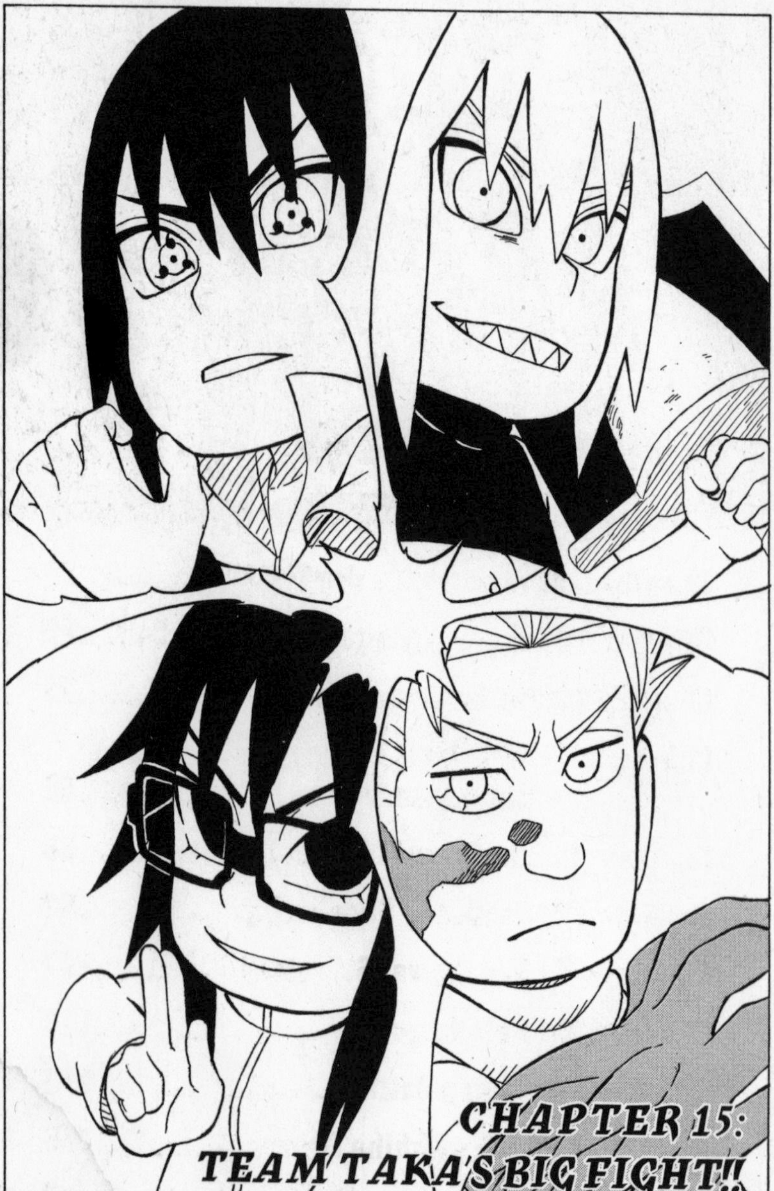
CHAPTER 15:
TEAM TAKA'S BIG FIGHT!!

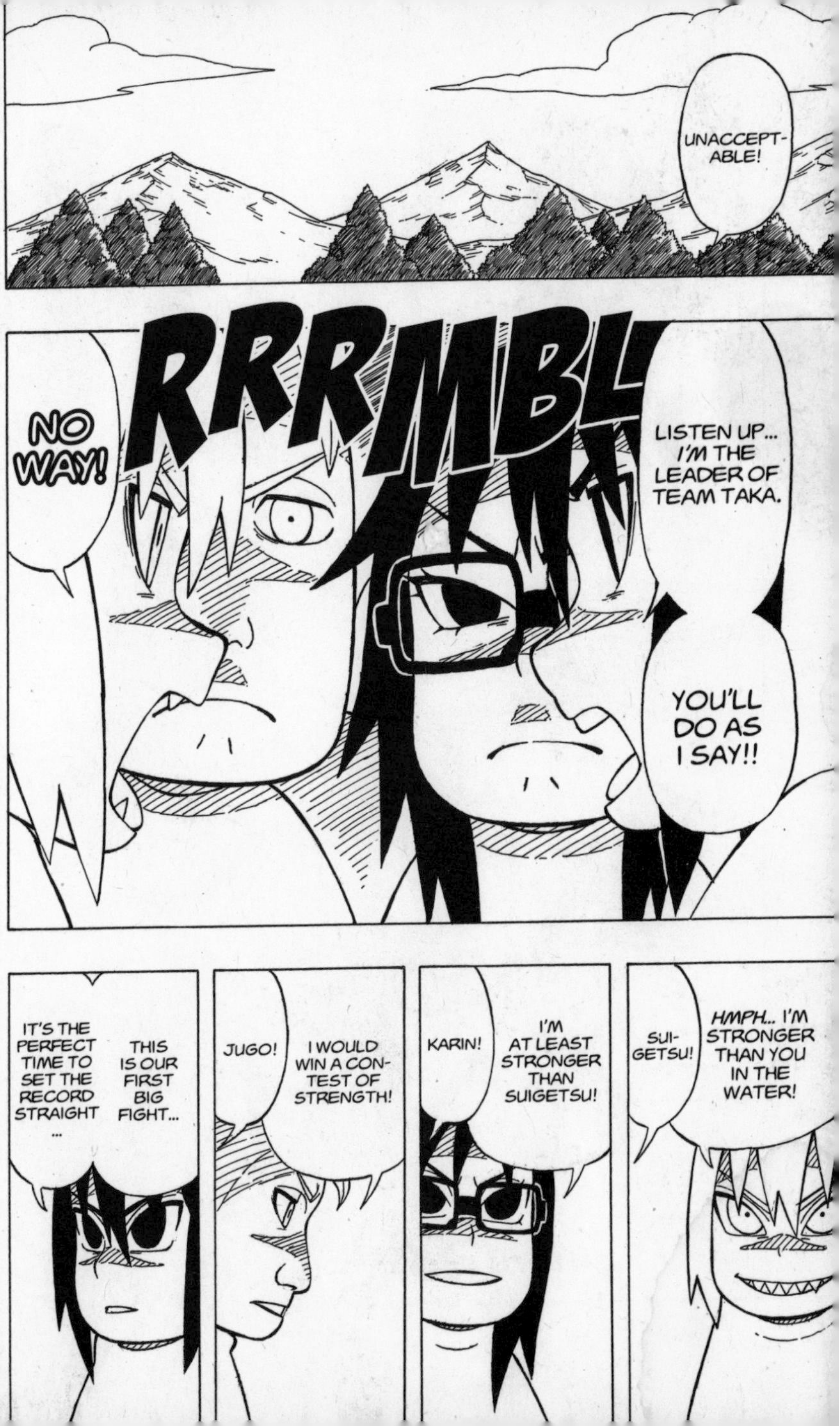
UNACCEPT-ABLE!
LISTEN UP... I'M THE LEADER OF TEAM TAKA.
YOU'LL DO AS I SAY!!
RRRMBL
NO WAY!
HMPH... I'M STRONGER THAN YOU IN THE WATER!
SUI-GETSU!
I'M AT LEAST STRONGER THAN SUIGETSU!
KARIN!
I WOULD WIN A CON-TEST OF STRENGTH!
JUGO!
THIS IS OUR FIRST BIG FIGHT...
IT'S THE PERFECT TIME TO SET THE RECORD STRAIGHT ...

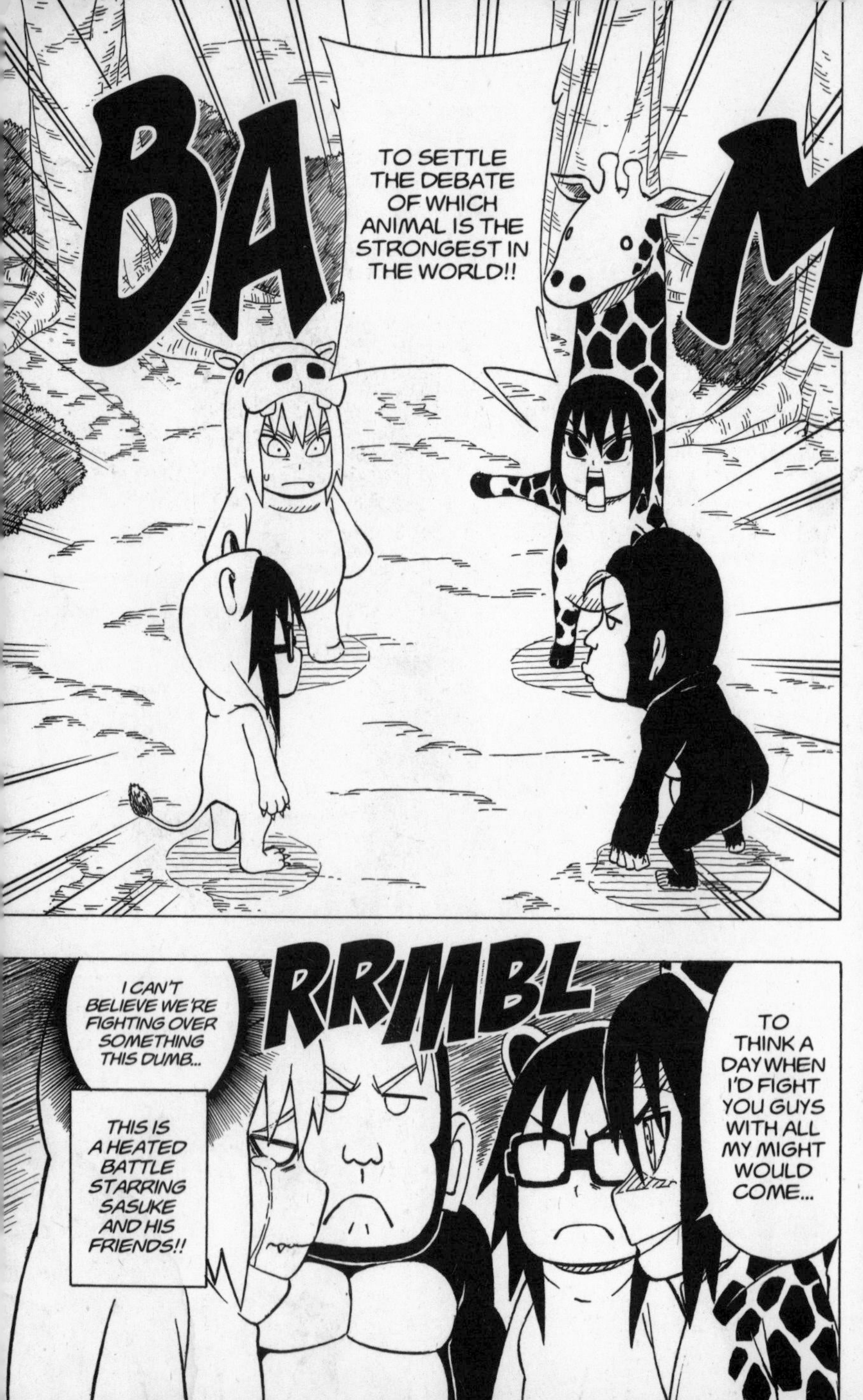
BAM
TO SETTLE THE DEBATE OF WHICH ANIMAL IS THE STRONGEST IN THE WORLD!!
TO THINK A DAY WHEN I'D FIGHT YOU GUYS WITH ALL MY MIGHT WOULD COME...
RRMBL
I CAN'T BELIEVE WE'RE FIGHTING OVER SOMETHING THIS DUMB...
THIS IS A HEATED BATTLE STARRING SASUKE AND HIS FRIENDS!!

GIRAFFE

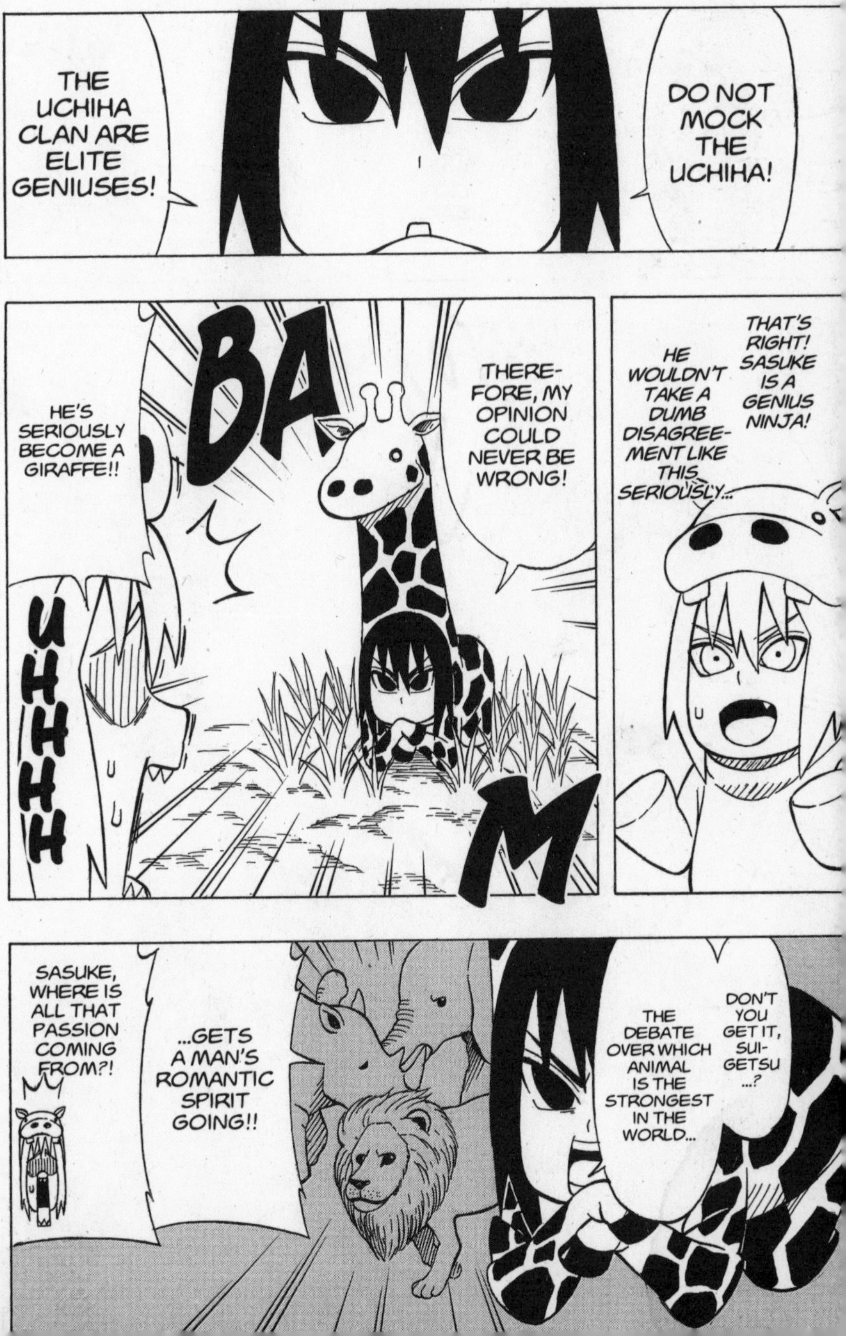
DO NOT MOCK THE UCHIHA!
THE UCHIHA CLAN ARE ELITE GENIUSES!
THAT'S RIGHT! SASUKE IS A GENIUS NINJA!
HE WOULDN'T TAKE A DUMB DISAGREEMENT LIKE THIS SERIOUSLY...
THEREFORE, MY OPINION COULD NEVER BE WRONG!
BAM
HE'S SERIOUSLY BECOME A GIRAFFE!!
UHHHHH
DON'T YOU GET IT, SUI-GETSU...?
THE DEBATE OVER WHICH ANIMAL IS THE STRONGEST IN THE WORLD...
...GETS A MAN'S ROMANTIC SPIRIT GOING!!
SASUKE, WHERE IS ALL THAT PASSION COMING FROM?!

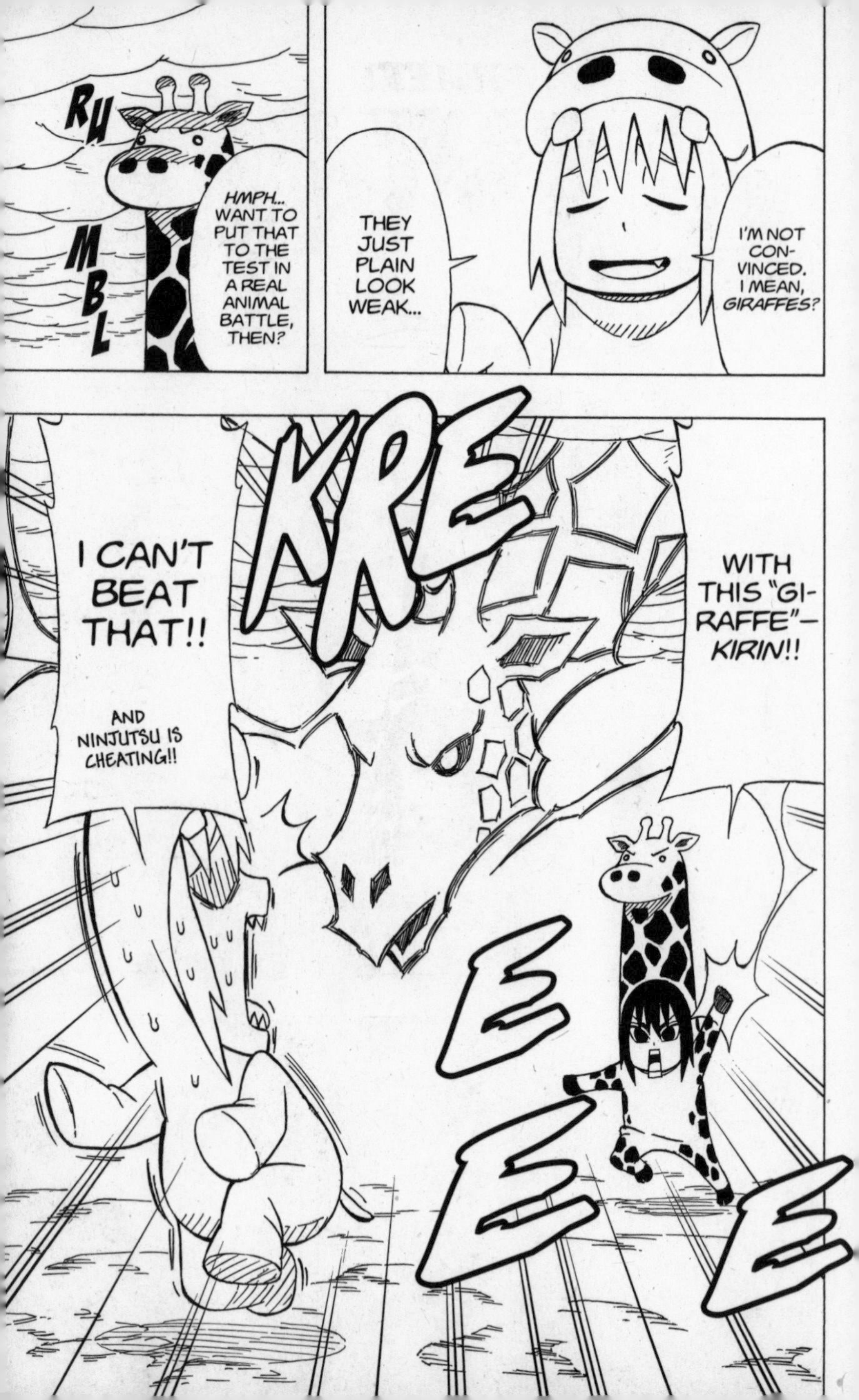
I'M NOT CONVINCED. I MEAN, GIRAFFES?
THEY JUST PLAIN LOOK WEAK...
RUMBL
HMPH... WANT TO PUT THAT TO THE TEST IN A REAL ANIMAL BATTLE, THEN?
WITH THIS "GIRAFFE"—KIRIN!!
KREEEE
I CAN'T BEAT THAT!!
AND NINJUTSU IS CHEATING!!

HIPPO

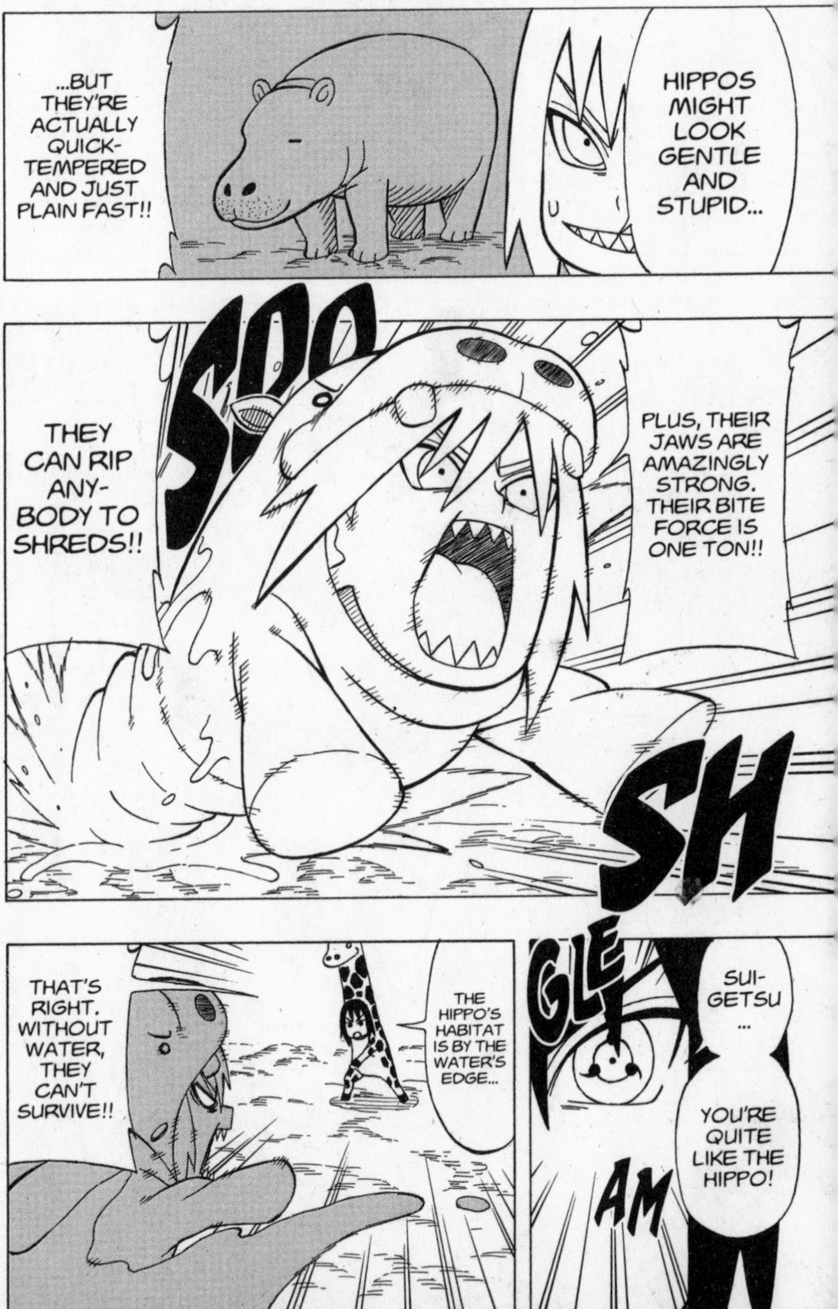
HIPPOS MIGHT LOOK GENTLE AND STUPID...
...BUT THEY'RE ACTUALLY QUICK-TEMPERED AND JUST PLAIN FAST!!
PLUS, THEIR JAWS ARE AMAZINGLY STRONG. THEIR BITE FORCE IS ONE TON!!
THEY CAN RIP ANY-BODY TO SHREDS!!
SUI-GETSU ...
YOU'RE QUITE LIKE THE HIPPO!
THE HIPPO'S HABITAT IS BY THE WATER'S EDGE...
THAT'S RIGHT. WITHOUT WATER, THEY CAN'T SURVIVE!!

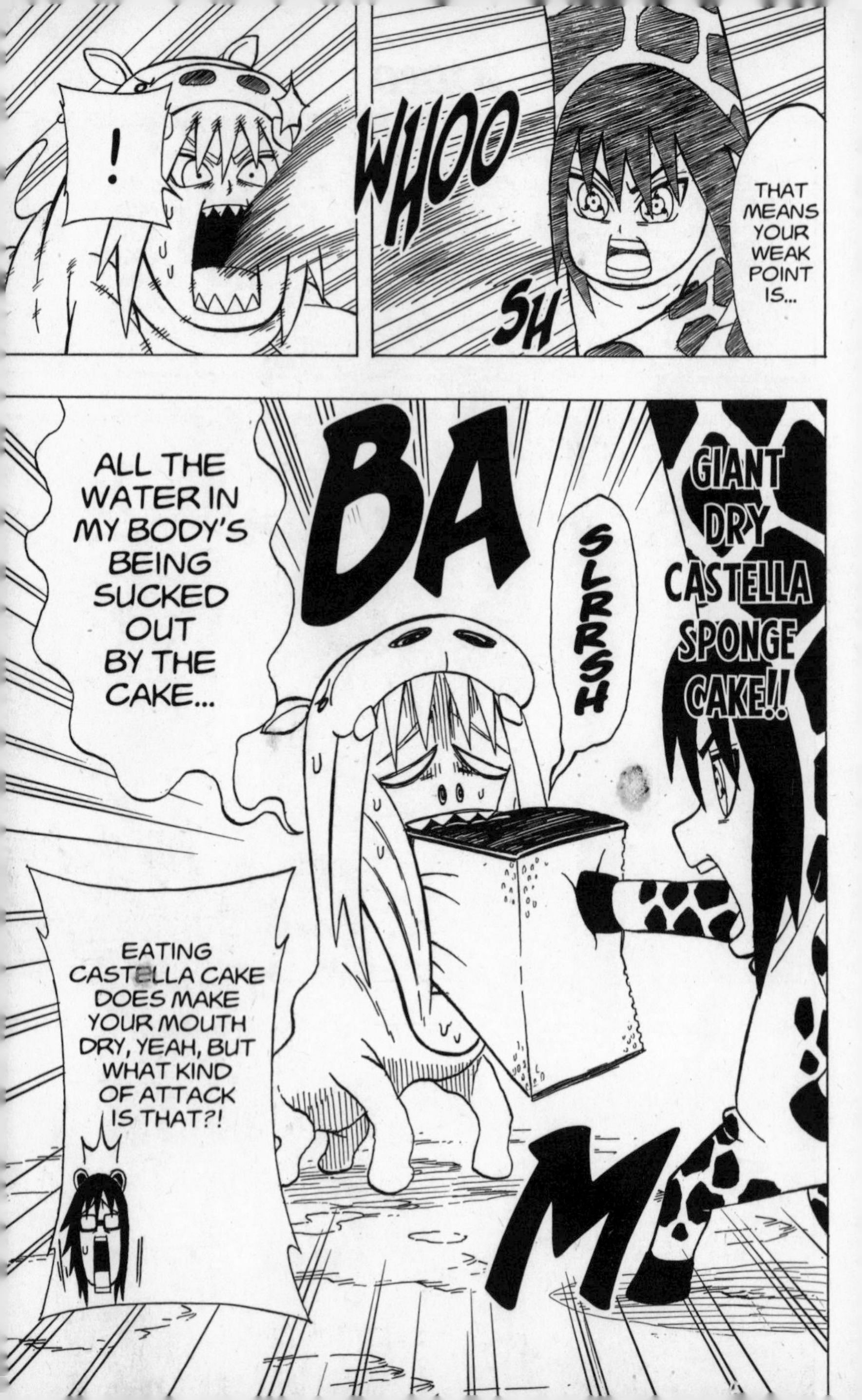
THAT MEANS YOUR WEAK POINT IS...
WHOO
SH
!
GIANT DRY CASTELLA SPONGE CAKE!!
BA
SLRRSH
ALL THE WATER IN MY BODY'S BEING SUCKED OUT BY THE CAKE...
M
EATING CASTELLA CAKE DOES MAKE YOUR MOUTH DRY, YEAH, BUT WHAT KIND OF ATTACK IS THAT?!

LION

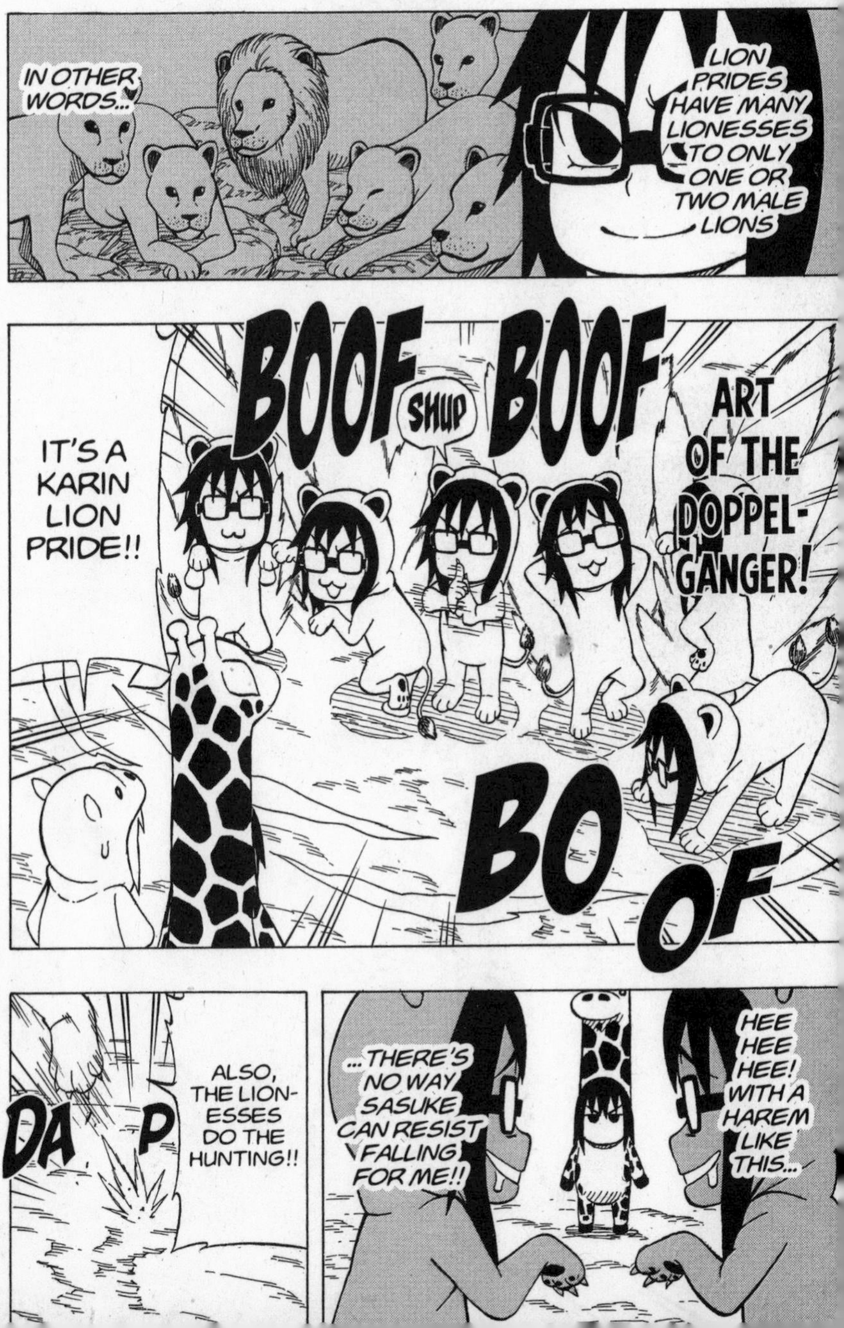

LION PRIDES HAVE MANY LIONESSES TO ONLY ONE OR TWO MALE LIONS
IN OTHER WORDS...
BOOF
SHUP
BOOF
ART OF THE DOPPEL-GANGER!
BOOF
IT'S A KARIN LION PRIDE!!
HEE HEE HEE! WITH A HAREM LIKE THIS...
...THERE'S NO WAY SASUKE CAN RESIST FALLING FOR ME!!
ALSO, THE LION-ESSES DO THE HUNTING!!
DAP

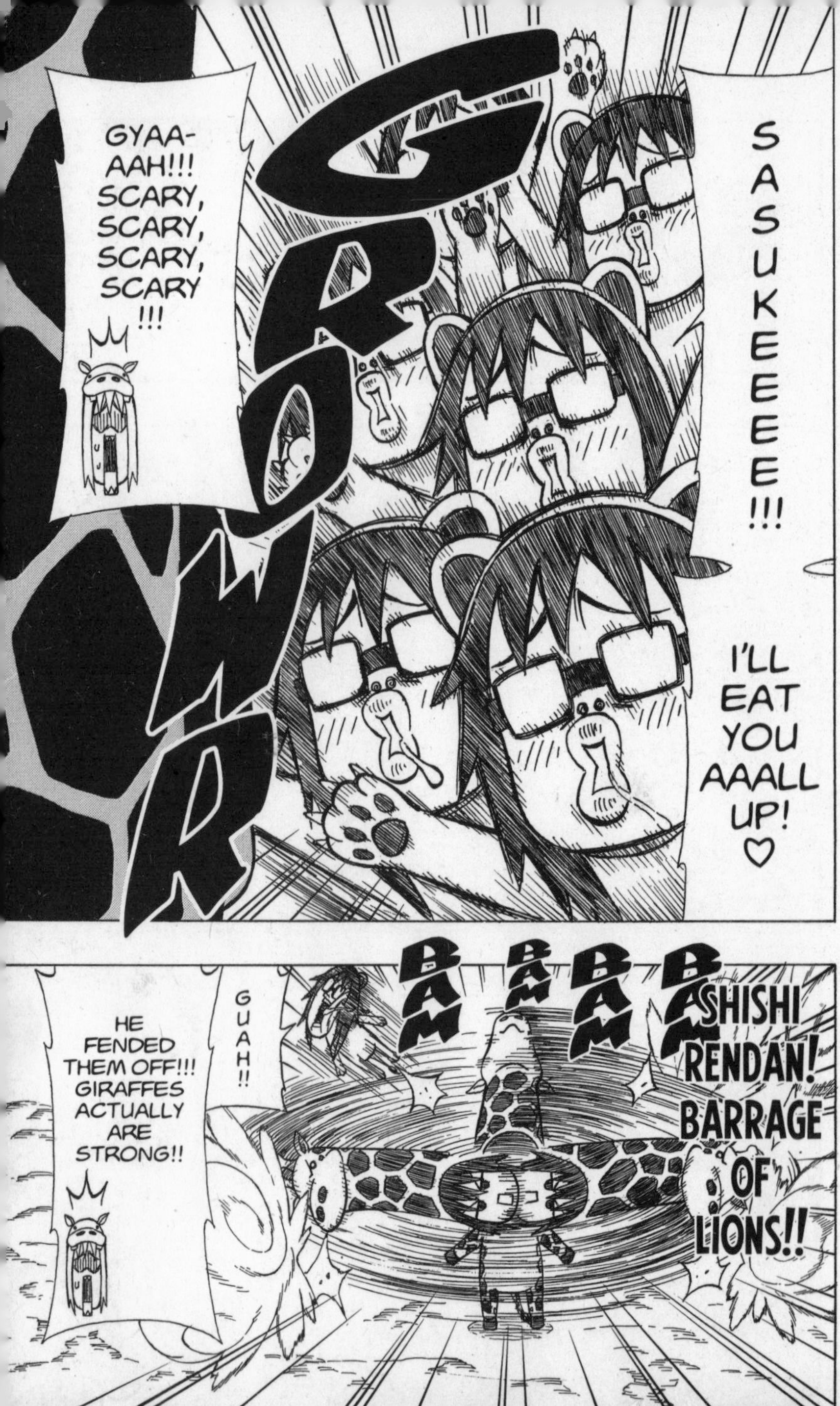
SASUKEEEE!!!
I'LL EAT YOU AAALL UP! ♡
GROWR
GYAA-AAH!!! SCARY, SCARY, SCARY, SCARY!!!
SHISHI RENDAN! BARRAGE OF LIONS!!
BAM BAM BAM BAM
GUAH!!
HE FENDED THEM OFF!!! GIRAFFES ACTUALLY ARE STRONG!!

GORILLA

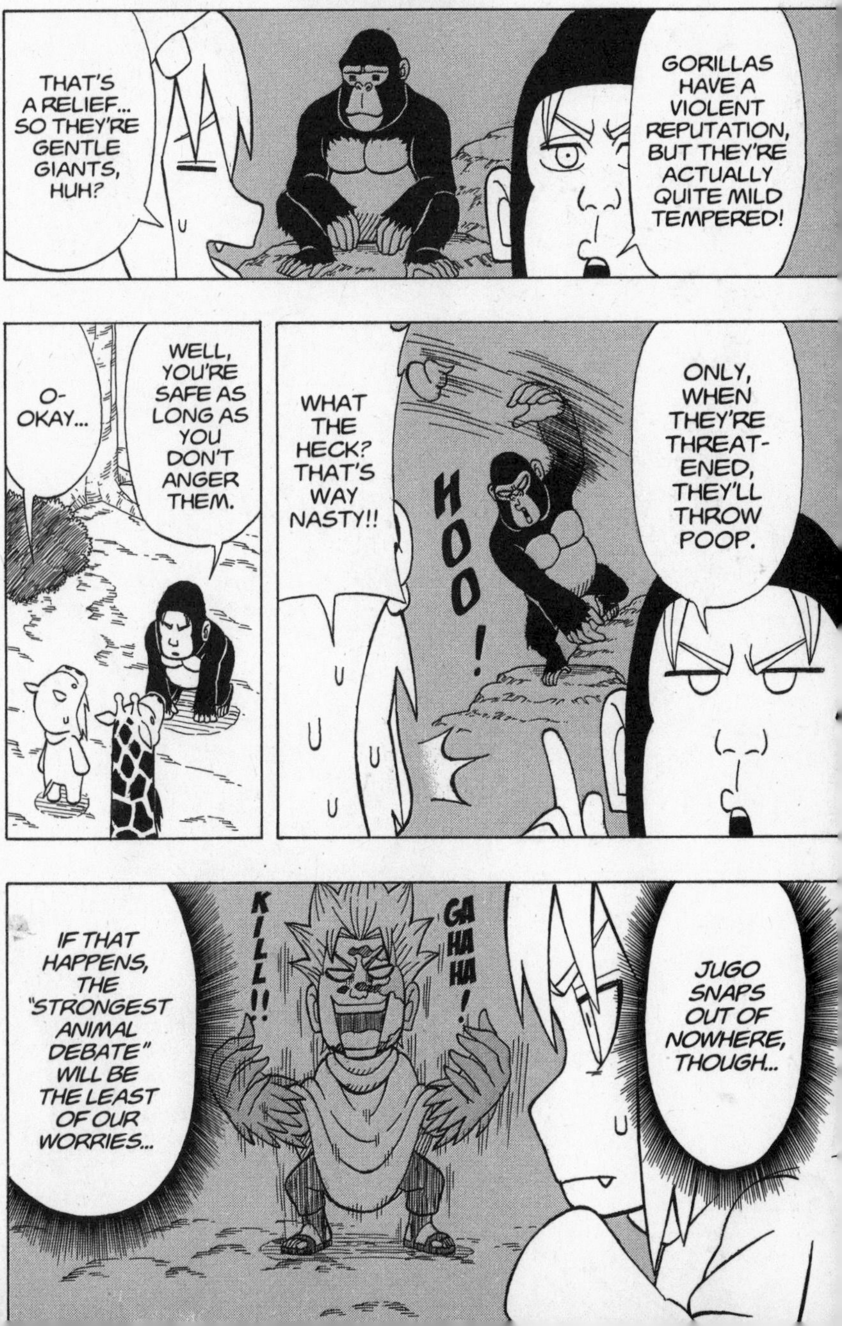

GORILLAS HAVE A VIOLENT REPUTATION, BUT THEY'RE ACTUALLY QUITE MILD TEMPERED!
THAT'S A RELIEF... SO THEY'RE GENTLE GIANTS, HUH?
ONLY, WHEN THEY'RE THREAT-ENED, THEY'LL THROW POOP.
HOO!
WHAT THE HECK? THAT'S WAY NASTY!!
WELL, YOU'RE SAFE AS LONG AS YOU DON'T ANGER THEM.
O-OKAY...
JUGO SNAPS OUT OF NOWHERE, THOUGH...
GAHAHA!
KILL!!
IF THAT HAPPENS, THE "STRONGEST ANIMAL DEBATE" WILL BE THE LEAST OF OUR WORRIES...

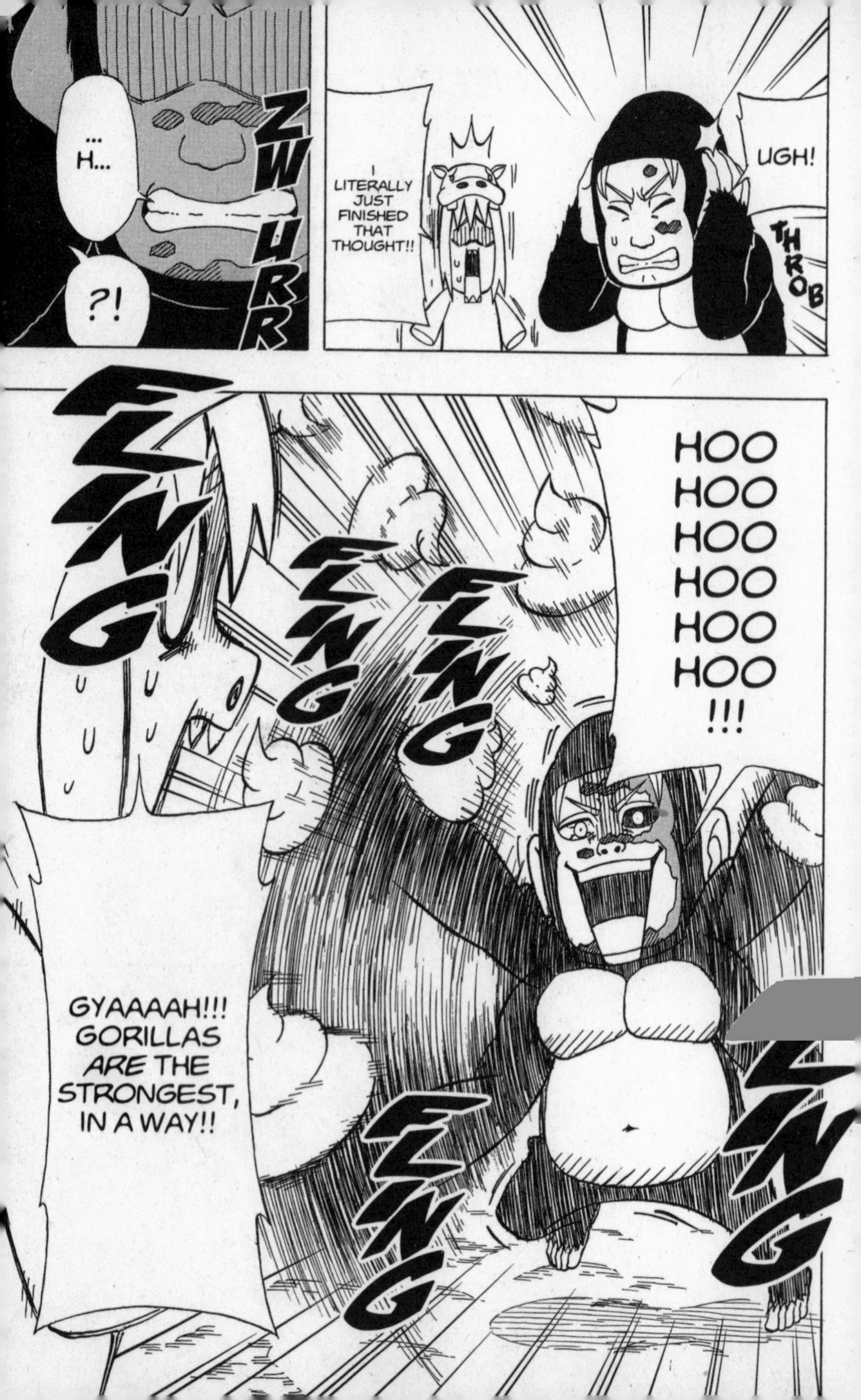
UGH!
THROB
I LITERALLY JUST FINISHED THAT THOUGHT!!
ZWURR
... H...
?!
HOO HOO HOO HOO HOO HOO !!!
FLING
FLING
FLING
FLING
GYAAAAH!!! GORILLAS ARE THE STRONGEST, IN A WAY!!

THE STRONGEST ANIMAL

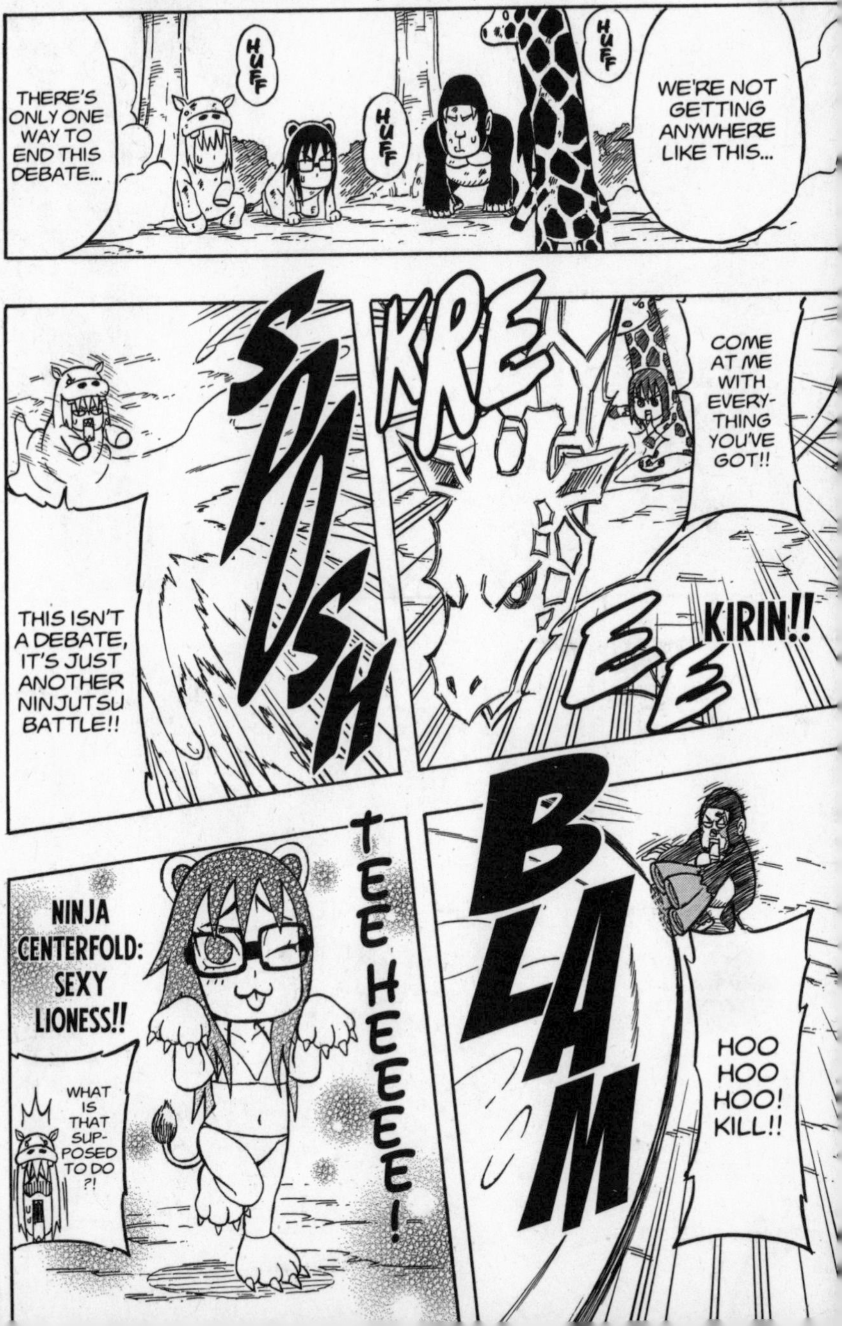
WE'RE NOT GETTING ANYWHERE LIKE THIS...
HUFF
HUFF
HUFF
THERE'S ONLY ONE WAY TO END THIS DEBATE...
COME AT ME WITH EVERY-THING YOU'VE GOT!!
KREEEE
KIRIN!!
THIS ISN'T A DEBATE, IT'S JUST ANOTHER NINJUTSU BATTLE!!
BLAM
HOO HOO HOO! KILL!!
NINJA CENTERFOLD: SEXY LIONESS!!
TEE HEEEEE!
WHAT IS THAT SUP-POSED TO DO ?!

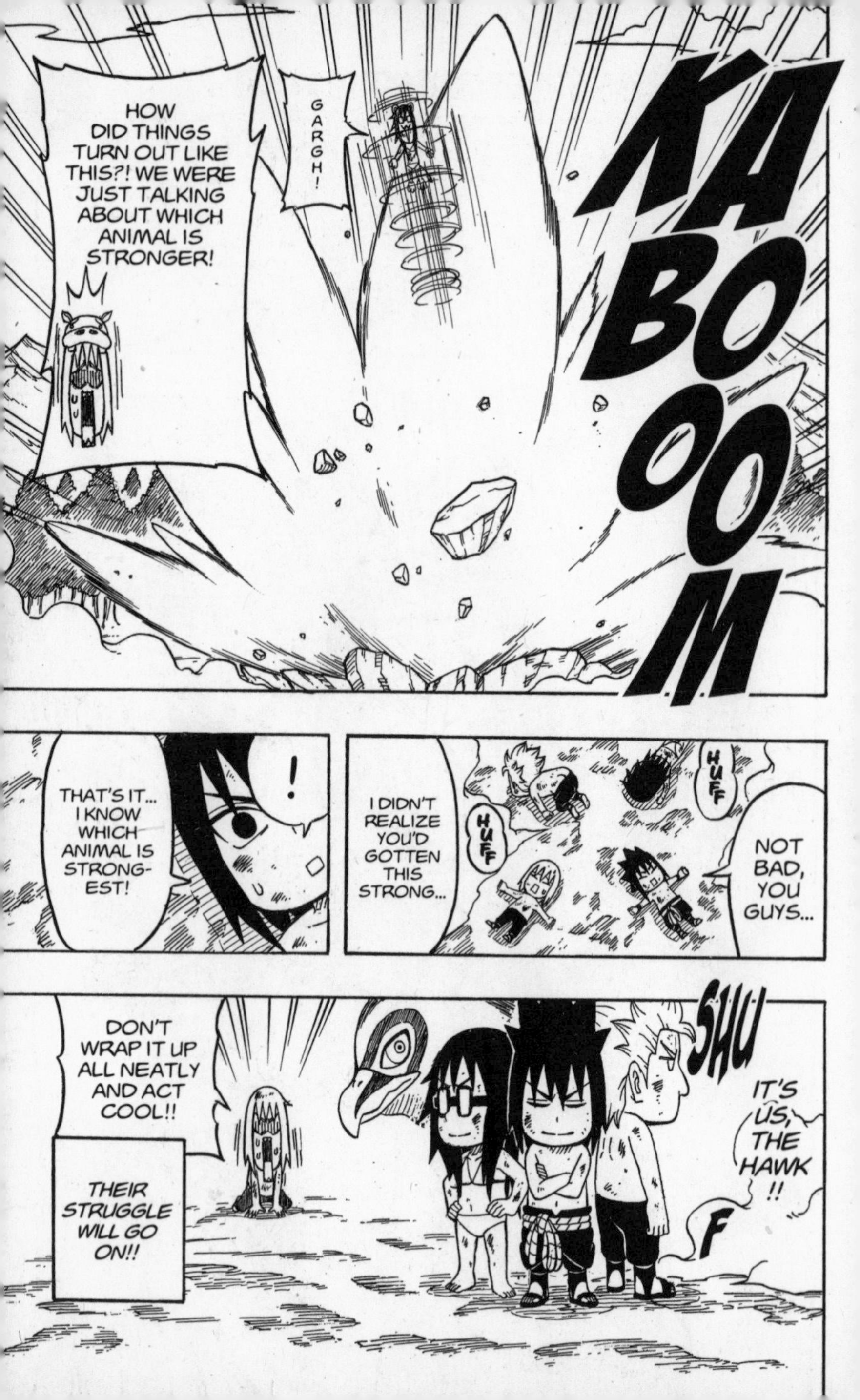
KABOOOM
GARGH!
HOW DID THINGS TURN OUT LIKE THIS?! WE WERE JUST TALKING ABOUT WHICH ANIMAL IS STRONGER!
NOT BAD, YOU GUYS...
HUFF
HUFF
I DIDN'T REALIZE YOU'D GOTTEN THIS STRONG...
!
THAT'S IT... I KNOW WHICH ANIMAL IS STRONG-EST!
SHU F
IT'S US, THE HAWK!!
DON'T WRAP IT UP ALL NEATLY AND ACT COOL!!
THEIR STRUGGLE WILL GO ON!!

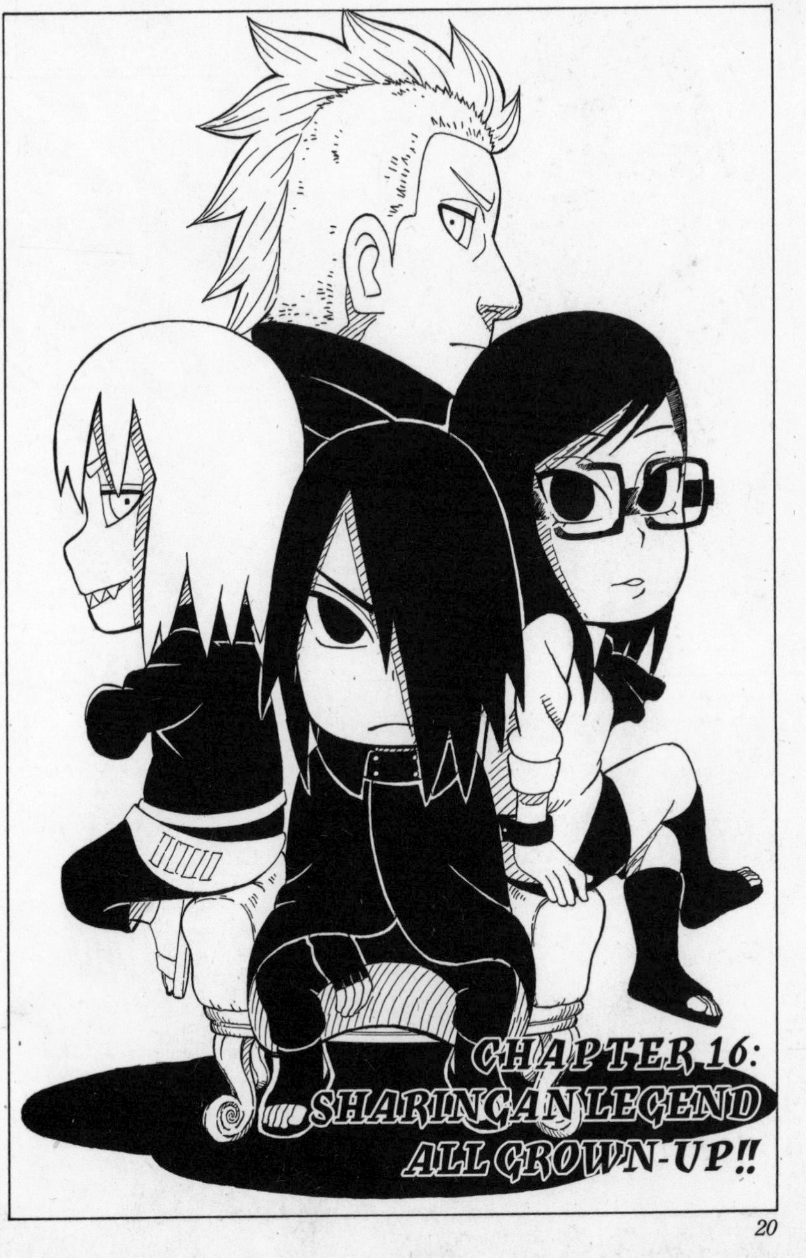
CHAPTER 16:
SHARINGAN LEGEND ALL GROWN-UP!!

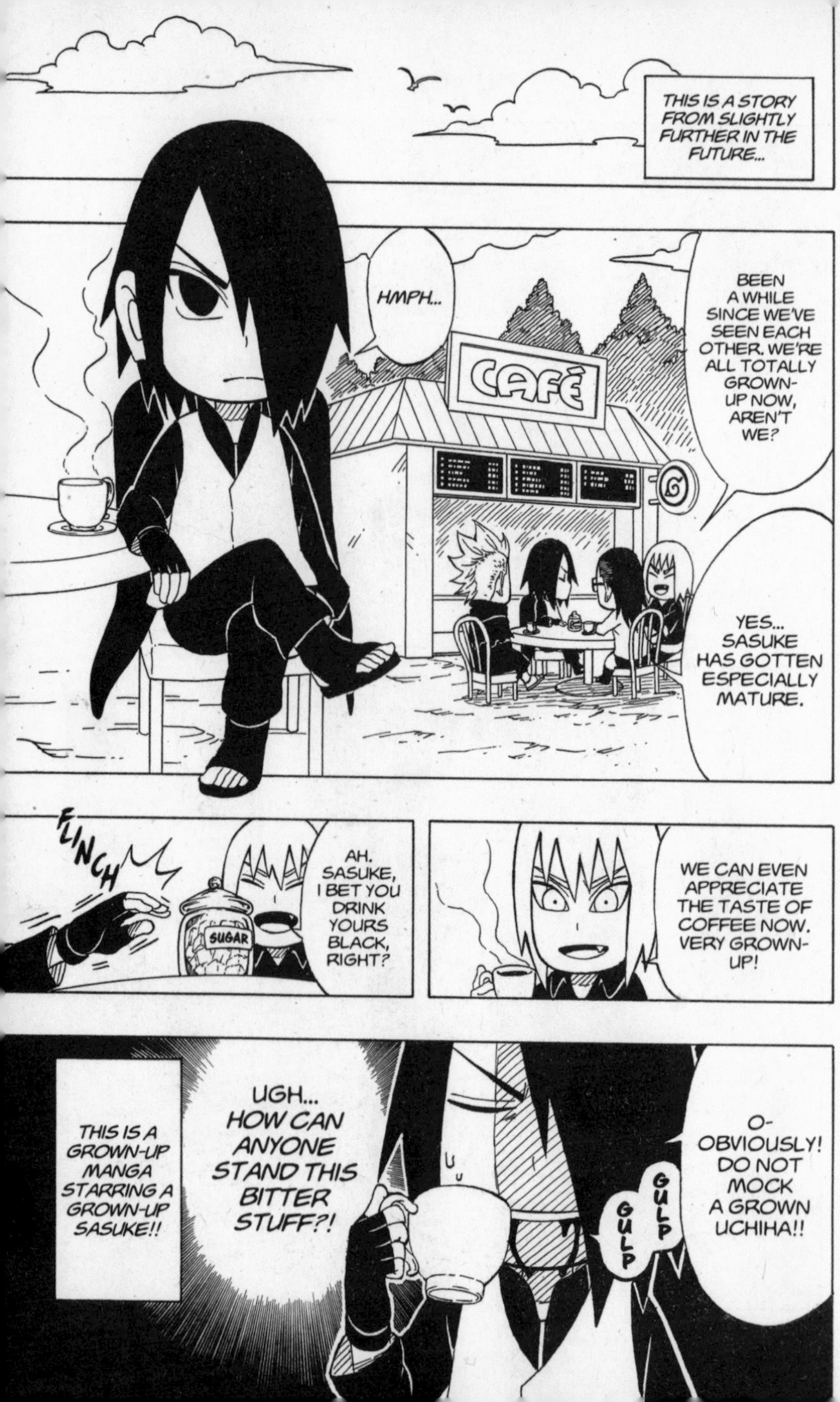
THIS IS A STORY FROM SLIGHTLY FURTHER IN THE FUTURE...
BEEN A WHILE SINCE WE'VE SEEN EACH OTHER. WE'RE ALL TOTALLY GROWN-UP NOW, AREN'T WE?
YES... SASUKE HAS GOTTEN ESPECIALLY MATURE.
CAFÉ
HMPH...
WE CAN EVEN APPRECIATE THE TASTE OF COFFEE NOW. VERY GROWN-UP!
AH. SASUKE, I BET YOU DRINK YOURS BLACK, RIGHT?
SUGAR
FLINCH
O-OBVIOUSLY! DO NOT MOCK A GROWN UCHIHA!!
GULP
GULP
UGH... HOW CAN ANYONE STAND THIS BITTER STUFF?!
THIS IS A GROWN-UP MANGA STARRING A GROWN-UP SASUKE!!

LATE NIGHTS FOR GROWN-UPS

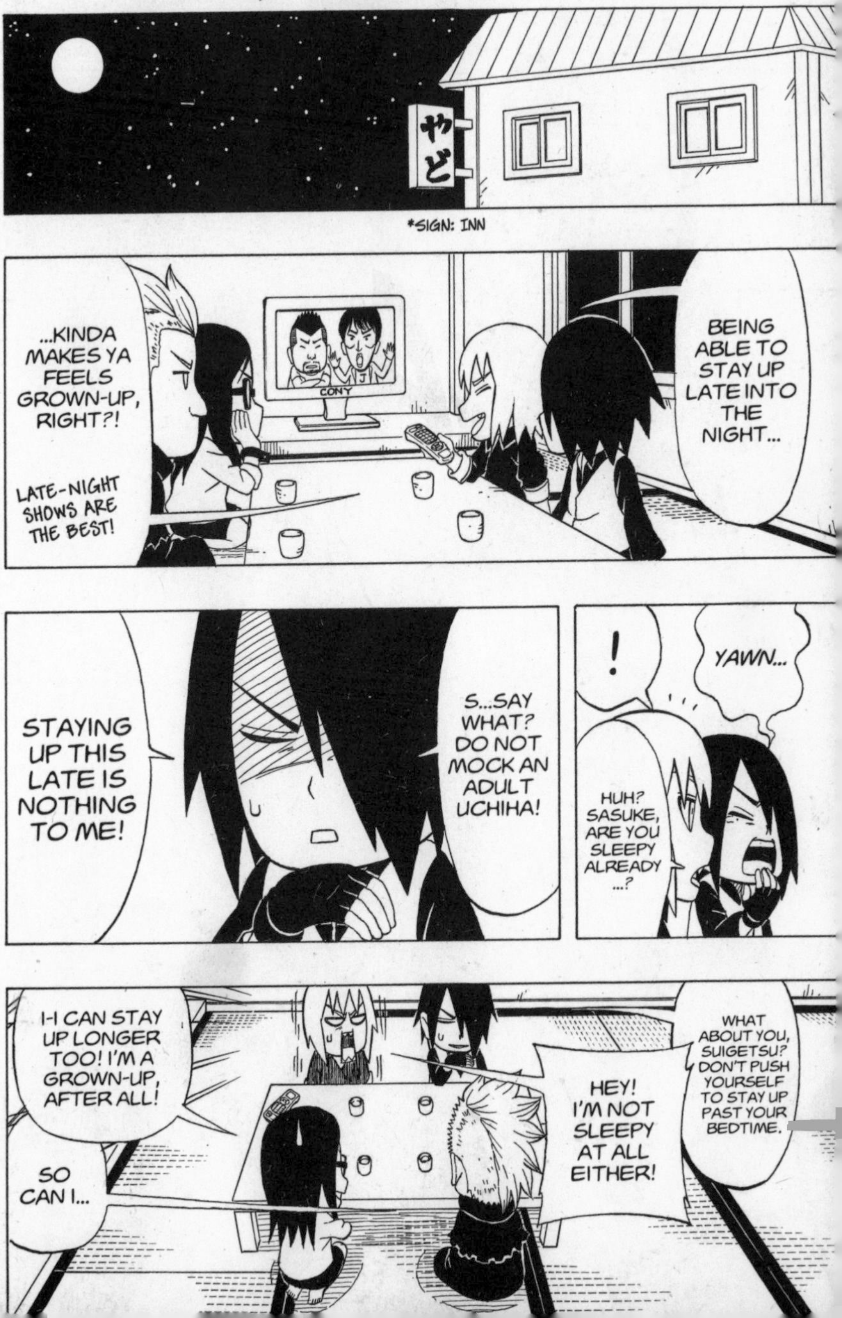

やど
*SIGN: INN
BEING ABLE TO STAY UP LATE INTO THE NIGHT...
...KINDA MAKES YA FEELS GROWN-UP, RIGHT?!
LATE-NIGHT SHOWS ARE THE BEST!
CONY
YAWN...
!
HUH? SASUKE, ARE YOU SLEEPY ALREADY ...?
S...SAY WHAT? DO NOT MOCK AN ADULT UCHIHA!
STAYING UP THIS LATE IS NOTHING TO ME!
WHAT ABOUT YOU, SUIGETSU? DON'T PUSH YOURSELF TO STAY UP PAST YOUR BEDTIME.
HEY! I'M NOT SLEEPY AT ALL EITHER!
I-I CAN STAY UP LONGER TOO! I'M A GROWN-UP, AFTER ALL!
SO CAN I...

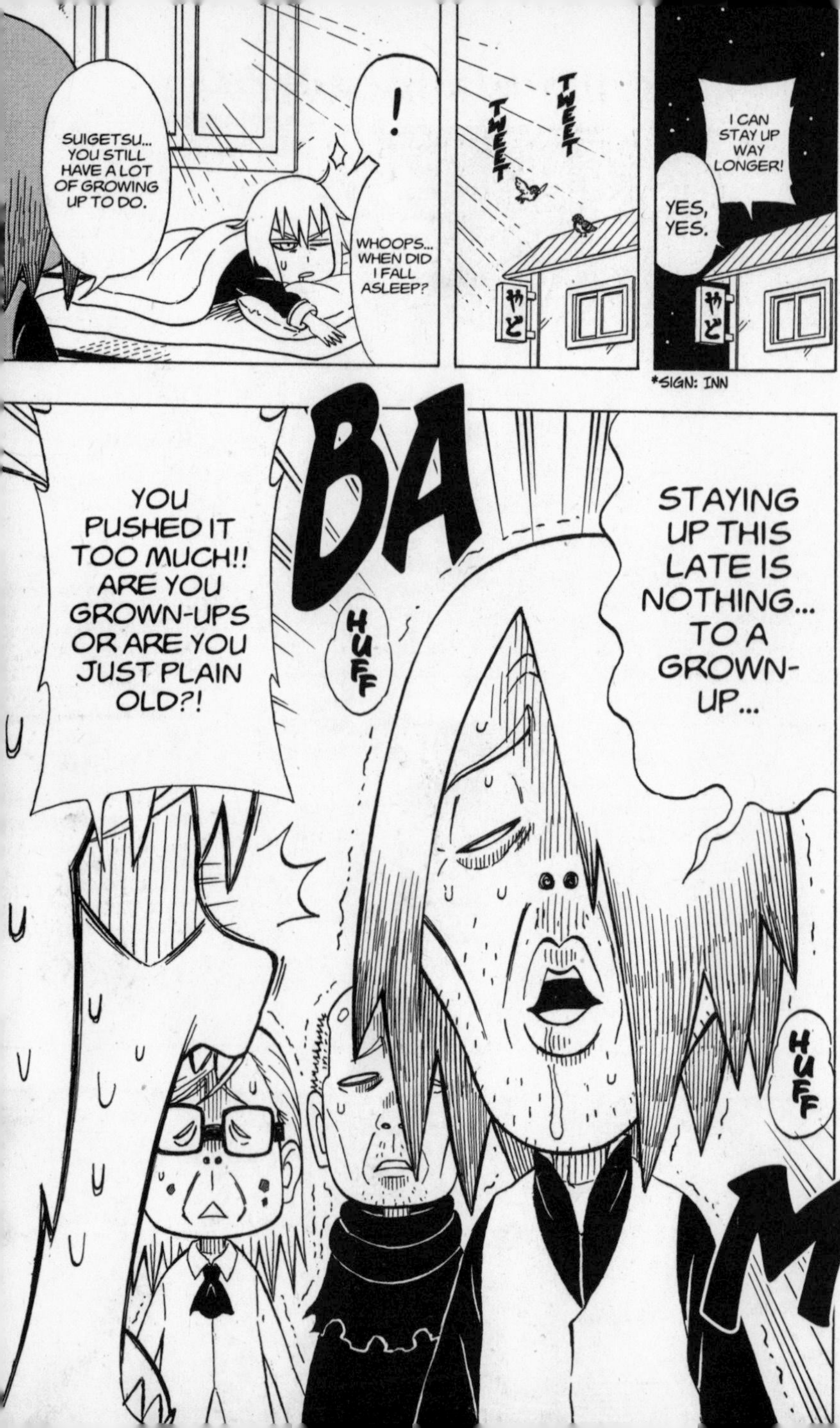
I CAN STAY UP WAY LONGER!
YES, YES.
やど
TWEET
TWEET
やど
!
WHOOPS... WHEN DID I FALL ASLEEP?
SUIGETSU... YOU STILL HAVE A LOT OF GROWING UP TO DO.
BA
STAYING UP THIS LATE IS NOTHING... TO A GROWN-UP...
YOU PUSHED IT TOO MUCH!! ARE YOU GROWN-UPS OR ARE YOU JUST PLAIN OLD?!
HUFF
HUFF
M
*SIGN: INN

GROWN-UP SEX APPEAL

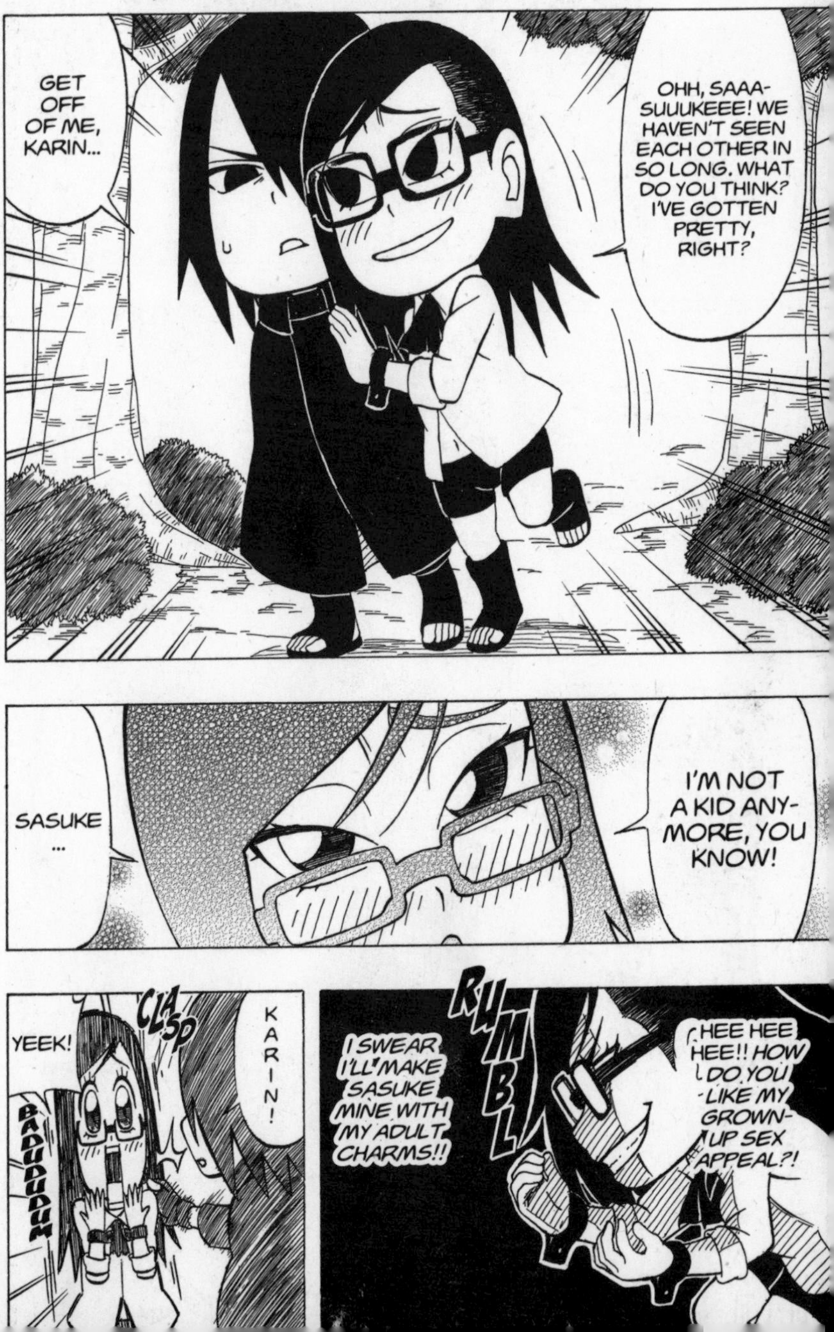

OHH, SAAA-SUUUKEEE! WE HAVEN'T SEEN EACH OTHER IN SO LONG. WHAT DO YOU THINK? I'VE GOTTEN PRETTY, RIGHT?
GET OFF OF ME, KARIN...
I'M NOT A KID ANY-MORE, YOU KNOW!
SASUKE ...
HEE HEE HEE!! HOW DO YOU LIKE MY GROWN-UP SEX APPEAL?!
RUMBL
I SWEAR I'LL MAKE SASUKE MINE WITH MY ADULT CHARMS!!
KARIN!
CLASP
YEEK!
BADUDUDUM

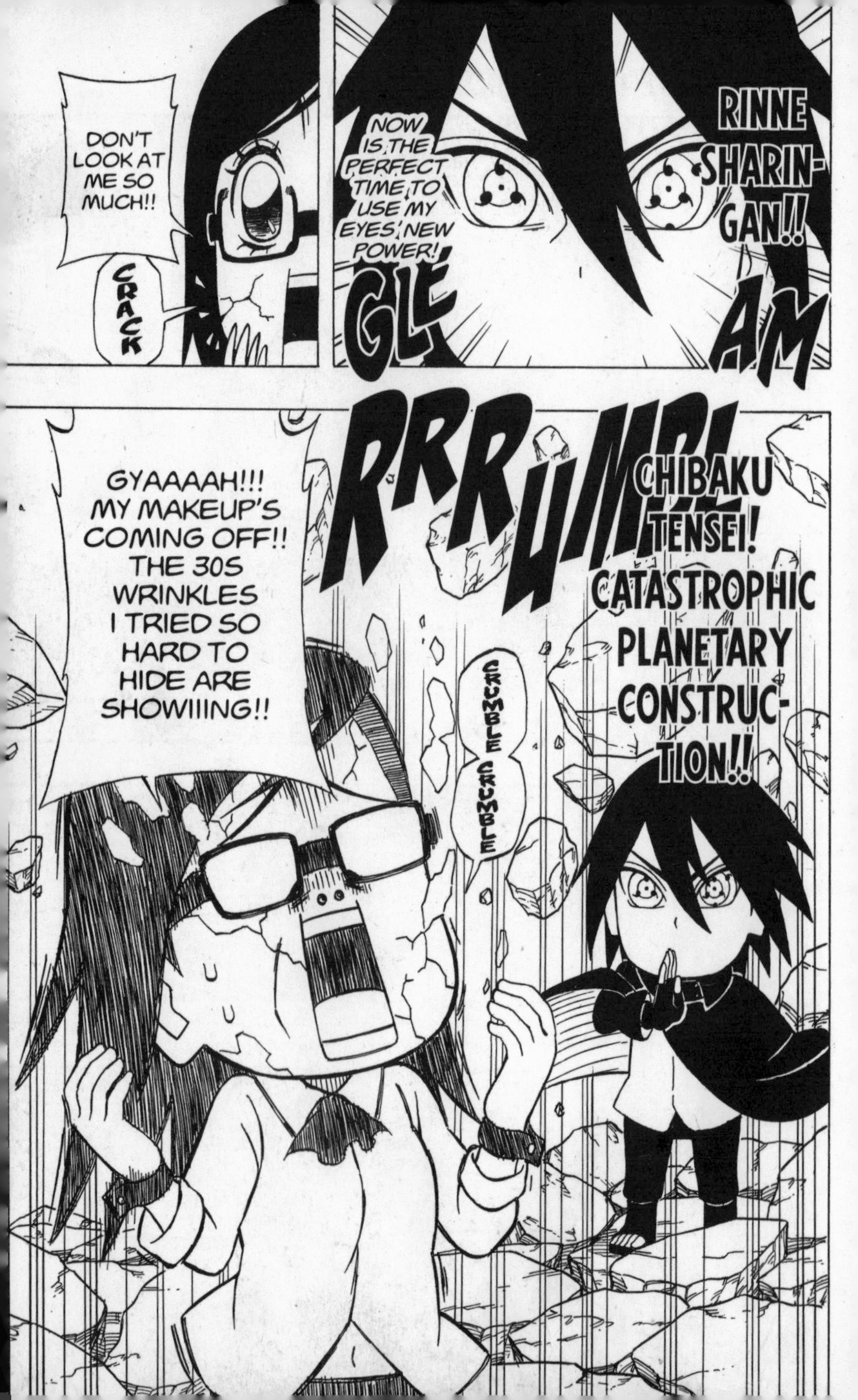
NOW IS THE PERFECT TIME TO USE MY EYES' NEW POWER!
RINNE SHARINGAN!!
GLE
AM
DON'T LOOK AT ME SO MUCH!!
CRACK
RRRUMBL
CHIBAKU TENSEI! CATASTROPHIC PLANETARY CONSTRUCTION!!
GYAAAAH!!! MY MAKEUP'S COMING OFF!! THE 30S WRINKLES I TRIED SO HARD TO HIDE ARE SHOWIIING!!
CRUMBLE CRUMBLE

GROWN-UP FIGHT

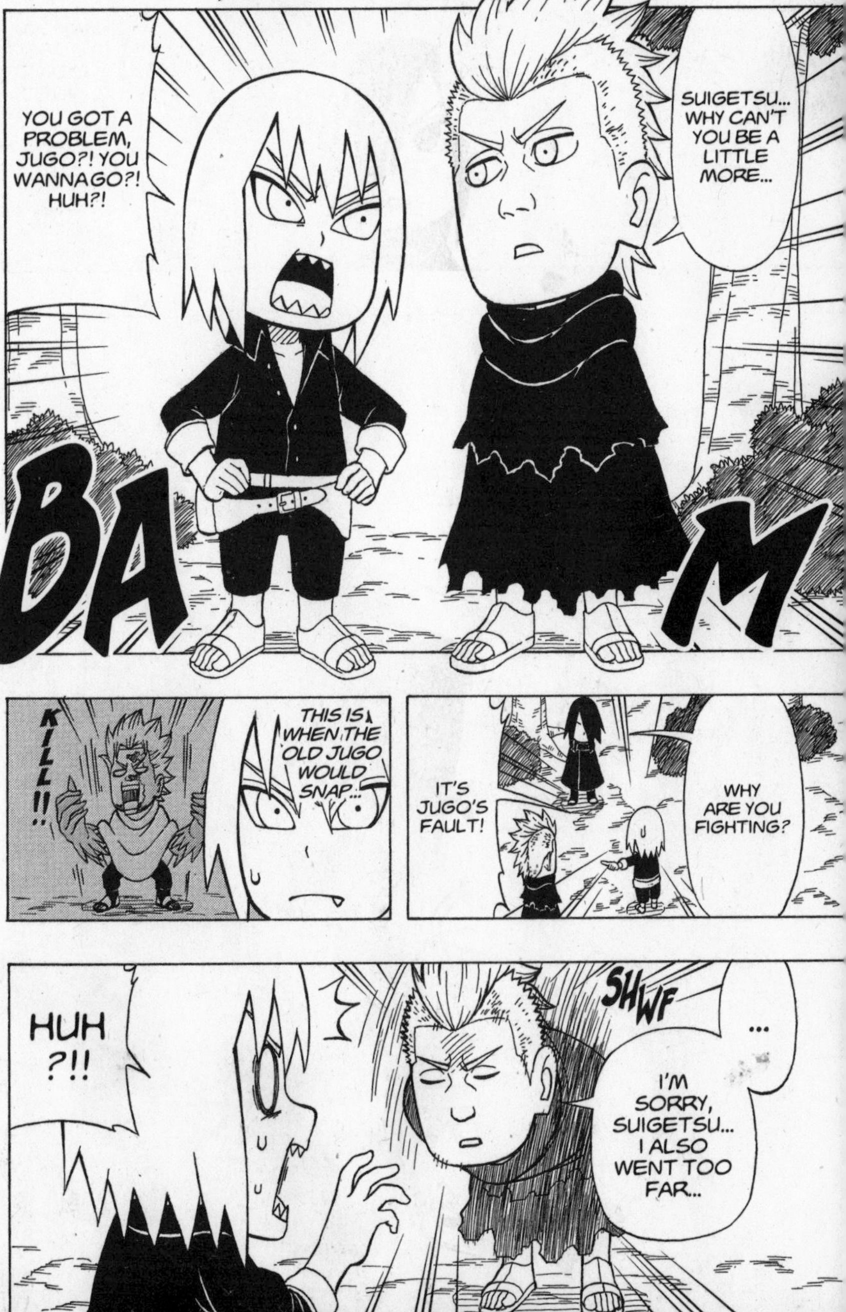

SUIGETSU... WHY CAN'T YOU BE A LITTLE MORE...
YOU GOT A PROBLEM, JUGO?! YOU WANNA GO?! HUH?!
BAM
WHY ARE YOU FIGHTING?
IT'S JUGO'S FAULT!
THIS IS WHEN THE OLD JUGO WOULD SNAP...
KILL!!
SHWF
...
I'M SORRY, SUIGETSU... I ALSO WENT TOO FAR...
HUH ?!!

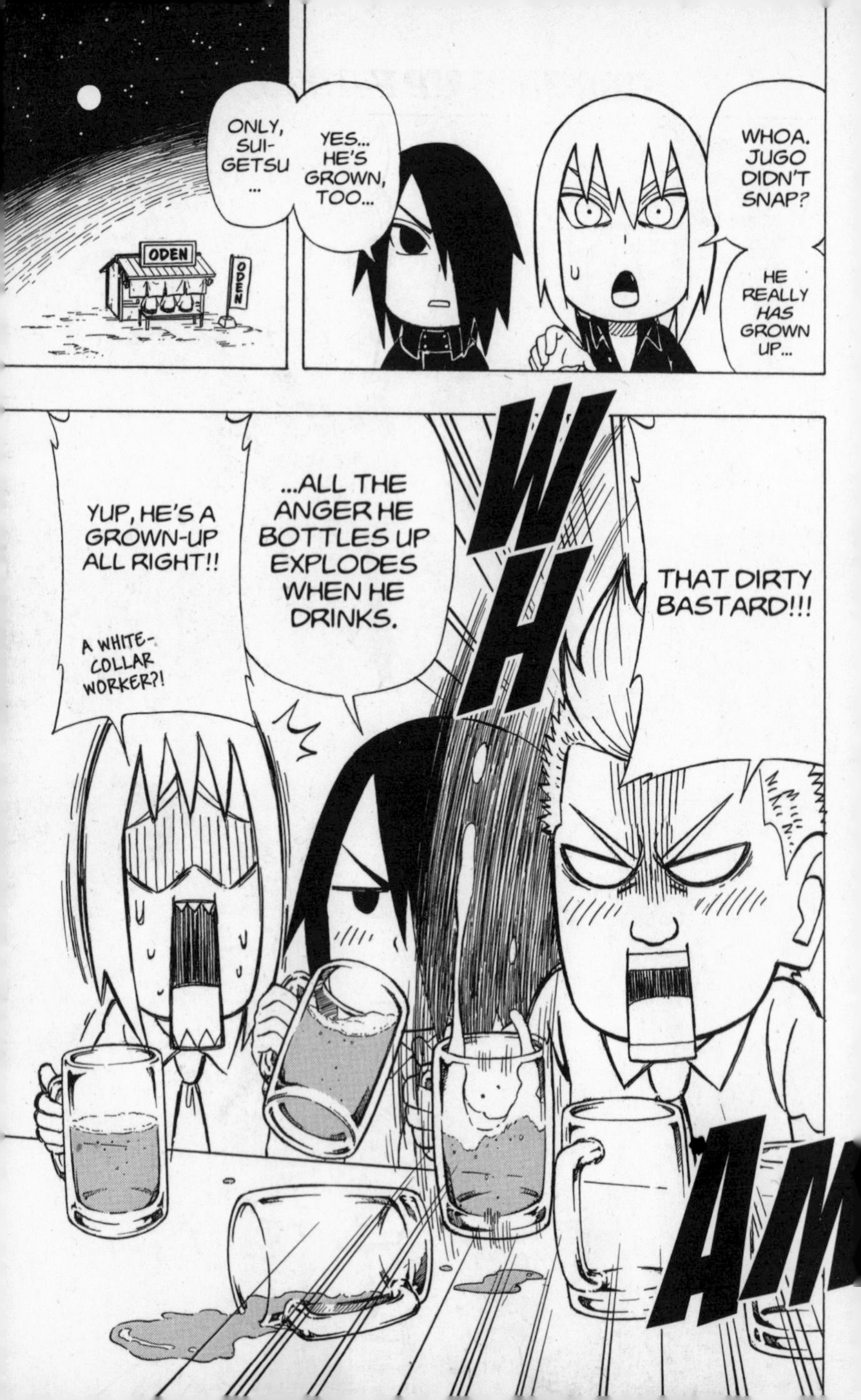
WHOA. JUGO DIDN'T SNAP?
HE REALLY HAS GROWN UP...
YES... HE'S GROWN, TOO...
ONLY, SUI-GETSU ...
ODEN
ODEN
WH
AM
THAT DIRTY BASTARD!!!
...ALL THE ANGER HE BOTTLES UP EXPLODES WHEN HE DRINKS.
YUP, HE'S A GROWN-UP ALL RIGHT!!
A WHITE-COLLAR WORKER?!

GROWN-UP BATTLE!!

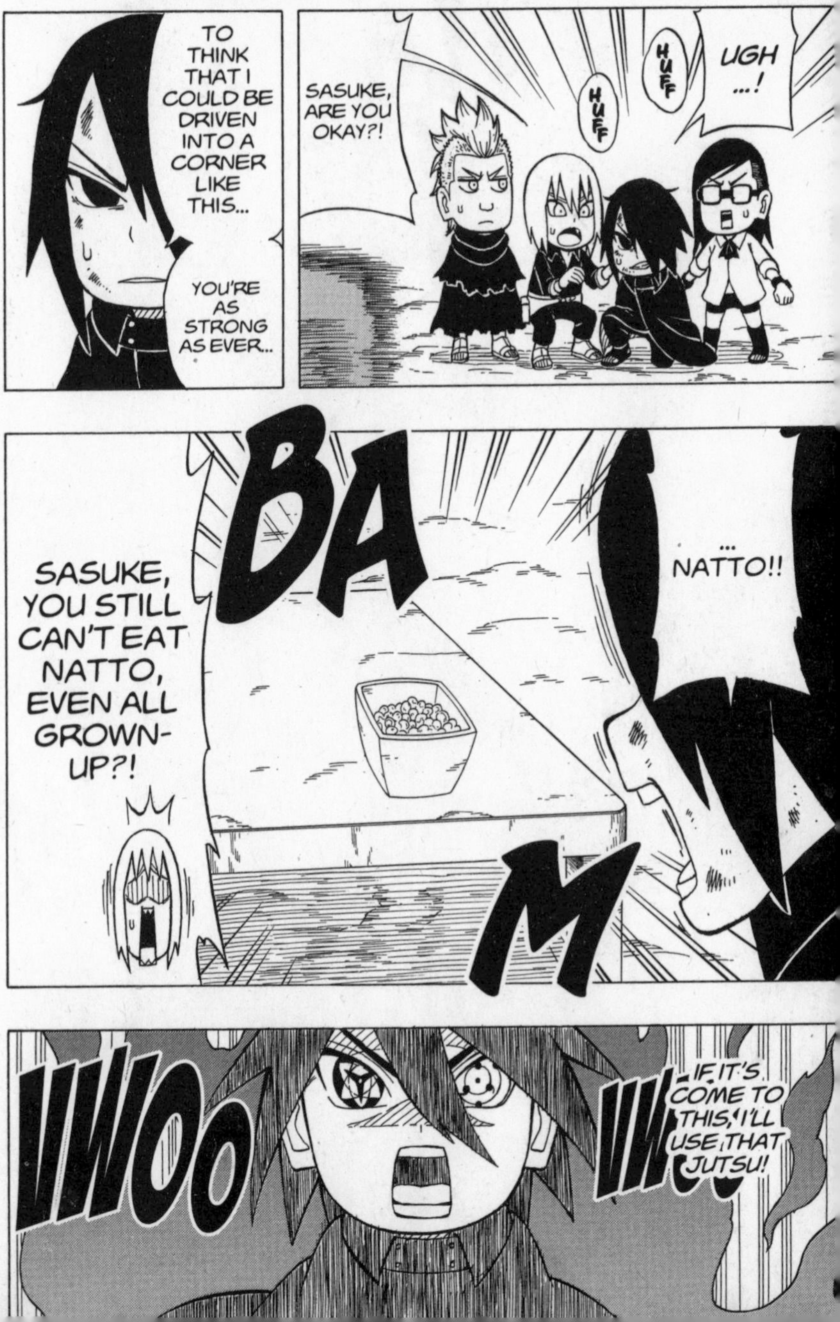
UGH ...!
HUFF
HUFF
SASUKE, ARE YOU OKAY?!
TO THINK THAT I COULD BE DRIVEN INTO A CORNER LIKE THIS...
YOU'RE AS STRONG AS EVER...
... NATTO!!
BAM
SASUKE, YOU STILL CAN'T EAT NATTO, EVEN ALL GROWN-UP?!
IF IT'S COME TO THIS, I'LL USE THAT JUTSU!
VWOOM

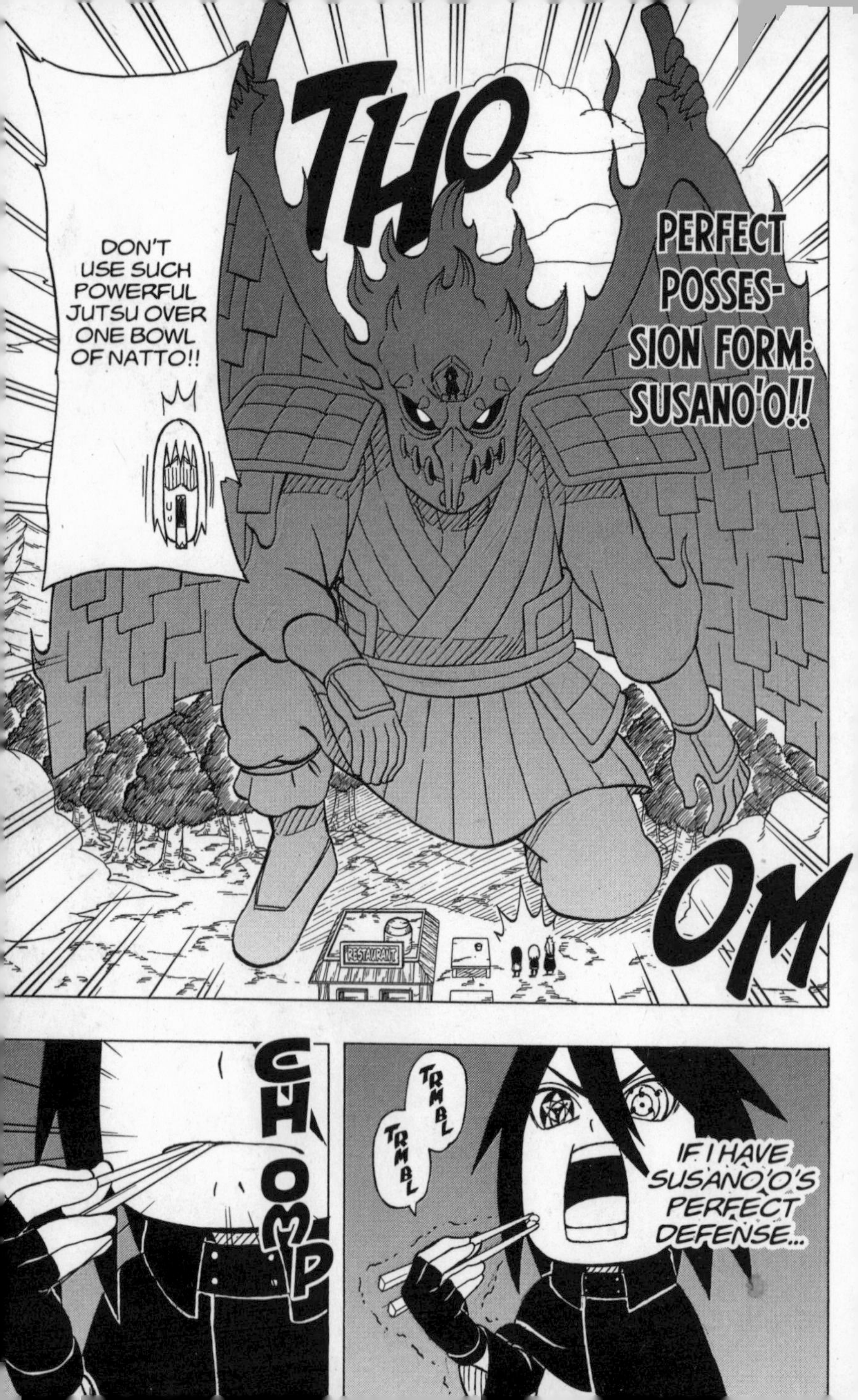
THO
OM
PERFECT POSSES-SION FORM: SUSANO'O!!
DON'T USE SUCH POWERFUL JUTSU OVER ONE BOWL OF NATTO!!
RESTAURANT
IF I HAVE SUSANO'O'S PERFECT DEFENSE...
TRMBL
TRMBL
CHOMP

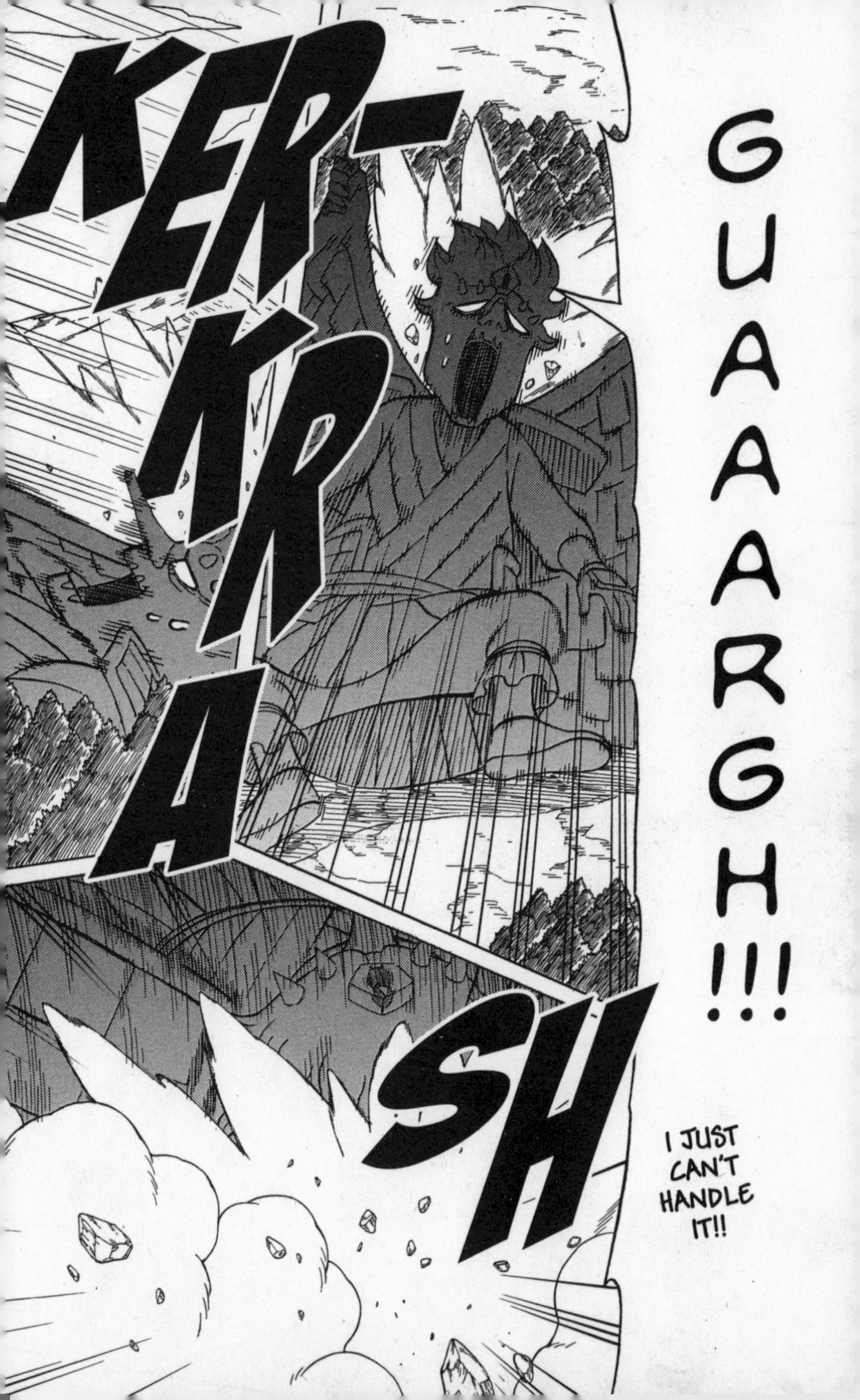
GUAAARGH!!!
I JUST CAN'T HANDLE IT!!
KER-AK-AA
-SH

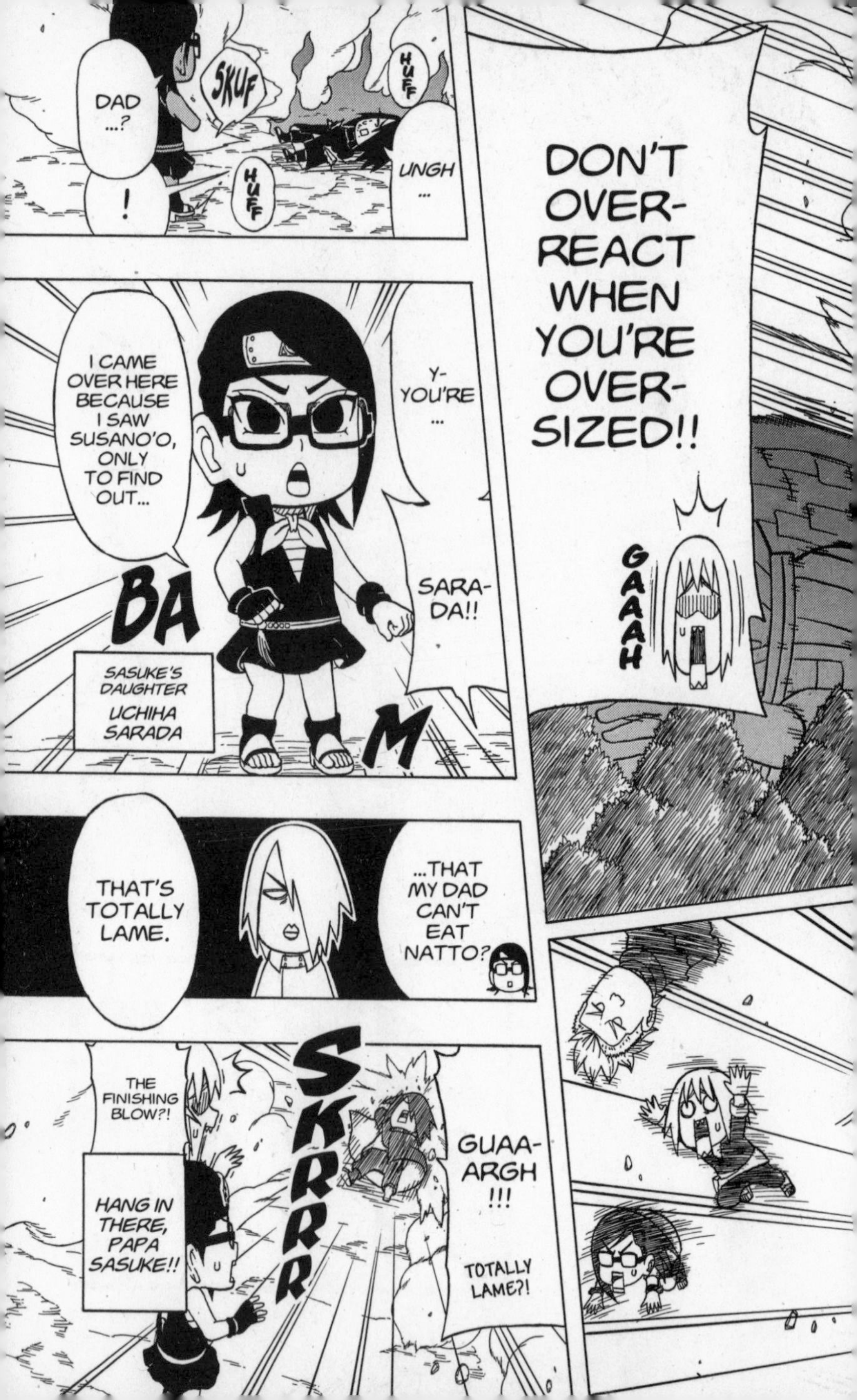
DON'T OVER-REACT WHEN YOU'RE OVER-SIZED!!
GAAAH
UNGH ...
HUFF HUFF
SKUF
DAD ...?
!
Y-YOU'RE ...
SARADA!!
I CAME OVER HERE BECAUSE I SAW SUSANO'O, ONLY TO FIND OUT...
BAM
SASUKE'S DAUGHTER UCHIHA SARADA
...THAT MY DAD CAN'T EAT NATTO?
THAT'S TOTALLY LAME.
GUAAARGH !!!
TOTALLY LAME?!
SKRRR
THE FINISHING BLOW?!
HANG IN THERE, PAPA SASUKE!!

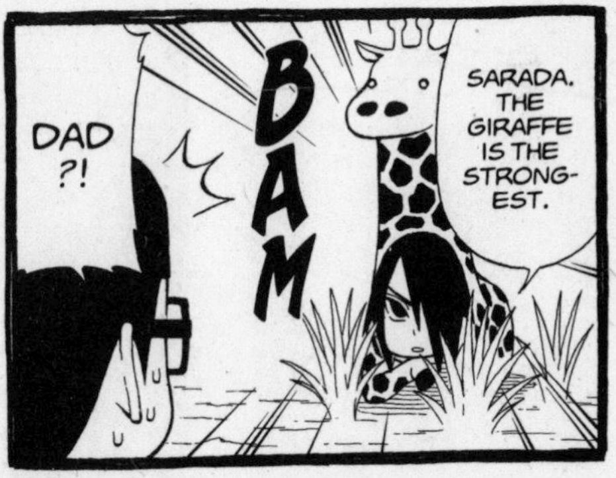
SARADA. THE GIRAFFE IS THE STRONGEST.
BAM
DAD ?!

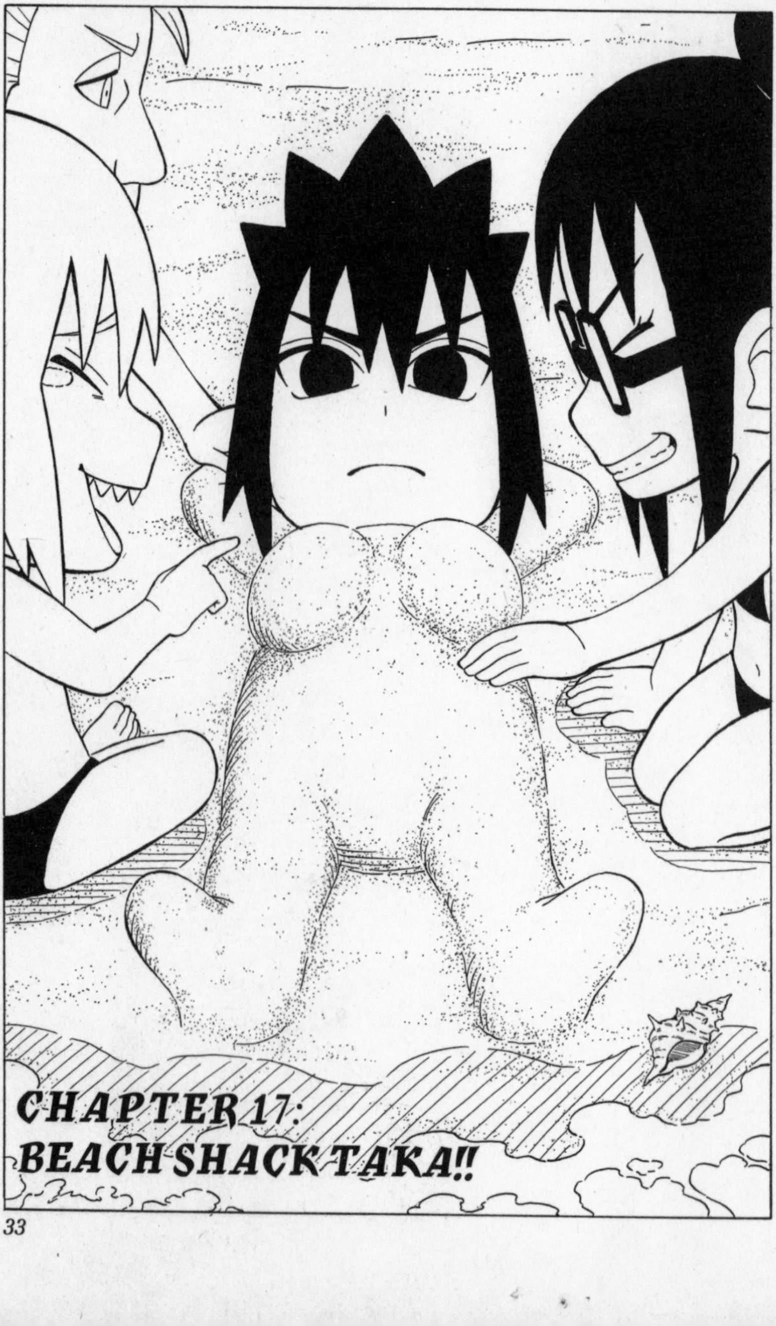
CHAPTER 17:
BEACH SHACK TAKA!!

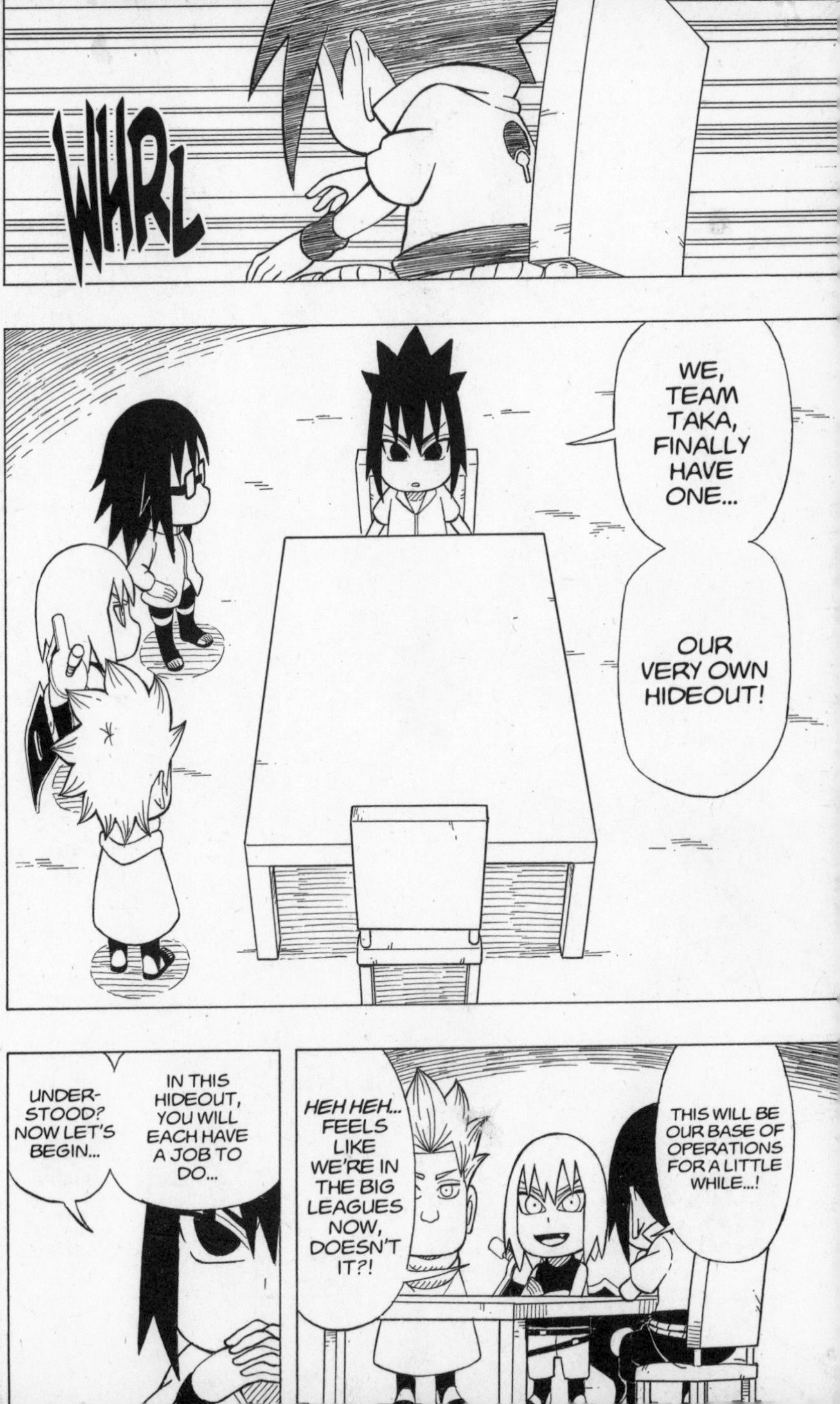
WHRL
WE, TEAM TAKA, FINALLY HAVE ONE...
OUR VERY OWN HIDEOUT!
THIS WILL BE OUR BASE OF OPERATIONS FOR A LITTLE WHILE...!
HEH HEH... FEELS LIKE WE'RE IN THE BIG LEAGUES NOW, DOESN'T IT?!
IN THIS HIDEOUT, YOU WILL EACH HAVE A JOB TO DO...
UNDER-STOOD? NOW LET'S BEGIN...

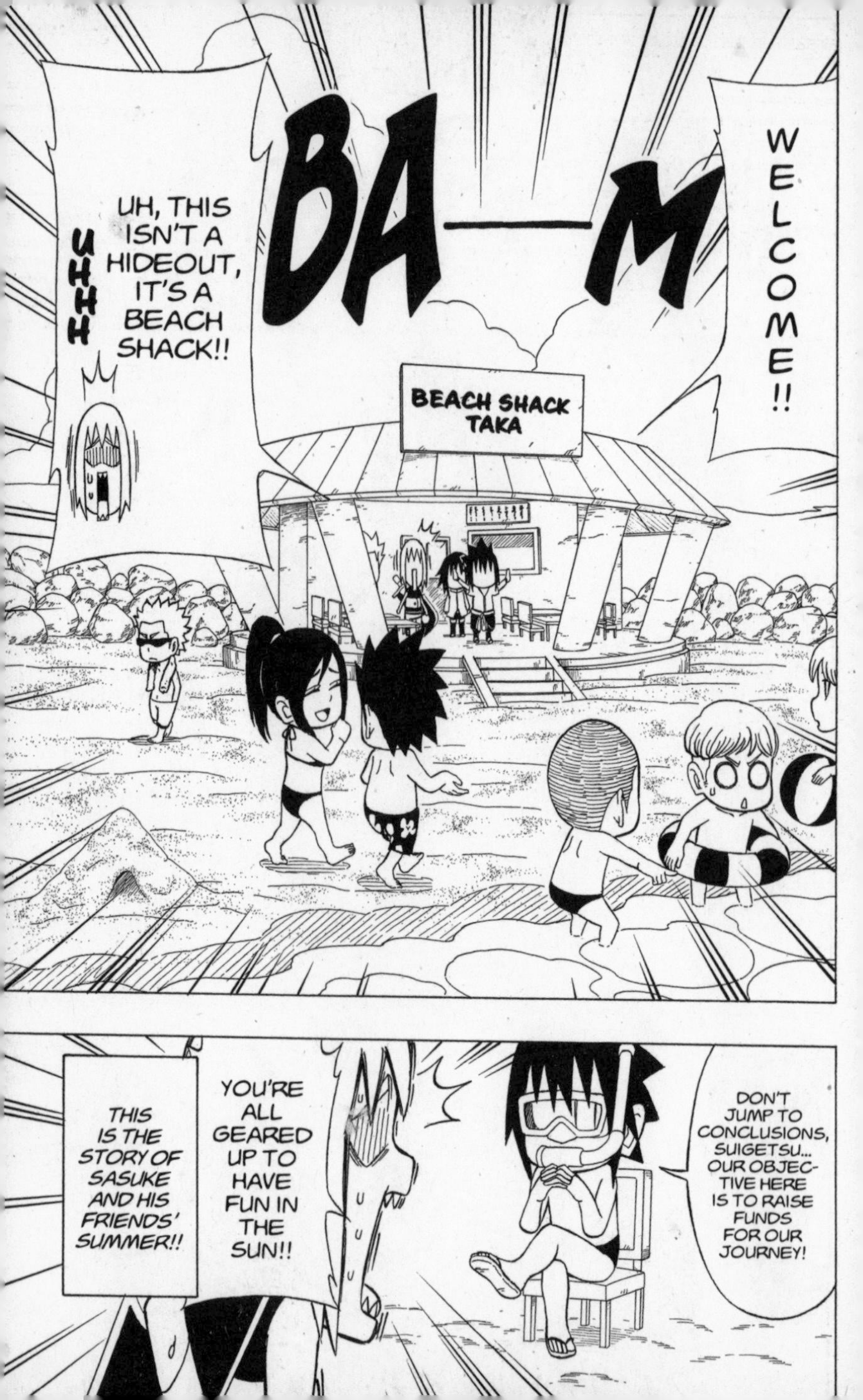
WELCOME!!
BA—M
UHHH
UH, THIS ISN'T A HIDEOUT, IT'S A BEACH SHACK!!
BEACH SHACK TAKA
DON'T JUMP TO CONCLUSIONS, SUIGETSU... OUR OBJECTIVE HERE IS TO RAISE FUNDS FOR OUR JOURNEY!
YOU'RE ALL GEARED UP TO HAVE FUN IN THE SUN!!
THIS IS THE STORY OF SASUKE AND HIS FRIENDS' SUMMER!!

BEACH TOYS

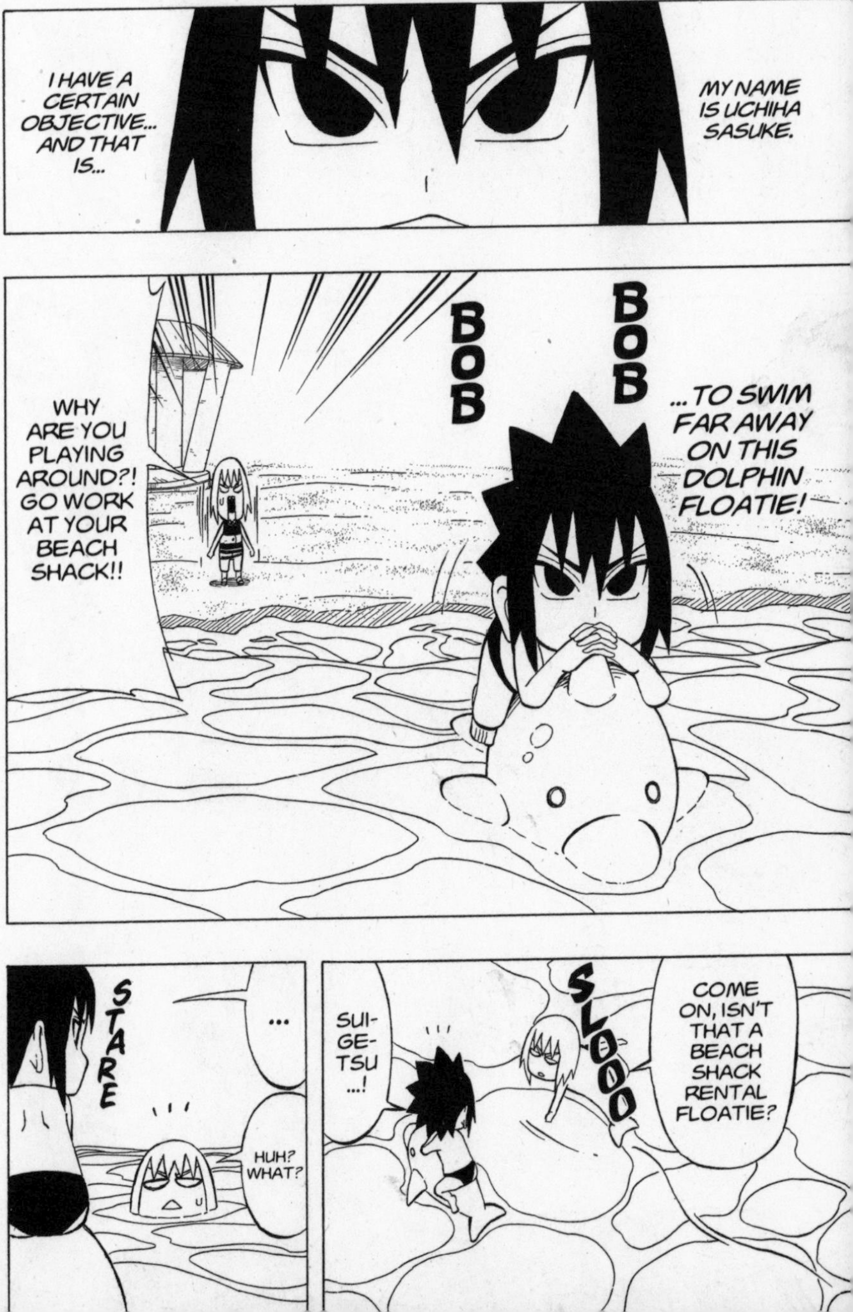
MY NAME IS UCHIHA SASUKE.
I HAVE A CERTAIN OBJECTIVE... AND THAT IS...
BOB BOB
...TO SWIM FAR AWAY ON THIS DOLPHIN FLOATIE!
WHY ARE YOU PLAYING AROUND?! GO WORK AT YOUR BEACH SHACK!!
COME ON, ISN'T THAT A BEACH SHACK RENTAL FLOATIE?
SLOOO
SUI-GE-TSU...!
...
STARE
HUH? WHAT?

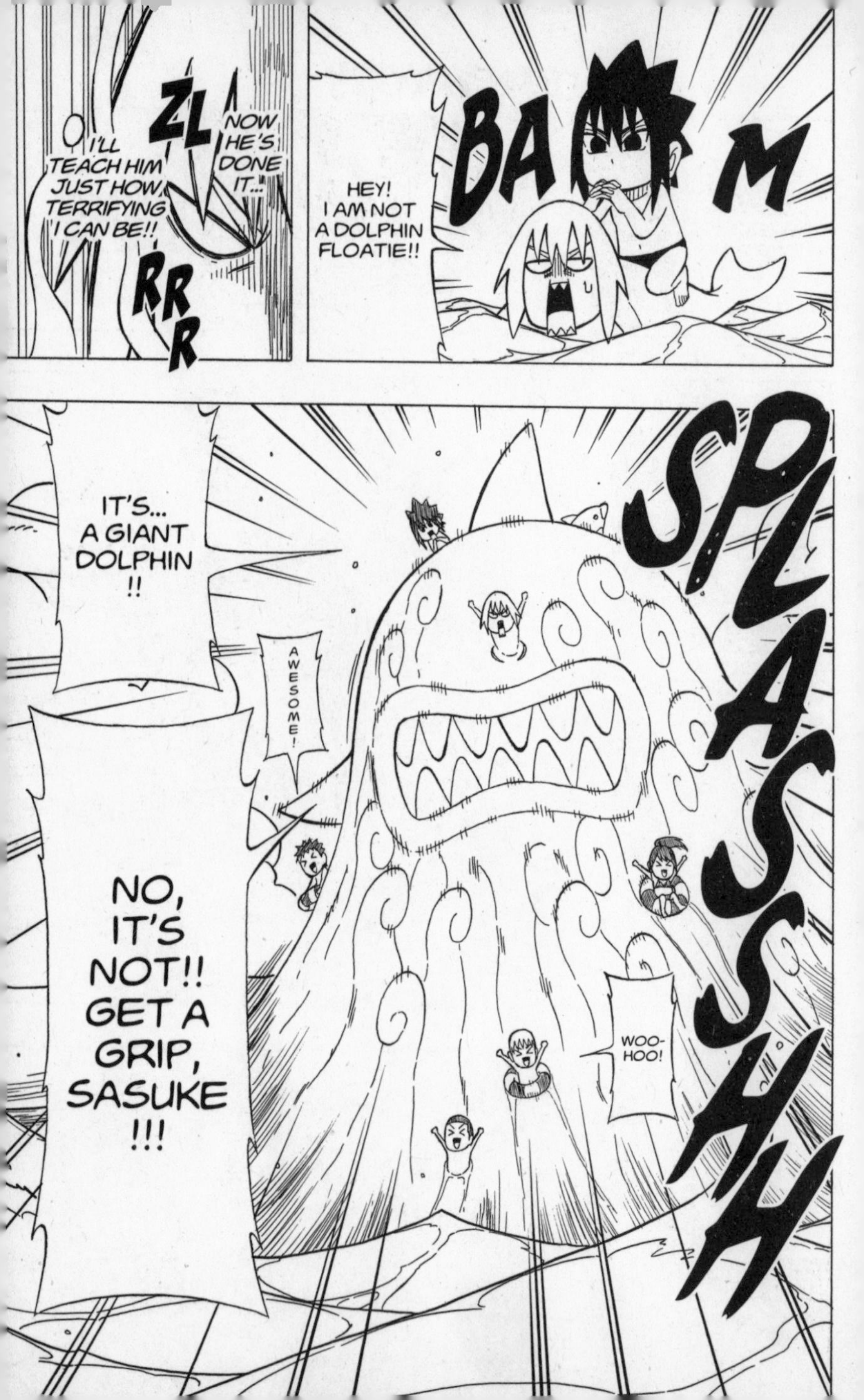
BAMM
HEY! I AM NOT A DOLPHIN FLOATIE!!
NOW HE'S DONE IT...
ZL
I'LL TEACH HIM JUST HOW TERRIFYING I CAN BE!!
RRR
SPLASHH
IT'S... A GIANT DOLPHIN!!
AWESOME!
WOO-HOO!
NO, IT'S NOT!! GET A GRIP, SASUKE!!!

PLAYBOY?

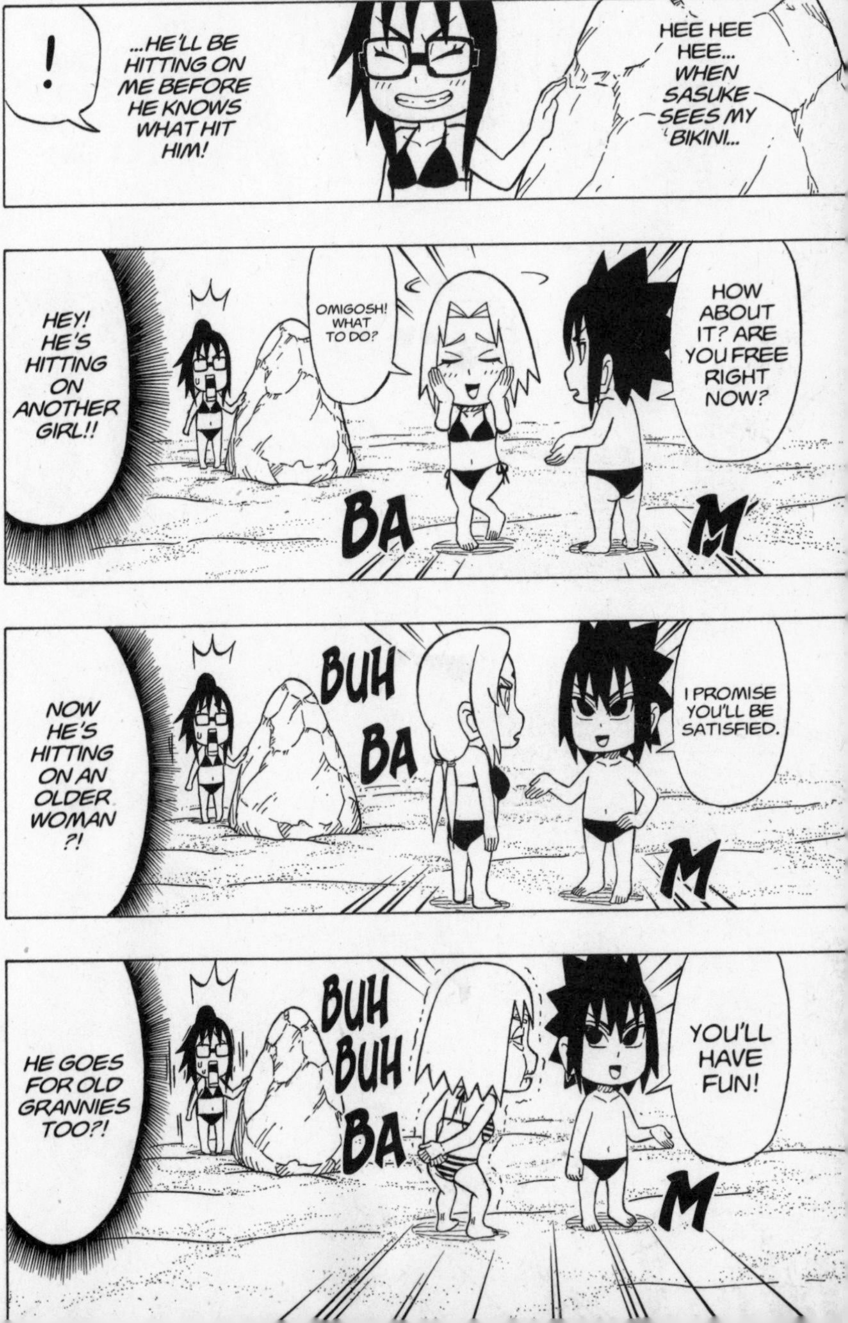
HEE HEE HEE... WHEN SASUKE SEES MY BIKINI...
...HE'LL BE HITTING ON ME BEFORE HE KNOWS WHAT HIT HIM!
!
HOW ABOUT IT? ARE YOU FREE RIGHT NOW?
BA M
OMIGOSH! WHAT TO DO?
HEY! HE'S HITTING ON ANOTHER GIRL!!
I PROMISE YOU'LL BE SATISFIED.
BUH BA M
NOW HE'S HITTING ON AN OLDER WOMAN?!
YOU'LL HAVE FUN!
BUH BUH BA M
HE GOES FOR OLD GRANNIES TOO?!

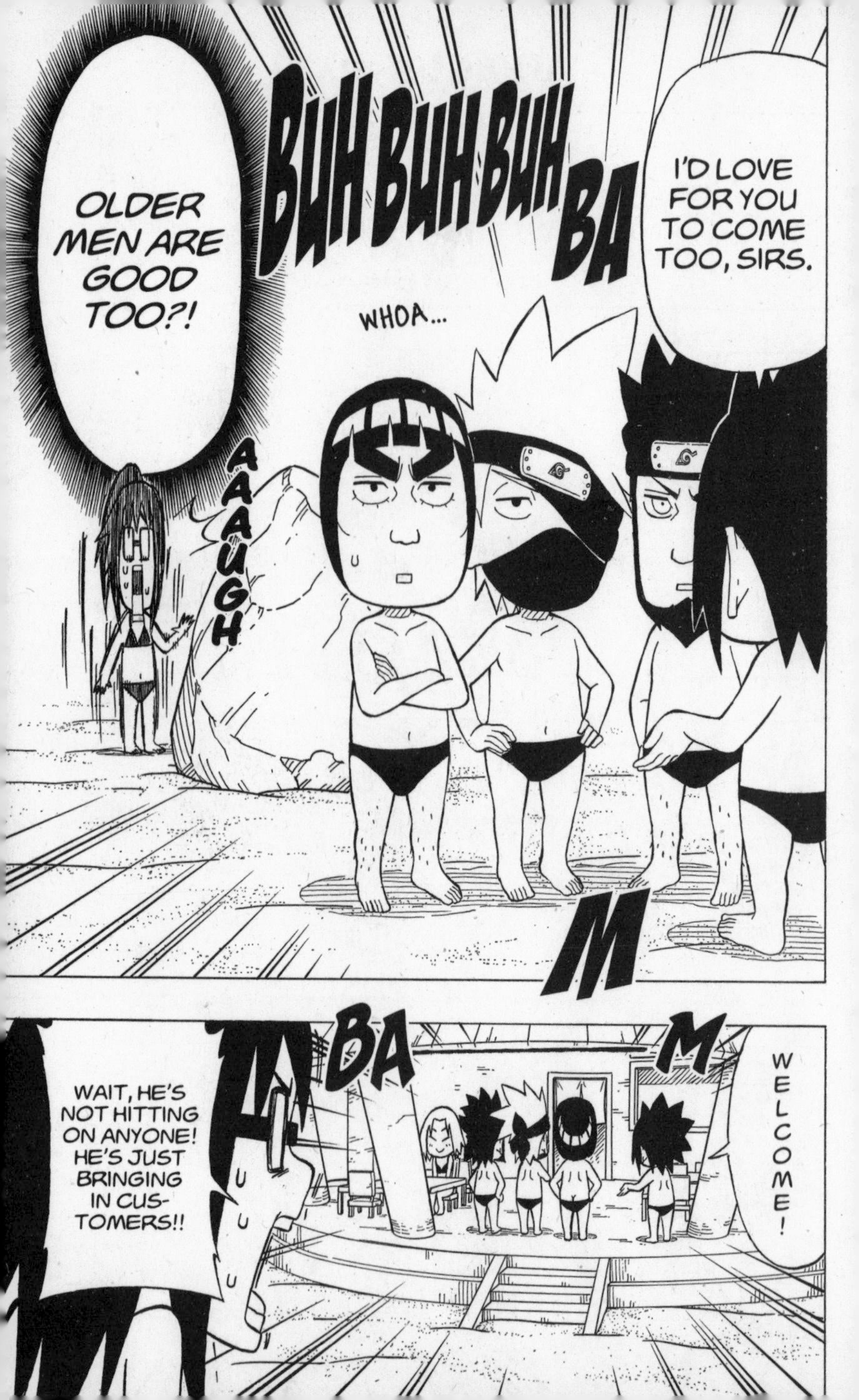
I'D LOVE FOR YOU TO COME TOO, SIRS.
BUH BUH BUH BA
WHOA...
OLDER MEN ARE GOOD TOO?!
AAAAUGH
M
WELCOME!
BA M
WAIT, HE'S NOT HITTING ON ANYONE! HE'S JUST BRINGING IN CUS-TOMERS!!

LIFEGUARD

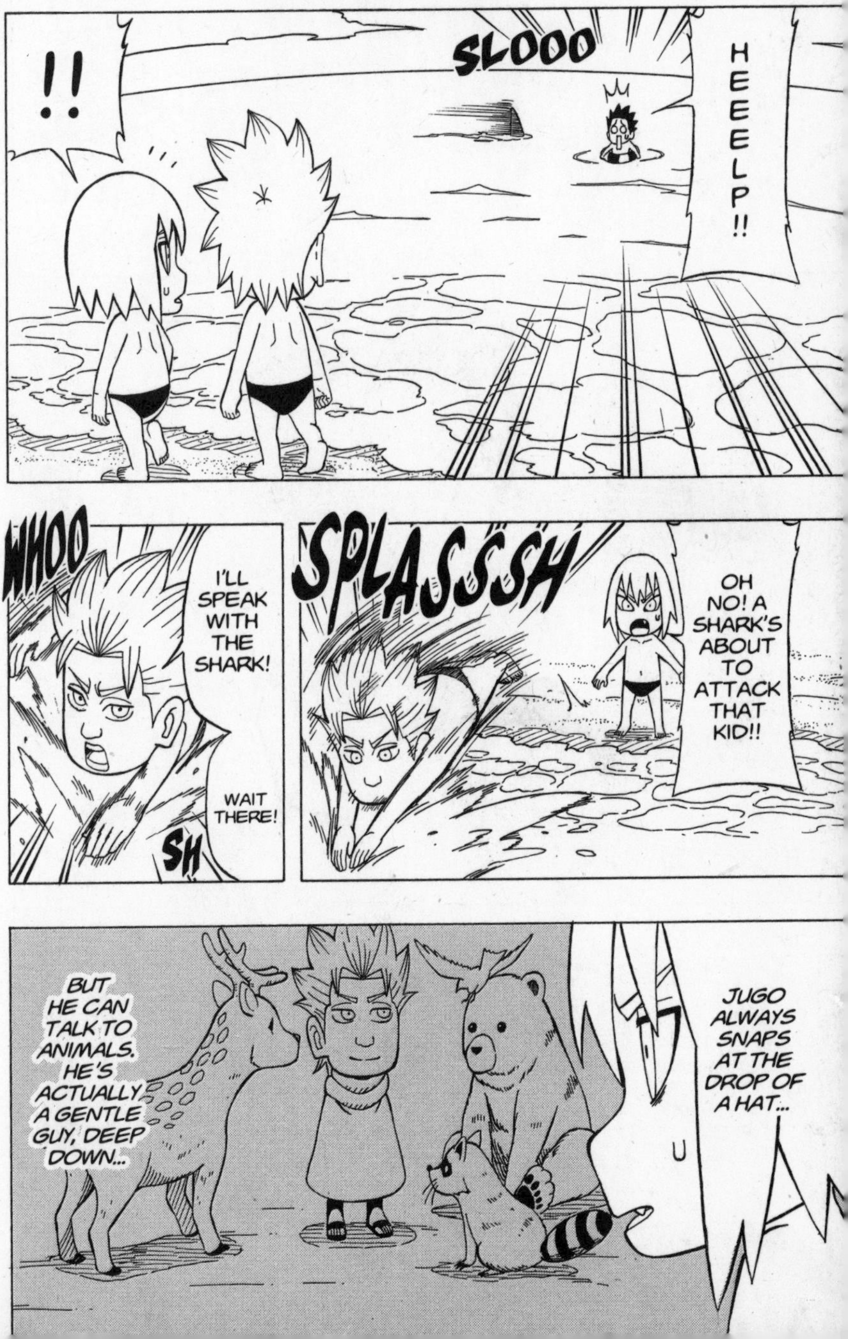
HEEEELP!!
SLOOO
!!
OH NO! A SHARK'S ABOUT TO ATTACK THAT KID!!
SPLASSSH
I'LL SPEAK WITH THE SHARK!
WAIT THERE!
WHOO
SH
JUGO ALWAYS SNAPS AT THE DROP OF A HAT...
BUT HE CAN TALK TO ANIMALS. HE'S ACTUALLY A GENTLE GUY, DEEP DOWN...

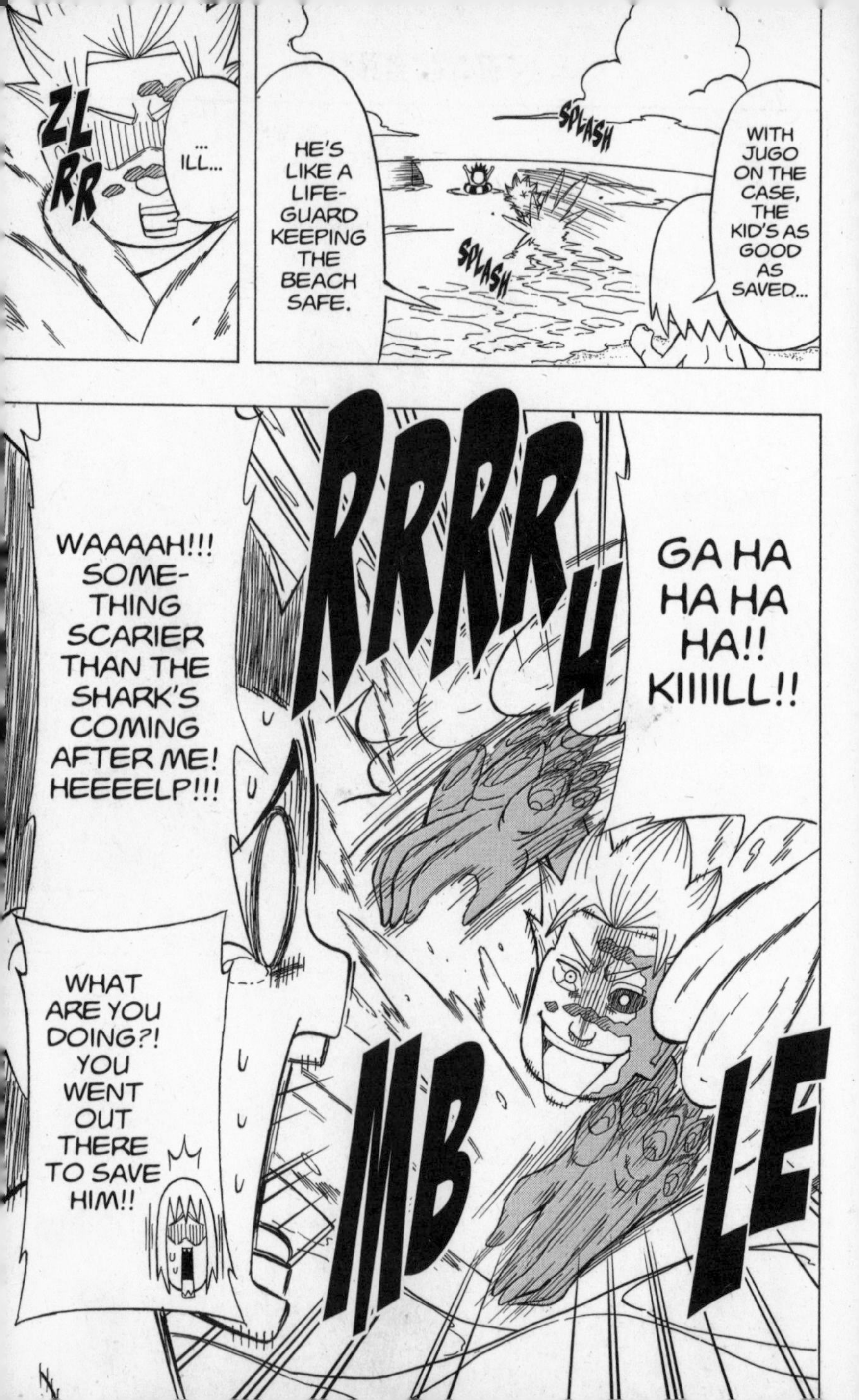
WITH JUGO ON THE CASE, THE KID'S AS GOOD AS SAVED...
SPLASH
SPLASH
HE'S LIKE A LIFE-GUARD KEEPING THE BEACH SAFE.
ZLRR
... ILL...
RRRRU
GA HA HA HA HA!! KIIIILL!!
WAAAAH!!! SOME-THING SCARIER THAN THE SHARK'S COMING AFTER ME! HEEEEELP!!!
MB
LE
WHAT ARE YOU DOING?! YOU WENT OUT THERE TO SAVE HIM!!

SUNTAN

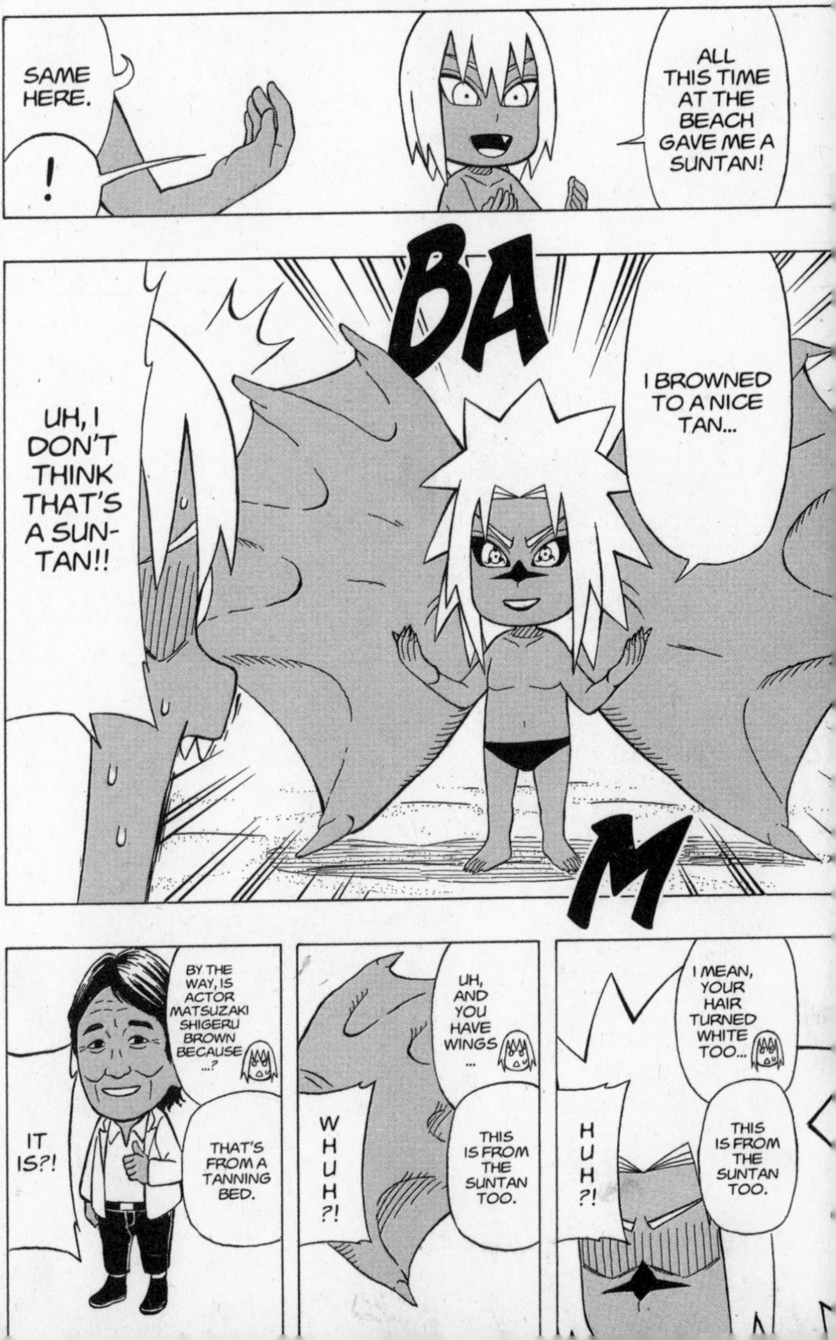
ALL THIS TIME AT THE BEACH GAVE ME A SUNTAN!
!
SAME HERE.
BAM
I BROWNED TO A NICE TAN...
UH, I DON'T THINK THAT'S A SUN-TAN!!
I MEAN, YOUR HAIR TURNED WHITE TOO...
THIS IS FROM THE SUNTAN TOO.
HUH?!
UH, AND YOU HAVE WINGS ...
THIS IS FROM THE SUNTAN TOO.
WHUH?!
BY THE WAY, IS ACTOR MATSUZAKI SHIGERU BROWN BECAUSE ...?
THAT'S FROM A TANNING BED.
IT IS?!

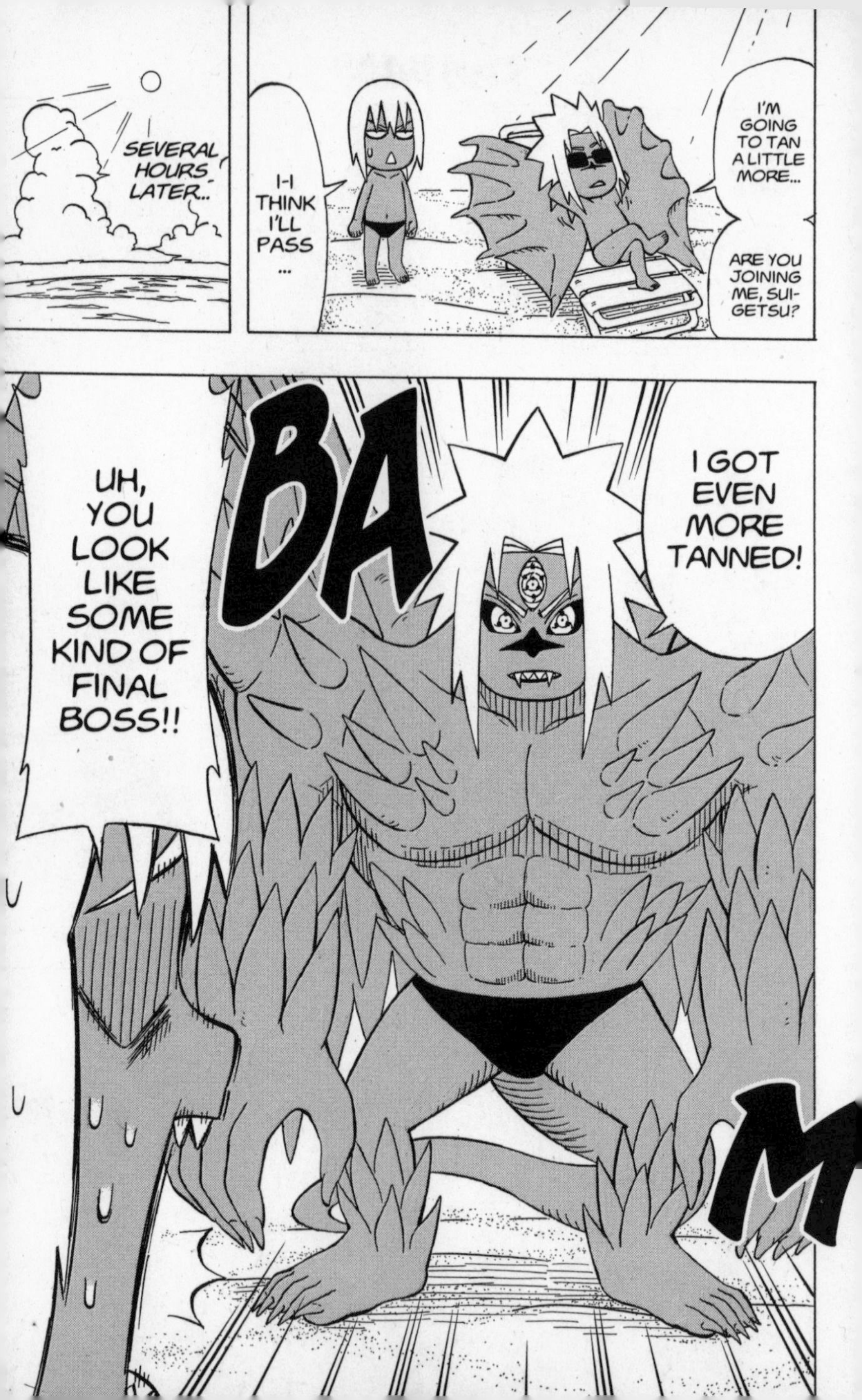
I'M GOING TO TAN A LITTLE MORE...
ARE YOU JOINING ME, SUI-GETSU?
I-I THINK I'LL PASS ...
SEVERAL HOURS LATER...
I GOT EVEN MORE TANNED!
BA
UH, YOU LOOK LIKE SOME KIND OF FINAL BOSS!!
M

SHOWER

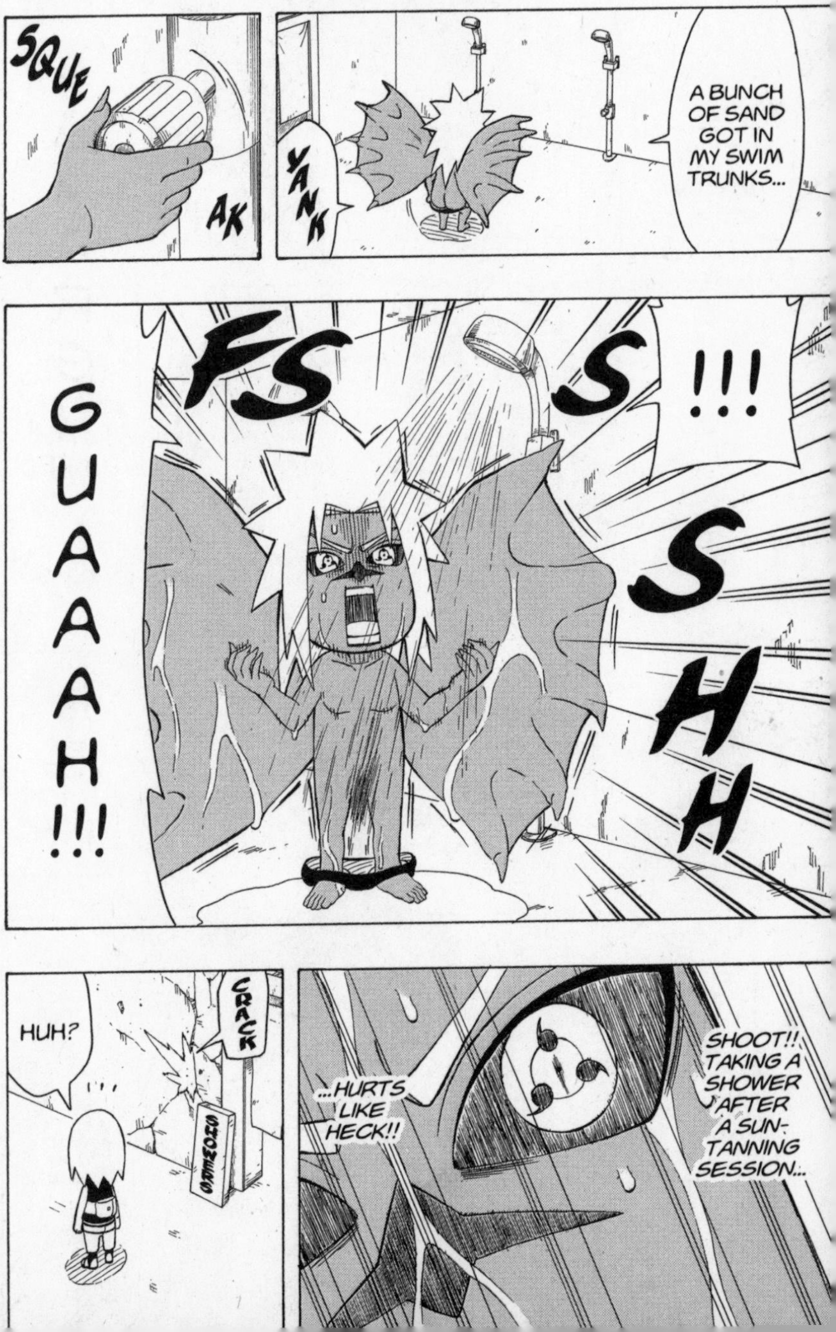
A BUNCH OF SAND GOT IN MY SWIM TRUNKS...
YANK
SQUEAK
FSSSHH!!!
GUAAAAH!!!
SHOOT!! TAKING A SHOWER AFTER A SUN-TANNING SESSION...
...HURTS LIKE HECK!!
CRACK
SHOWERS
HUH?

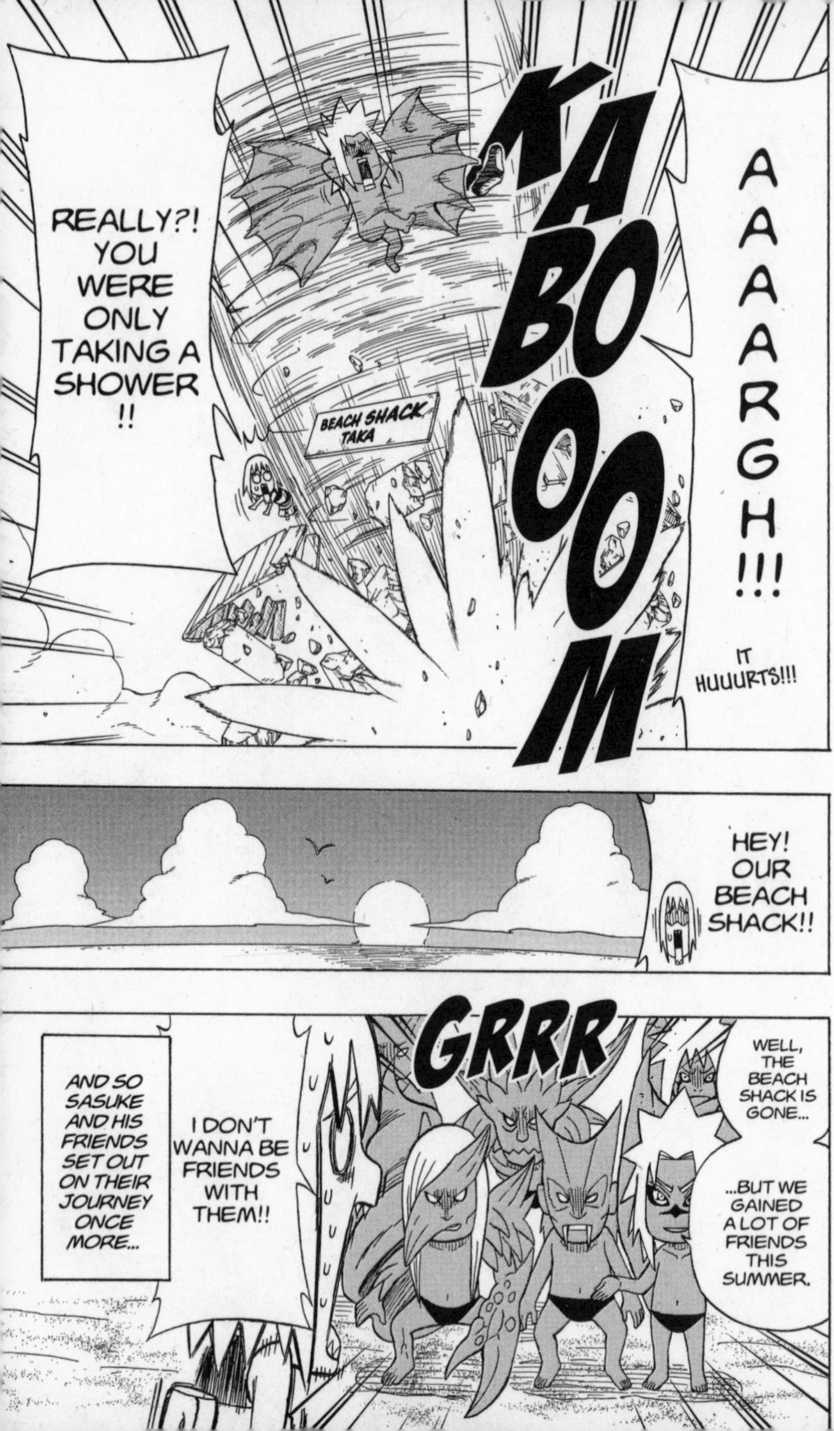
AAAARGH!!!
KABOOOOM
REALLY?! YOU WERE ONLY TAKING A SHOWER!!
BEACH SHACK TAKA
IT HUUURTS!!!
HEY! OUR BEACH SHACK!!
WELL, THE BEACH SHACK IS GONE...
GRRR
...BUT WE GAINED A LOT OF FRIENDS THIS SUMMER.
I DON'T WANNA BE FRIENDS WITH THEM!!
AND SO SASUKE AND HIS FRIENDS SET OUT ON THEIR JOURNEY ONCE MORE...

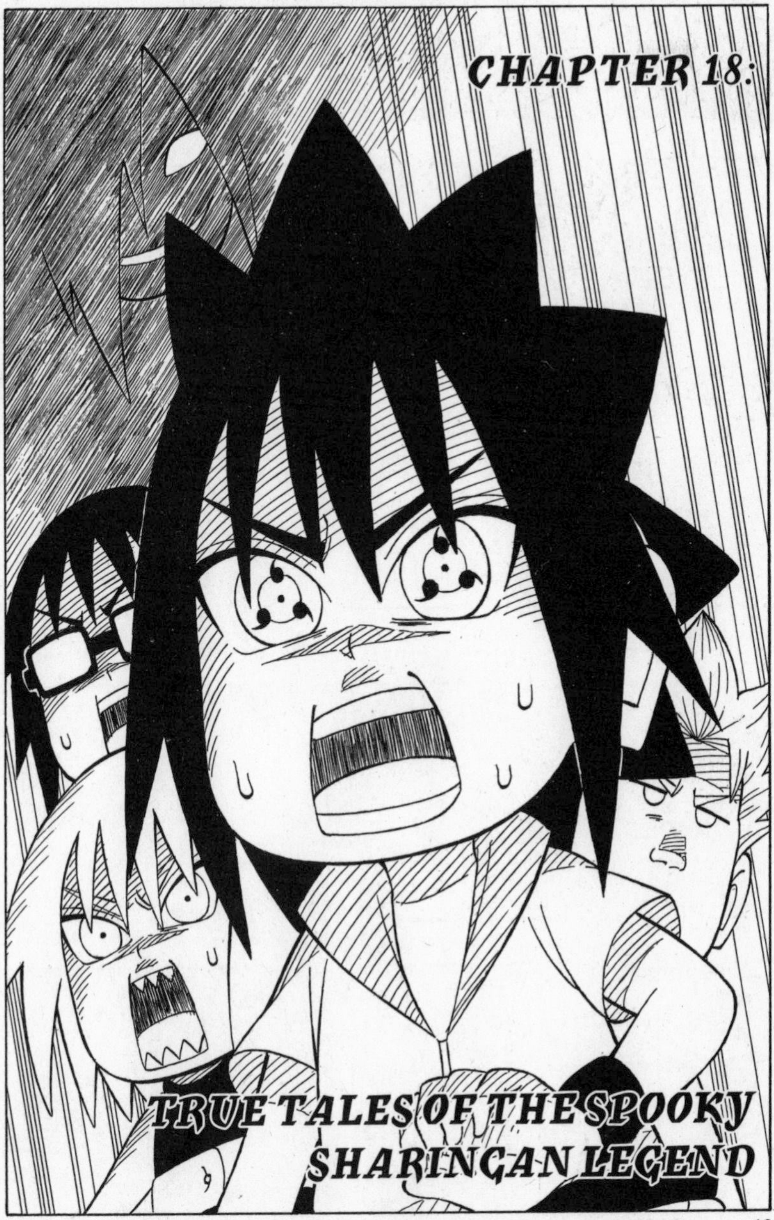
CHAPTER 18:
TRUE TALES OF THE SPOOKY SHARINGAN LEGEND

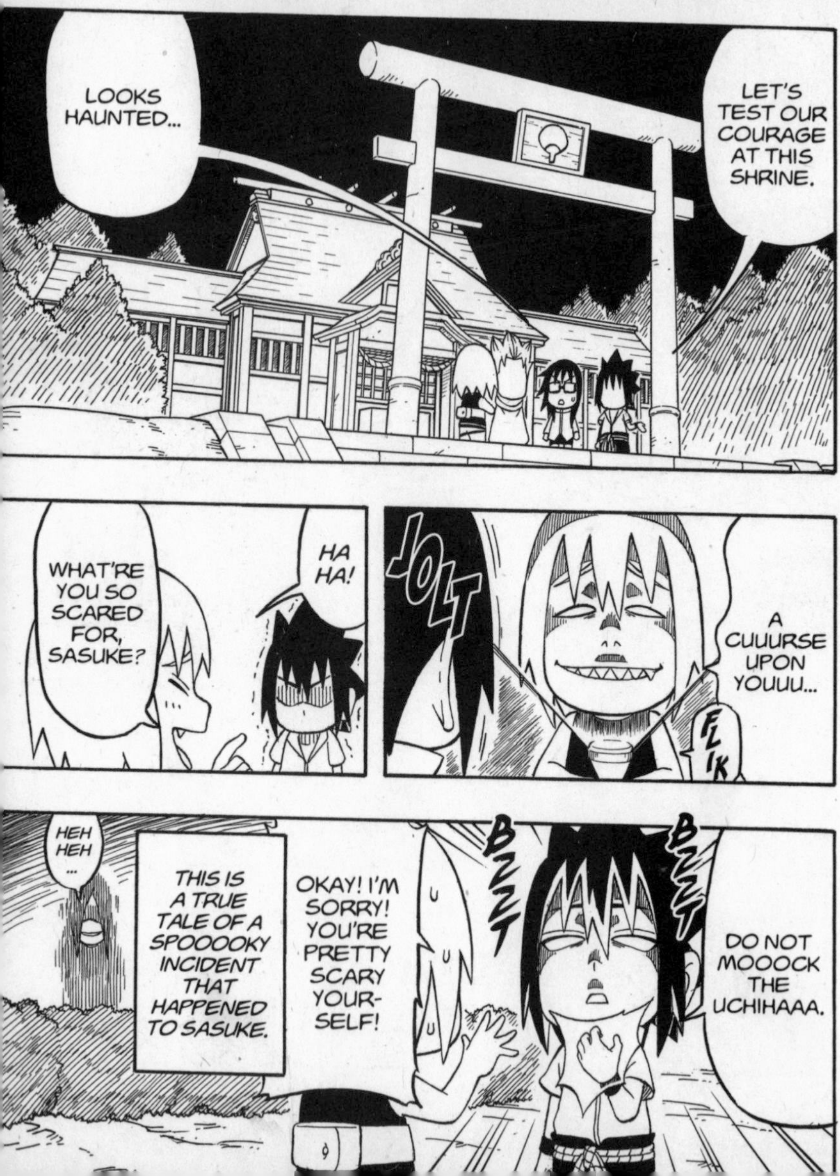
LET'S TEST OUR COURAGE AT THIS SHRINE.
LOOKS HAUNTED...
A CUUURSE UPON YOUUU...
JOLT
FLIK
HA HA!
WHAT'RE YOU SO SCARED FOR, SASUKE?
DO NOT MOOOCK THE UCHIHAAA.
BZZZT
BZZZT
OKAY! I'M SORRY! YOU'RE PRETTY SCARY YOUR-SELF!
THIS IS A TRUE TALE OF A SPOOOOKY INCIDENT THAT HAPPENED TO SASUKE.
HEH HEH ...

SASUKE VS. THE GHOST!!

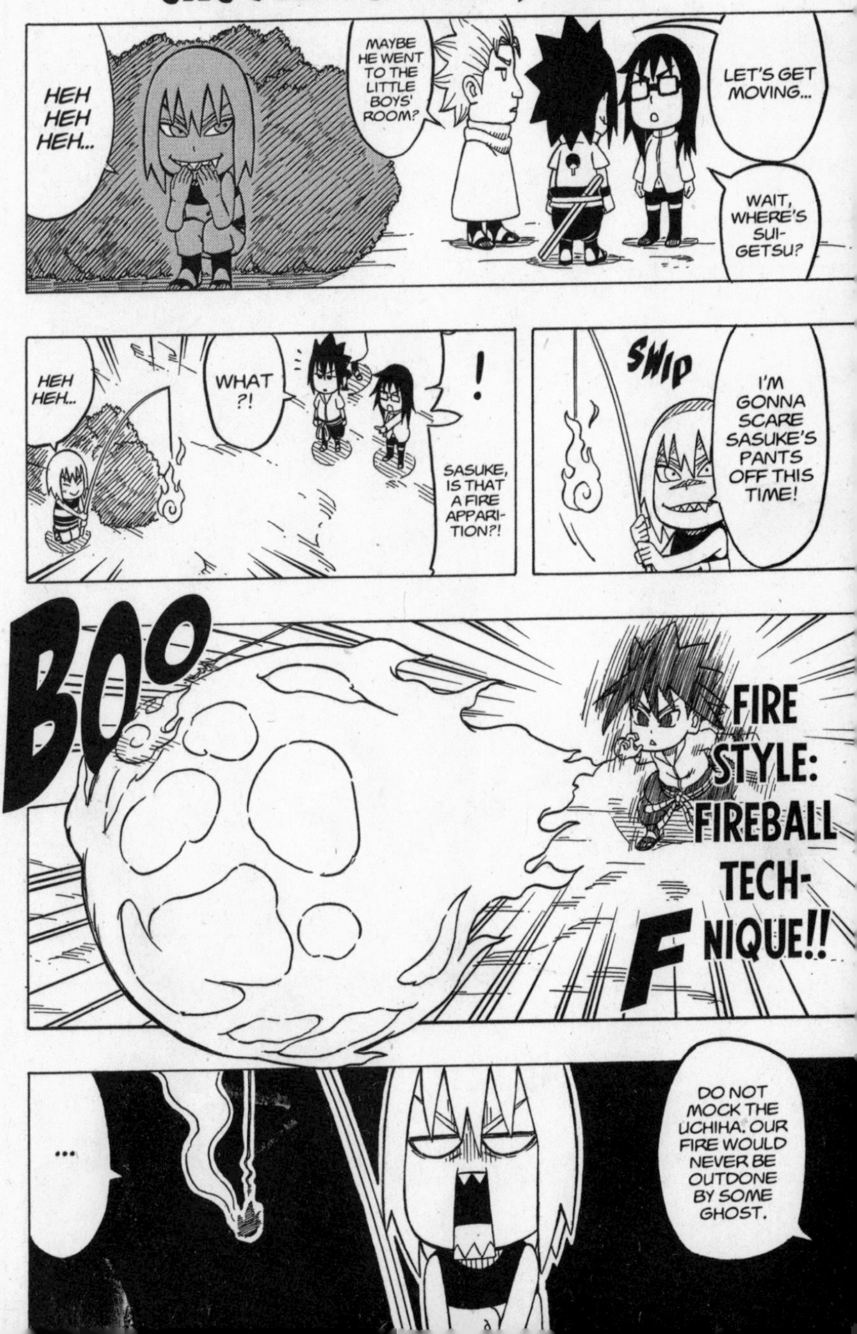
LET'S GET MOVING...
WAIT, WHERE'S SUI-GETSU?
MAYBE HE WENT TO THE LITTLE BOYS' ROOM?
HEH HEH HEH...
SWIP
I'M GONNA SCARE SASUKE'S PANTS OFF THIS TIME!
!
SASUKE, IS THAT A FIRE APPARITION?!
WHAT ?!
HEH HEH...
FIRE STYLE: FIREBALL TECH-NIQUE!!
F
BOO
DO NOT MOCK THE UCHIHA. OUR FIRE WOULD NEVER BE OUTDONE BY SOME GHOST.
...

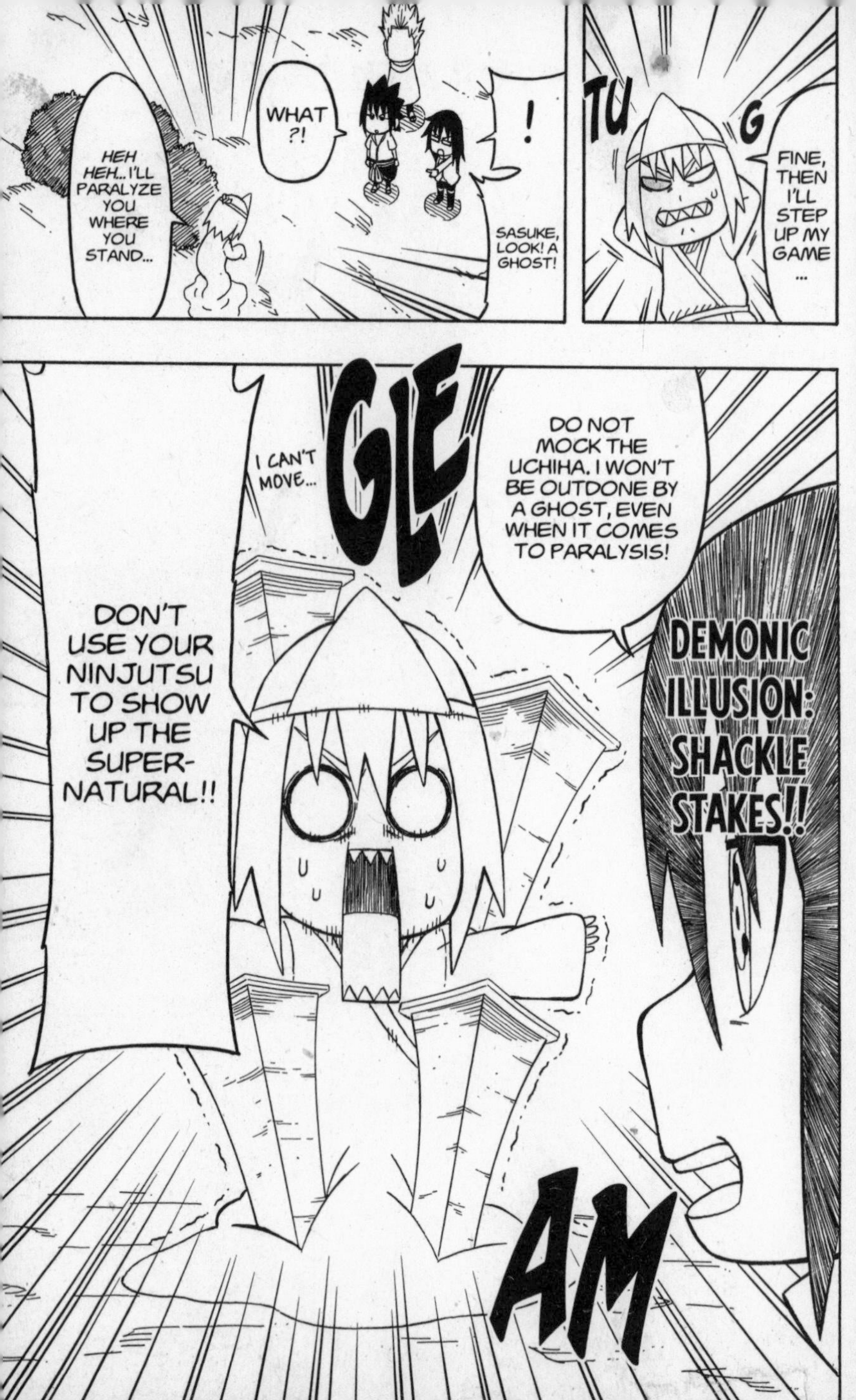
TU
G
FINE, THEN I'LL STEP UP MY GAME ...
!
SASUKE, LOOK! A GHOST!
WHAT ?!
HEH HEH... I'LL PARALYZE YOU WHERE YOU STAND...
DO NOT MOCK THE UCHIHA. I WON'T BE OUTDONE BY A GHOST, EVEN WHEN IT COMES TO PARALYSIS!
DEMONIC ILLUSION: SHACKLE STAKES!!
GLE
I CAN'T MOVE...
DON'T USE YOUR NINJUTSU TO SHOW UP THE SUPER-NATURAL!!
AM

CHANCE FOR ROMANCE?!

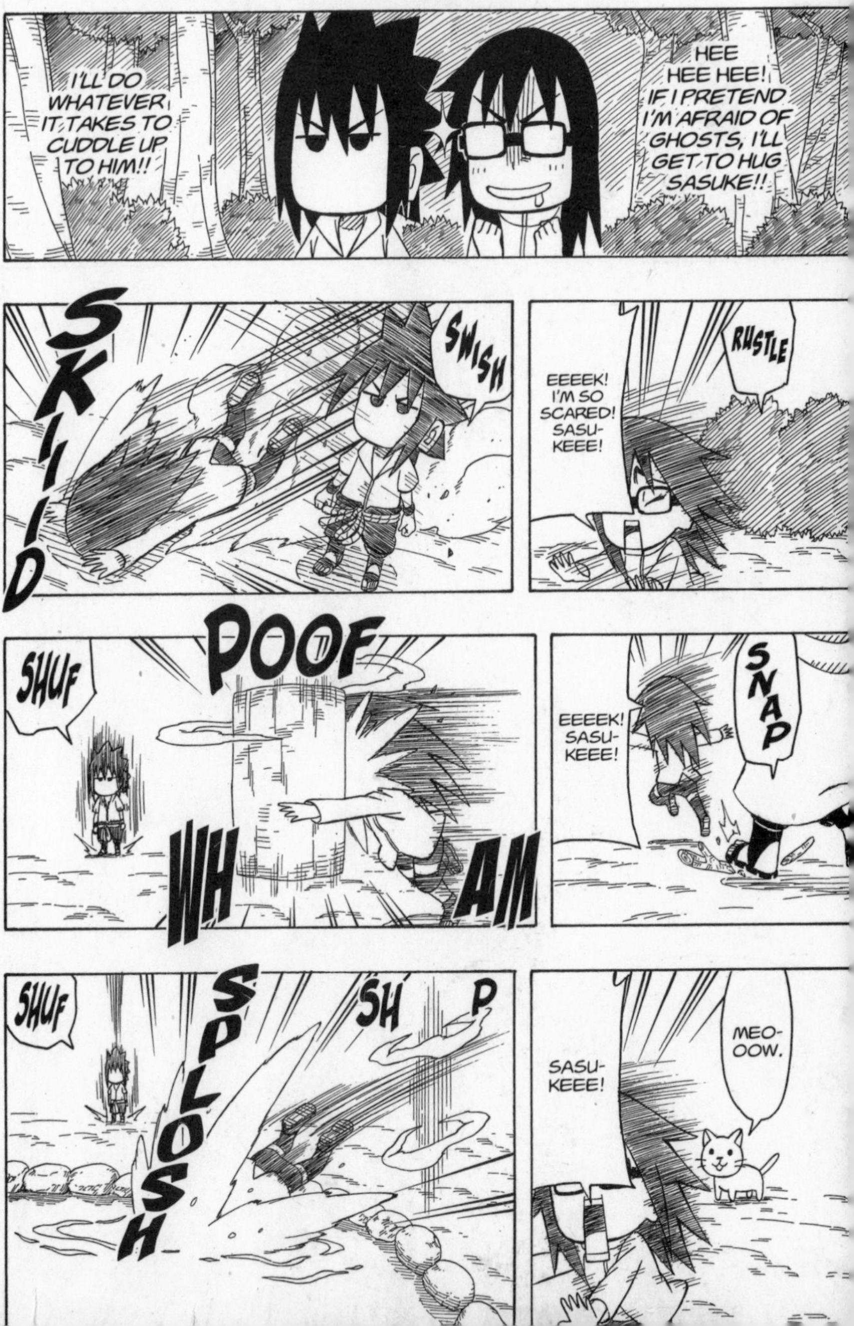
HEE HEE HEE! IF I PRETEND I'M AFRAID OF GHOSTS, I'LL GET TO HUG SASUKE!!
I'LL DO WHATEVER IT TAKES TO CUDDLE UP TO HIM!!
RUSTLE
EEEEK! I'M SO SCARED! SASU-KEEE!
SWISH
SKIIID
SNAP
EEEEK! SASU-KEEE!
POOF
SHUF
WHAM
MEO-OOW.
SASU-KEEE!
SHP
SPLOSH
SHUF

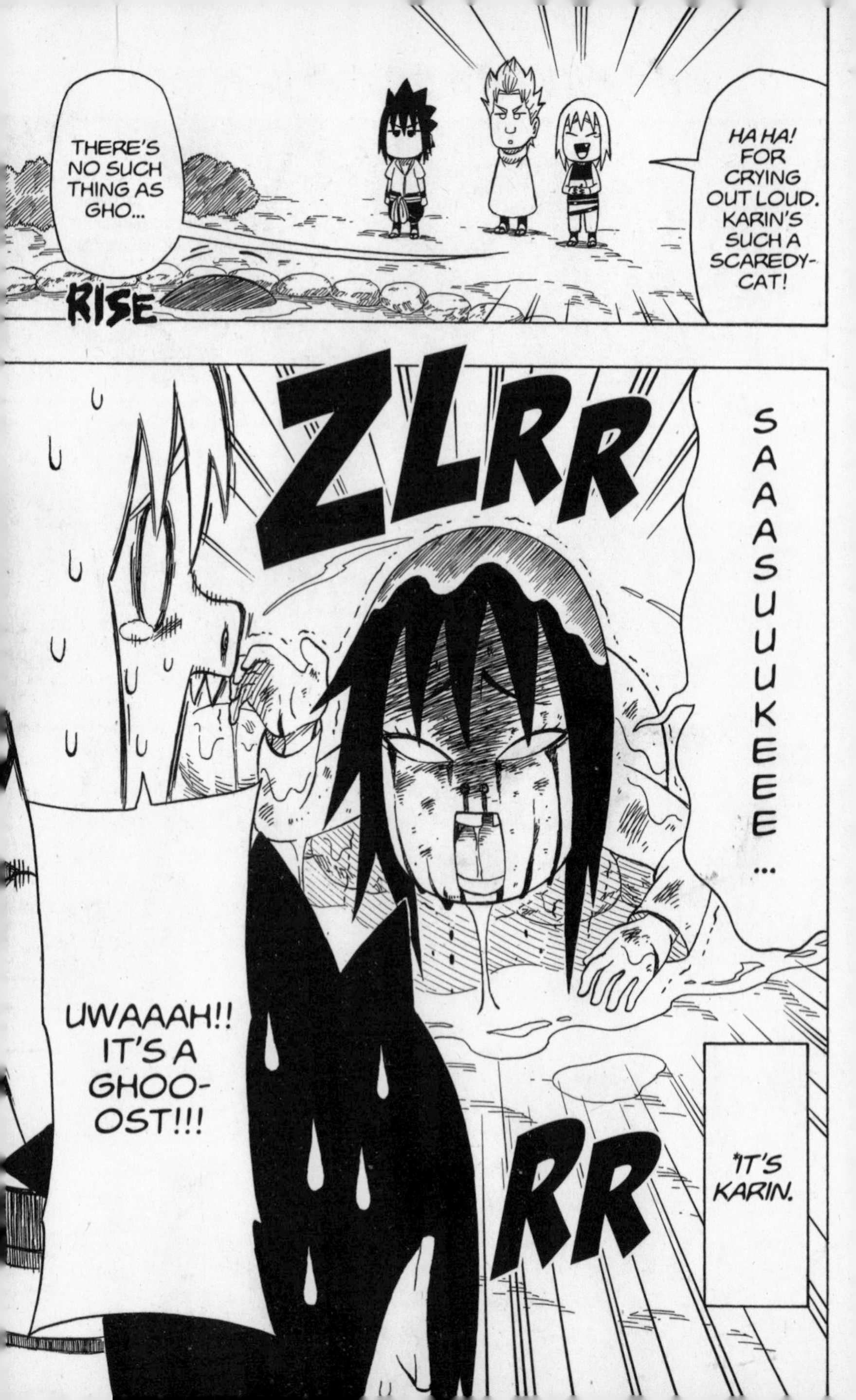
HA HA! FOR CRYING OUT LOUD. KARIN'S SUCH A SCAREDY-CAT!
THERE'S NO SUCH THING AS GHO...
RISE
SAAAASUUUKEEE...
ZLRR
*IT'S KARIN.
UWAAAH!! IT'S A GHOO-OST!!!
RR

ONE EXTRA PERSON...?!

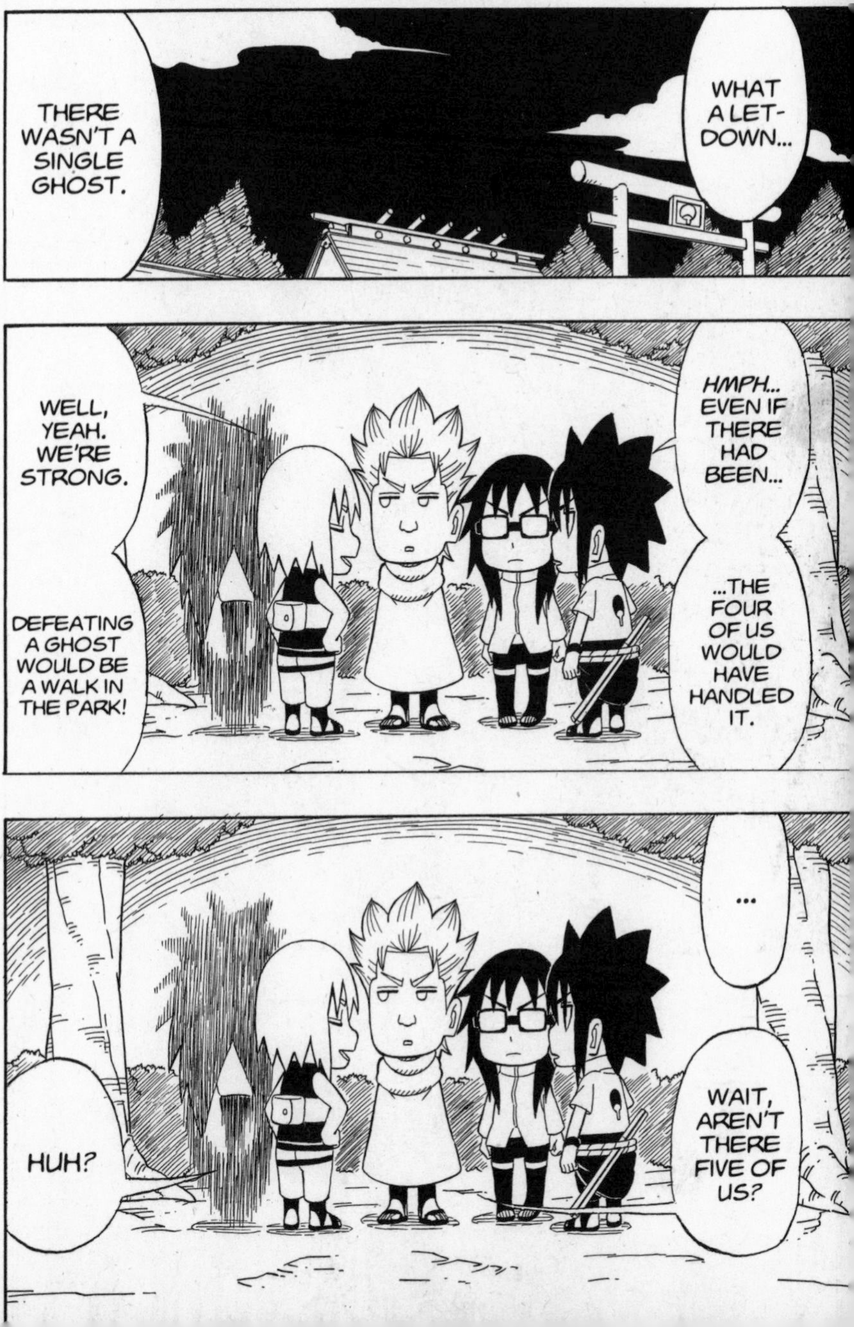
WHAT A LET-DOWN...
THERE WASN'T A SINGLE GHOST.
HMPH... EVEN IF THERE HAD BEEN...
...THE FOUR OF US WOULD HAVE HANDLED IT.
WELL, YEAH. WE'RE STRONG.
DEFEATING A GHOST WOULD BE A WALK IN THE PARK!
...
WAIT, AREN'T THERE FIVE OF US?
HUH?

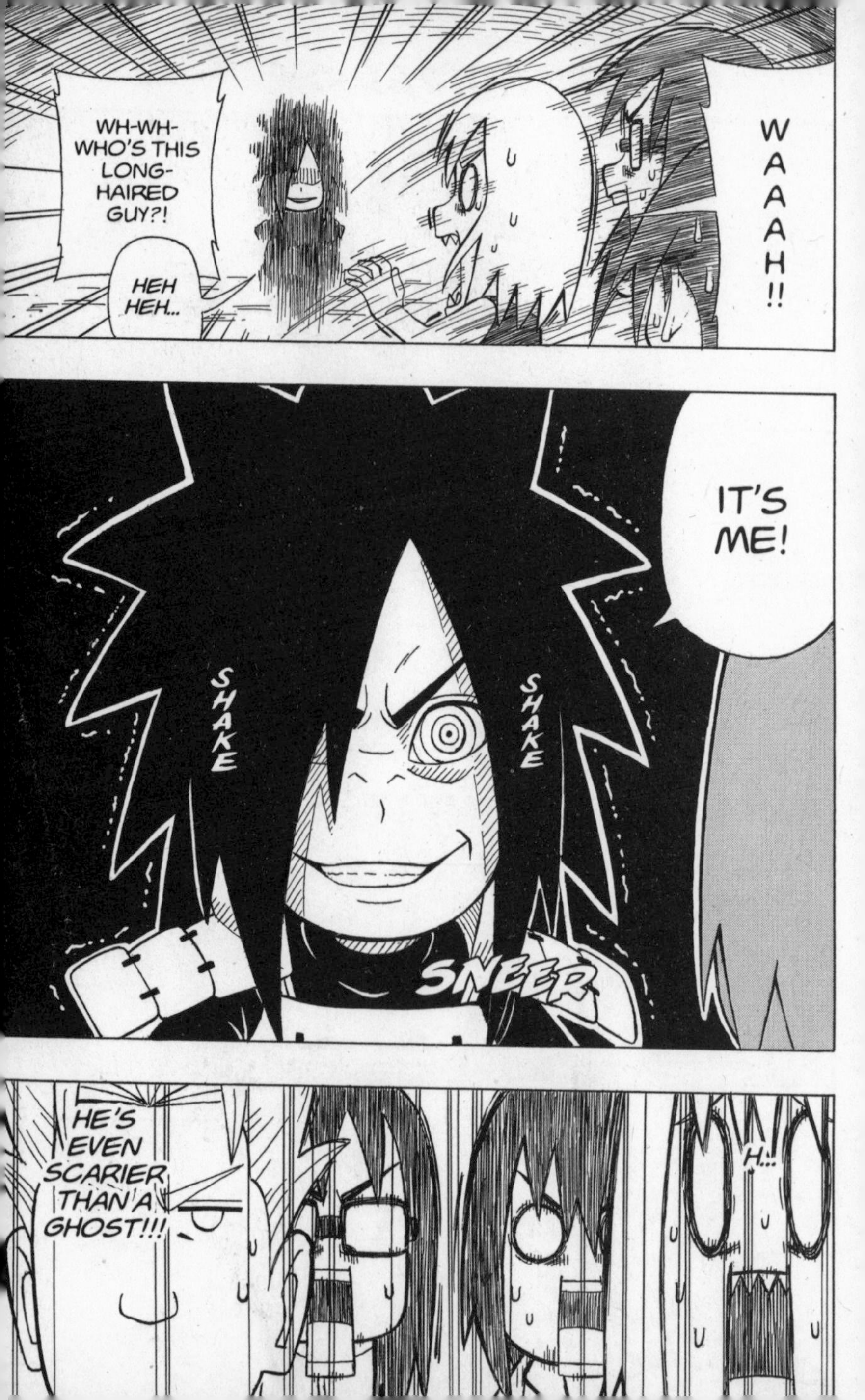
WAAAAH!!
WH-WH-WHO'S THIS LONG-HAIRED GUY?!
HEH HEH...
IT'S ME!
SHAKE
SHAKE
SNEER
H...
HE'S EVEN SCARIER THAN A GHOST!!!

UCHIHA MADARA

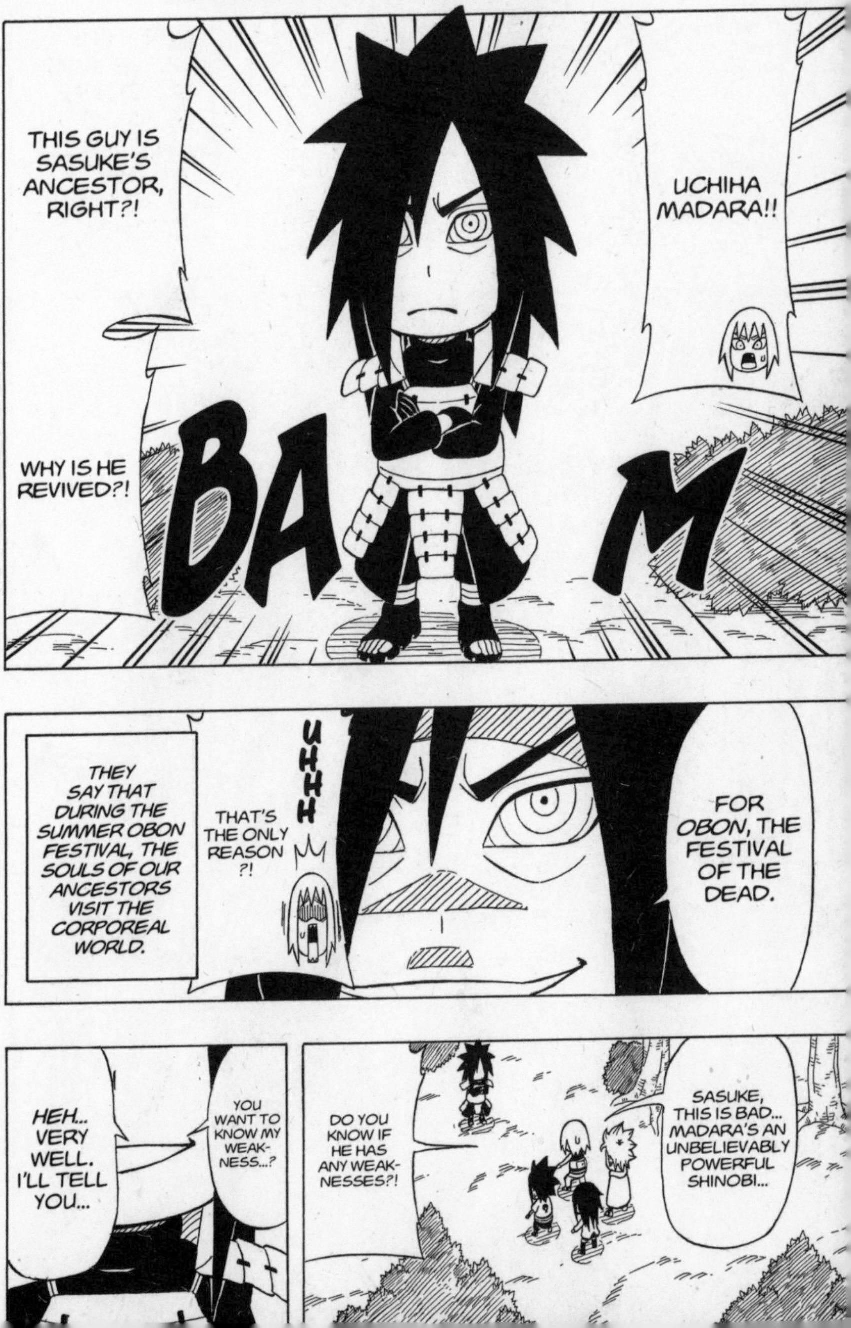
UCHIHA MADARA!!
THIS GUY IS SASUKE'S ANCESTOR, RIGHT?!
WHY IS HE REVIVED?!
BA M
FOR OBON, THE FESTIVAL OF THE DEAD.
UHHH
THAT'S THE ONLY REASON ?!
THEY SAY THAT DURING THE SUMMER OBON FESTIVAL, THE SOULS OF OUR ANCESTORS VISIT THE CORPOREAL WORLD.
SASUKE, THIS IS BAD... MADARA'S AN UNBELIEVABLY POWERFUL SHINOBI...
DO YOU KNOW IF HE HAS ANY WEAK-NESSES?!
YOU WANT TO KNOW MY WEAK-NESS...?
HEH... VERY WELL. I'LL TELL YOU...

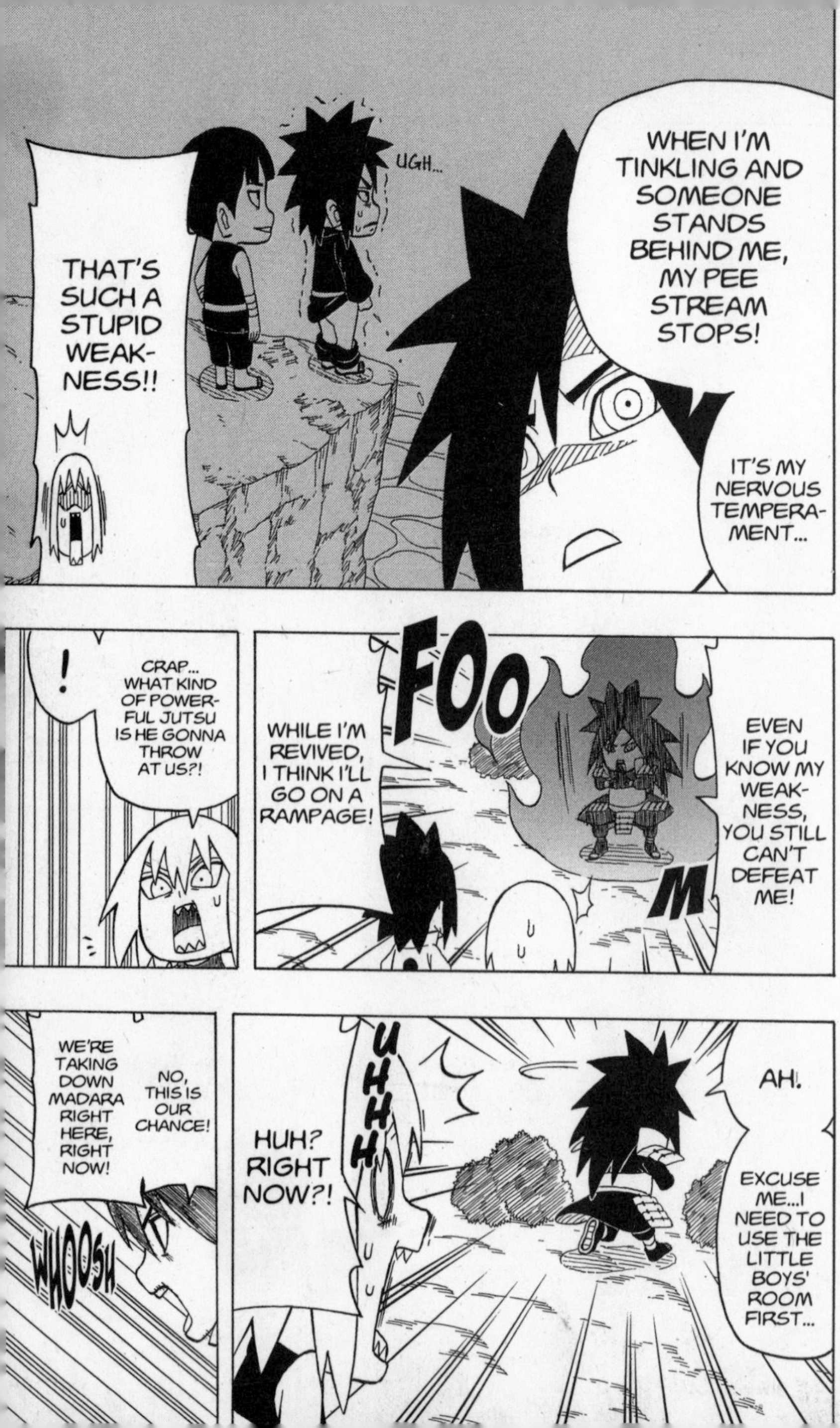
WHEN I'M TINKLING AND SOMEONE STANDS BEHIND ME, MY PEE STREAM STOPS!
IT'S MY NERVOUS TEMPERA-MENT...
UGH...
THAT'S SUCH A STUPID WEAK-NESS!!
EVEN IF YOU KNOW MY WEAK-NESS, YOU STILL CAN'T DEFEAT ME!
FOOM
WHILE I'M REVIVED, I THINK I'LL GO ON A RAMPAGE!
!
CRAP... WHAT KIND OF POWER-FUL JUTSU IS HE GONNA THROW AT US?!
AH!
EXCUSE ME...I NEED TO USE THE LITTLE BOYS' ROOM FIRST...
UHHHH
HUH? RIGHT NOW?!
NO, THIS IS OUR CHANCE!
WE'RE TAKING DOWN MADARA RIGHT HERE, RIGHT NOW!
WHOOSH

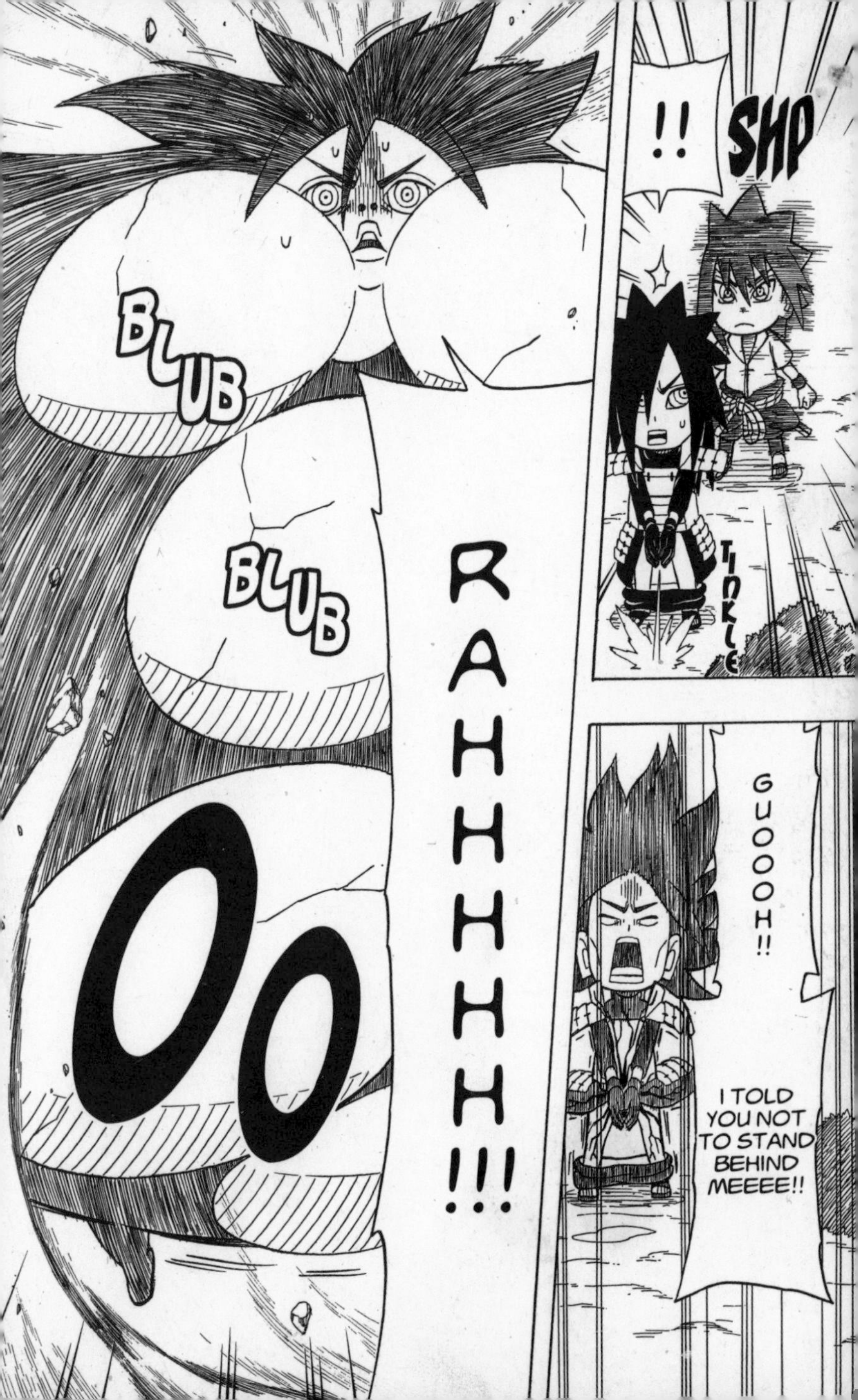
!!
SHP
TINKLE
GUOOOH!!
I TOLD YOU NOT TO STAND BEHIND MEEEE!!
BLUB
BLUB
OO
RAHHHHH!!!

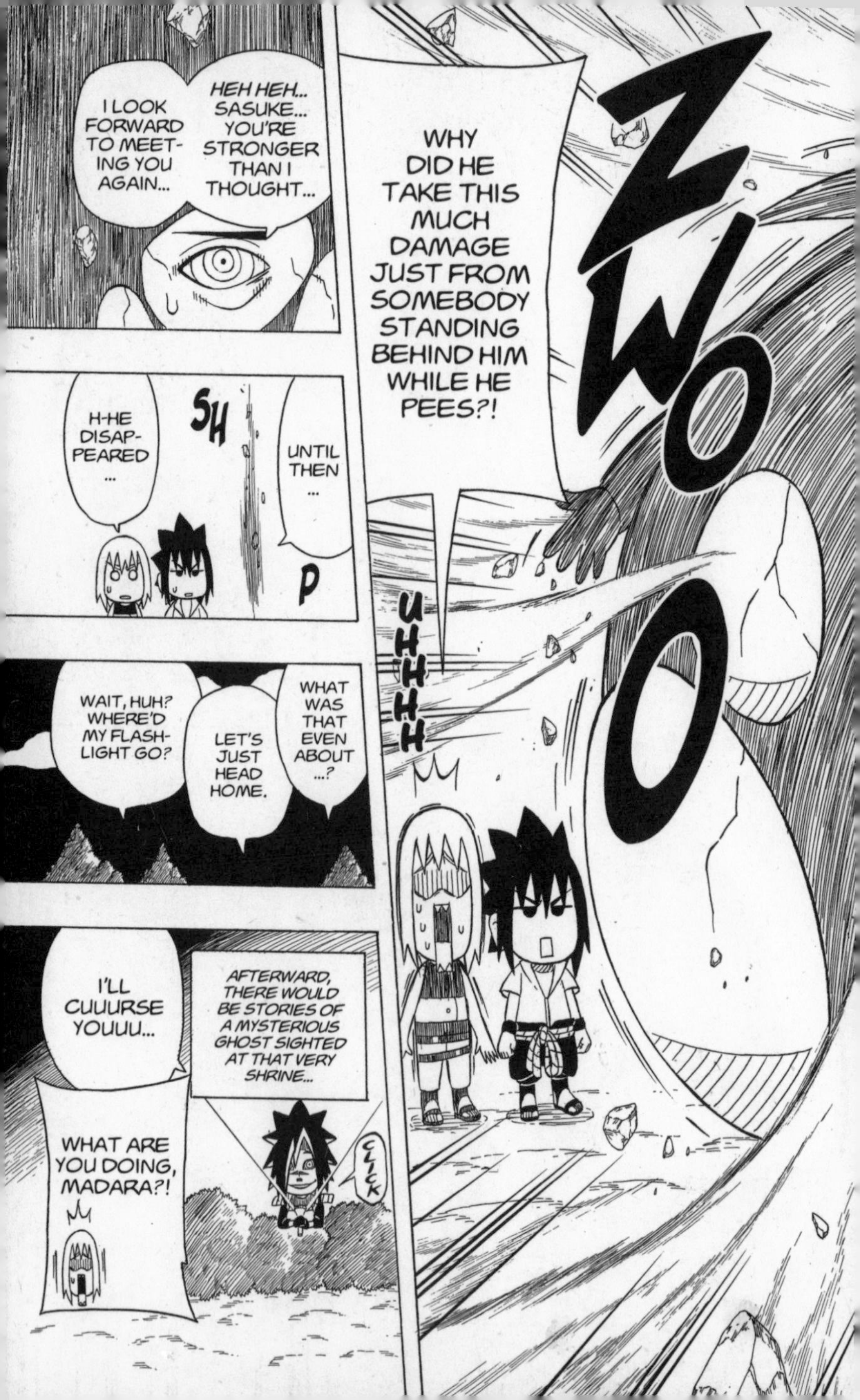
ZWOOO
WHY DID HE TAKE THIS MUCH DAMAGE JUST FROM SOMEBODY STANDING BEHIND HIM WHILE HE PEES?!
UHHHHH
HEH HEH... SASUKE... YOU'RE STRONGER THAN I THOUGHT...
I LOOK FORWARD TO MEETING YOU AGAIN...
UNTIL THEN ...
SHP
H-HE DISAPPEARED ...
WHAT WAS THAT EVEN ABOUT ...?
LET'S JUST HEAD HOME.
WAIT, HUH? WHERE'D MY FLASHLIGHT GO?
AFTERWARD, THERE WOULD BE STORIES OF A MYSTERIOUS GHOST SIGHTED AT THAT VERY SHRINE...
I'LL CUUURSE YOUUU...
CLICK
WHAT ARE YOU DOING, MADARA?!

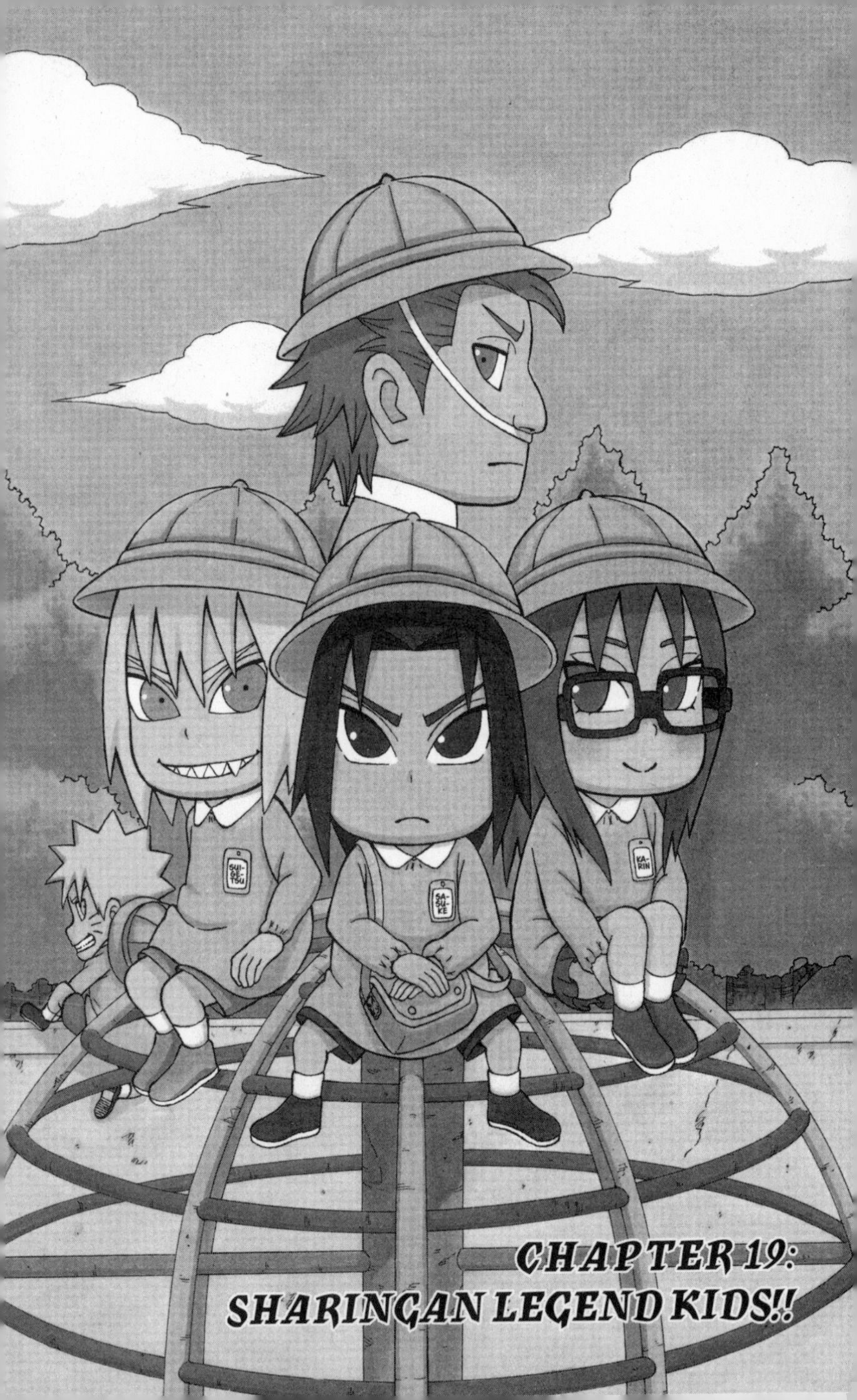
SUI-GE-TSU
SA-SU-KE
KA-RIN

CHAPTER 19: SHARINGAN LEGEND KIDS!!

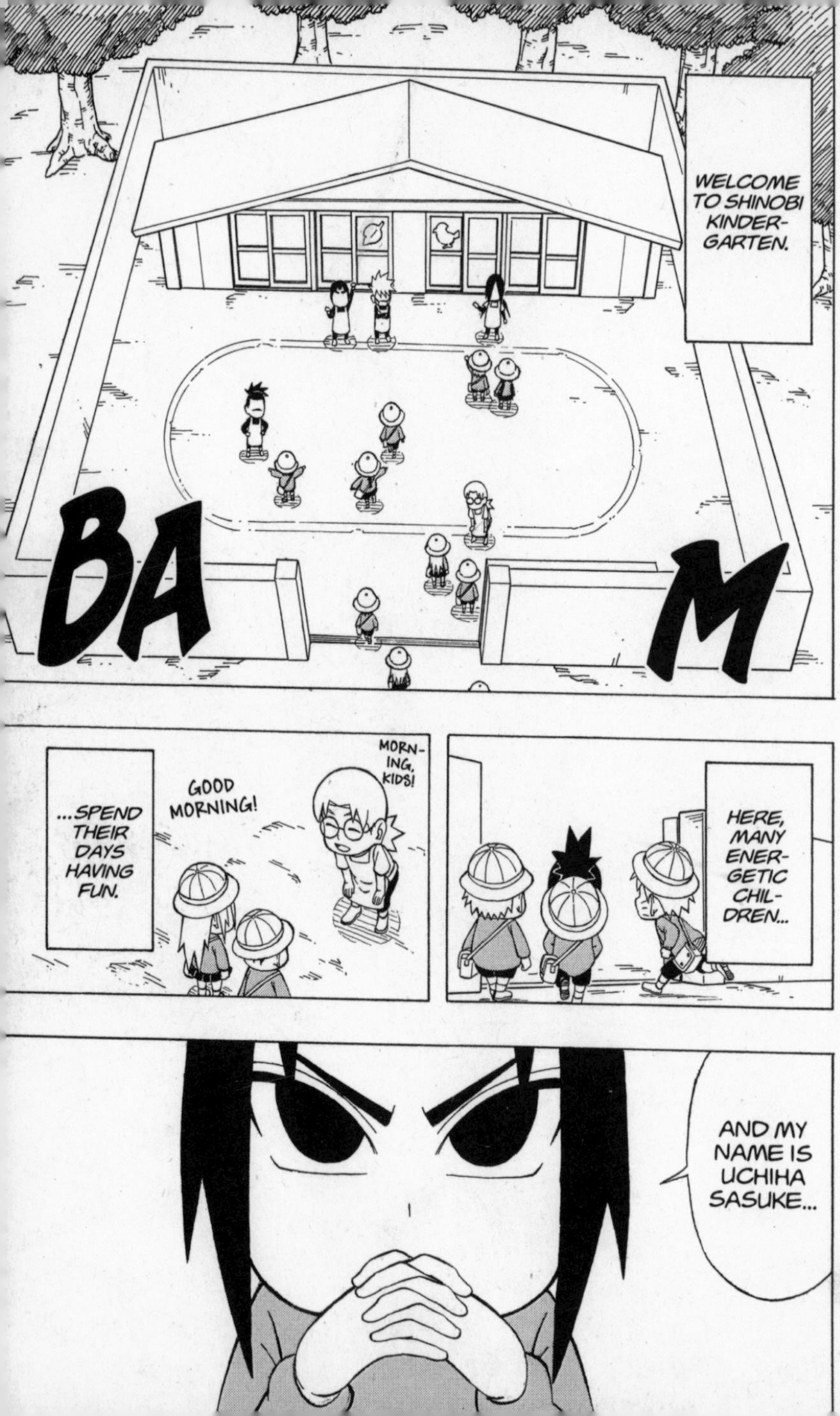
WELCOME TO SHINOBI KINDER-GARTEN.
BAM
HERE, MANY ENER-GETIC CHIL-DREN...
MORN-ING, KIDS!
GOOD MORNING!
...SPEND THEIR DAYS HAVING FUN.
AND MY NAME IS UCHIHA SASUKE...

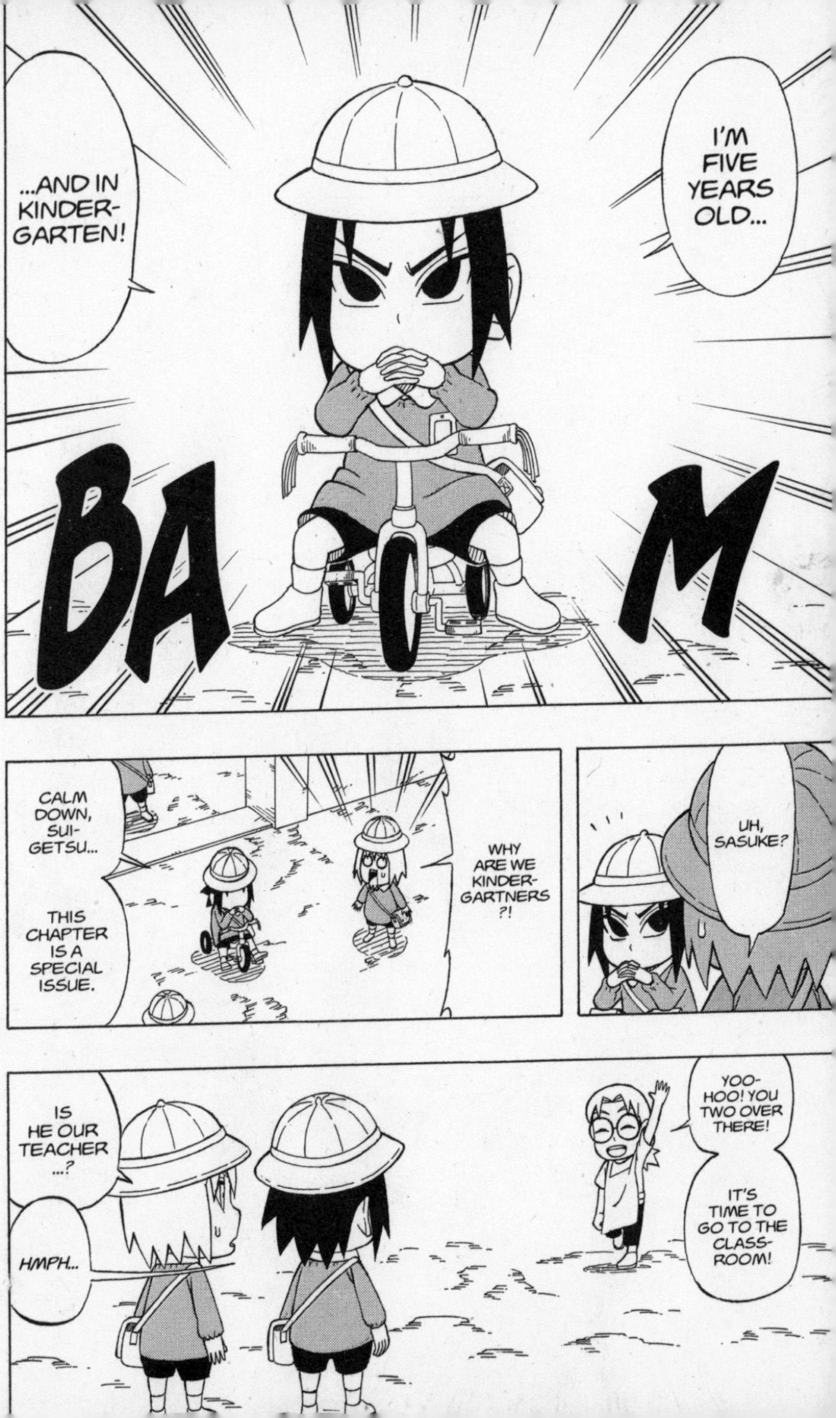
I'M FIVE YEARS OLD...
...AND IN KINDERGARTEN!
BAM
UH, SASUKE?
WHY ARE WE KINDERGARTNERS?!
CALM DOWN, SUIGETSU...
THIS CHAPTER IS A SPECIAL ISSUE.
YOO-HOO! YOU TWO OVER THERE!
IT'S TIME TO GO TO THE CLASSROOM!
IS HE OUR TEACHER...?
HMPH...

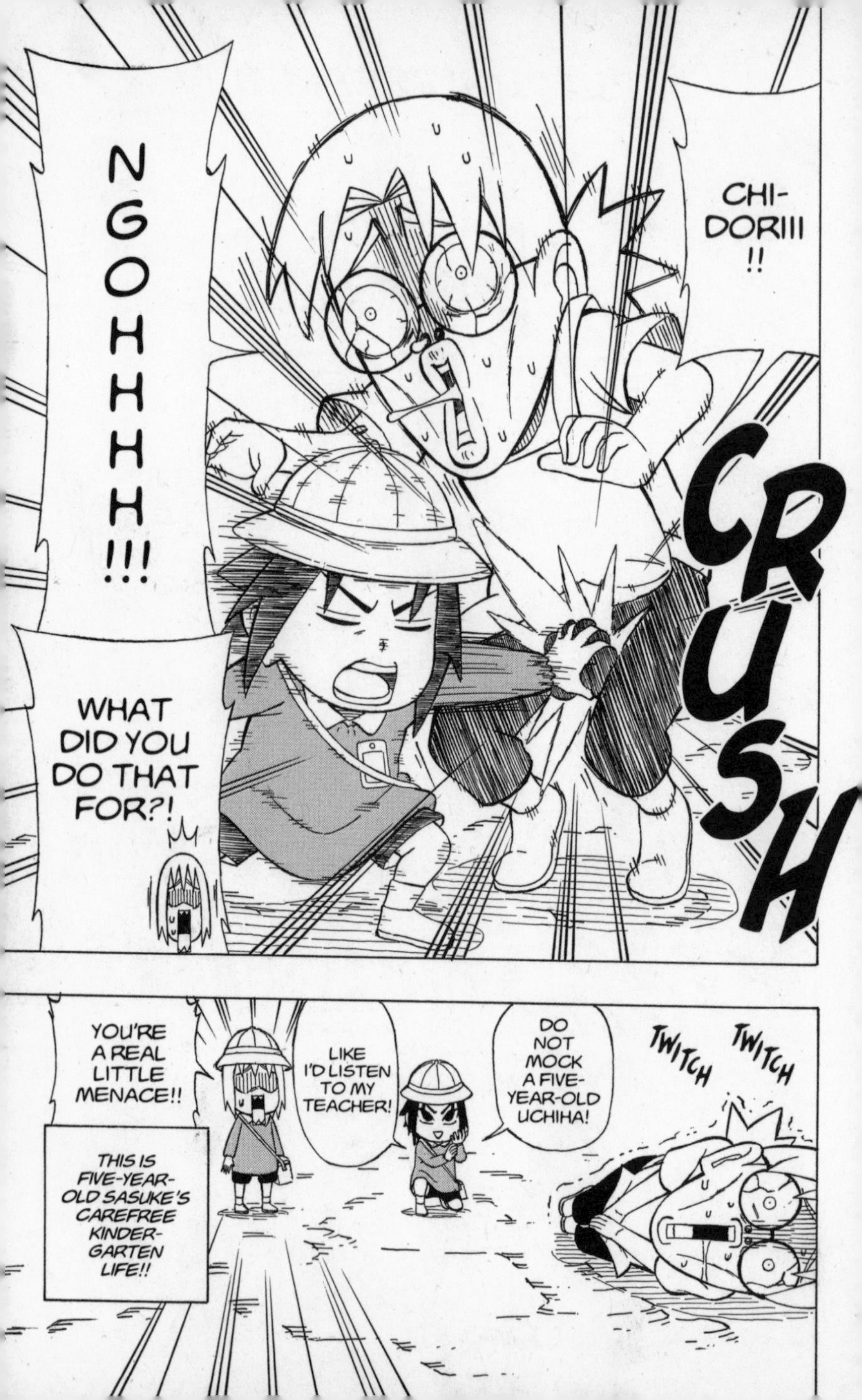
CHI-DORIII!!
NGOHHHH!!!
CRUSH
WHAT DID YOU DO THAT FOR?!
TWITCH TWITCH
DO NOT MOCK A FIVE-YEAR-OLD UCHIHA!
LIKE I'D LISTEN TO MY TEACHER!
YOU'RE A REAL LITTLE MENACE!!
THIS IS FIVE-YEAR-OLD SASUKE'S CAREFREE KINDERGARTEN LIFE!!

PLAYING PRETEND

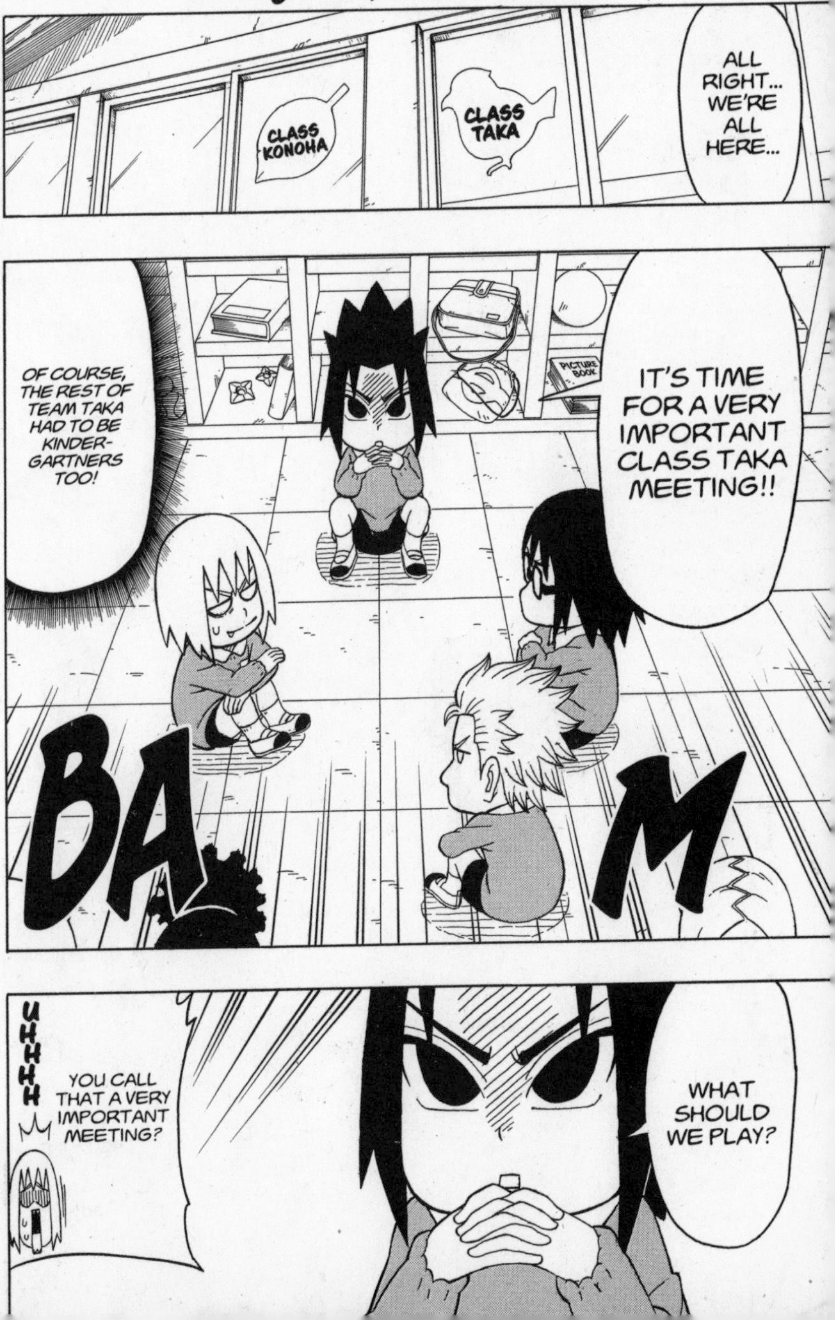

ALL RIGHT... WE'RE ALL HERE...
CLASS TAKA
CLASS KONOHA
IT'S TIME FOR A VERY IMPORTANT CLASS TAKA MEETING!!
PICTURE BOOK
OF COURSE, THE REST OF TEAM TAKA HAD TO BE KINDER-GARTNERS TOO!
BAM
WHAT SHOULD WE PLAY?
UHHHH
YOU CALL THAT A VERY IMPORTANT MEETING?

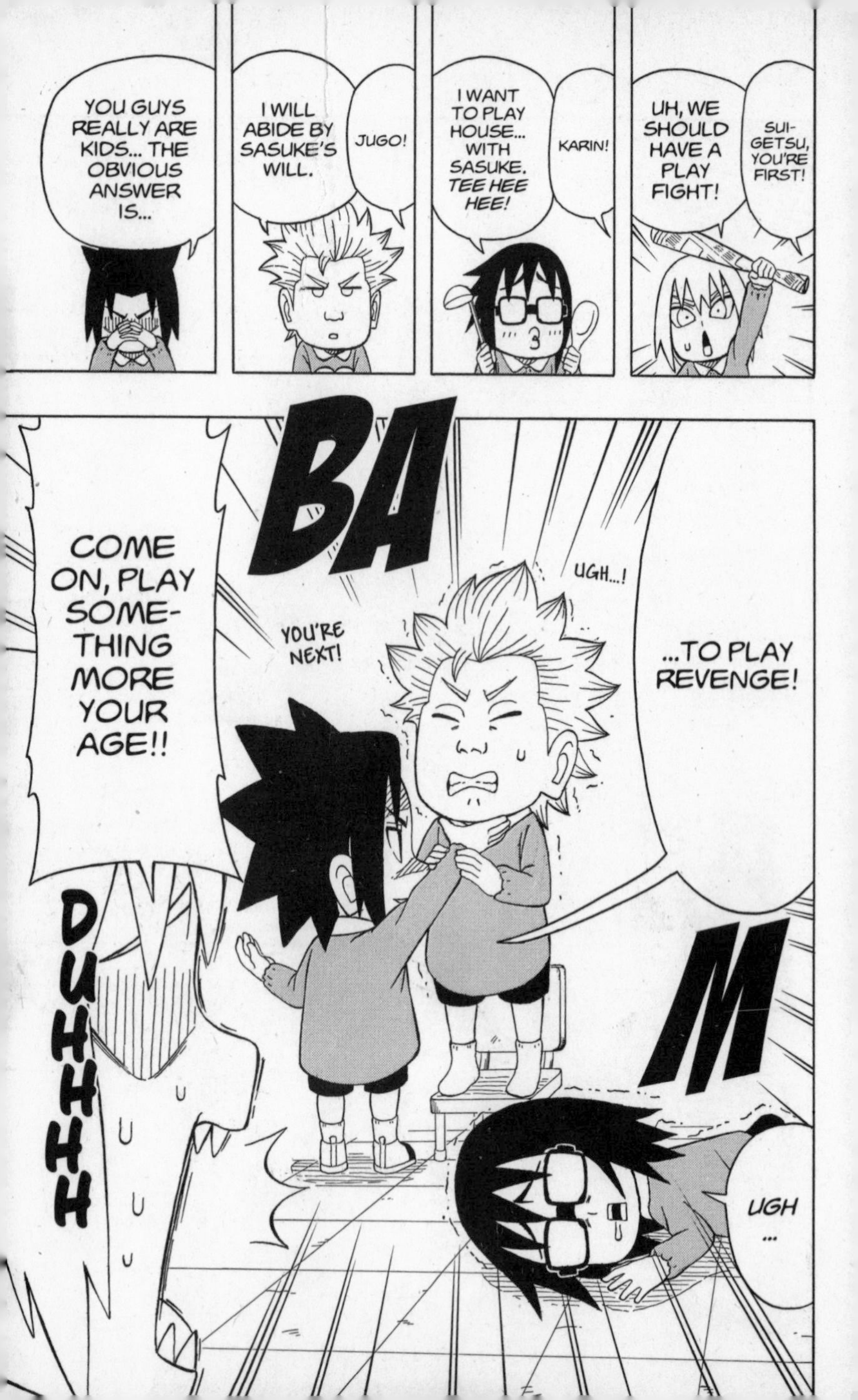
SUI-GETSU, YOU'RE FIRST!
UH, WE SHOULD HAVE A PLAY FIGHT!
KARIN!
I WANT TO PLAY HOUSE... WITH SASUKE. TEE HEE HEE!
JUGO!
I WILL ABIDE BY SASUKE'S WILL.
YOU GUYS REALLY ARE KIDS... THE OBVIOUS ANSWER IS...
...TO PLAY REVENGE!
UGH...!
BA
YOU'RE NEXT!
M
COME ON, PLAY SOME-THING MORE YOUR AGE!!
UGH ...
DUHHHH

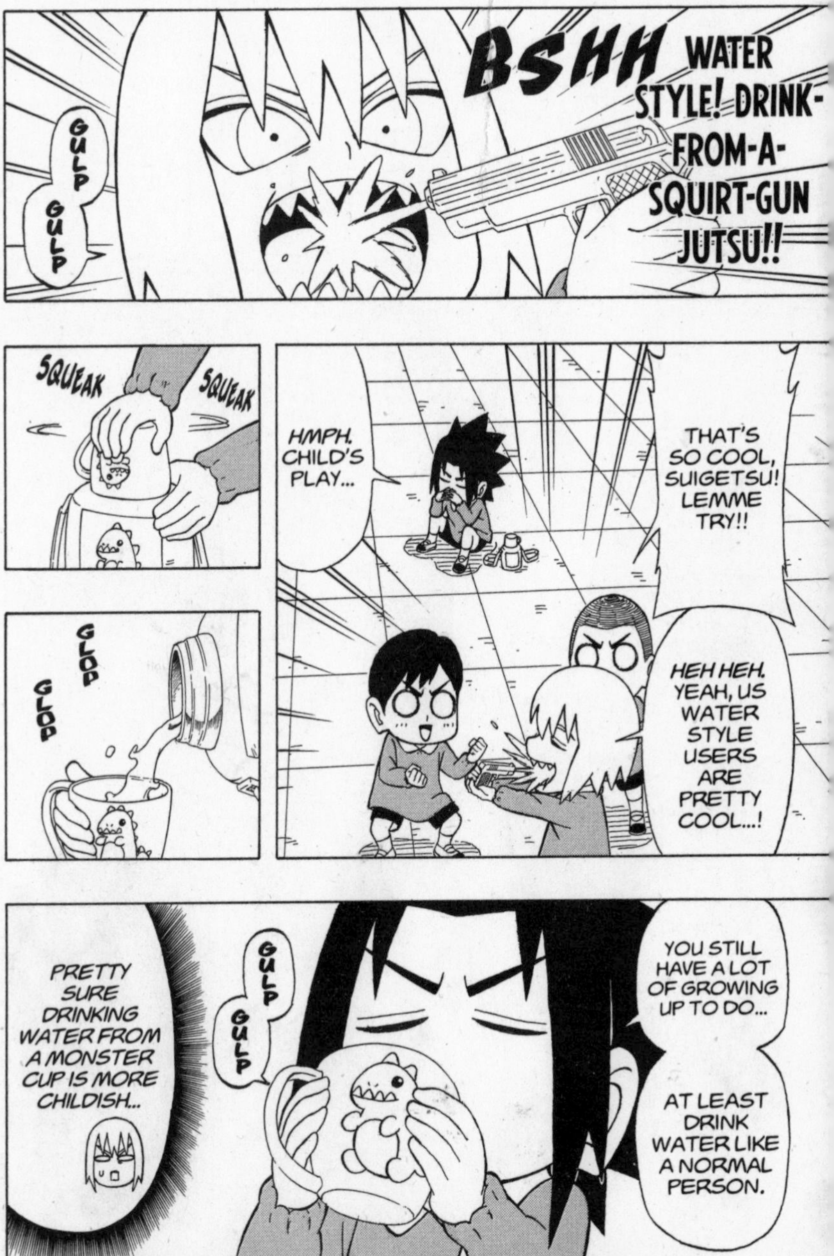
BSHH
WATER STYLE! DRINK-FROM-A-SQUIRT-GUN JUTSU!!
GULP GULP
THAT'S SO COOL, SUIGETSU! LEMME TRY!!
HMPH. CHILD'S PLAY...
HEH HEH. YEAH, US WATER STYLE USERS ARE PRETTY COOL...!
SQUEAK SQUEAK
GLOP GLOP
YOU STILL HAVE A LOT OF GROWING UP TO DO...
AT LEAST DRINK WATER LIKE A NORMAL PERSON.
GULP GULP
PRETTY SURE DRINKING WATER FROM A MONSTER CUP IS MORE CHILDISH...
SASUKE

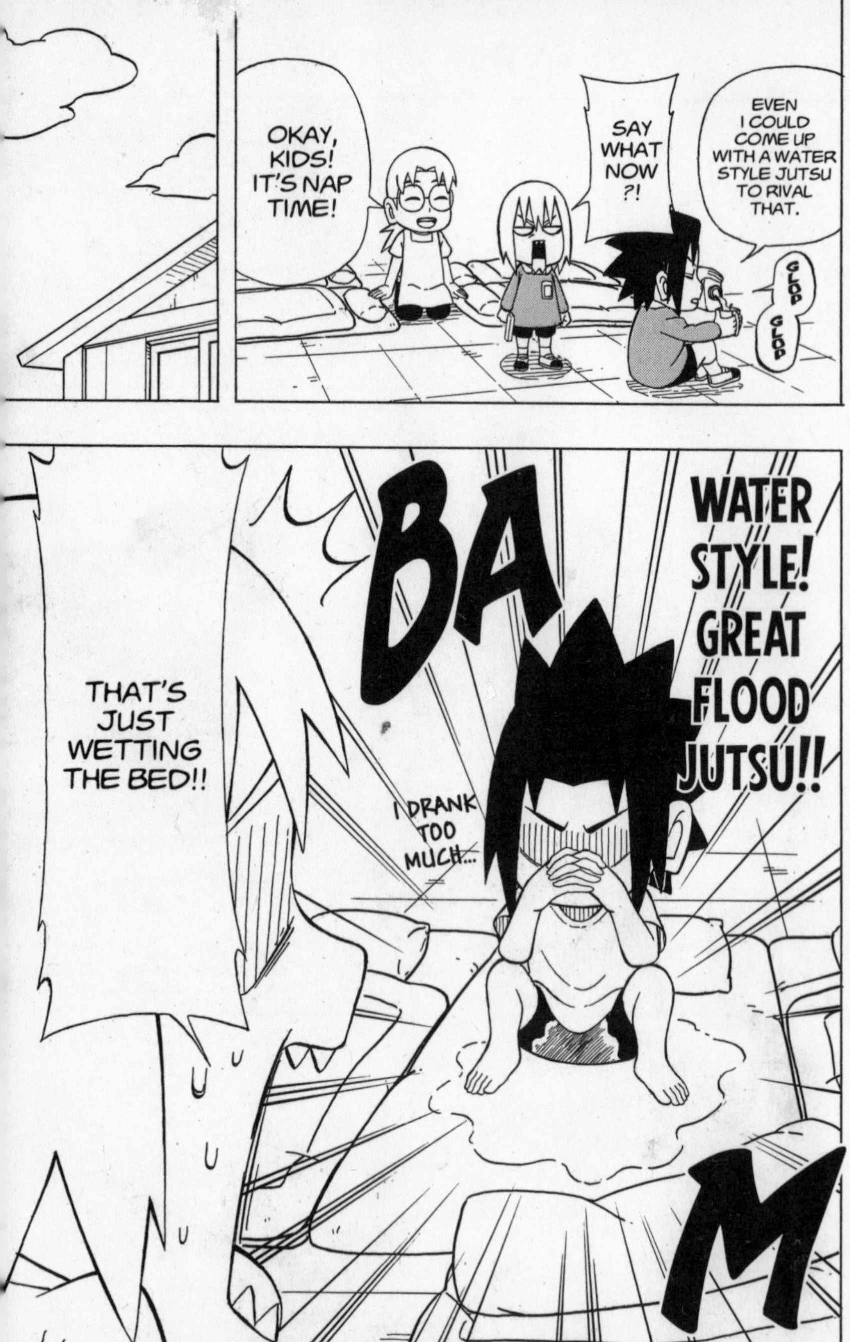
EVEN I COULD COME UP WITH A WATER STYLE JUTSU TO RIVAL THAT.
GLOP GLOP
SAY WHAT NOW ?!
OKAY, KIDS! IT'S NAP TIME!
WATER STYLE! GREAT FLOOD JUTSU!!
BAM
I DRANK TOO MUCH...
THAT'S JUST WETTING THE BED!!

PLAYING HOUSE

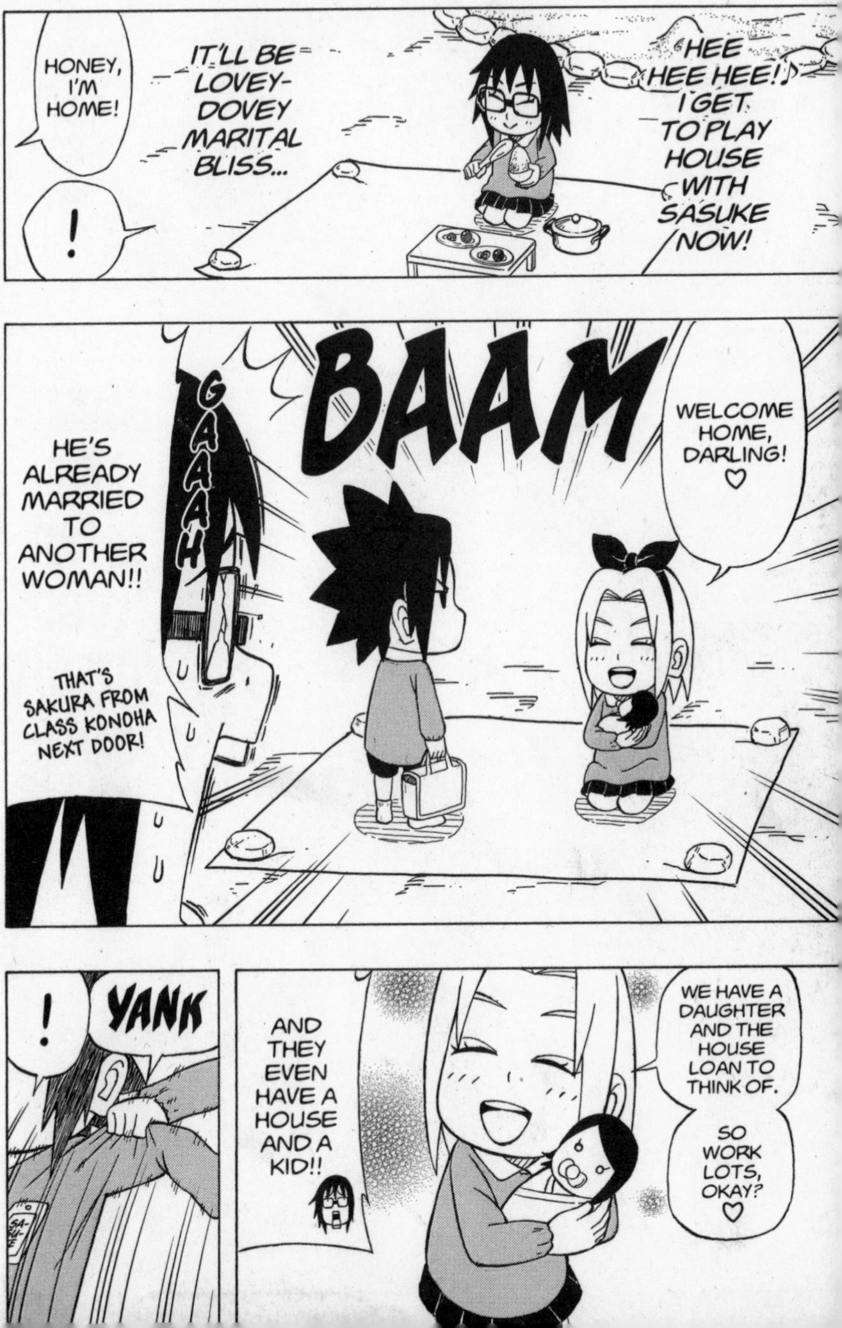
HEE HEE HEE!♪ I GET TO PLAY HOUSE WITH SASUKE NOW!
IT'LL BE LOVEY-DOVEY MARITAL BLISS...
HONEY, I'M HOME!
!
WELCOME HOME, DARLING! ♡
BAAM
GAAAAH
HE'S ALREADY MARRIED TO ANOTHER WOMAN!!
THAT'S SAKURA FROM CLASS KONOHA NEXT DOOR!
WE HAVE A DAUGHTER AND THE HOUSE LOAN TO THINK OF.
SO WORK LOTS, OKAY? ♡
AND THEY EVEN HAVE A HOUSE AND A KID!!
YANK
!

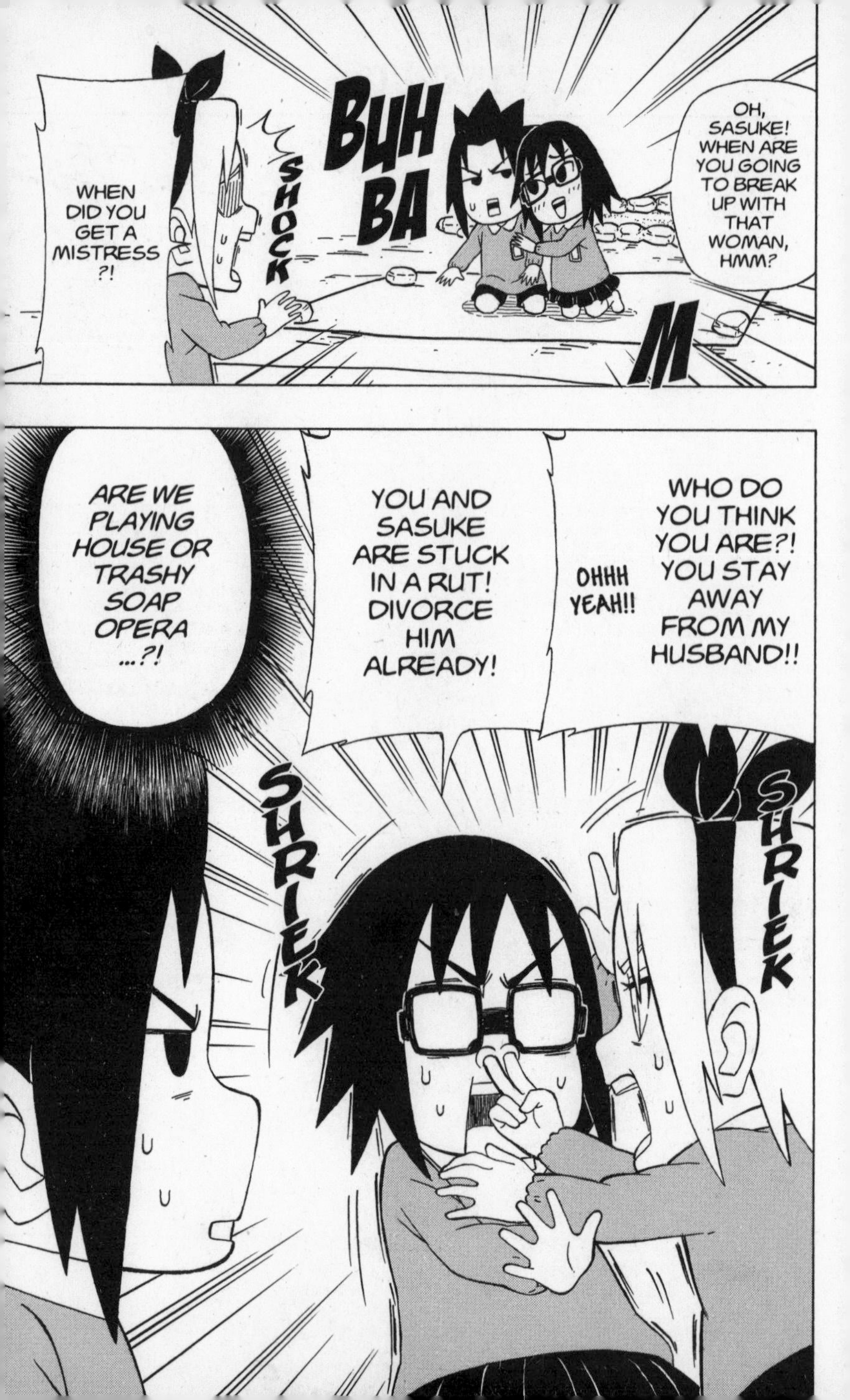
OH, SASUKE! WHEN ARE YOU GOING TO BREAK UP WITH THAT WOMAN, HMM?
BUH BA
SHOCK
WHEN DID YOU GET A MISTRESS ?!
M
WHO DO YOU THINK YOU ARE?! YOU STAY AWAY FROM MY HUSBAND!!
OHHH YEAH!!
YOU AND SASUKE ARE STUCK IN A RUT! DIVORCE HIM ALREADY!
ARE WE PLAYING HOUSE OR TRASHY SOAP OPERA ...?!
SHRIEK
SHRIEK

FIGHT

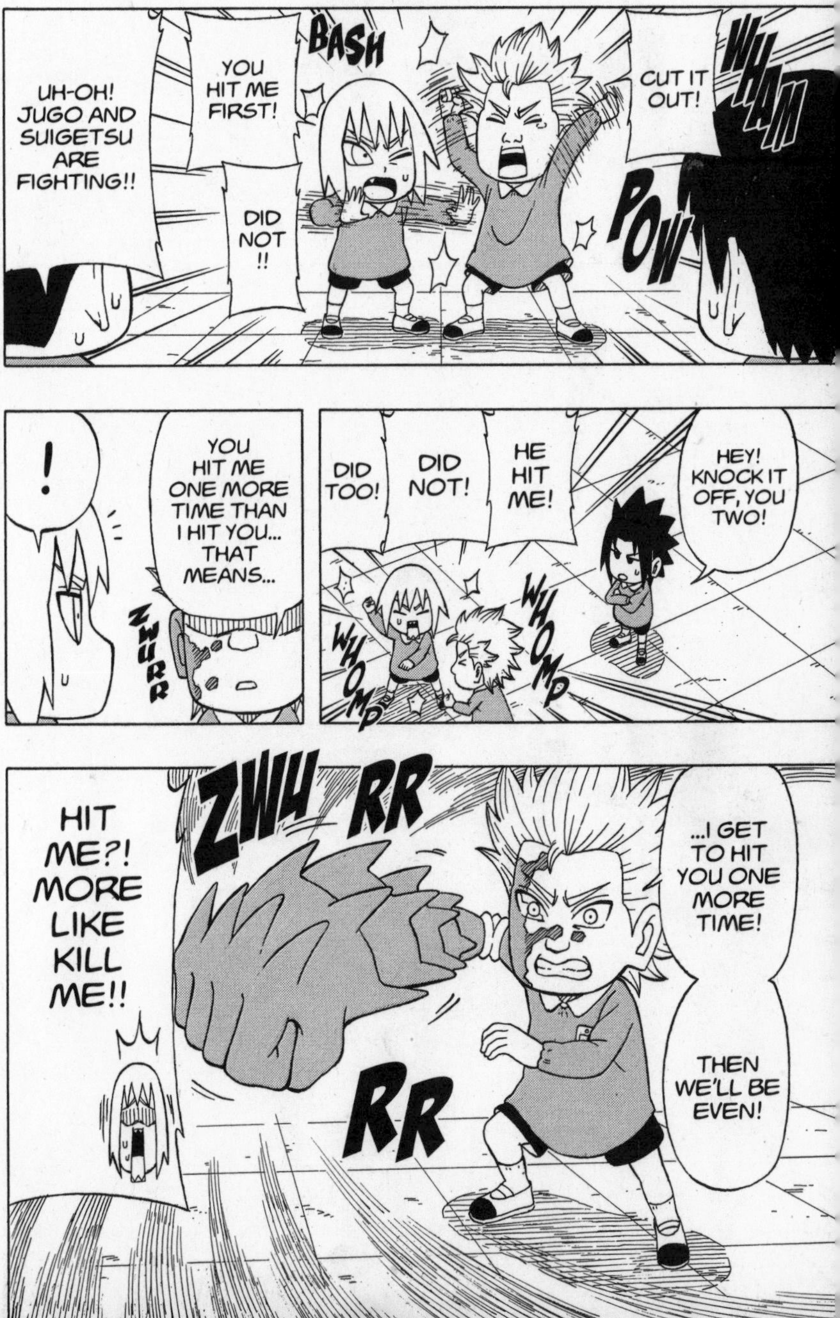
WHAM
CUT IT OUT!
POW
BASH
YOU HIT ME FIRST!
DID NOT !!
UH-OH! JUGO AND SUIGETSU ARE FIGHTING!!
HEY! KNOCK IT OFF, YOU TWO!
HE HIT ME!
DID NOT!
DID TOO!
WHOMP
WHOMP
YOU HIT ME ONE MORE TIME THAN I HIT YOU... THAT MEANS...
ZWURR
!
...I GET TO HIT YOU ONE MORE TIME!
THEN WE'LL BE EVEN!
ZWUU RR
RR
HIT ME?! MORE LIKE KILL ME!!

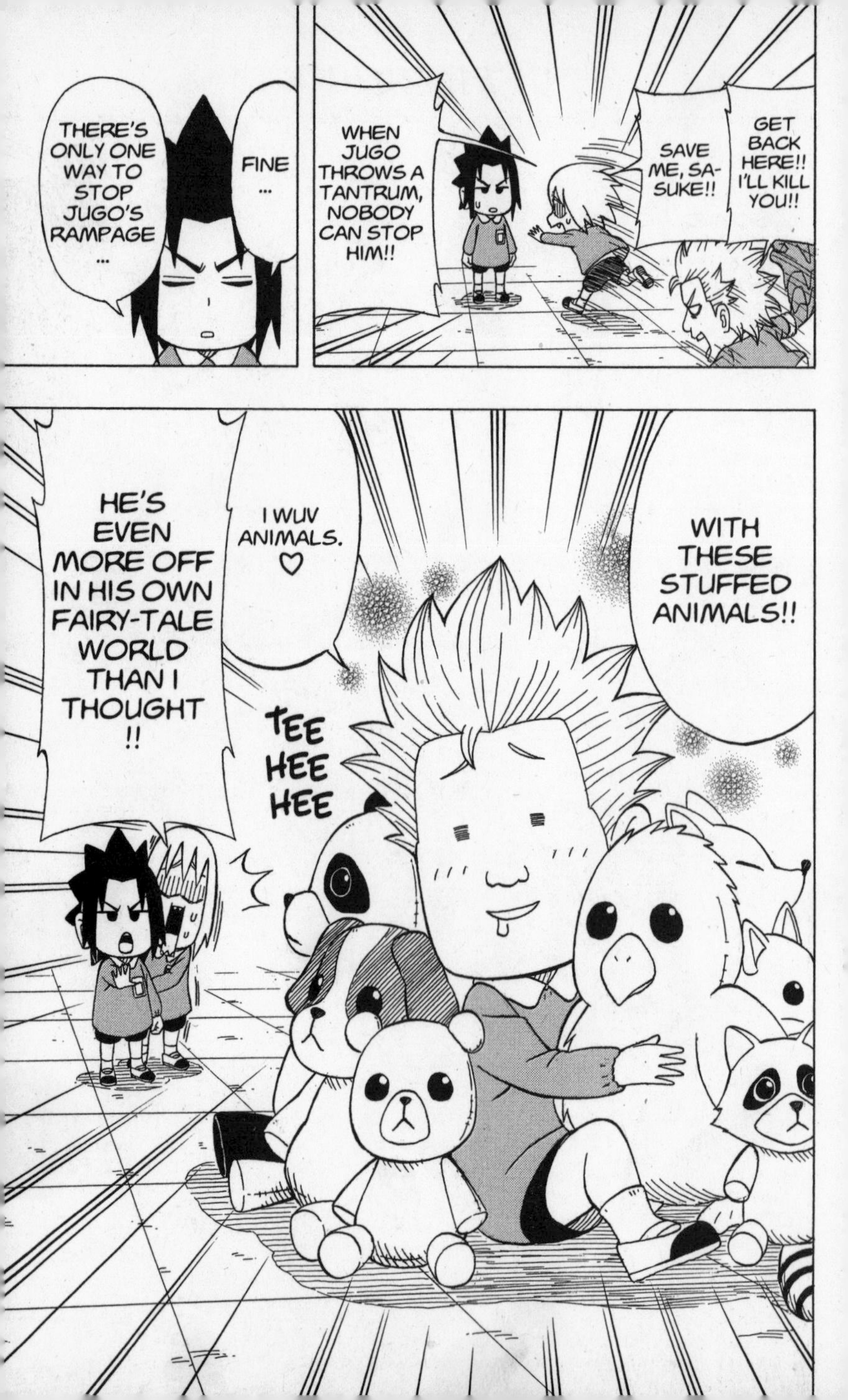
GET BACK HERE!! I'LL KILL YOU!!
SAVE ME, SA-SUKE!!
WHEN JUGO THROWS A TANTRUM, NOBODY CAN STOP HIM!!
FINE ...
THERE'S ONLY ONE WAY TO STOP JUGO'S RAMPAGE ...
WITH THESE STUFFED ANIMALS!!
I WUV ANIMALS. ♡
TEE HEE HEE
HE'S EVEN MORE OFF IN HIS OWN FAIRY-TALE WORLD THAN I THOUGHT !!

PUPPET SHOW

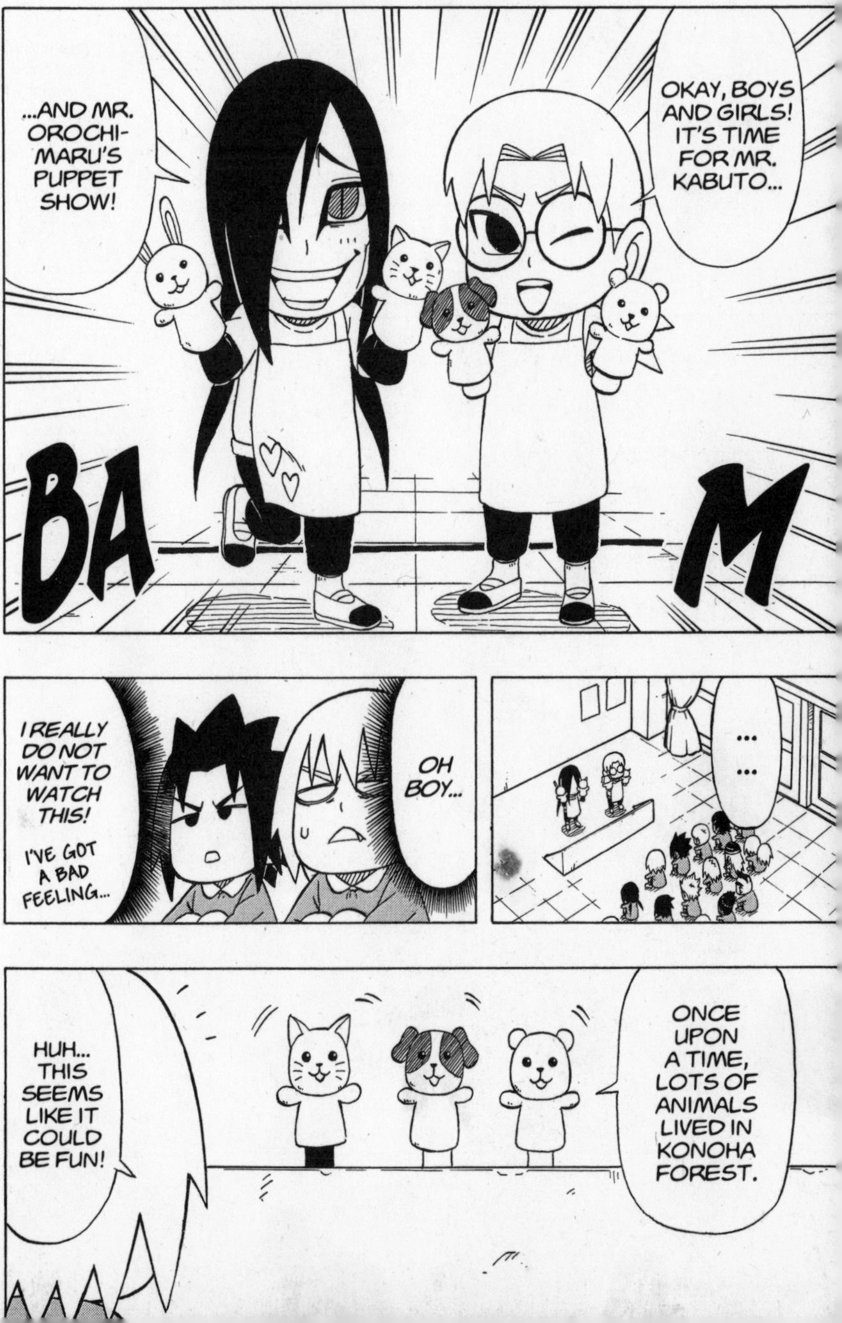

OKAY, BOYS AND GIRLS! IT'S TIME FOR MR. KABUTO...
...AND MR. OROCHI-MARU'S PUPPET SHOW!
BAM
...
...
OH BOY...
I REALLY DO NOT WANT TO WATCH THIS!
I'VE GOT A BAD FEELING...
ONCE UPON A TIME, LOTS OF ANIMALS LIVED IN KONOHA FOREST.
HUH... THIS SEEMS LIKE IT COULD BE FUN!

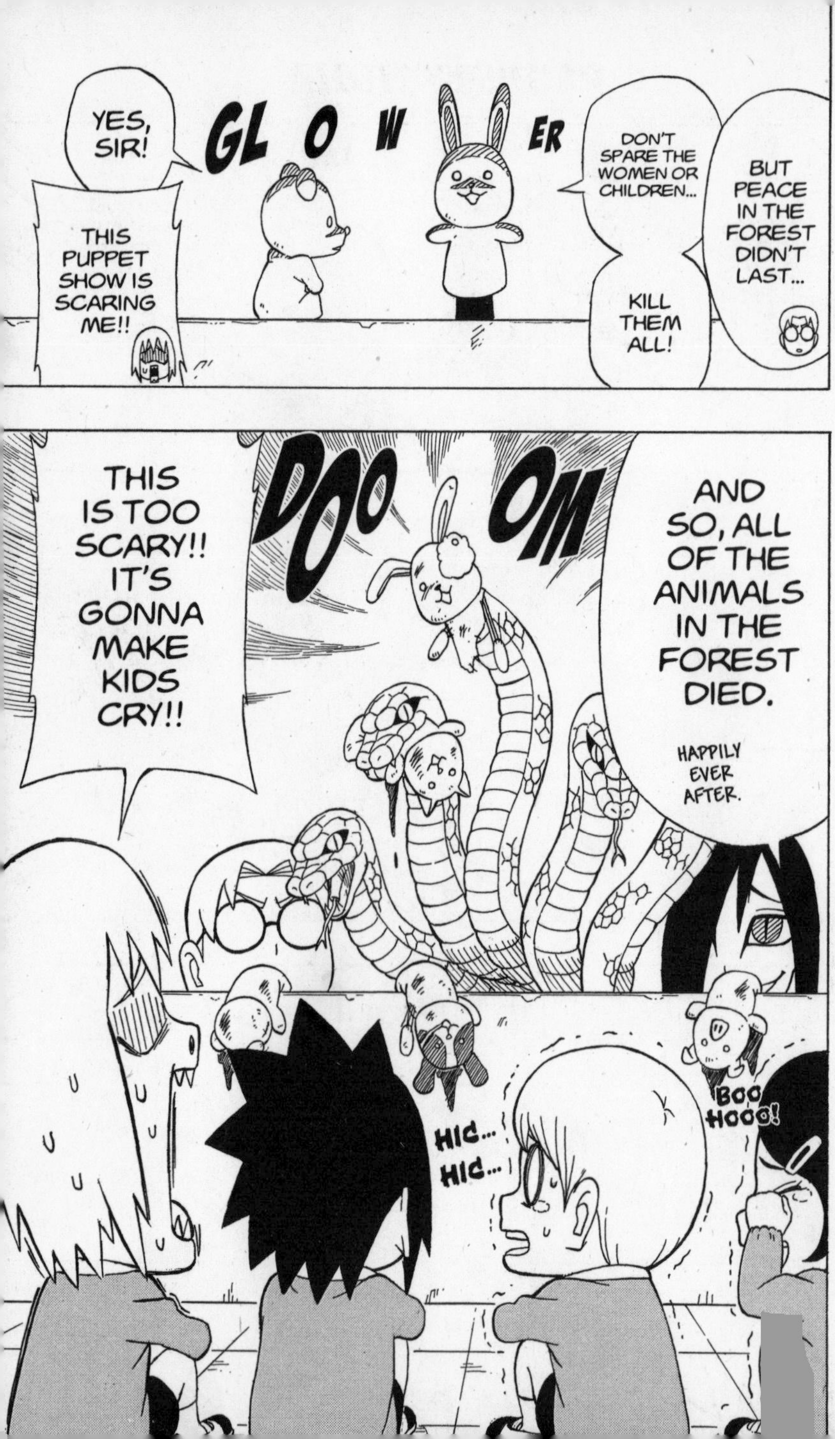
BUT PEACE IN THE FOREST DIDN'T LAST...
DON'T SPARE THE WOMEN OR CHILDREN...
KILL THEM ALL!
GLOWER
YES, SIR!
THIS PUPPET SHOW IS SCARING ME!!
AND SO, ALL OF THE ANIMALS IN THE FOREST DIED.
HAPPILY EVER AFTER.
DOOOM
THIS IS TOO SCARY!! IT'S GONNA MAKE KIDS CRY!!
BOO HOOO!
HIC... HIC...

CLASS KONOHA

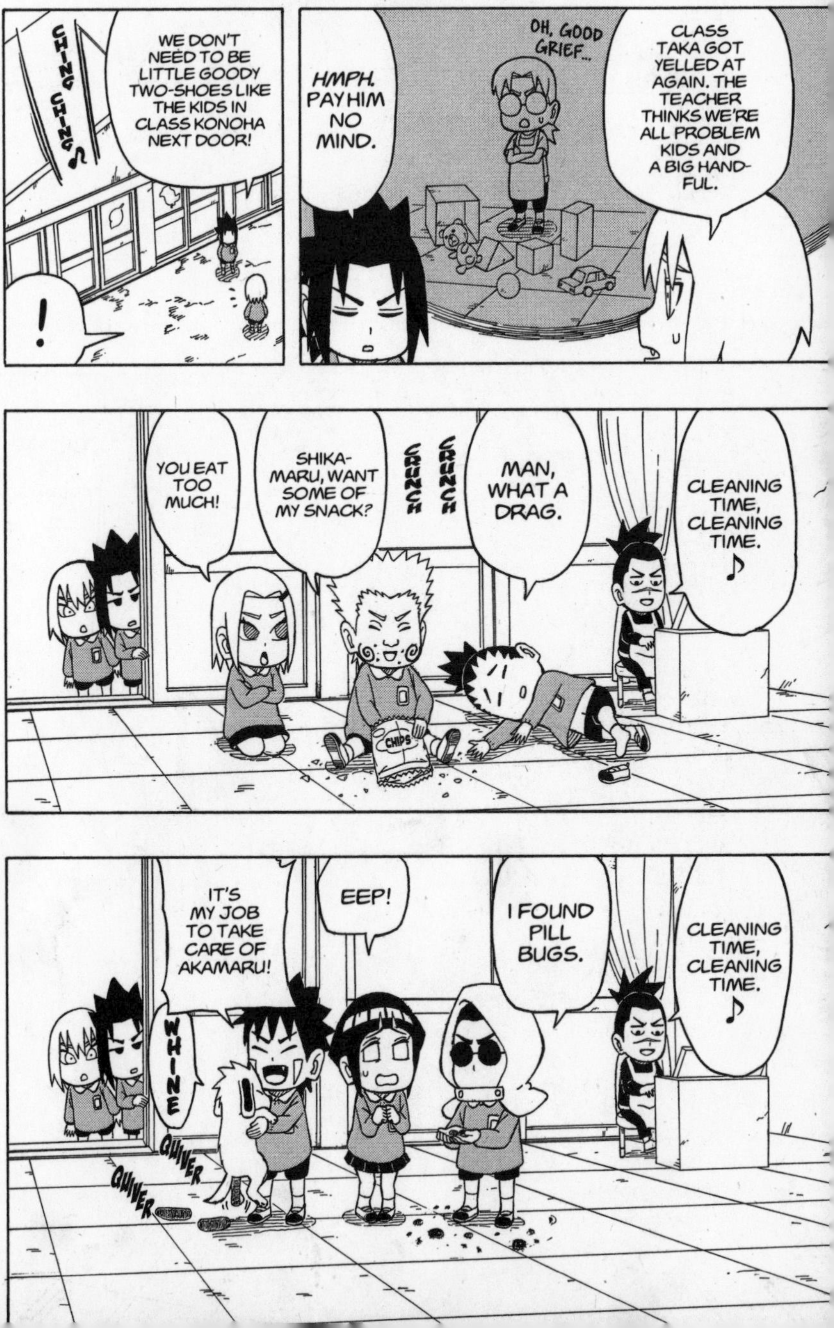
CLASS TAKA GOT YELLED AT AGAIN. THE TEACHER THINKS WE'RE ALL PROBLEM KIDS AND A BIG HAND-FUL.
OH, GOOD GRIEF...
HMPH. PAY HIM NO MIND.
WE DON'T NEED TO BE LITTLE GOODY TWO-SHOES LIKE THE KIDS IN CLASS KONOHA NEXT DOOR!
CHING CHING♪
!
CLEANING TIME, CLEANING TIME. ♪
MAN, WHAT A DRAG.
CRUNCH CRUNCH
SHIKA-MARU, WANT SOME OF MY SNACK?
YOU EAT TOO MUCH!
CHIPS
CLEANING TIME, CLEANING TIME. ♪
I FOUND PILL BUGS.
EEP!
IT'S MY JOB TO TAKE CARE OF AKAMARU!
WHINE
QUIVER QUIVER

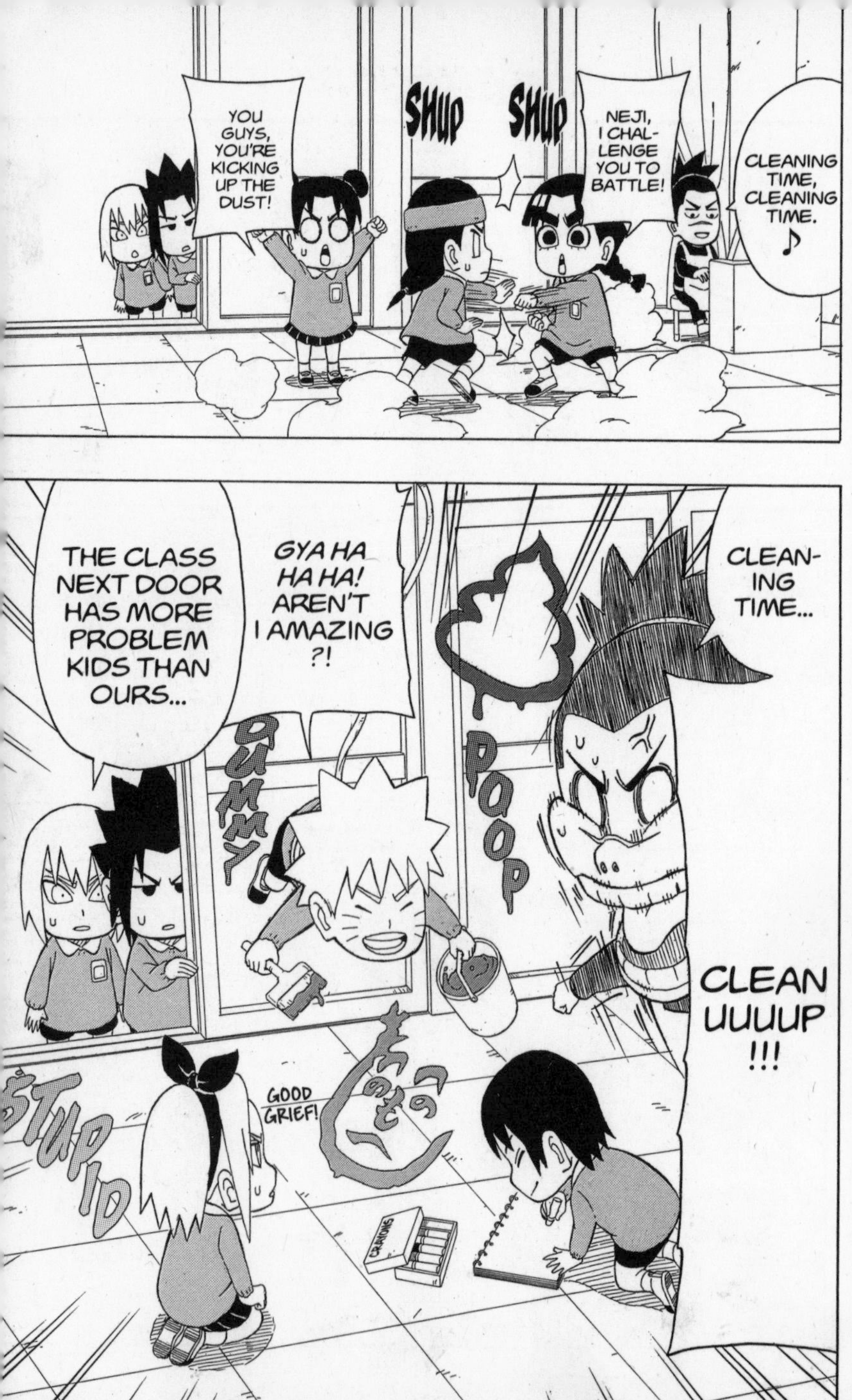
CLEANING TIME, CLEANING TIME. ♪
NEJI, I CHAL- LENGE YOU TO BATTLE!
SHUP SHUP
YOU GUYS, YOU'RE KICKING UP THE DUST!
CLEAN- ING TIME...
CLEAN UUUUP !!!
POOP
GYA HA HA HA! AREN'T I AMAZING ?!
DUMMY
THE CLASS NEXT DOOR HAS MORE PROBLEM KIDS THAN OURS...
GOOD GRIEF!
STUPID
CRAYONS

DUEL

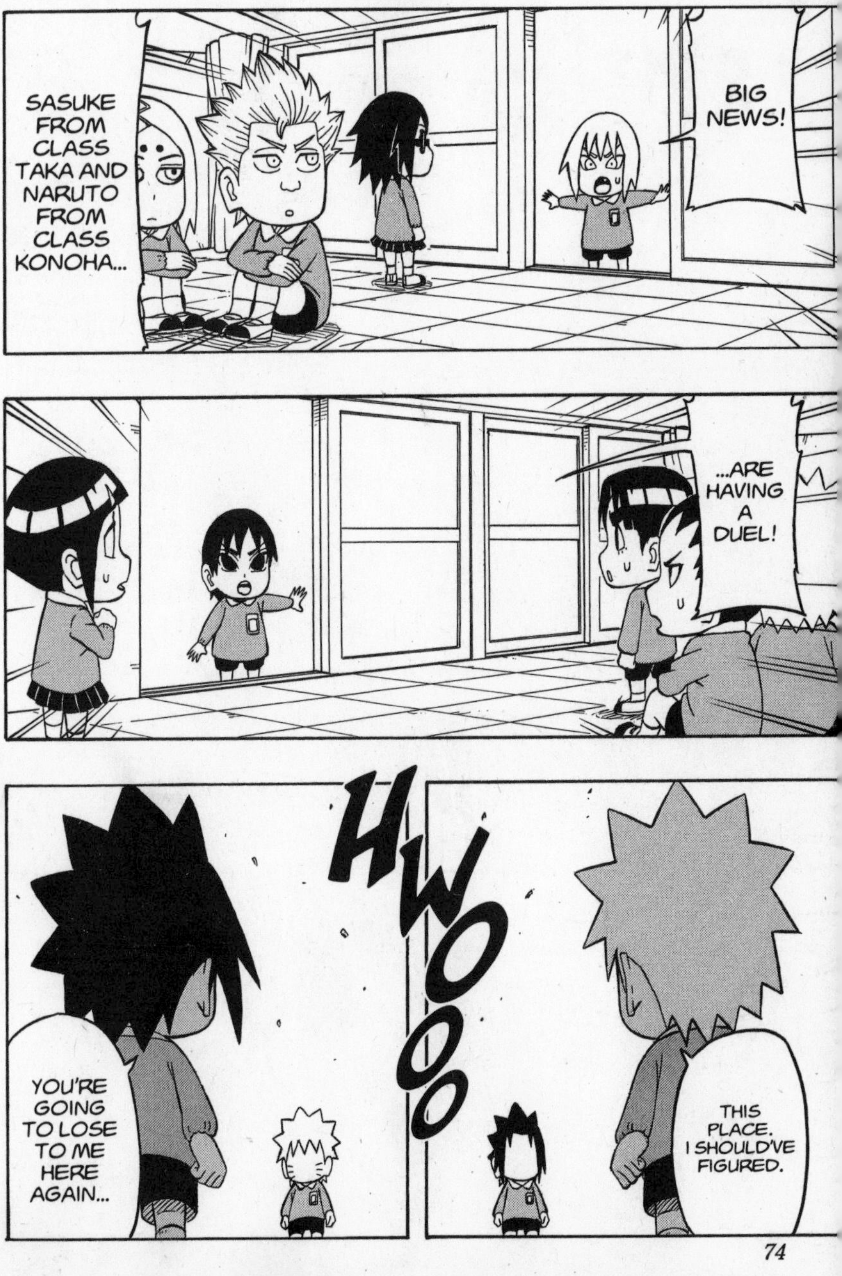
BIG NEWS!
SASUKE FROM CLASS TAKA AND NARUTO FROM CLASS KONOHA...
...ARE HAVING A DUEL!
THIS PLACE. I SHOULD'VE FIGURED.
HWOOOO
YOU'RE GOING TO LOSE TO ME HERE AGAIN...

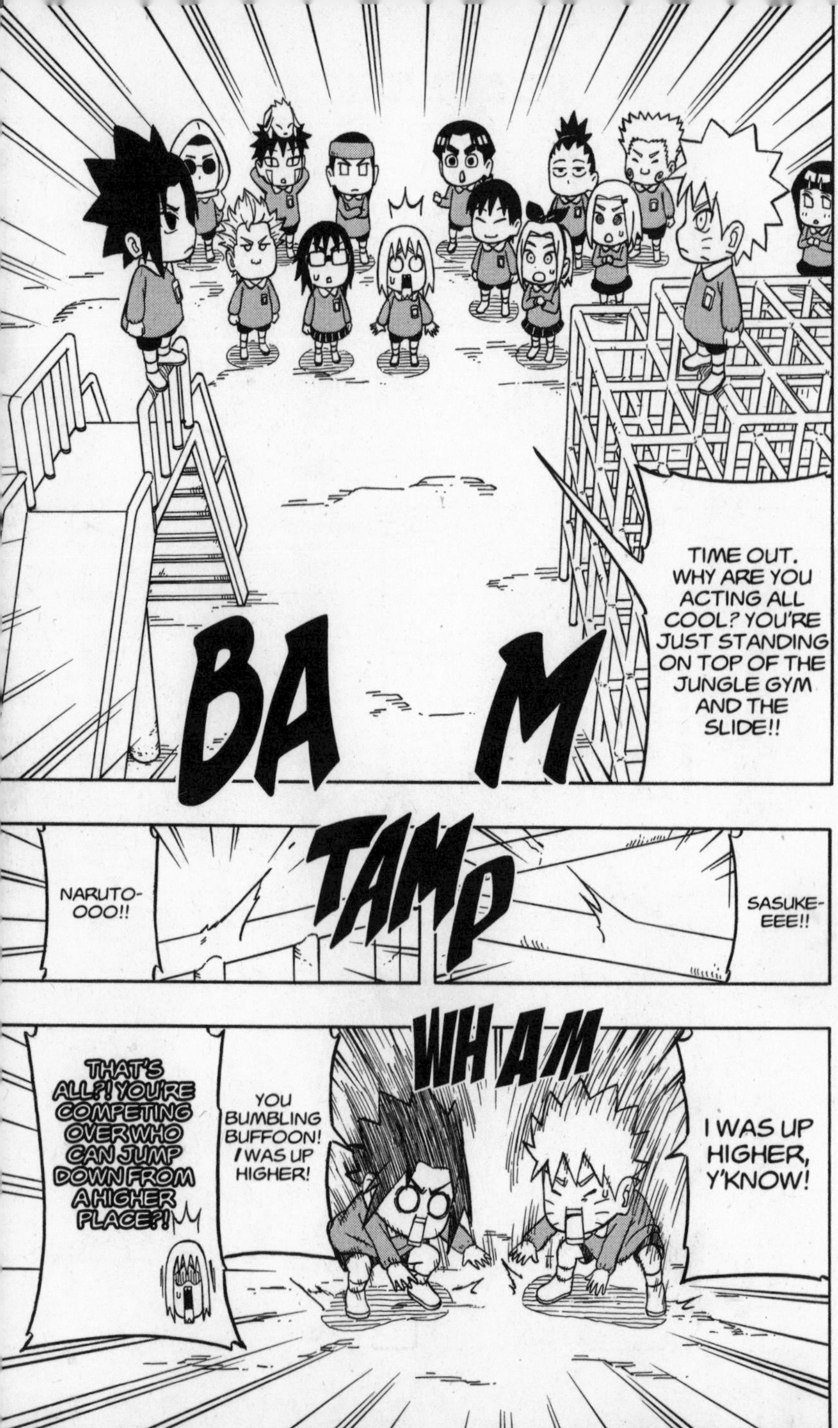
BAM
TIME OUT. WHY ARE YOU ACTING ALL COOL? YOU'RE JUST STANDING ON TOP OF THE JUNGLE GYM AND THE SLIDE!!
SASUKE-EEE!!
TAMP
NARUTO-OOO!!
WHAM
I WAS UP HIGHER, Y'KNOW!
YOU BUMBLING BUFFOON! I WAS UP HIGHER!
THAT'S ALL?! YOU'RE COMPETING OVER WHO CAN JUMP DOWN FROM A HIGHER PLACE?!

PLAY FIGHT

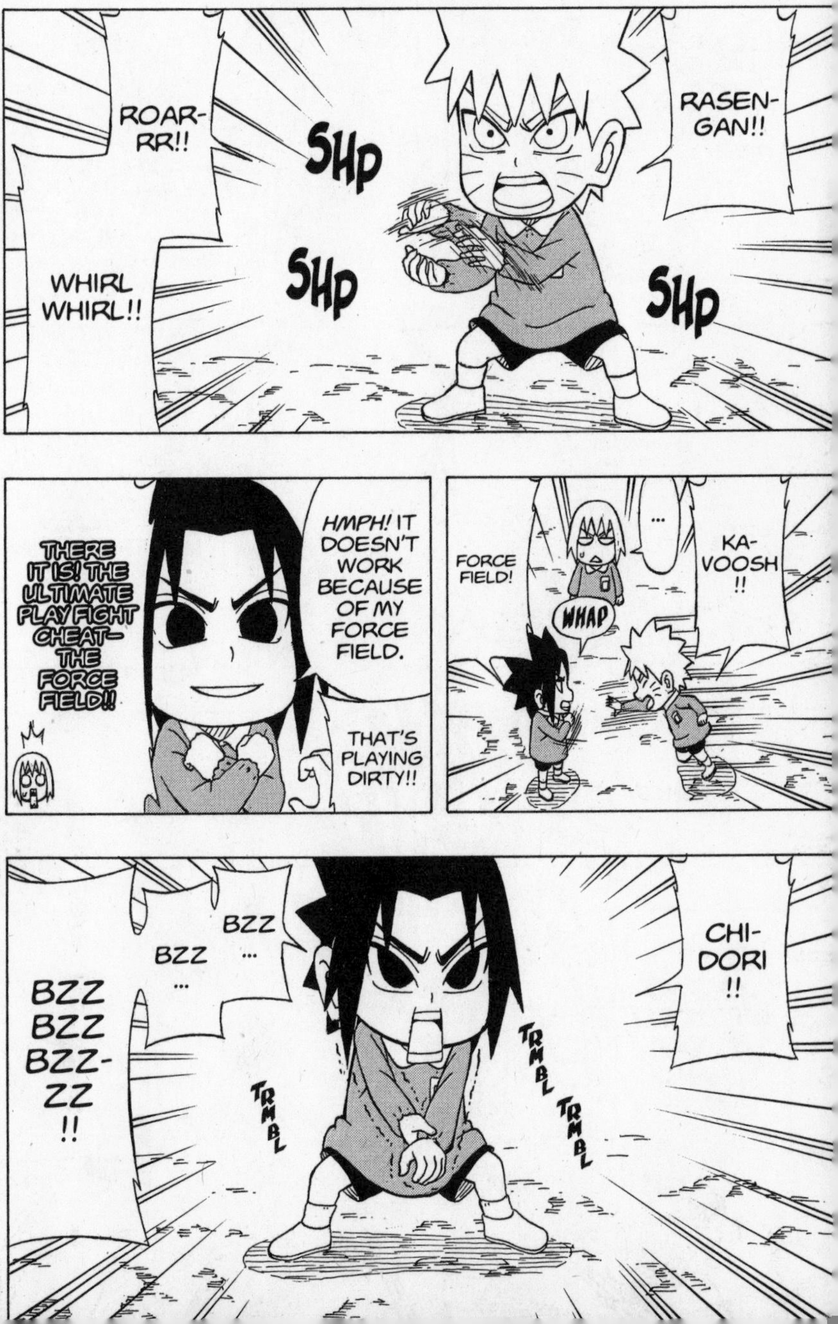
RASEN-GAN!!
SHP
SHP
ROAR-RR!!
SHP
WHIRL WHIRL!!
KA-VOOSH!!
...
FORCE FIELD!
WHAP
HMPH! IT DOESN'T WORK BECAUSE OF MY FORCE FIELD.
THERE IT IS! THE ULTIMATE PLAY FIGHT CHEAT—THE FORCE FIELD!!
THAT'S PLAYING DIRTY!!
CHI-DORI!!
BZZ...
BZZ...
TRMBL
TRMBL
TRMBL
BZZ BZZ BZZ-ZZ!!

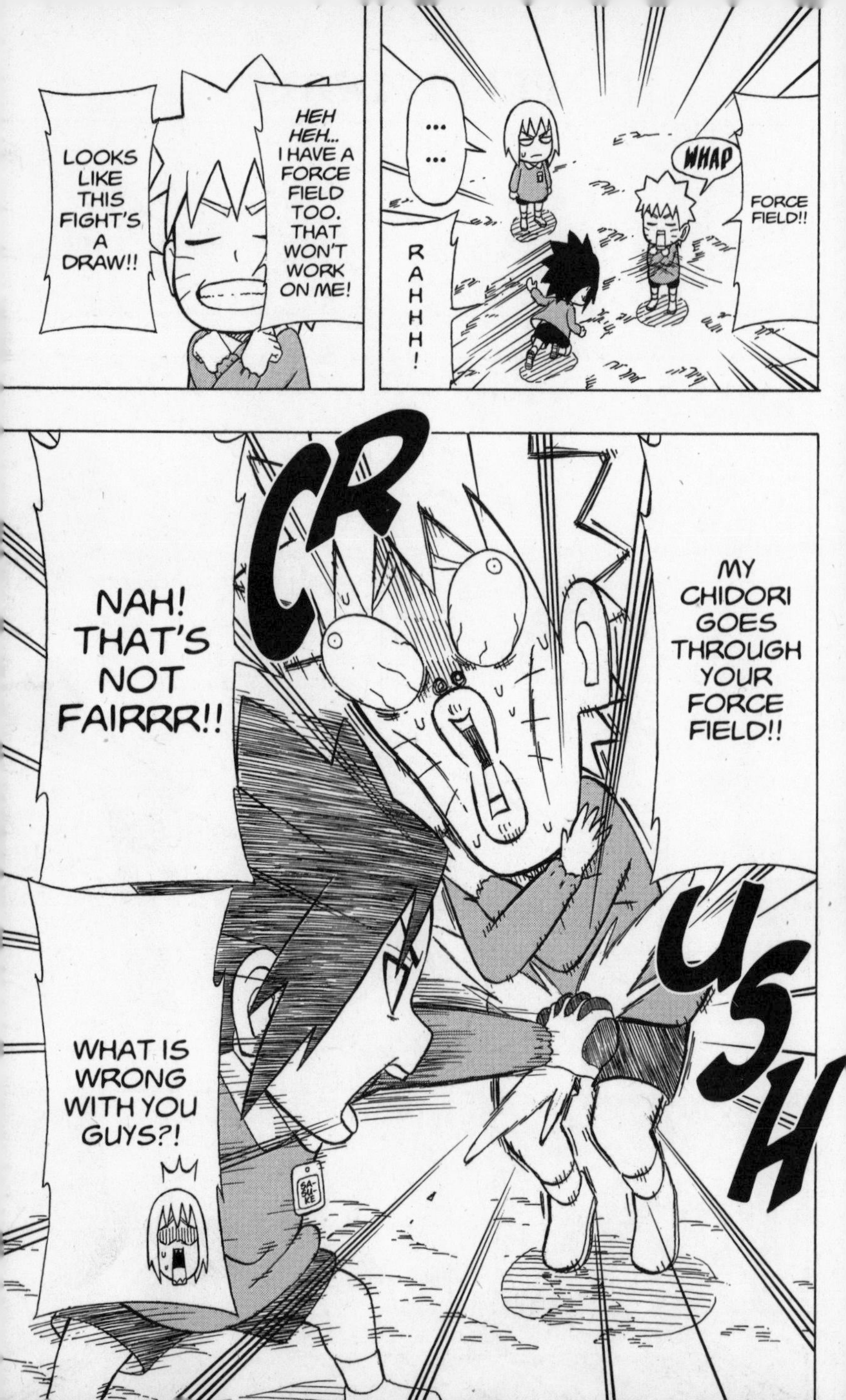
FORCE FIELD!!
WHAP
......
RAHHH!
HEH HEH... I HAVE A FORCE FIELD TOO. THAT WON'T WORK ON ME!
LOOKS LIKE THIS FIGHT'S A DRAW!!
MY CHIDORI GOES THROUGH YOUR FORCE FIELD!!
CR
NAH! THAT'S NOT FAIRRR!!
USH
WHAT IS WRONG WITH YOU GUYS?!
SASUKE

PLAY FIGHT PART 2

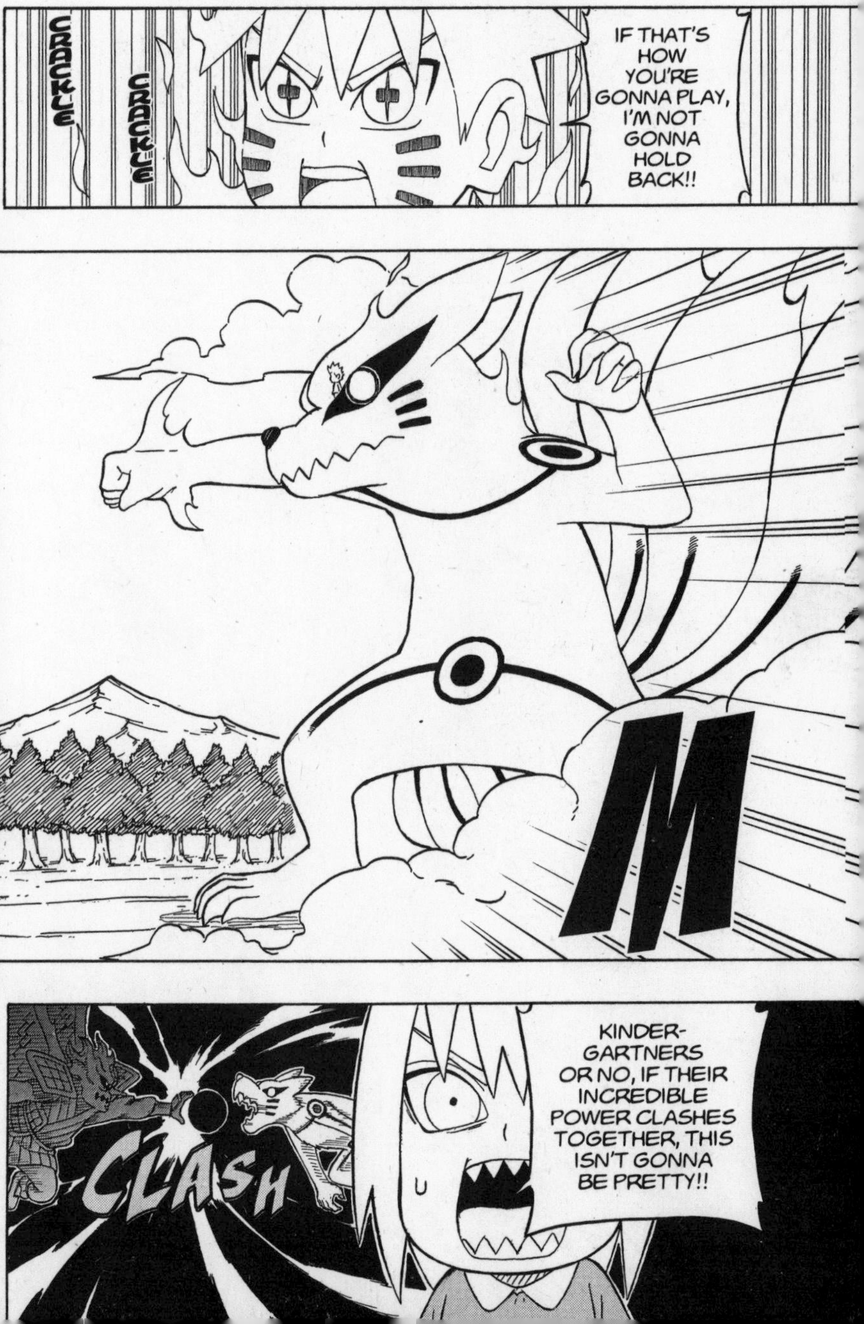
IF THAT'S HOW YOU'RE GONNA PLAY, I'M NOT GONNA HOLD BACK!!
CRACKLE
CRACKLE
M
KINDER-GARTNERS OR NO, IF THEIR INCREDIBLE POWER CLASHES TOGETHER, THIS ISN'T GONNA BE PRETTY!!
CLASH

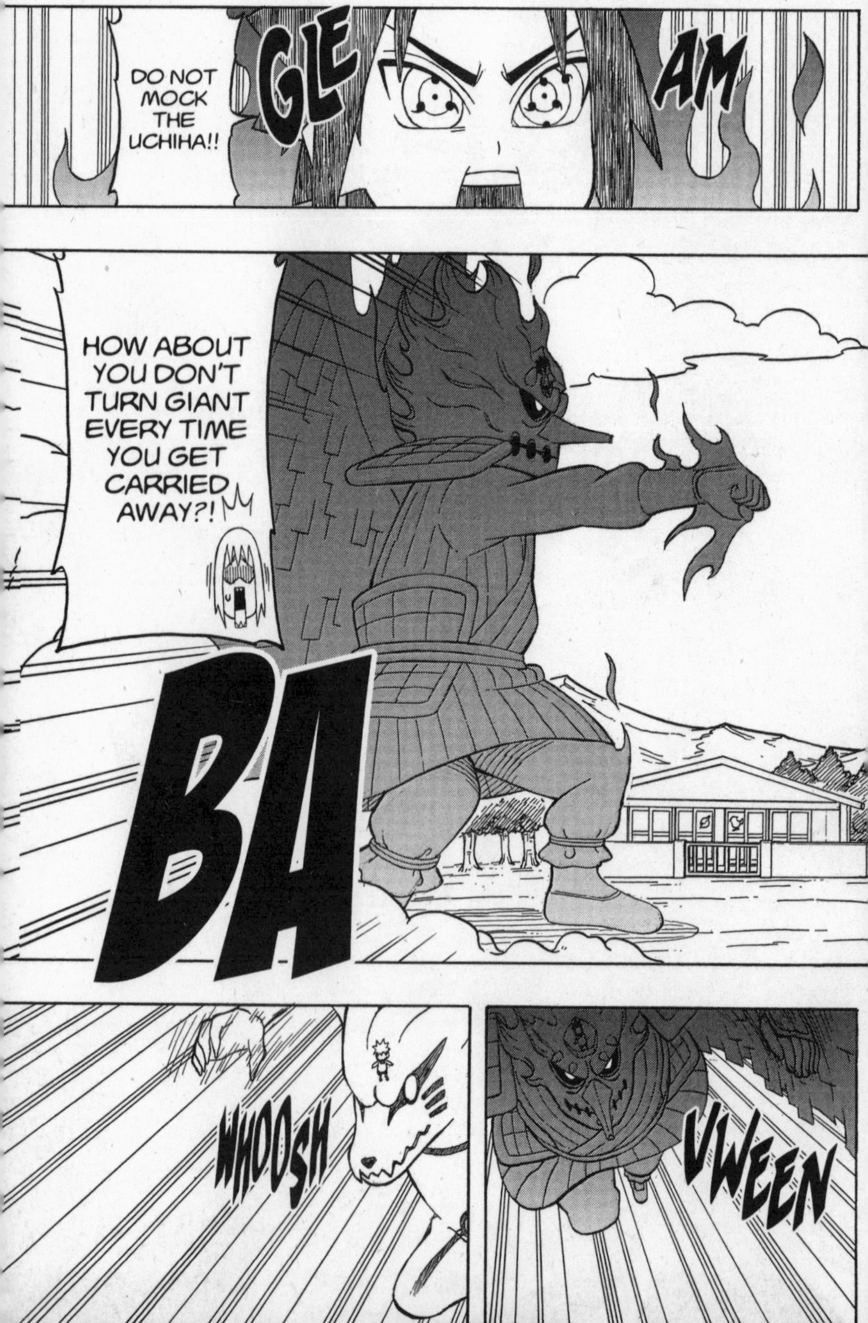
GLEAM
DO NOT MOCK THE UCHIHA!!
HOW ABOUT YOU DON'T TURN GIANT EVERY TIME YOU GET CARRIED AWAY?!
BA
VWEEN
WHOOSH

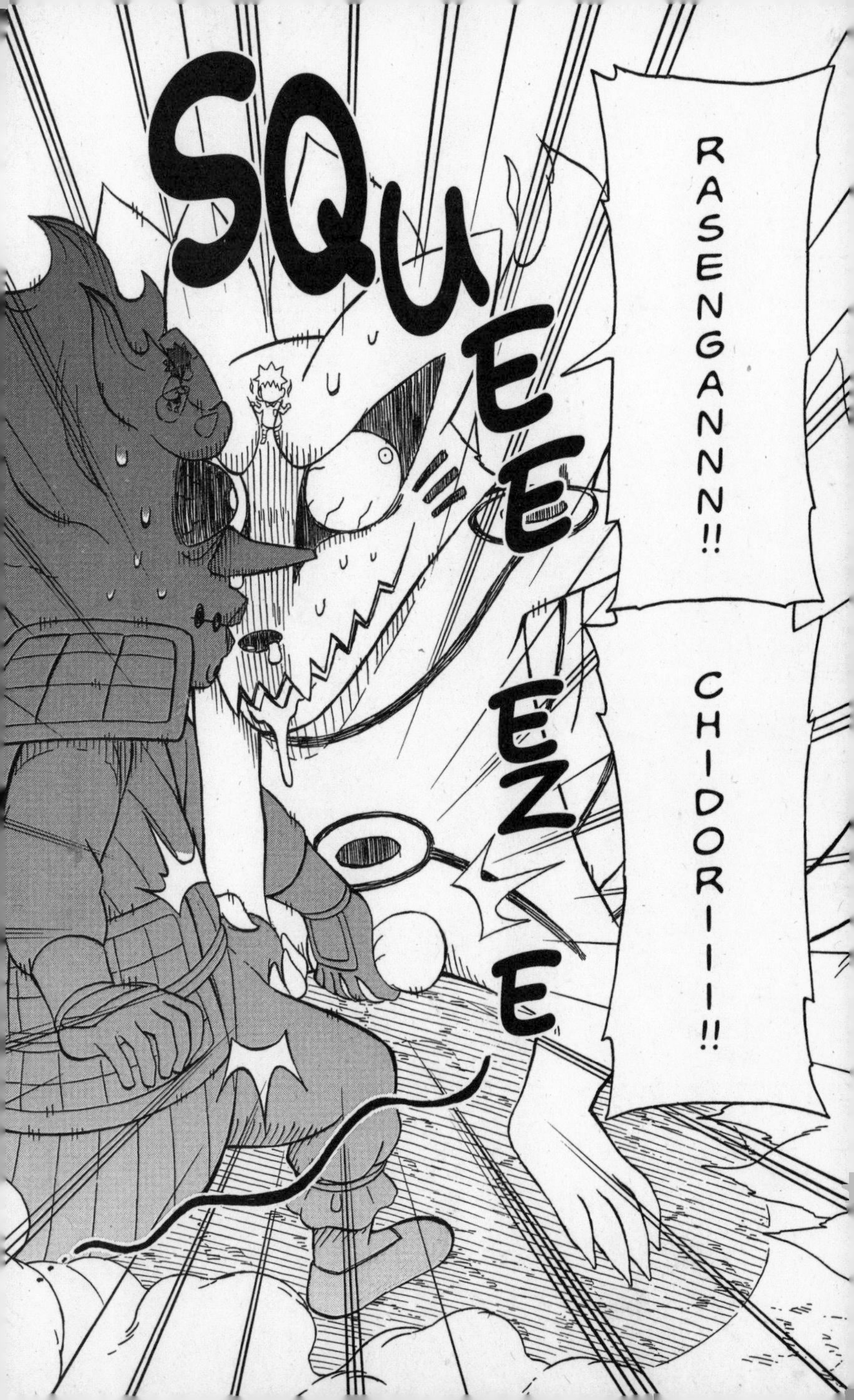
RASENGANNN!!
CHIDORIII!!
SQUEEEZE

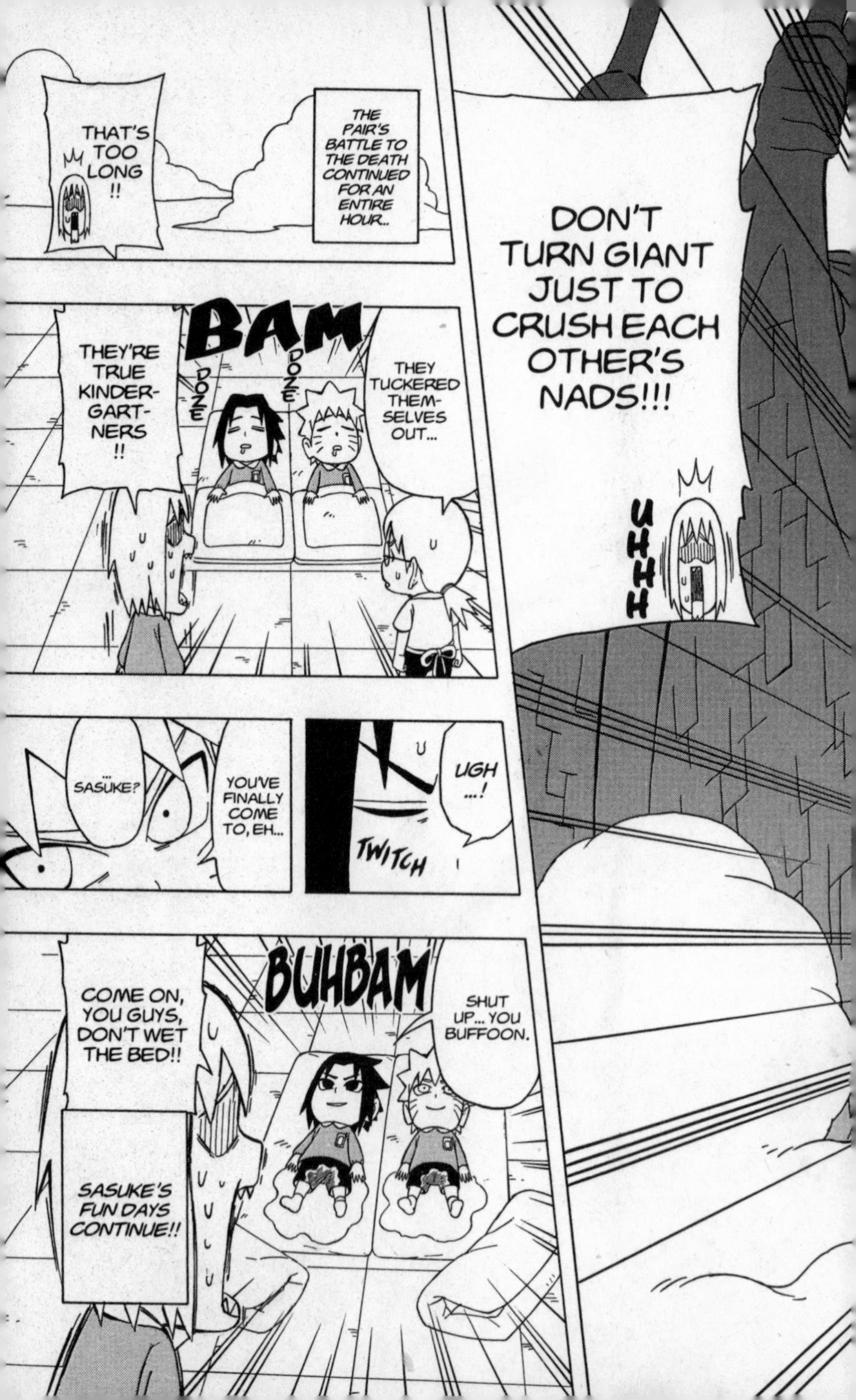
DON'T TURN GIANT JUST TO CRUSH EACH OTHER'S NADS!!!
UHHH
THE PAIR'S BATTLE TO THE DEATH CONTINUED FOR AN ENTIRE HOUR...
THAT'S TOO LONG!!
BAM
THEY TUCKERED THEMSELVES OUT...
DOZE
DOZE
THEY'RE TRUE KINDERGARTNERS!!
UGH...!
TWITCH
YOU'VE FINALLY COME TO, EH...
...SASUKE?
BUHBAM
SHUT UP... YOU BUFFOON.
COME ON, YOU GUYS, DON'T WET THE BED!!
SASUKE'S FUN DAYS CONTINUE!!

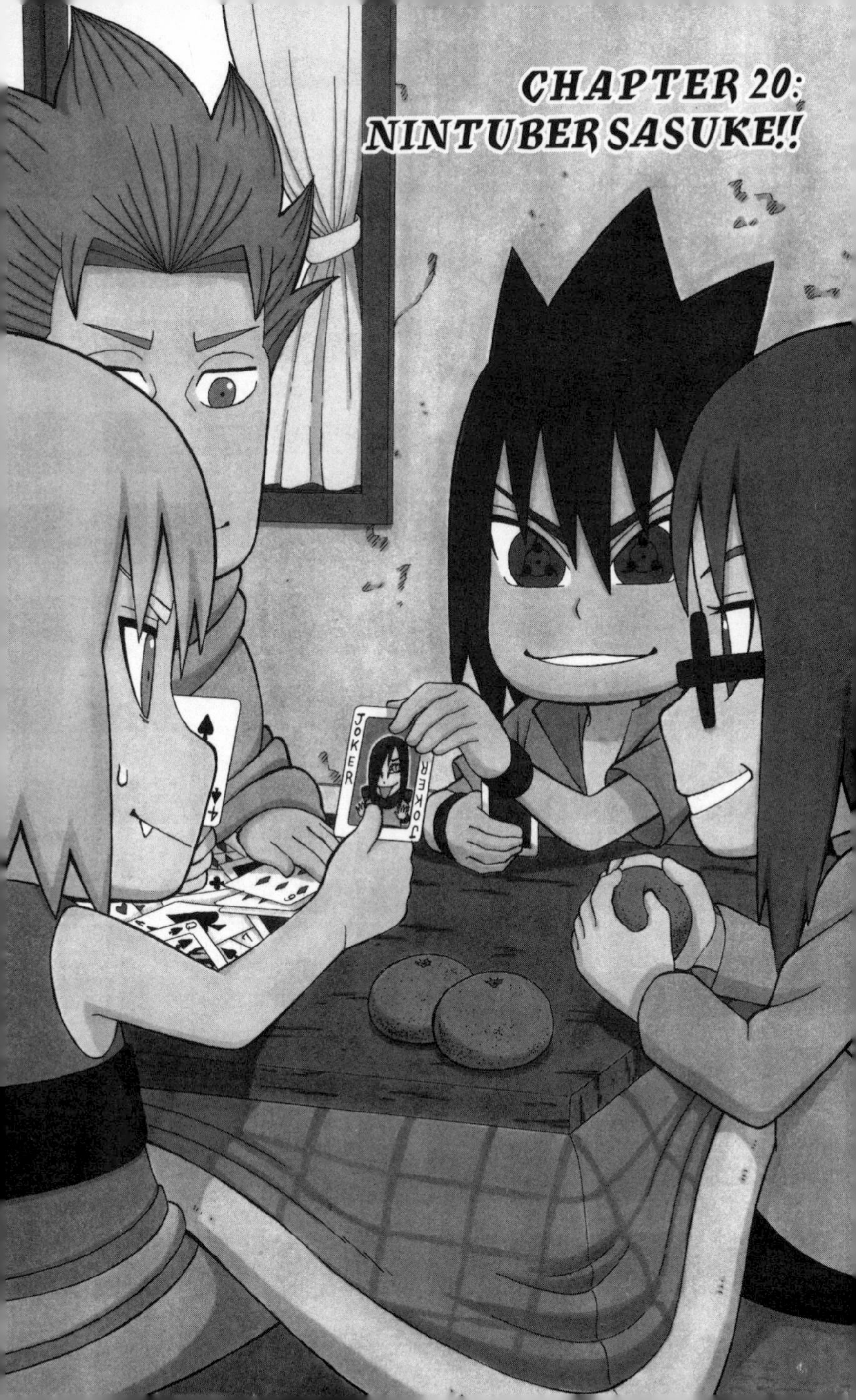
CHAPTER 20:
NINTUBER SASUKE!!
JOKER
JOKER

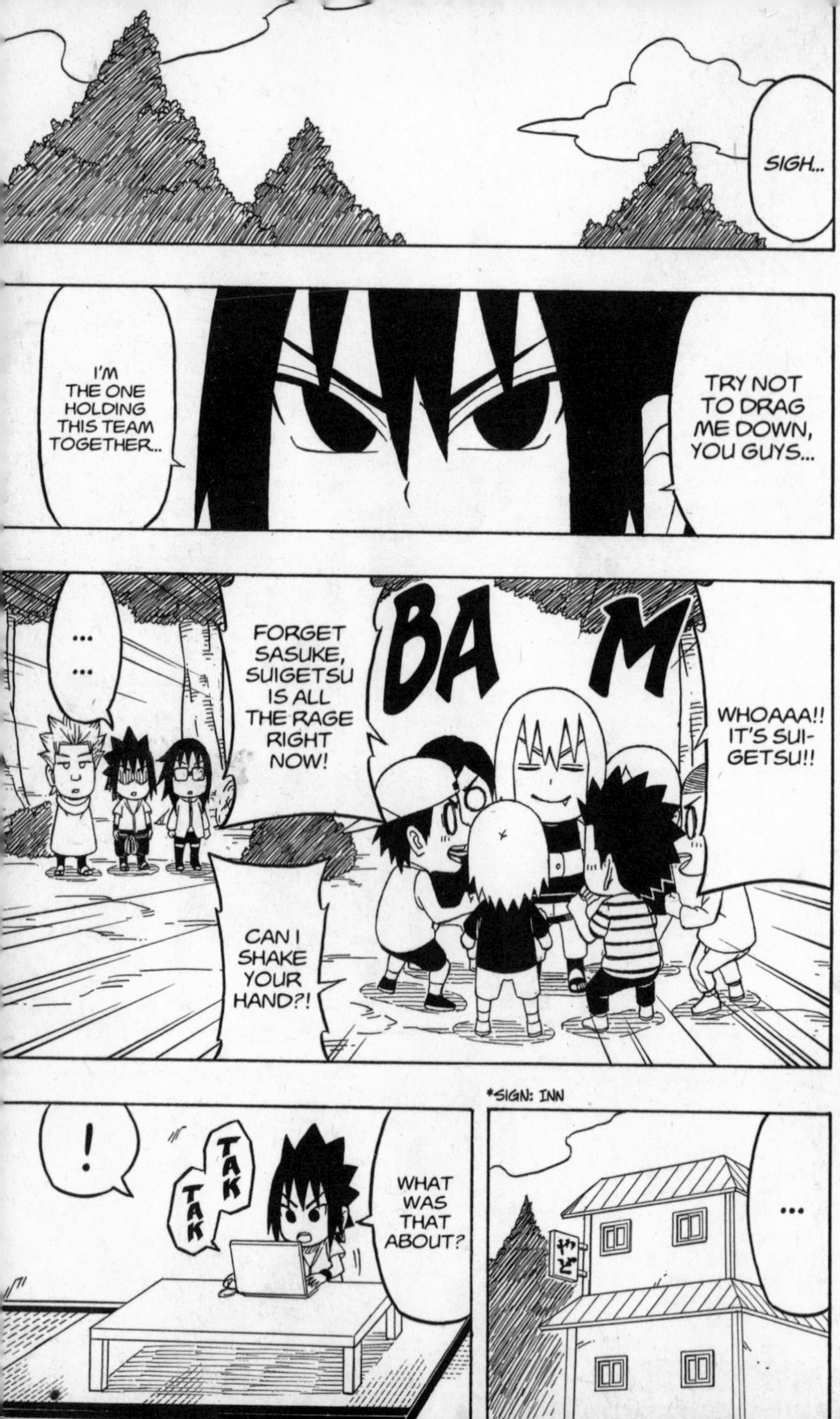
SIGH...
TRY NOT TO DRAG ME DOWN, YOU GUYS...
I'M THE ONE HOLDING THIS TEAM TOGETHER...
WHOAAA!! IT'S SUI-GETSU!!
BAM
FORGET SASUKE, SUIGETSU IS ALL THE RAGE RIGHT NOW!
... ...
CAN I SHAKE YOUR HAND?!
*SIGN: INN
...
WHAT WAS THAT ABOUT?
TAK TAK TAK
!

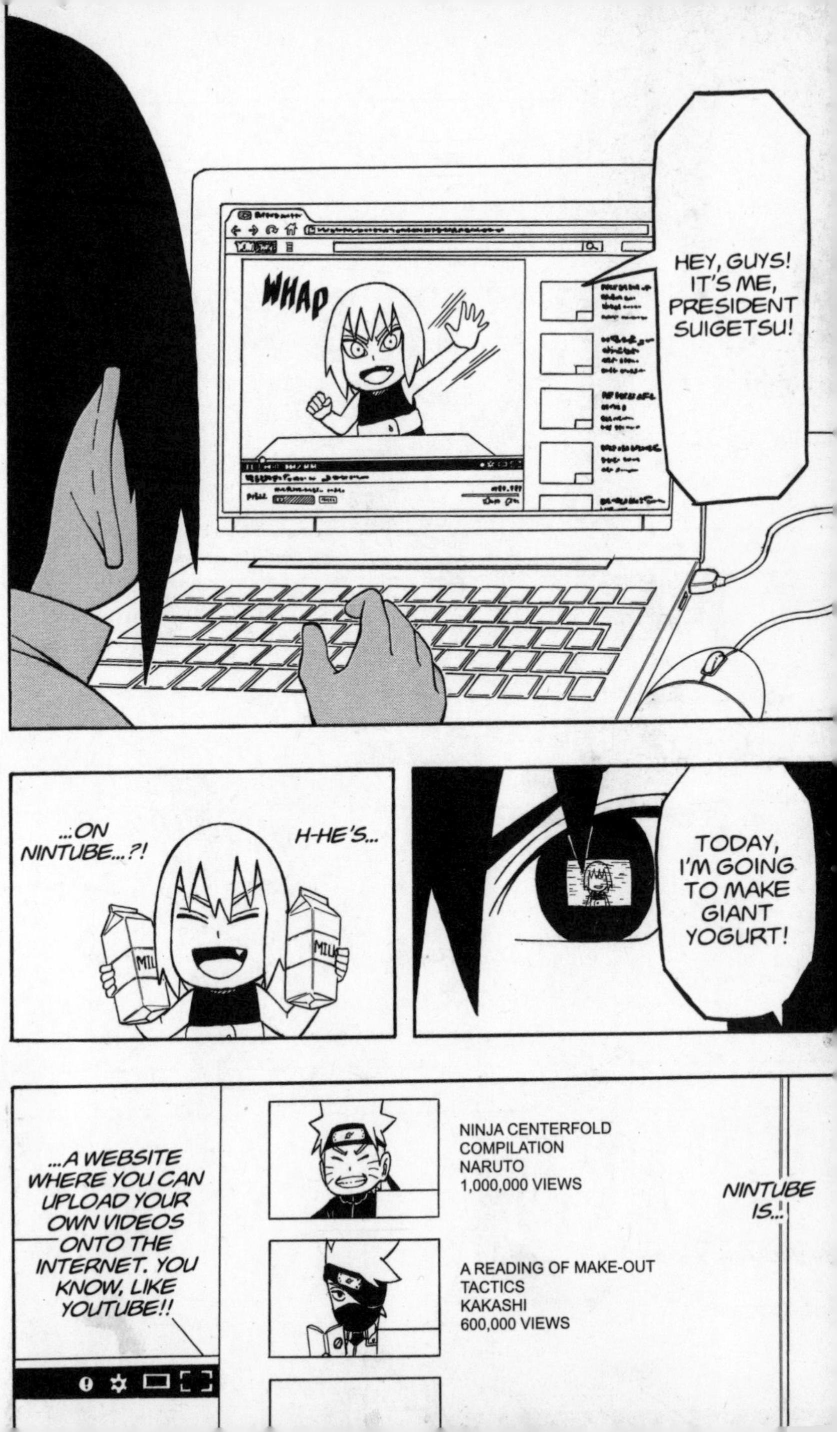
WHAP
HEY, GUYS! IT'S ME, PRESIDENT SUIGETSU!
TODAY, I'M GOING TO MAKE GIANT YOGURT!
H-HE'S...
...ON NINTUBE...?!
NINTUBE IS...
NINJA CENTERFOLD COMPILATION
NARUTO
1,000,000 VIEWS
A READING OF MAKE-OUT TACTICS
KAKASHI
600,000 VIEWS
...A WEBSITE WHERE YOU CAN UPLOAD YOUR OWN VIDEOS ONTO THE INTERNET. YOU KNOW, LIKE YOUTUBE!!

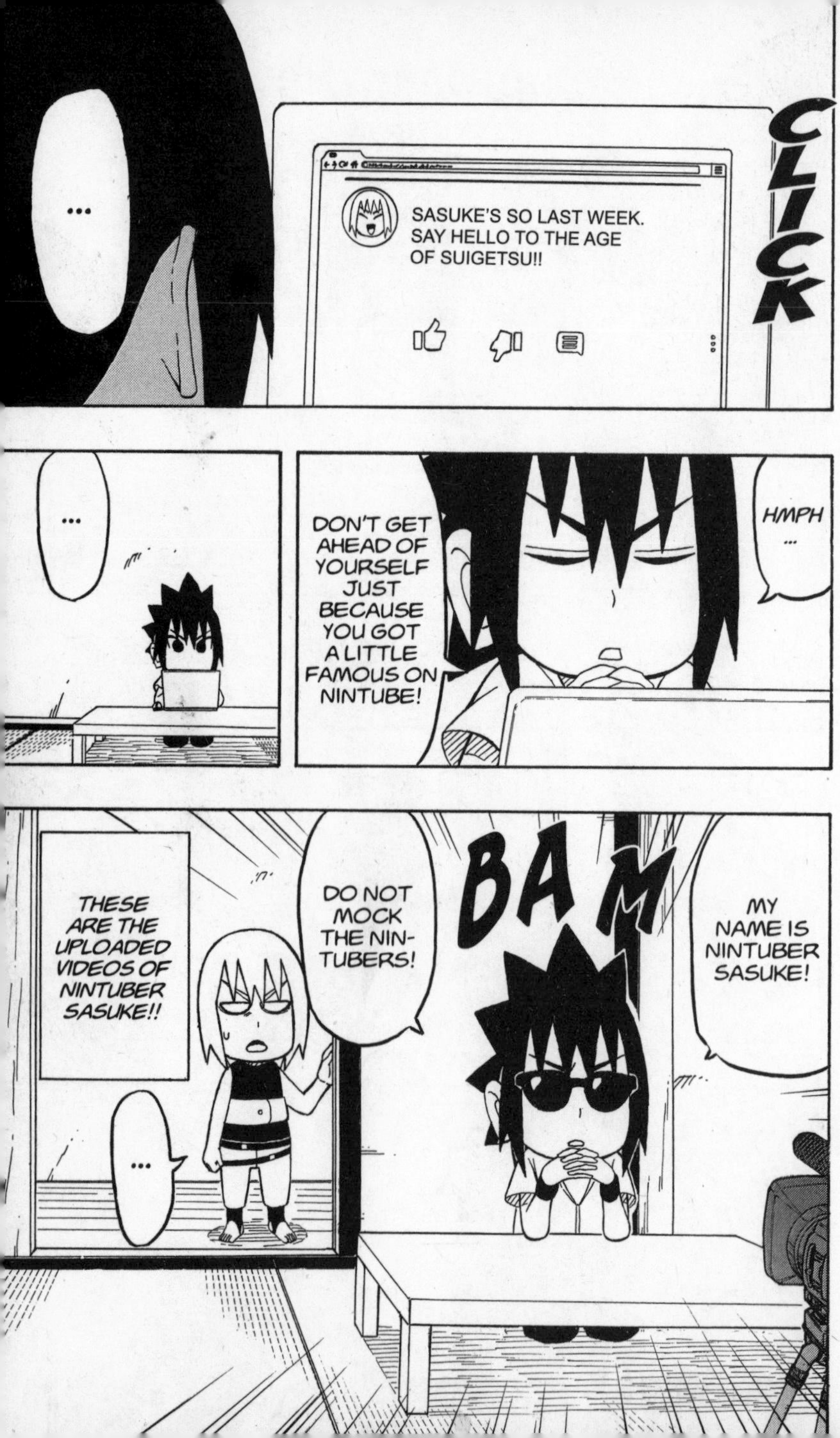
CLICK
SASUKE'S SO LAST WEEK. SAY HELLO TO THE AGE OF SUIGETSU!!
...
HMPH ...
DON'T GET AHEAD OF YOURSELF JUST BECAUSE YOU GOT A LITTLE FAMOUS ON NINTUBE!
...
MY NAME IS NINTUBER SASUKE!
BAM
DO NOT MOCK THE NIN-TUBERS!
THESE ARE THE UPLOADED VIDEOS OF NINTUBER SASUKE!!
...

CARD OPENING

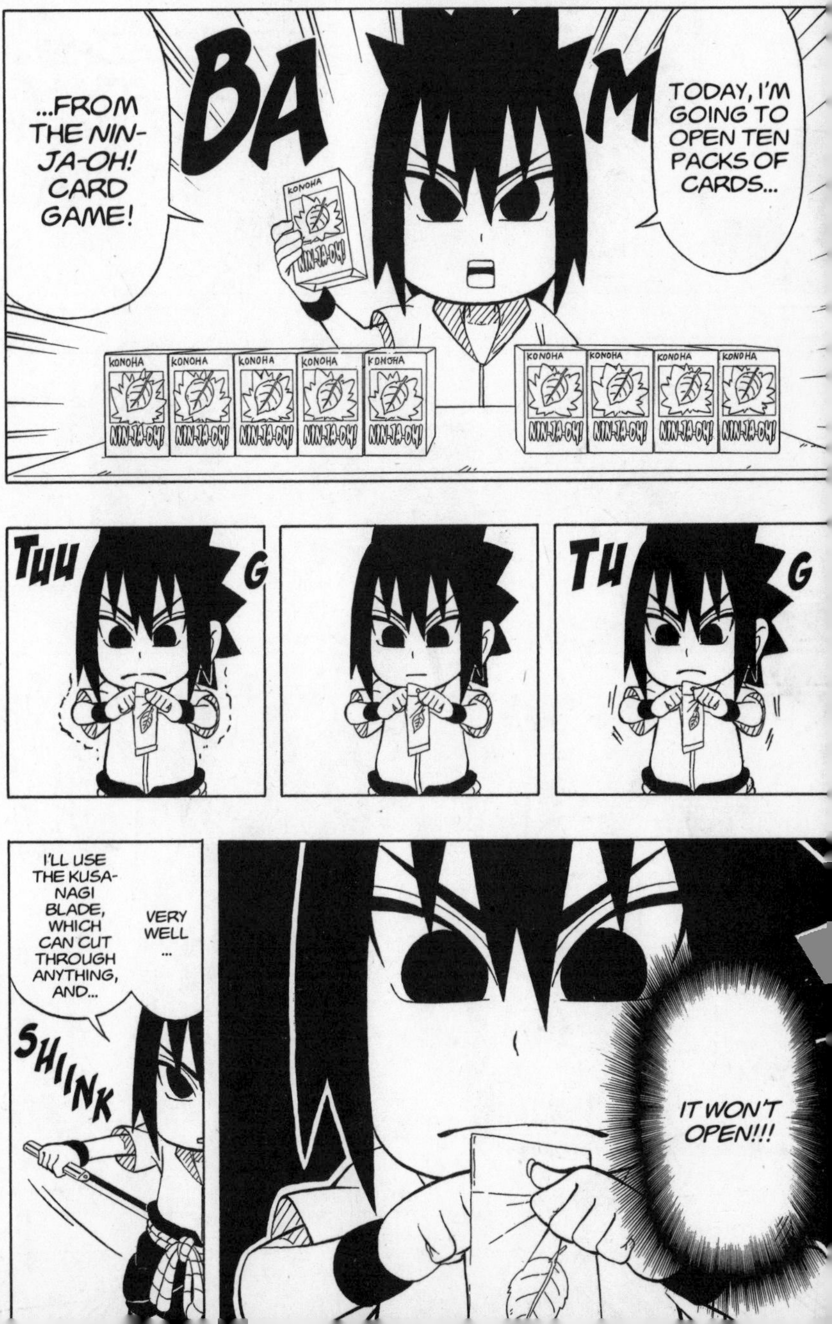
TODAY, I'M GOING TO OPEN TEN PACKS OF CARDS...
BAM
...FROM THE NIN-JA-OH! CARD GAME!
KONOHA
NIN-JA-OH!
TUG
TUUG
IT WON'T OPEN!!!
VERY WELL ...
I'LL USE THE KUSA-NAGI BLADE, WHICH CAN CUT THROUGH ANYTHING, AND...
SHIINK

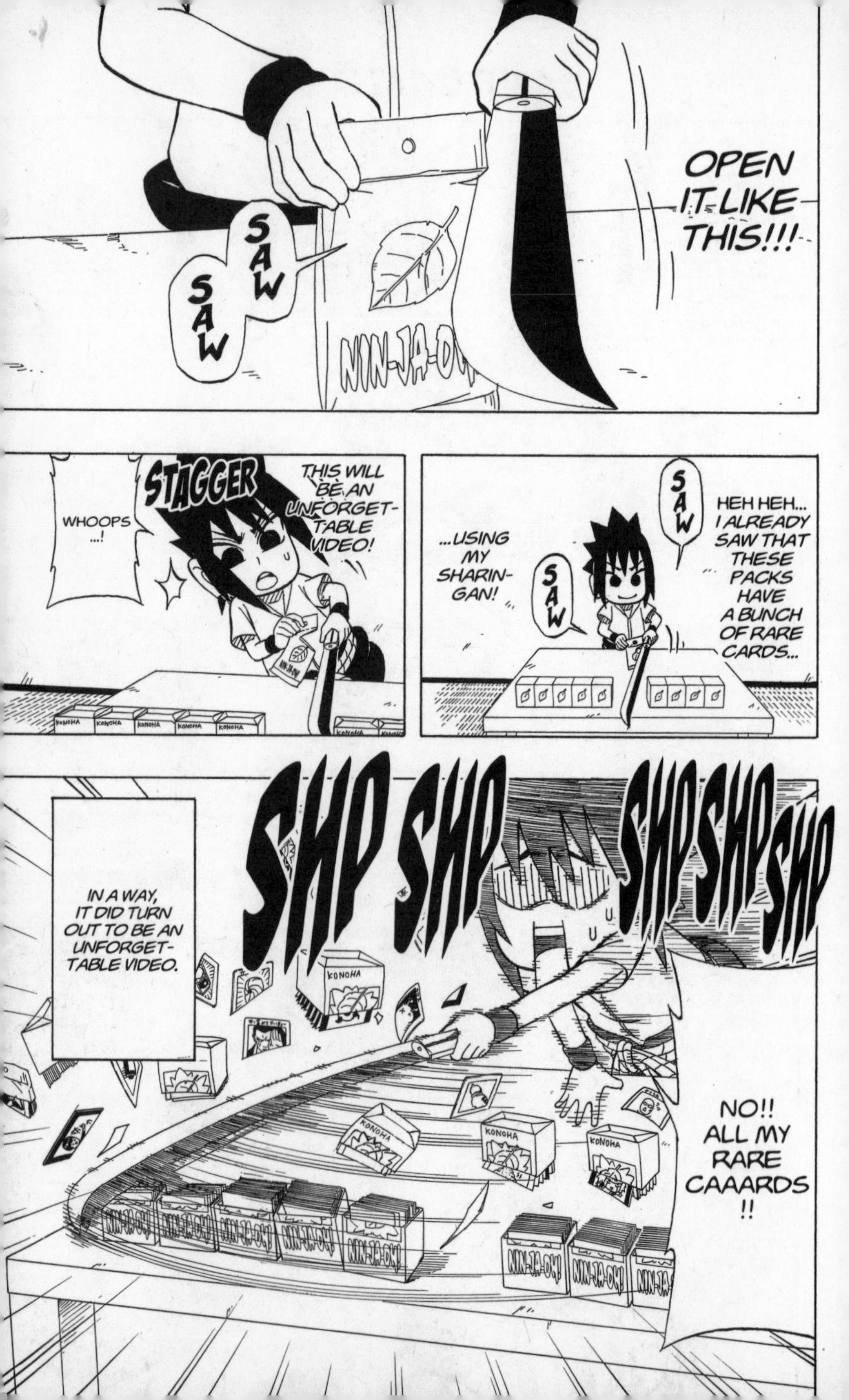
OPEN IT LIKE THIS!!!
SAW SAW
SAW SAW
NIN-JA-OH!
HEH HEH... I ALREADY SAW THAT THESE PACKS HAVE A BUNCH OF RARE CARDS...
SAW SAW
...USING MY SHARIN-GAN!
SAW SAW
THIS WILL BE AN UNFORGET-TABLE VIDEO!
STAGGER
WHOOPS ...!
KONOHA
SHP SHP SHP
SHP SHP
NO!! ALL MY RARE CAAARDS !!
IN A WAY, IT DID TURN OUT TO BE AN UNFORGET-TABLE VIDEO.
KONOHA
NIN-JA-OH!

VR GAME

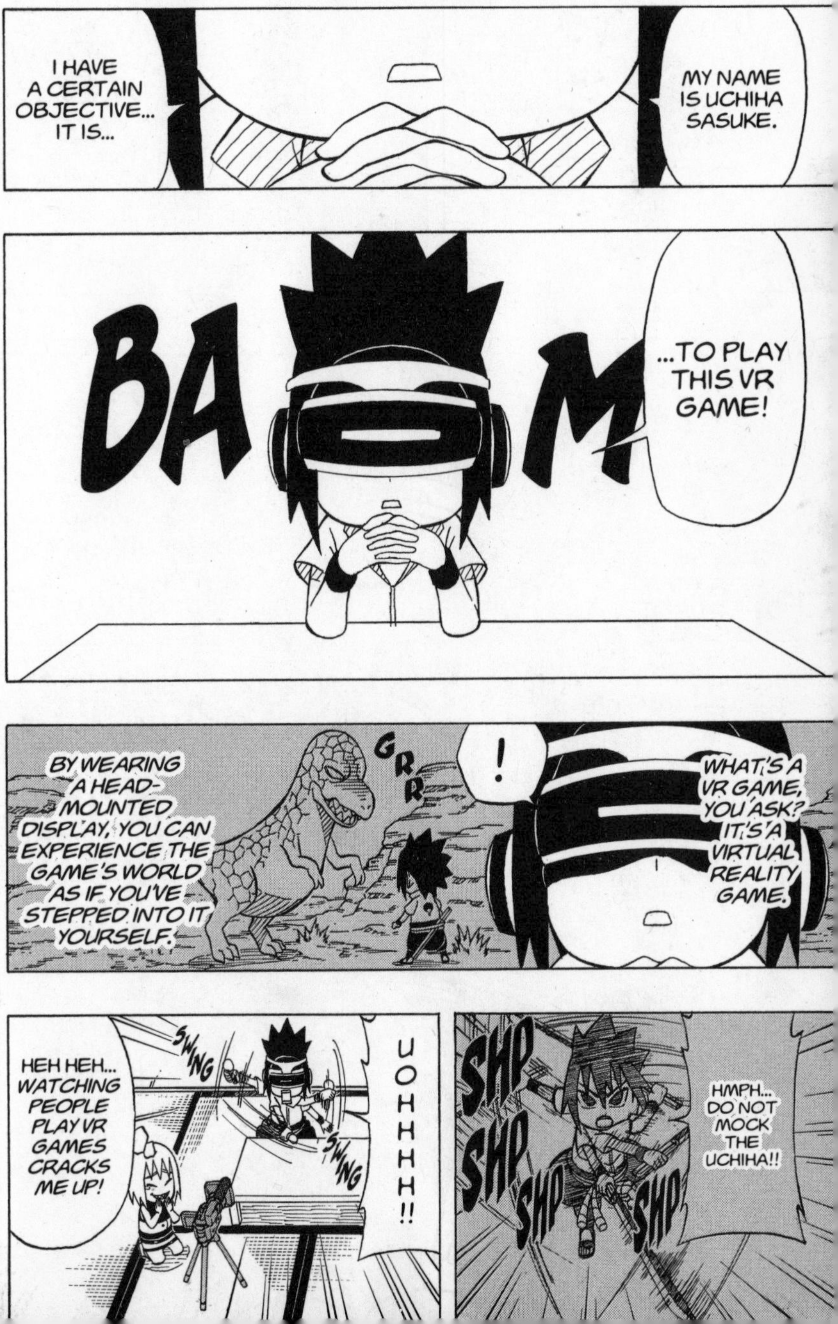
MY NAME IS UCHIHA SASUKE.
I HAVE A CERTAIN OBJECTIVE... IT IS...
...TO PLAY THIS VR GAME!
BAM
!
WHAT'S A VR GAME, YOU ASK? IT'S A VIRTUAL REALITY GAME.
GRR
BY WEARING A HEAD-MOUNTED DISPLAY, YOU CAN EXPERIENCE THE GAME'S WORLD AS IF YOU'VE STEPPED INTO IT YOURSELF.
HMPH... DO NOT MOCK THE UCHIHA!!
SHP SHP SHP SHP
UOHHHHH!!
SWING
SWING
HEH HEH... WATCHING PEOPLE PLAY VR GAMES CRACKS ME UP!

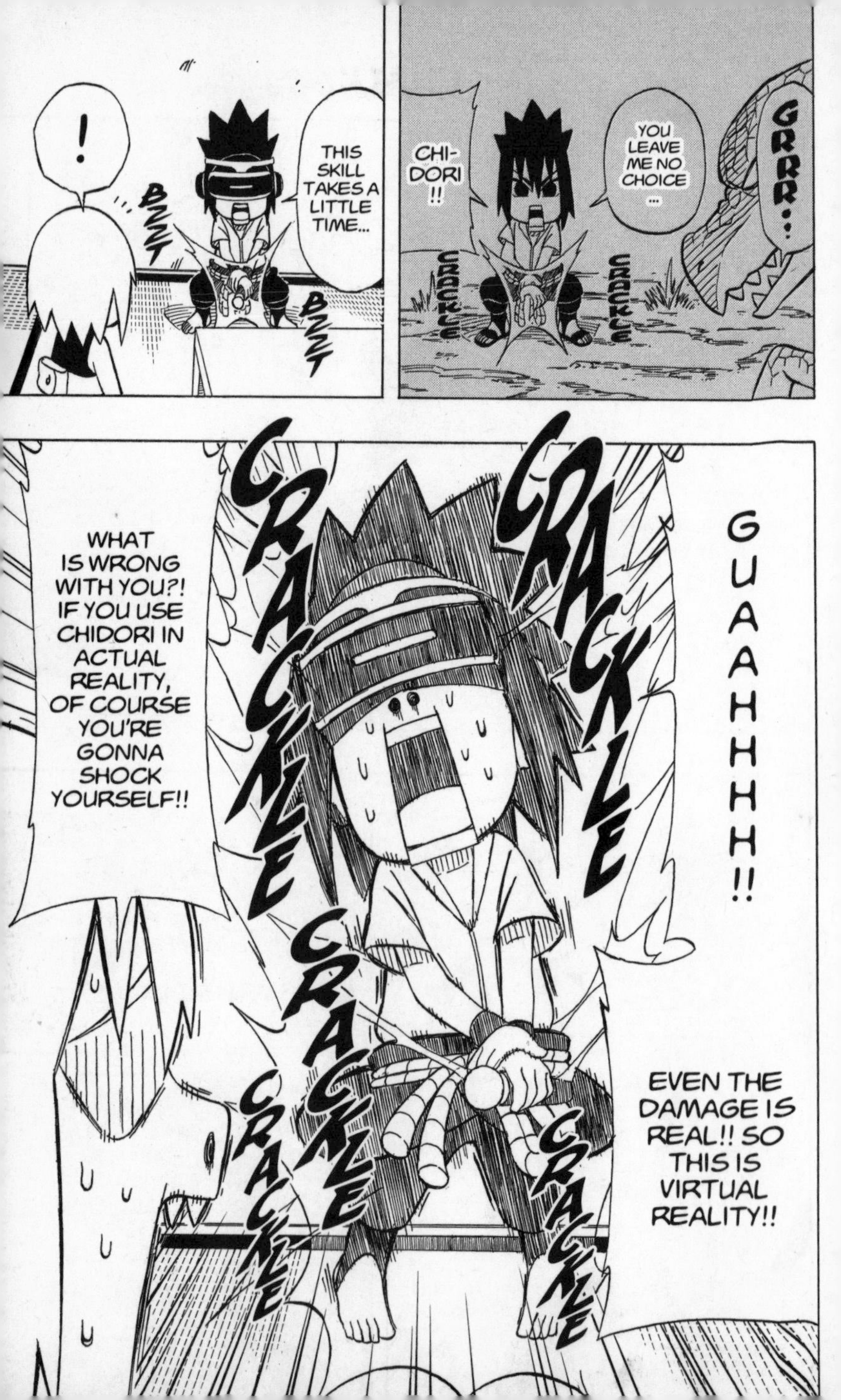
GRRR...
YOU LEAVE ME NO CHOICE...
CHI-DORI!!
CRACKLE
CRACKLE
THIS SKILL TAKES A LITTLE TIME...
!
BZZT
BZZT
GUAAHHHH!!
CRACKLE
CRACKLE
WHAT IS WRONG WITH YOU?! IF YOU USE CHIDORI IN ACTUAL REALITY, OF COURSE YOU'RE GONNA SHOCK YOURSELF!!
CRACKLE
CRACKLE
CRACKLE
EVEN THE DAMAGE IS REAL!! SO THIS IS VIRTUAL REALITY!!

SURPRISE SHOCK

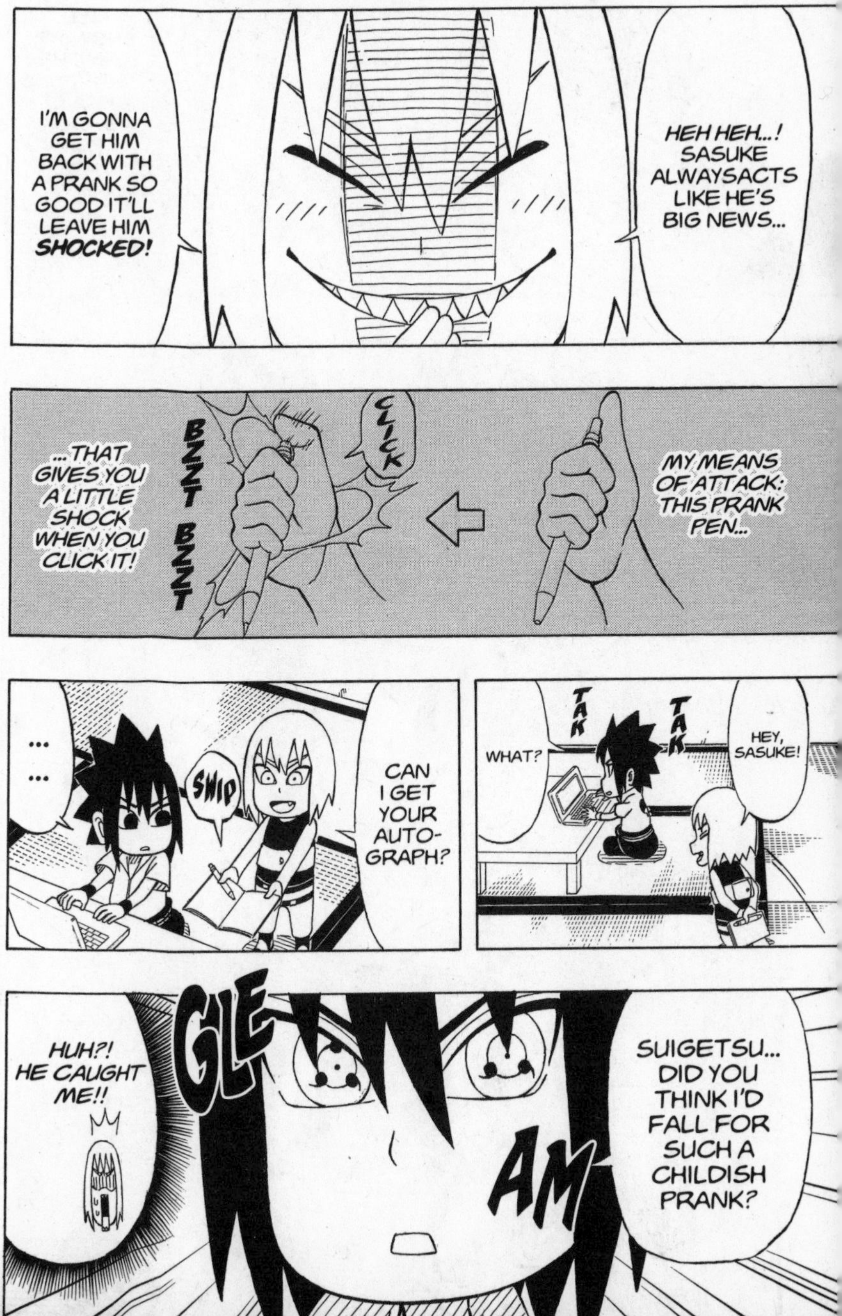

HEH HEH...! SASUKE ALWAYSACTS LIKE HE'S BIG NEWS...
I'M GONNA GET HIM BACK WITH A PRANK SO GOOD IT'LL LEAVE HIM **SHOCKED!**
MY MEANS OF ATTACK: THIS PRANK PEN...
CLICK
BZZT BZZT
...THAT GIVES YOU A LITTLE SHOCK WHEN YOU CLICK IT!
HEY, SASUKE!
TAK TAK
WHAT?
CAN I GET YOUR AUTO-GRAPH?
SWIP
... ...
SUIGETSU... DID YOU THINK I'D FALL FOR SUCH A CHILDISH PRANK?
GLEAM
HUH?! HE CAUGHT ME!!

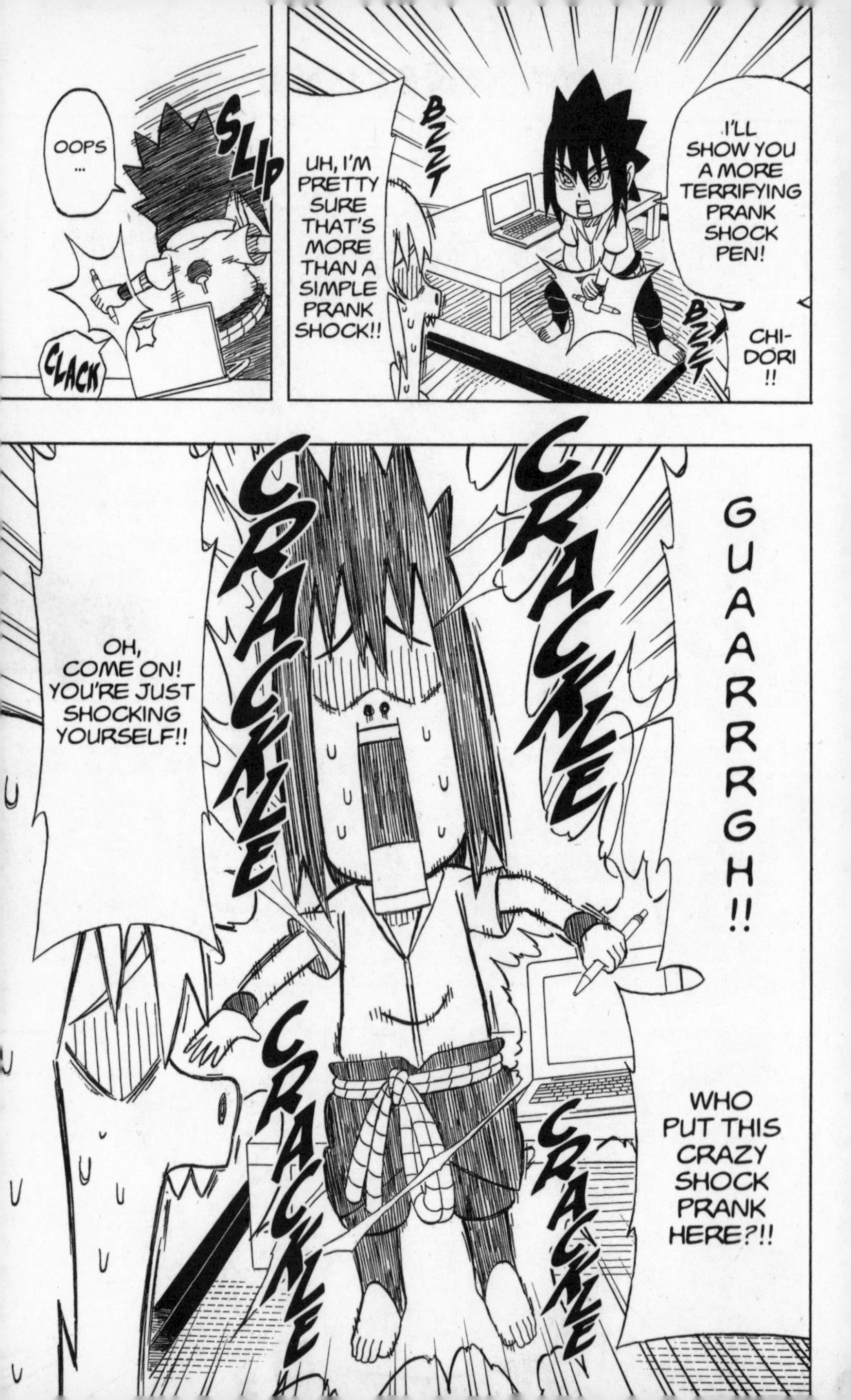
I'LL SHOW YOU A MORE TERRIFYING PRANK SHOCK PEN!
CHI-DORI !!
BZZZT
BZZZT
UH, I'M PRETTY SURE THAT'S MORE THAN A SIMPLE PRANK SHOCK!!
SLIP
OOPS ...
CLACK
GUAARRRGH!!
CRACKLE
CRACKLE
CRACKLE
CRACKLE
WHO PUT THIS CRAZY SHOCK PRANK HERE?!!
OH, COME ON! YOU'RE JUST SHOCKING YOURSELF!!

INTERNET IDOL

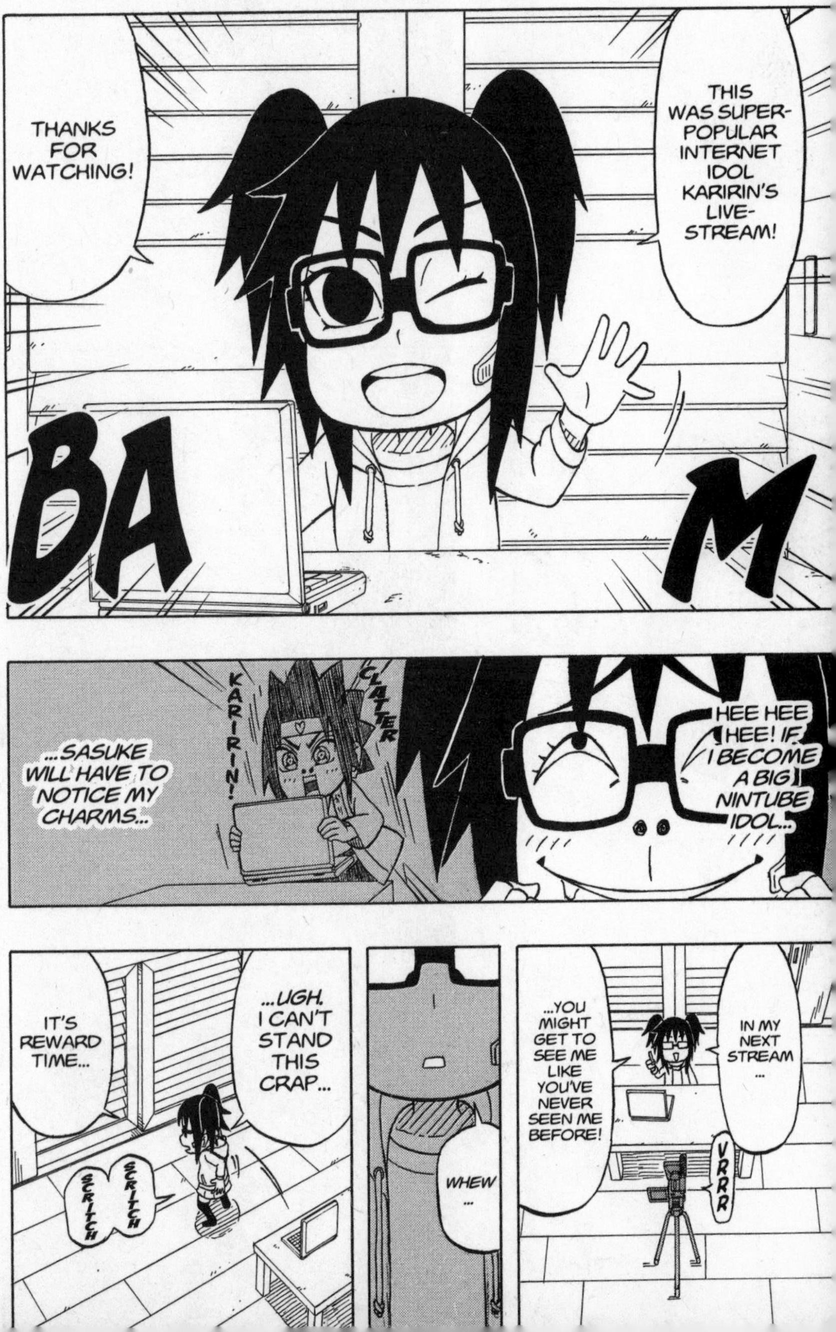
THIS WAS SUPER-POPULAR INTERNET IDOL KARIRIN'S LIVE-STREAM!
THANKS FOR WATCHING!
BAM
HEE HEE HEE! IF I BECOME A BIG NINTUBE IDOL...
CLATTER
KARIRIN!
...SASUKE WILL HAVE TO NOTICE MY CHARMS...
IN MY NEXT STREAM...
...YOU MIGHT GET TO SEE ME LIKE YOU'VE NEVER SEEN ME BEFORE!
VRRR
...UGH. I CAN'T STAND THIS CRAP...
WHEW...
IT'S REWARD TIME...
SCRITCH
SCRITCH

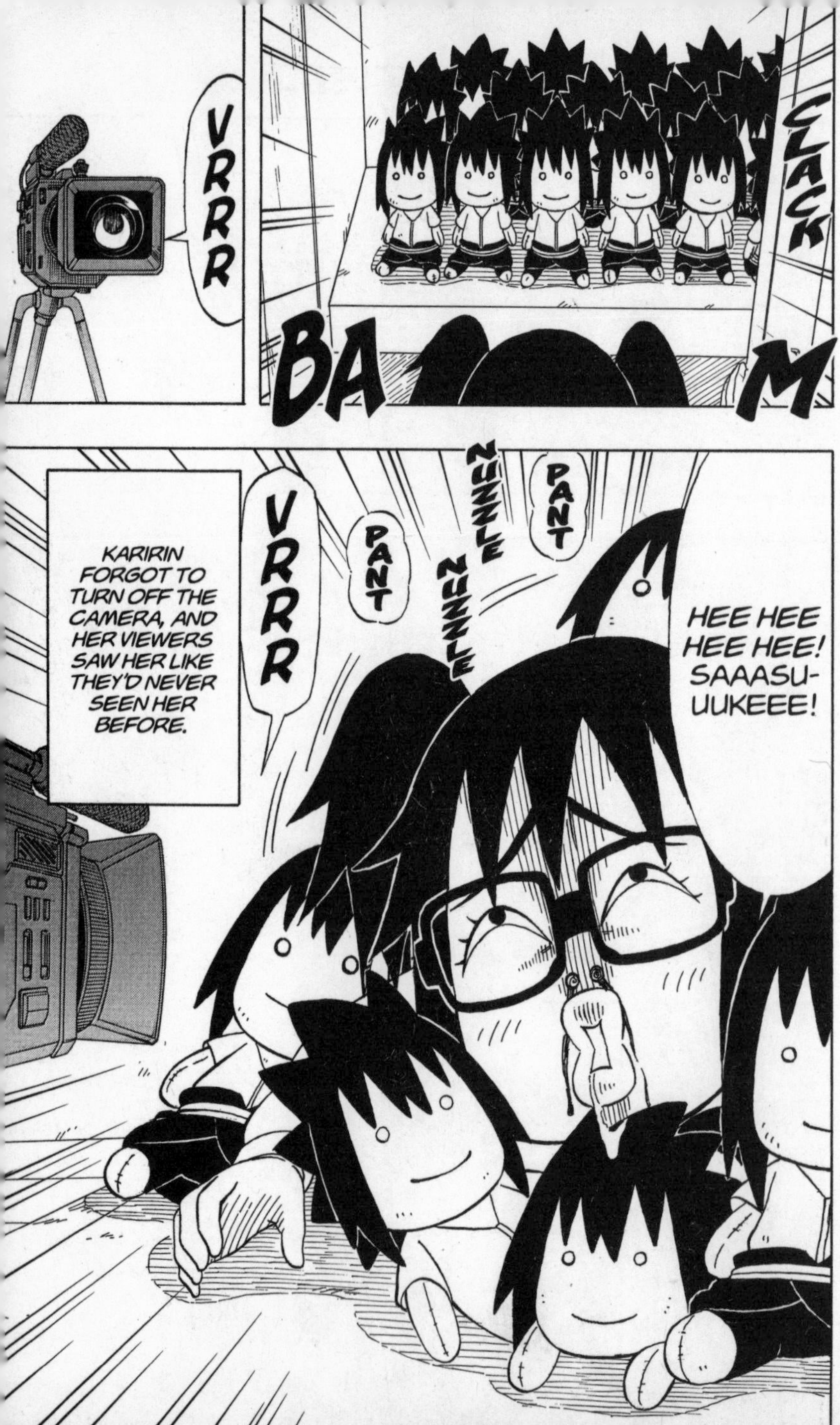
CLACK
BAM
VRRR
HEE HEE HEE HEE! SAAASU-UUKEEE!
PANT
NUZZLE NUZZLE
PANT
VRRR
KARIRIN FORGOT TO TURN OFF THE CAMERA, AND HER VIEWERS SAW HER LIKE THEY'D NEVER SEEN HER BEFORE.

PRODUCT REVIEW

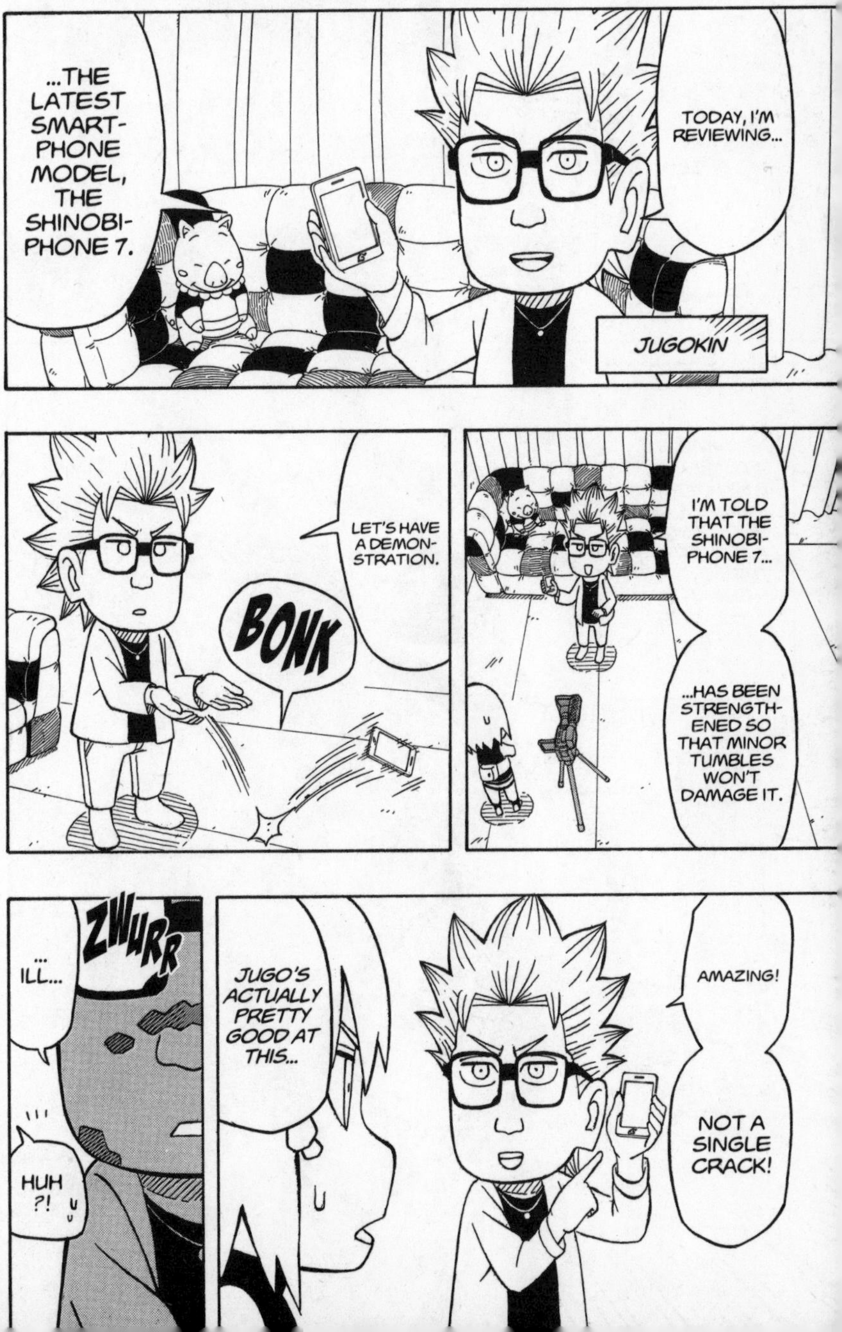
TODAY, I'M REVIEWING...
JUGOKIN
...THE LATEST SMART-PHONE MODEL, THE SHINOBI-PHONE 7.
I'M TOLD THAT THE SHINOBI-PHONE 7...
...HAS BEEN STRENGTH-ENED SO THAT MINOR TUMBLES WON'T DAMAGE IT.
LET'S HAVE A DEMON-STRATION.
BONK
AMAZING!
NOT A SINGLE CRACK!
JUGO'S ACTUALLY PRETTY GOOD AT THIS...
ZWURR
... ILL...
HUH ?!

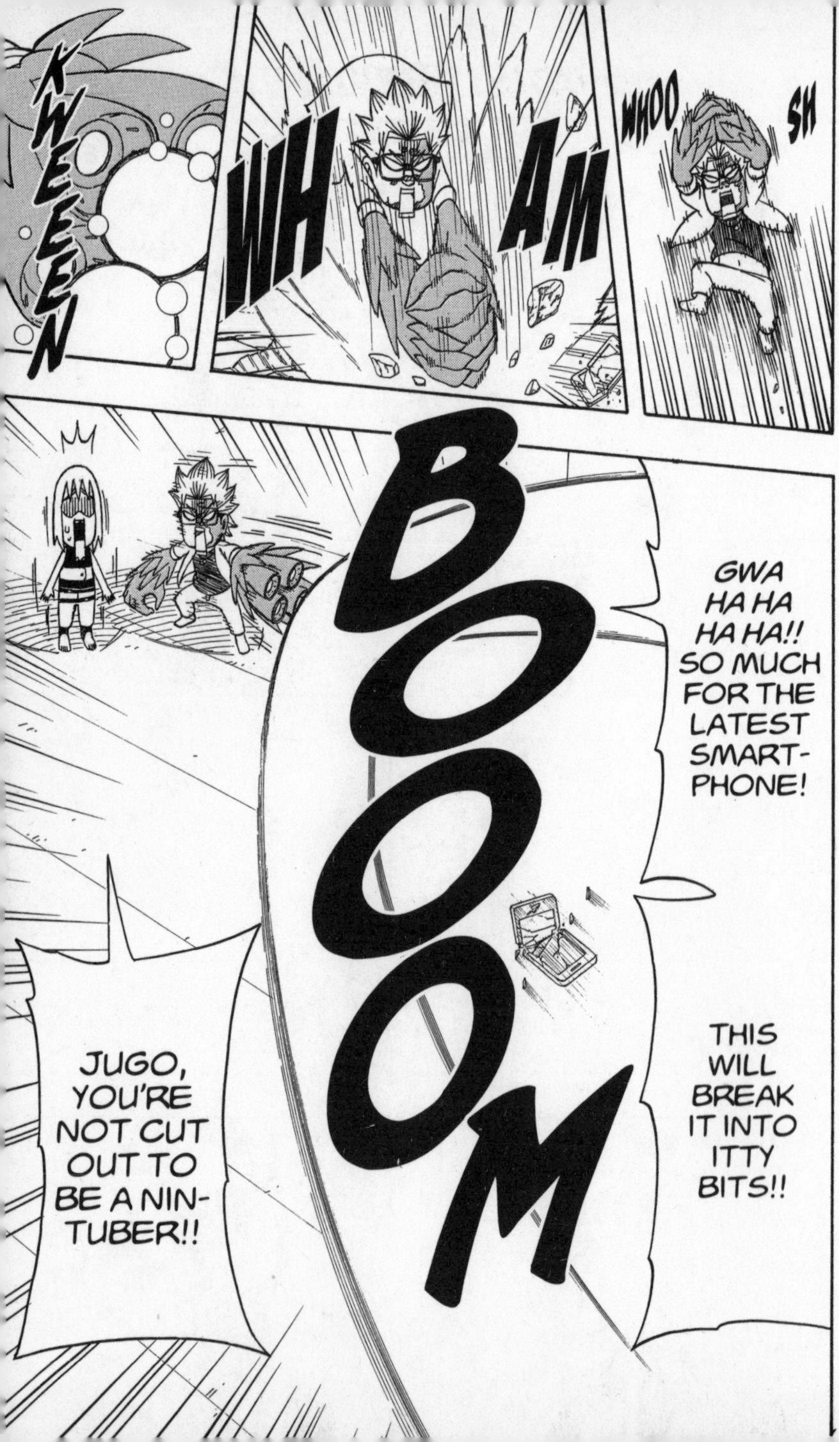
WHOOSH
WHAM
KWEEEEN
GWA HA HA HA HA!! SO MUCH FOR THE LATEST SMART-PHONE!
THIS WILL BREAK IT INTO ITTY BITS!!
BOOOOM
JUGO, YOU'RE NOT CUT OUT TO BE A NIN-TUBER!!

SASUTARO

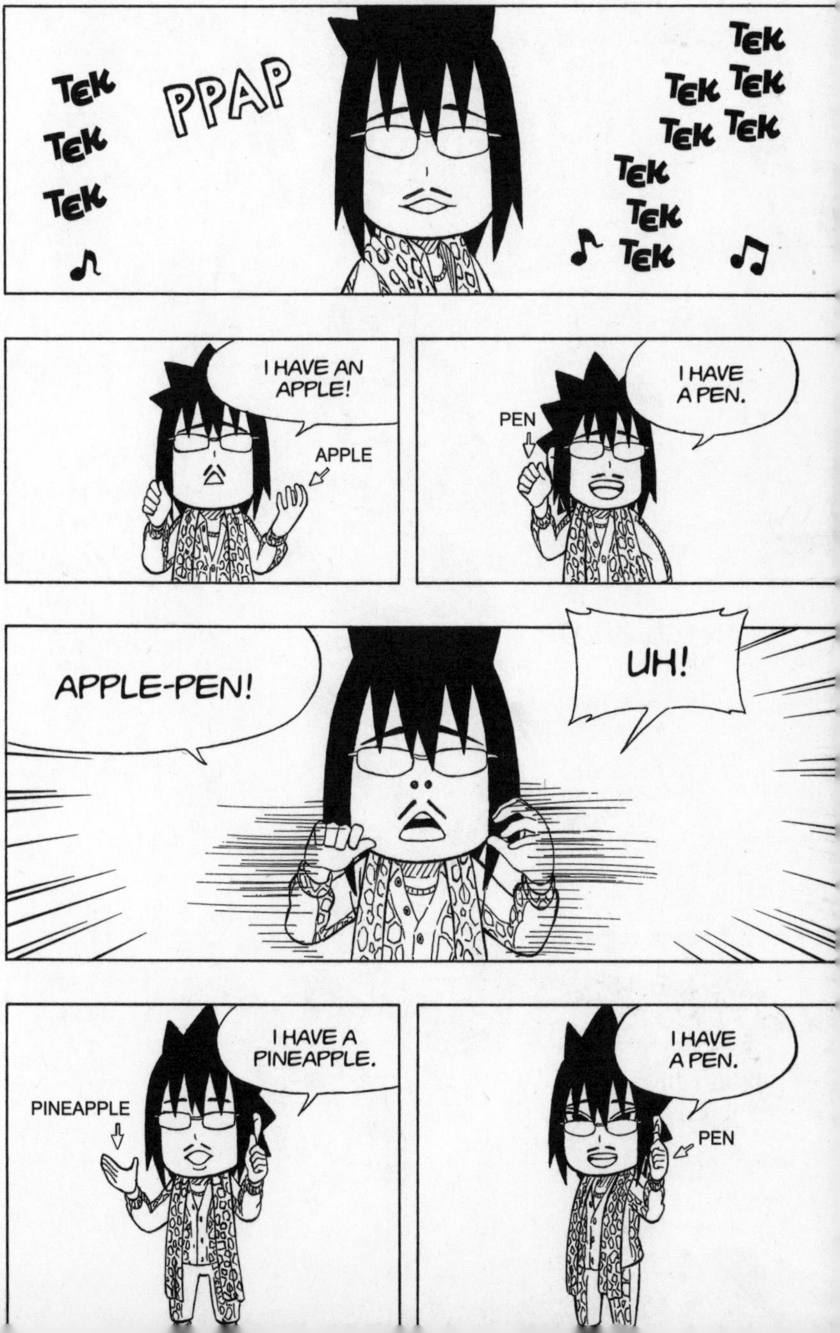
TEK
TEK
TEK
TEK
TEK
TEK
TEK
TEK
PPAP
TEK
TEK
TEK
I HAVE A PEN.
PEN
I HAVE AN APPLE!
APPLE
UH!
APPLE-PEN!
I HAVE A PEN.
PEN
I HAVE A PINEAPPLE.
PINEAPPLE

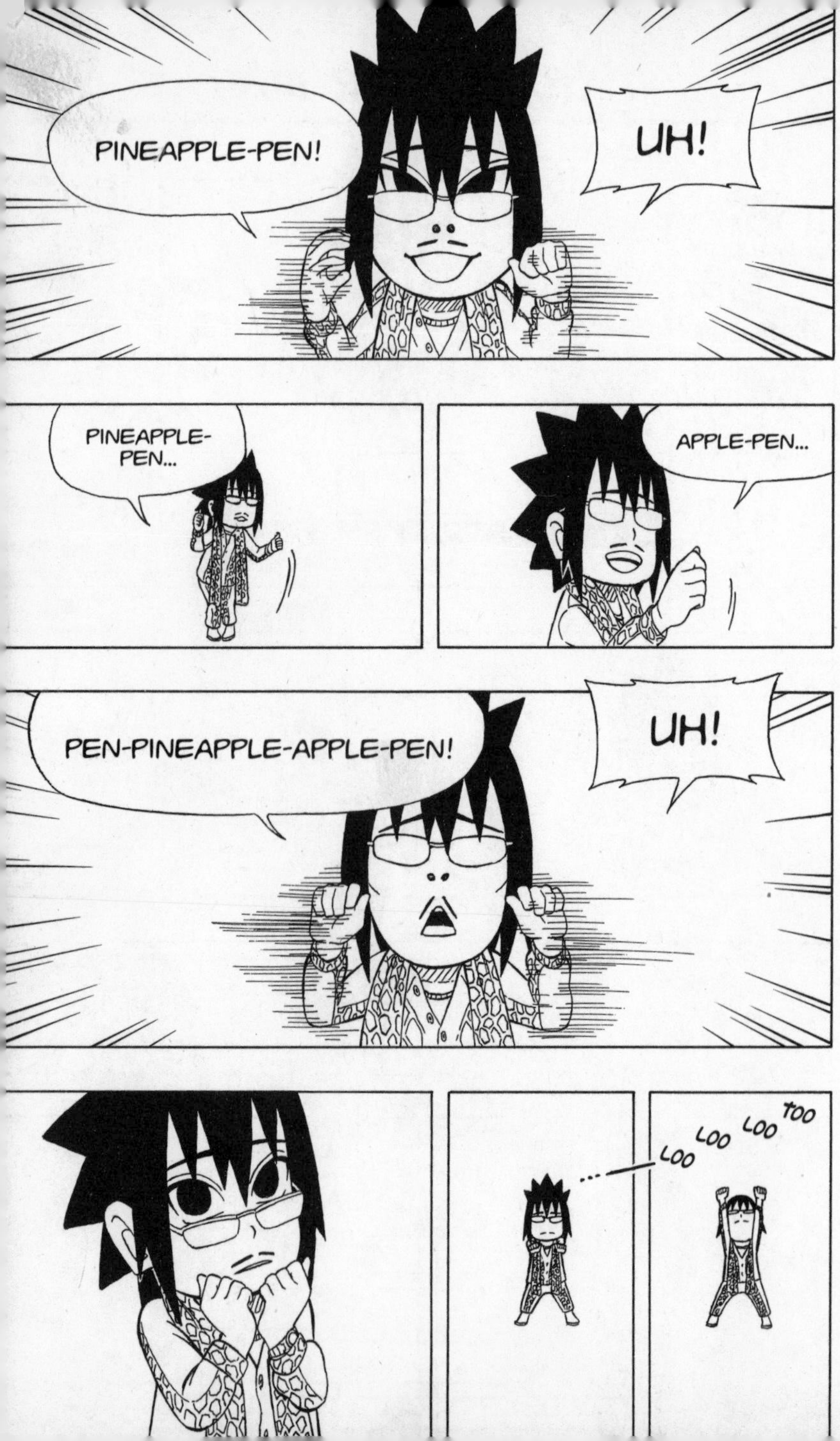
UH!
PINEAPPLE-PEN!
APPLE-PEN...
PINEAPPLE-PEN...
UH!
PEN-PINEAPPLE-APPLE-PEN!
LOO LOO LOO TOO
...

ITACHI CHANNEL

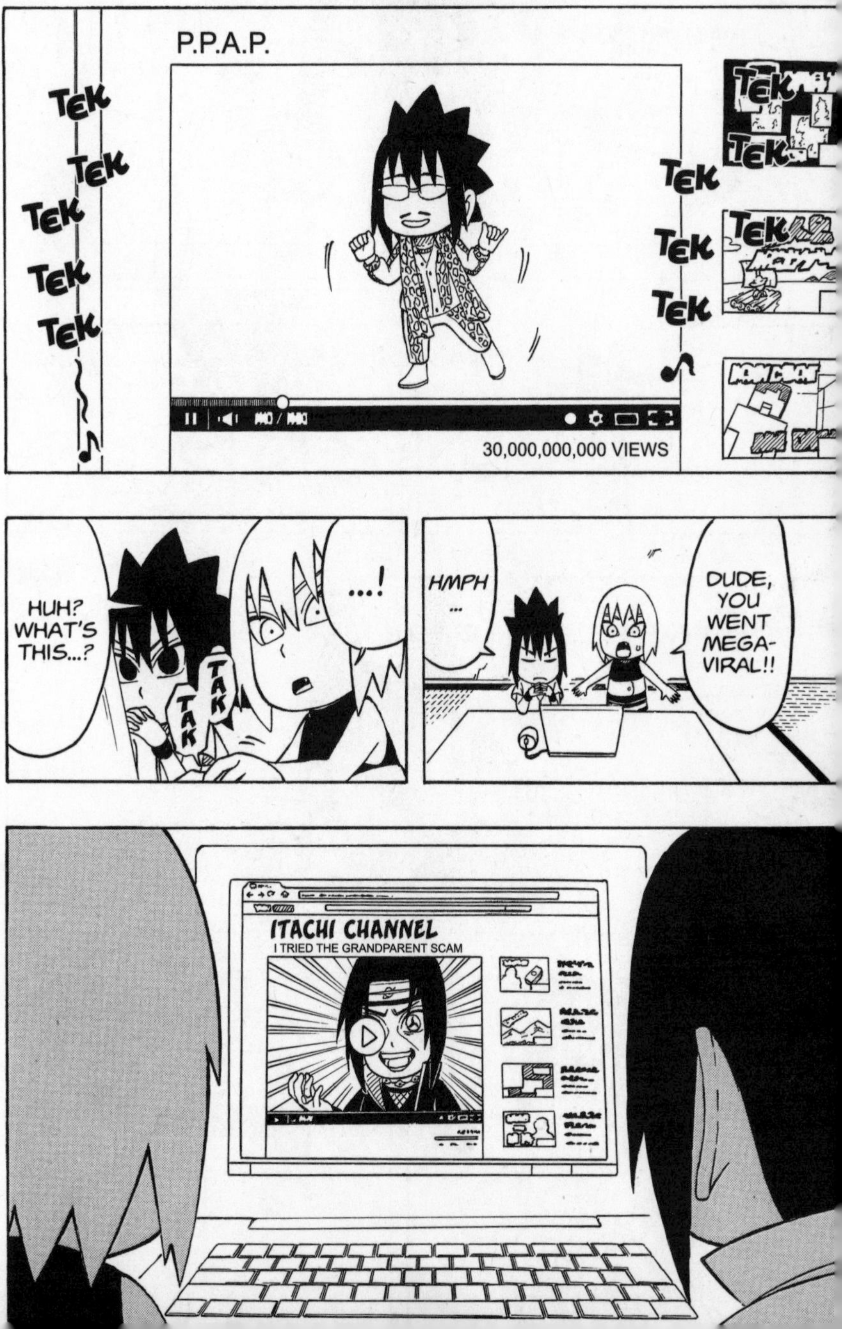
P.P.A.P.
TEK TEK TEK
30,000,000,000 VIEWS
TEK TEK TEK TEK TEK
DUDE, YOU WENT MEGA-VIRAL!!
HMPH ...
...!
TAK TAK
HUH? WHAT'S THIS...?
ITACHI CHANNEL
I TRIED THE GRANDPARENT SCAM

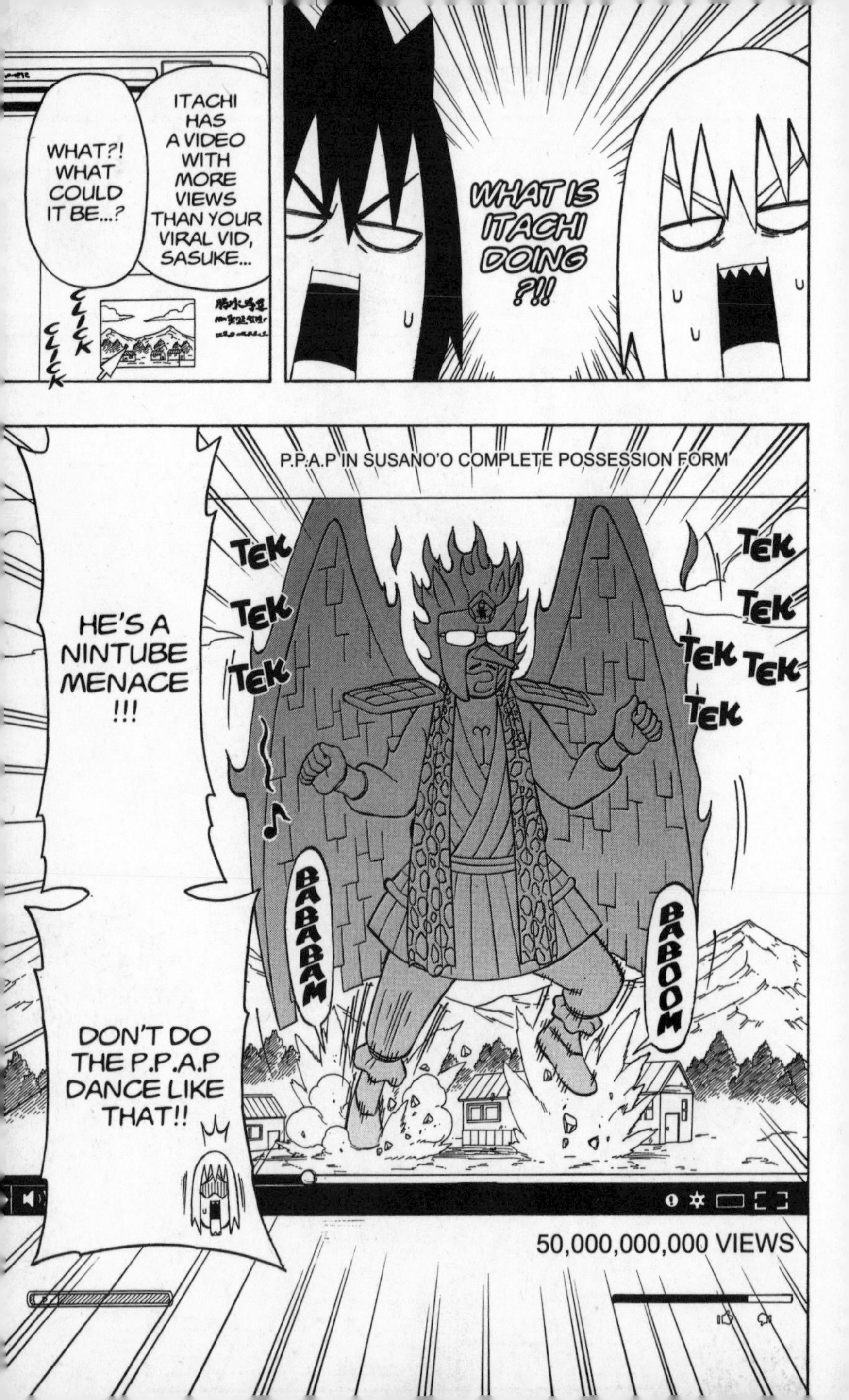
ITACHI HAS A VIDEO WITH MORE VIEWS THAN YOUR VIRAL VID, SASUKE...
WHAT?! WHAT COULD IT BE...?
CLICK CLICK
WHAT IS ITACHI DOING ?!!
P.P.A.P IN SUSANO'O COMPLETE POSSESSION FORM
HE'S A NINTUBE MENACE !!!
TEK TEK TEK
TEK TEK TEK TEK TEK
BABABAM
BABOOM
DON'T DO THE P.P.A.P DANCE LIKE THAT!!
50,000,000,000 VIEWS

ANIMAL VIDEOS

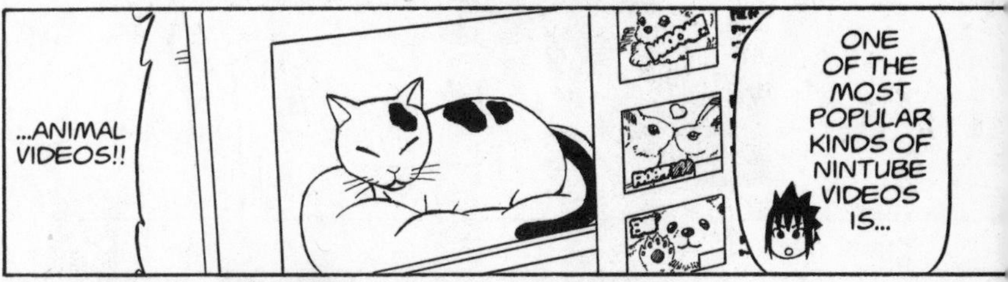
ONE OF THE MOST POPULAR KINDS OF NINTUBE VIDEOS IS...
...ANIMAL VIDEOS!!

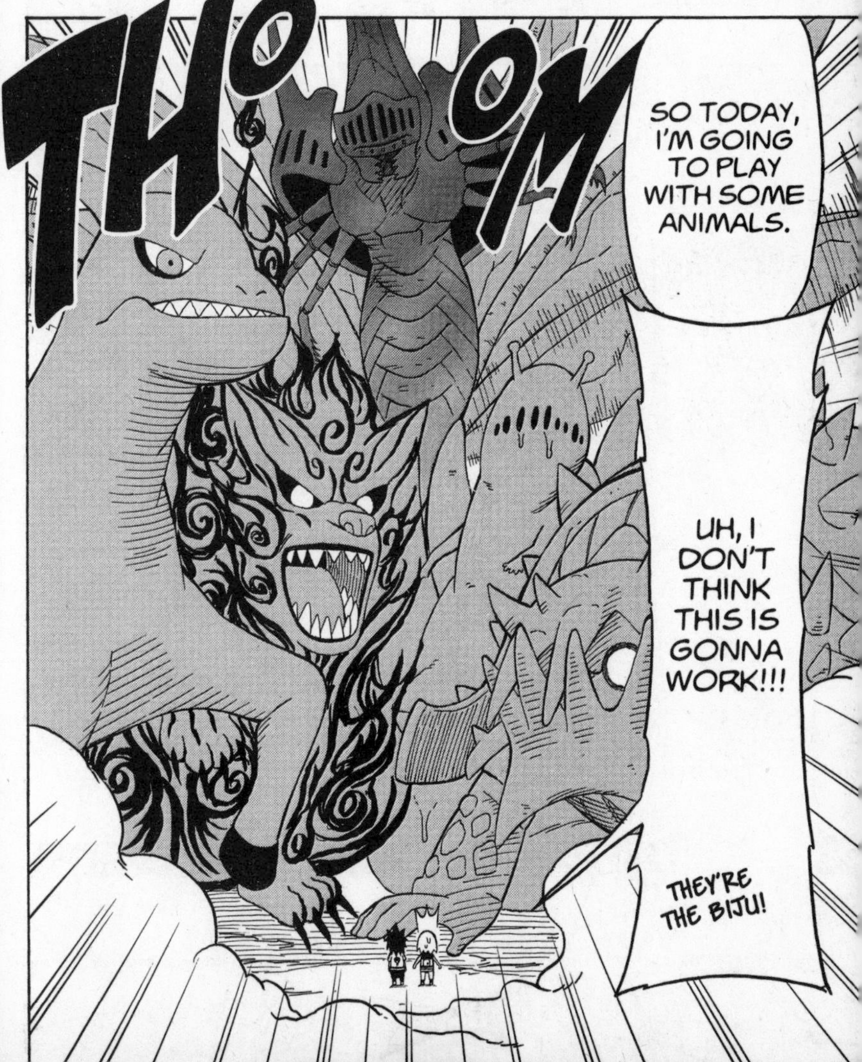
SO TODAY, I'M GOING TO PLAY WITH SOME ANIMALS.
THOOM
UH, I DON'T THINK THIS IS GONNA WORK!!!
THEY'RE THE BIJU!

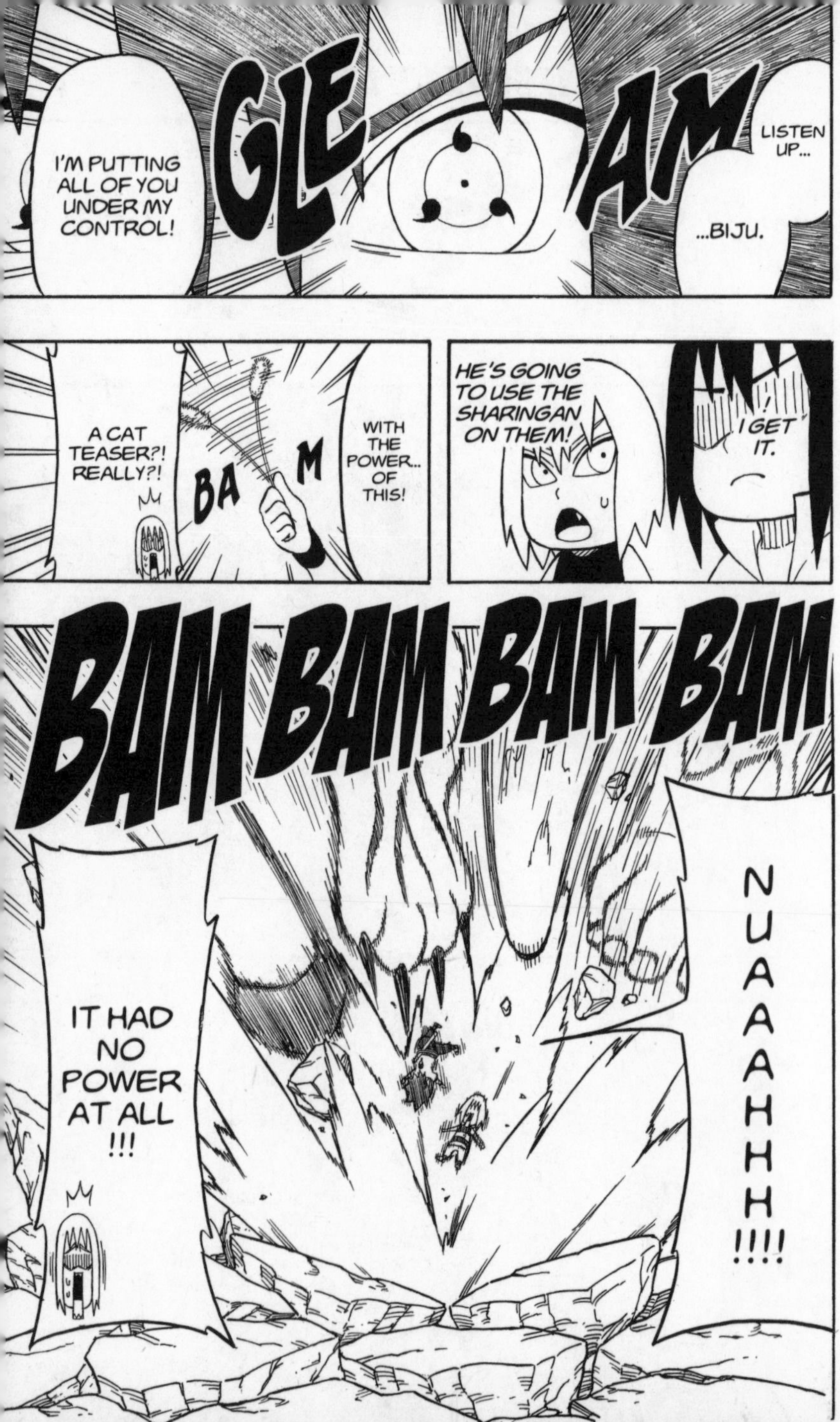
LISTEN UP... ...BIJU.
GLEAM
I'M PUTTING ALL OF YOU UNDER MY CONTROL!
! I GET IT.
HE'S GOING TO USE THE SHARINGAN ON THEM!
WITH THE POWER... OF THIS!
BAM
A CAT TEASER?! REALLY?!
BAM BAM BAM BAM
NUAAAAHHH!!!!
IT HAD NO POWER AT ALL!!!

VIDEO BATTLE!!

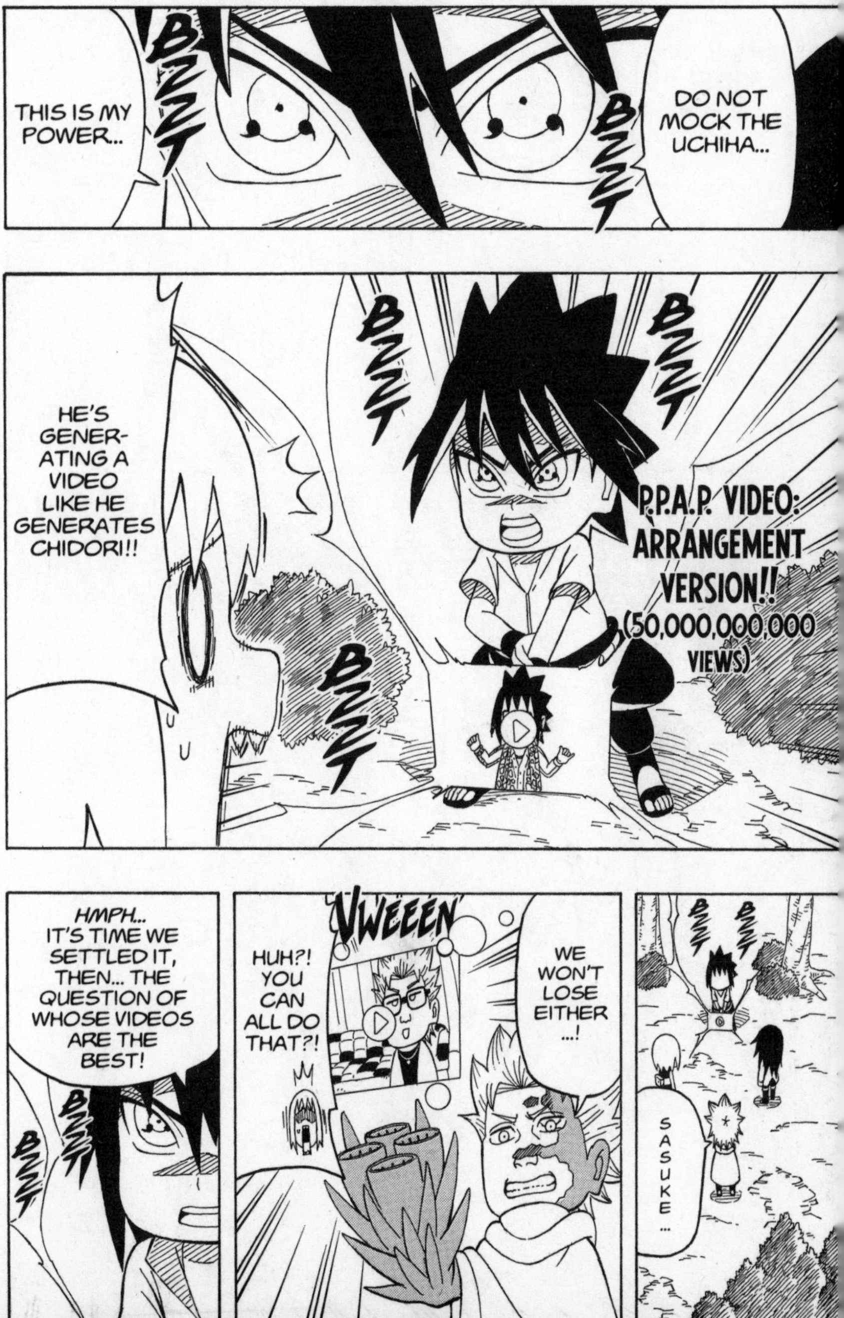
DO NOT MOCK THE UCHIHA...
BZZZT
BZZZT
THIS IS MY POWER...
BZZZT
BZZZT
P.P.A.P. VIDEO: ARRANGEMENT VERSION!! (50,000,000,000 VIEWS)
BZZZT
HE'S GENER-ATING A VIDEO LIKE HE GENERATES CHIDORI!!
BZZZT
BZZZT
SASUKE...
VWEEEN
WE WON'T LOSE EITHER ...!
HUH?! YOU CAN ALL DO THAT?!
HMPH... IT'S TIME WE SETTLED IT, THEN... THE QUESTION OF WHOSE VIDEOS ARE THE BEST!
BZZZT
BZZZT

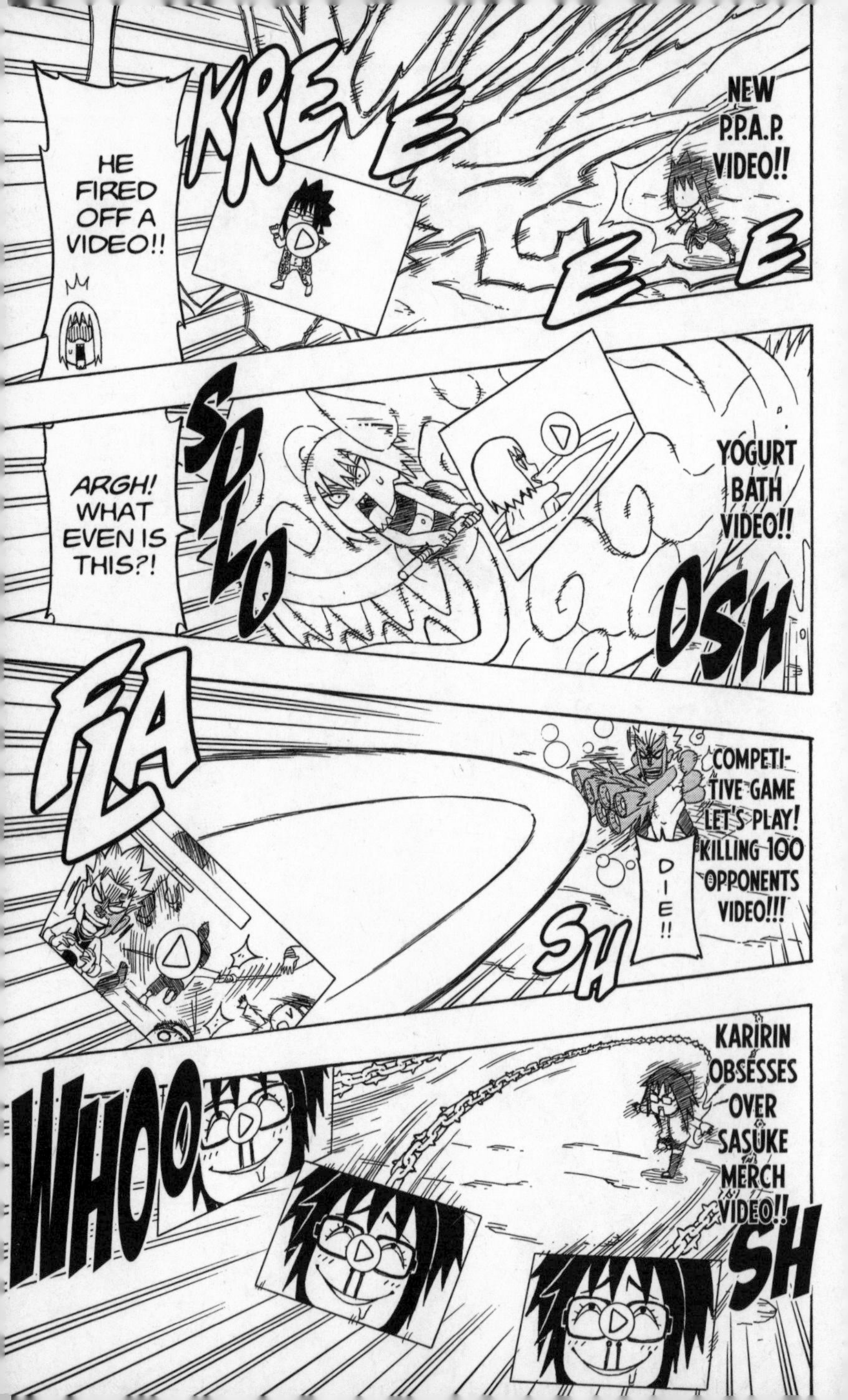

NEW P.P.A.P. VIDEO!!
KRE
E
E
E
HE FIRED OFF A VIDEO!!
YOGURT BATH VIDEO!!
SPLO
OSH
ARGH! WHAT EVEN IS THIS?!
COMPETITIVE GAME LET'S PLAY! KILLING 100 OPPONENTS VIDEO!!!
DIE!!
FLA
SH
KARIRIN OBSESSES OVER SASUKE MERCH VIDEO!!
WHOO
SH

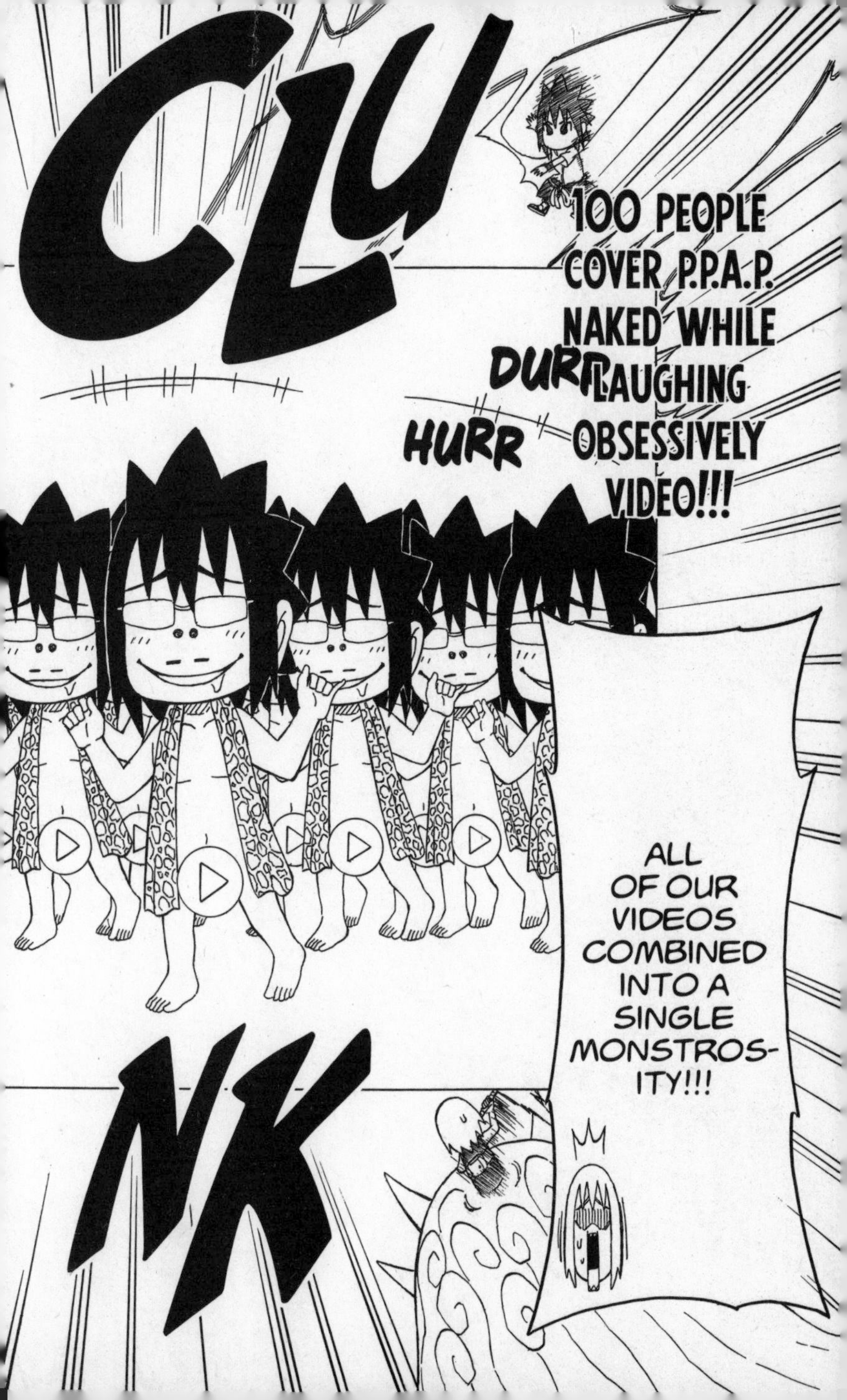
CLU
100 PEOPLE COVER P.P.A.P. NAKED WHILE LAUGHING OBSESSIVELY VIDEO!!!
DURR
HURR
NK
ALL OF OUR VIDEOS COMBINED INTO A SINGLE MONSTROS-ITY!!!

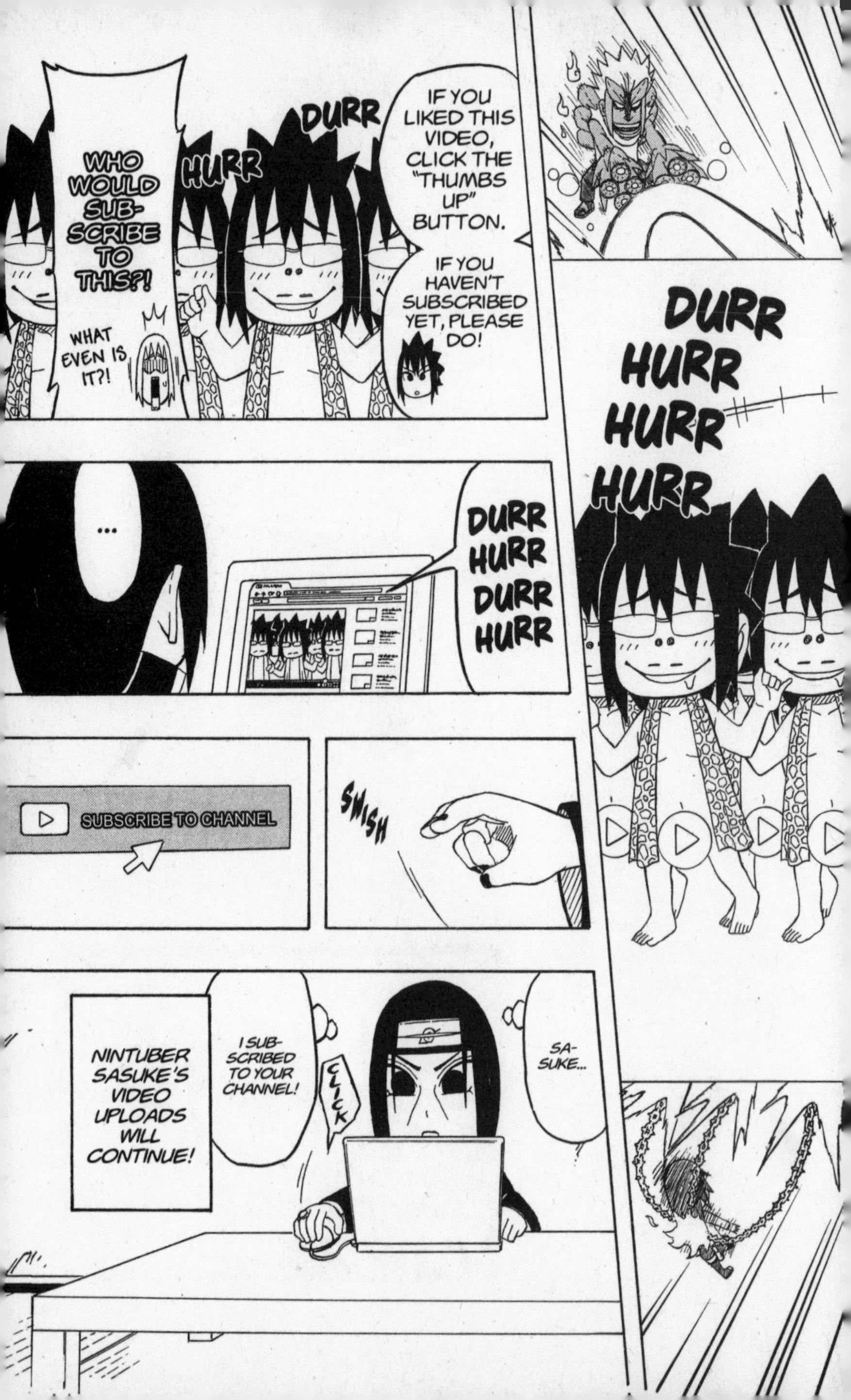
IF YOU LIKED THIS VIDEO, CLICK THE "THUMBS UP" BUTTON.
IF YOU HAVEN'T SUBSCRIBED YET, PLEASE DO!
DURR
HURR
WHO WOULD SUBSCRIBE TO THIS?!
WHAT EVEN IS IT?!
DURR HURR HURR HURR
DURR HURR DURR HURR
...
SWISH
SUBSCRIBE TO CHANNEL
SASUKE...
I SUBSCRIBED TO YOUR CHANNEL!
CLICK
NINTUBER SASUKE'S VIDEO UPLOADS WILL CONTINUE!

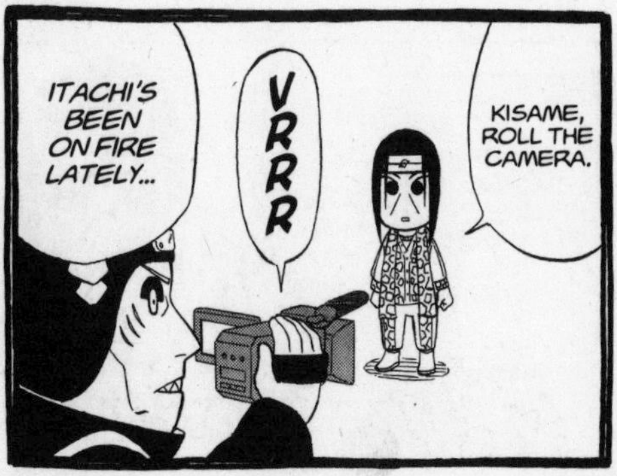
KISAME, ROLL THE CAMERA.
VRRR
ITACHI'S BEEN ON FIRE LATELY...

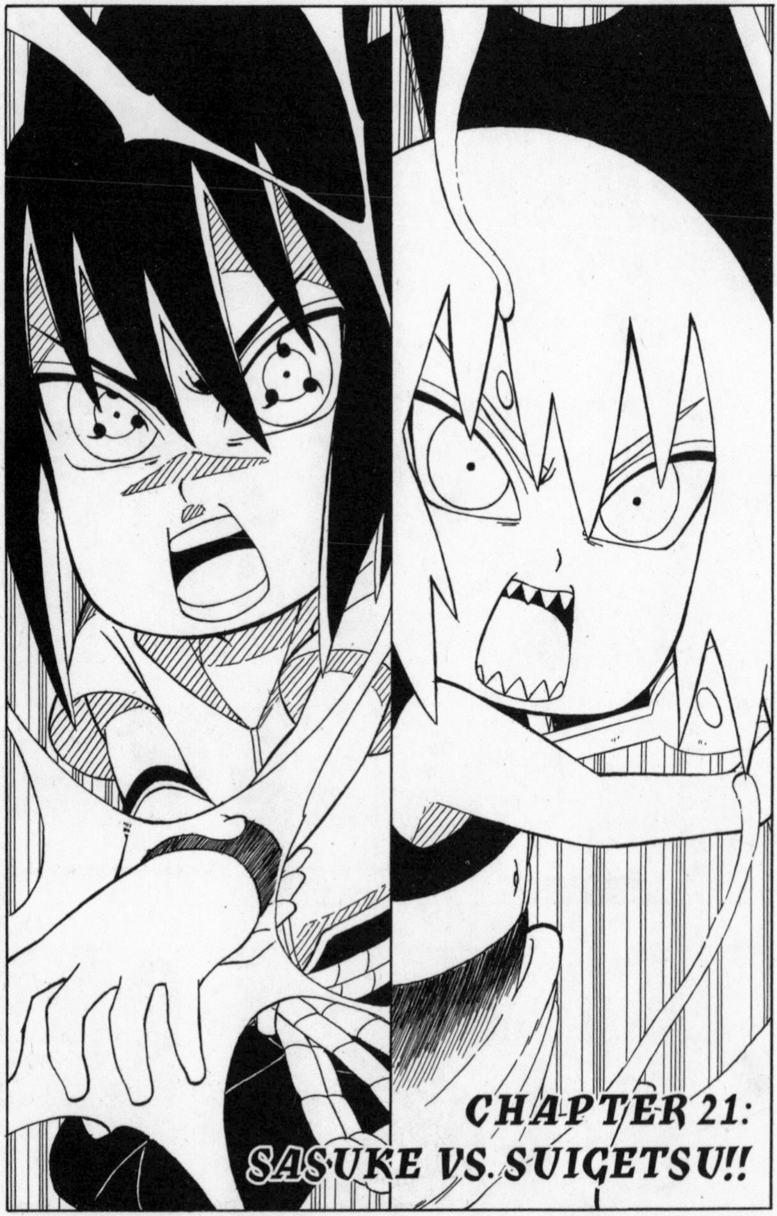
CHAPTER 21:
SASUKE VS. SUIGETSU!!

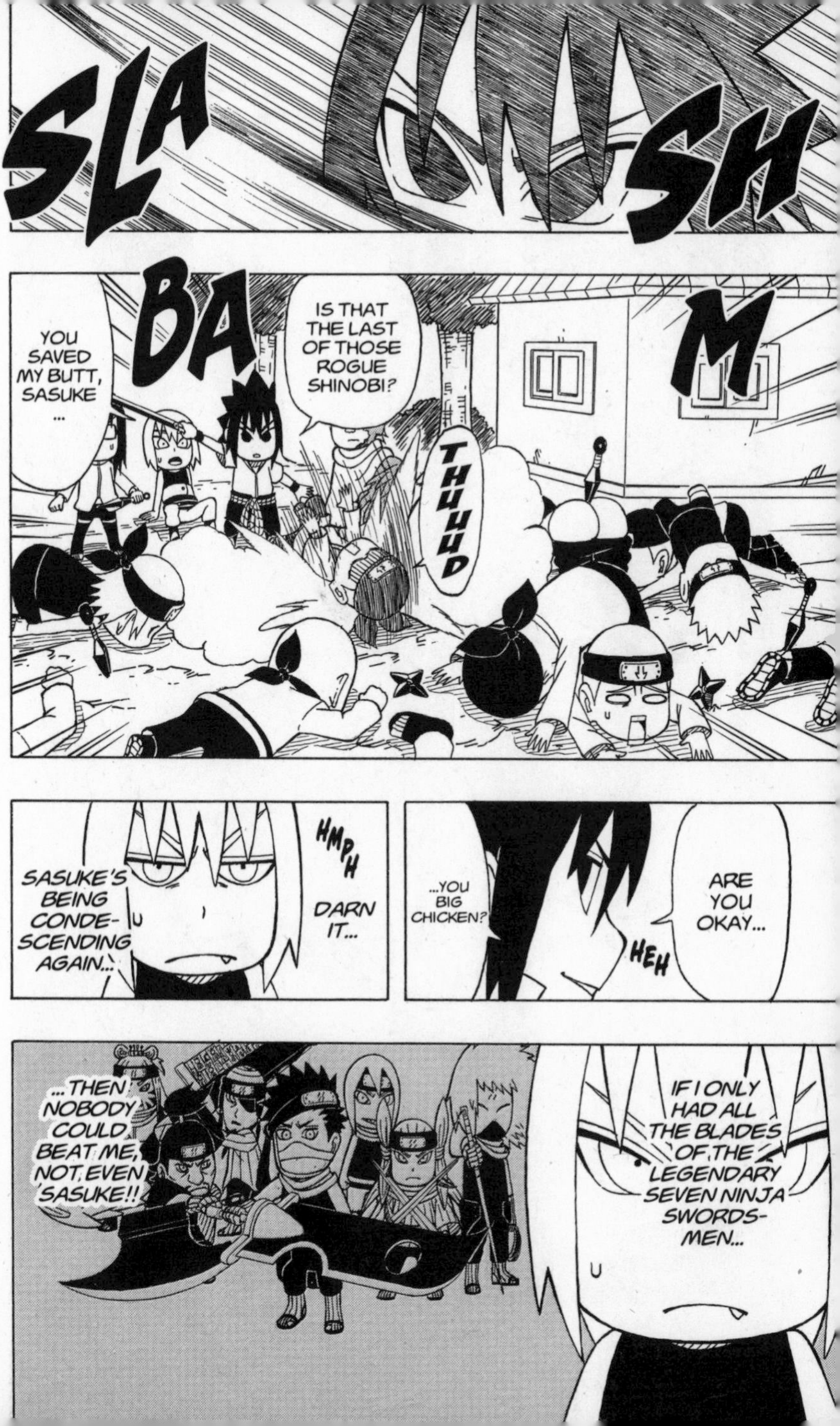
SLASH
BAM
IS THAT THE LAST OF THOSE ROGUE SHINOBI?
YOU SAVED MY BUTT, SASUKE ...
THUUUD
ARE YOU OKAY...
...YOU BIG CHICKEN?
HEH
HMPH
DARN IT...
SASUKE'S BEING CONDE-SCENDING AGAIN...
IF I ONLY HAD ALL THE BLADES OF THE LEGENDARY SEVEN NINJA SWORDS-MEN...
...THEN NOBODY COULD BEAT ME, NOT EVEN SASUKE!!

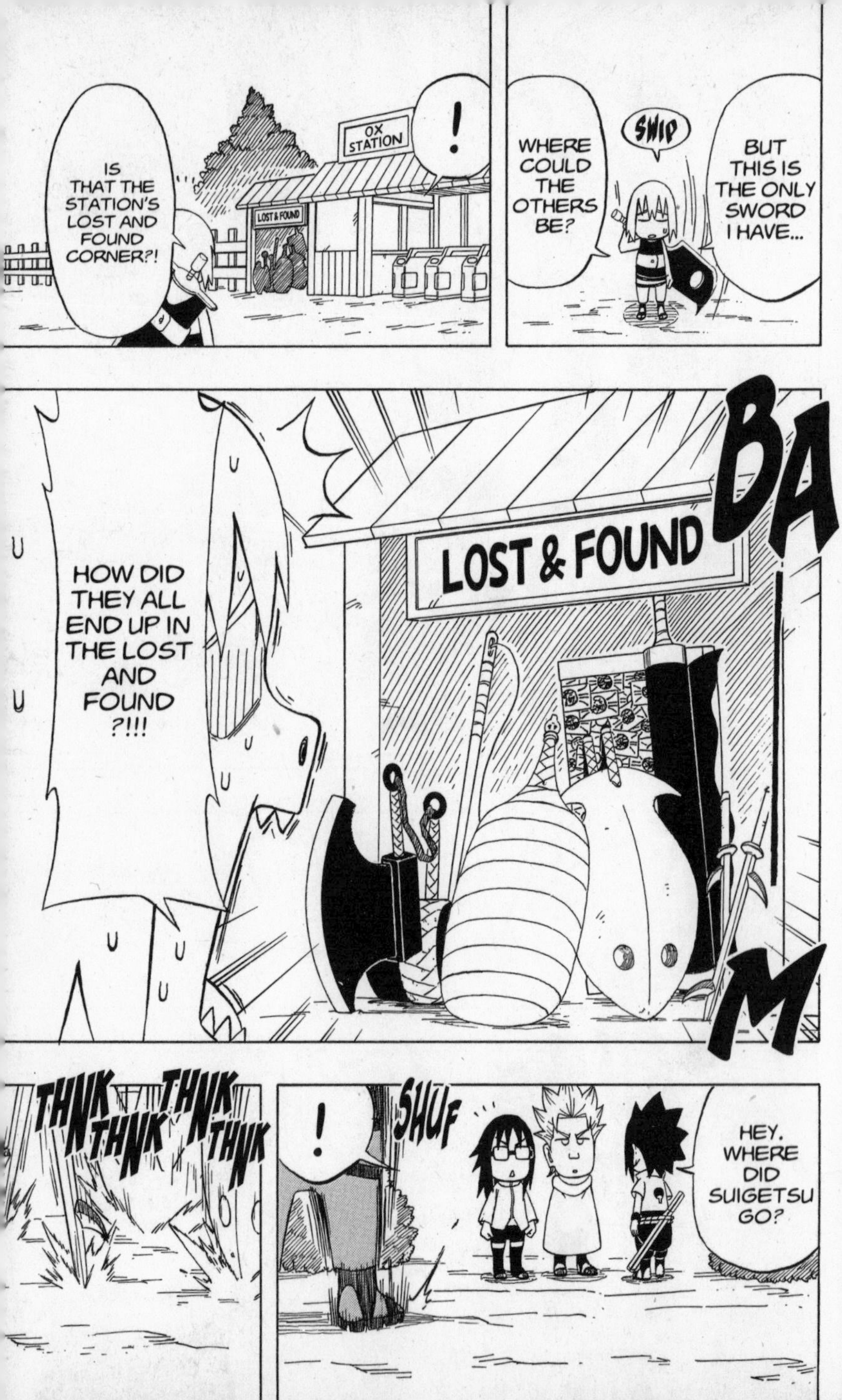
BUT THIS IS THE ONLY SWORD I HAVE...
SWIP
WHERE COULD THE OTHERS BE?
!
OX STATION
LOST & FOUND
IS THAT THE STATION'S LOST AND FOUND CORNER?!
BAM
LOST & FOUND
HOW DID THEY ALL END UP IN THE LOST AND FOUND ?!!!
HEY. WHERE DID SUIGETSU GO?
SHUF
!
THNK THNK THNK THNK THNK

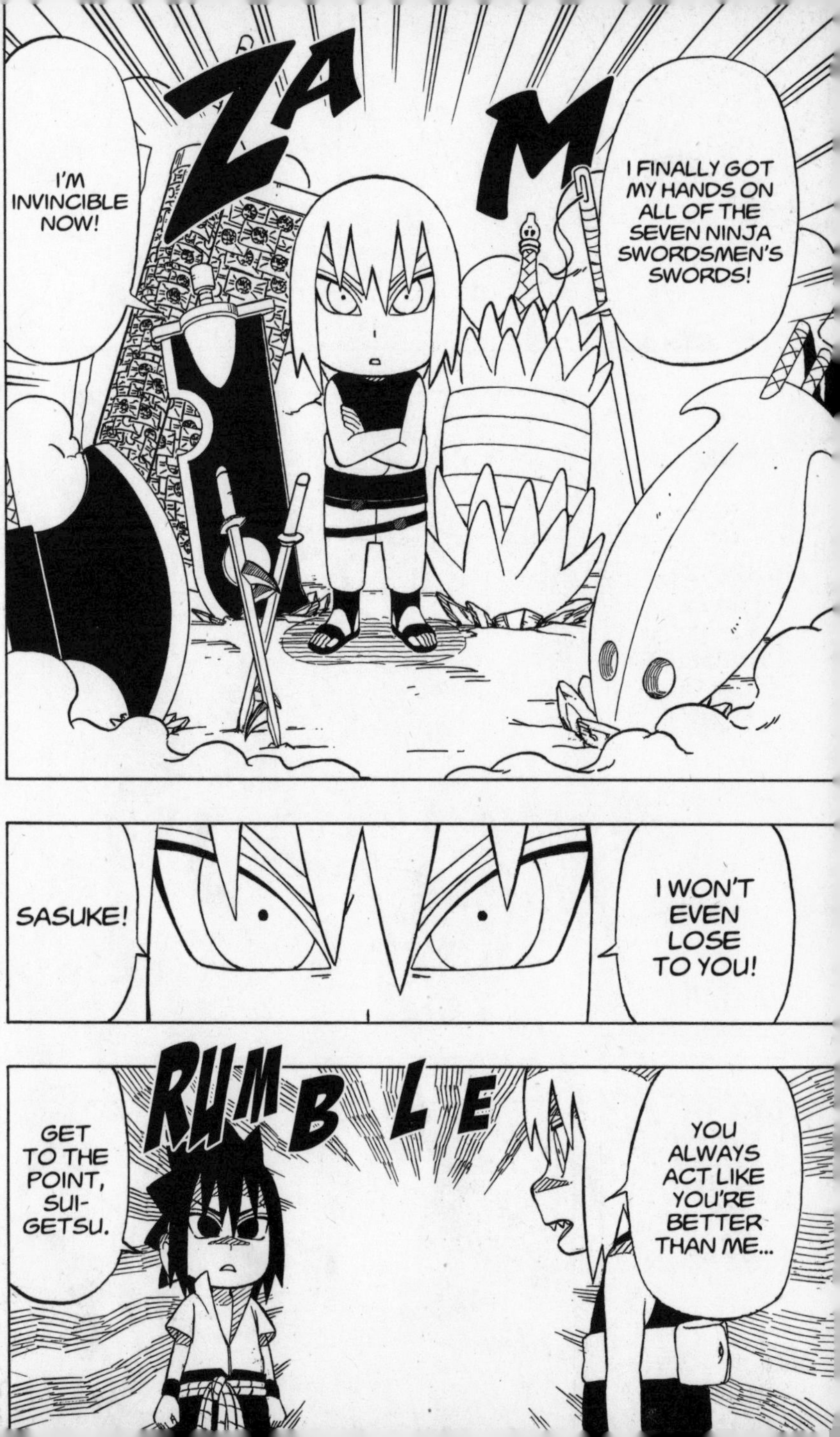
ZAM
I FINALLY GOT MY HANDS ON ALL OF THE SEVEN NINJA SWORDSMEN'S SWORDS!
I'M INVINCIBLE NOW!
I WON'T EVEN LOSE TO YOU!
SASUKE!
RUMBLE
YOU ALWAYS ACT LIKE YOU'RE BETTER THAN ME...
GET TO THE POINT, SUI-GETSU.

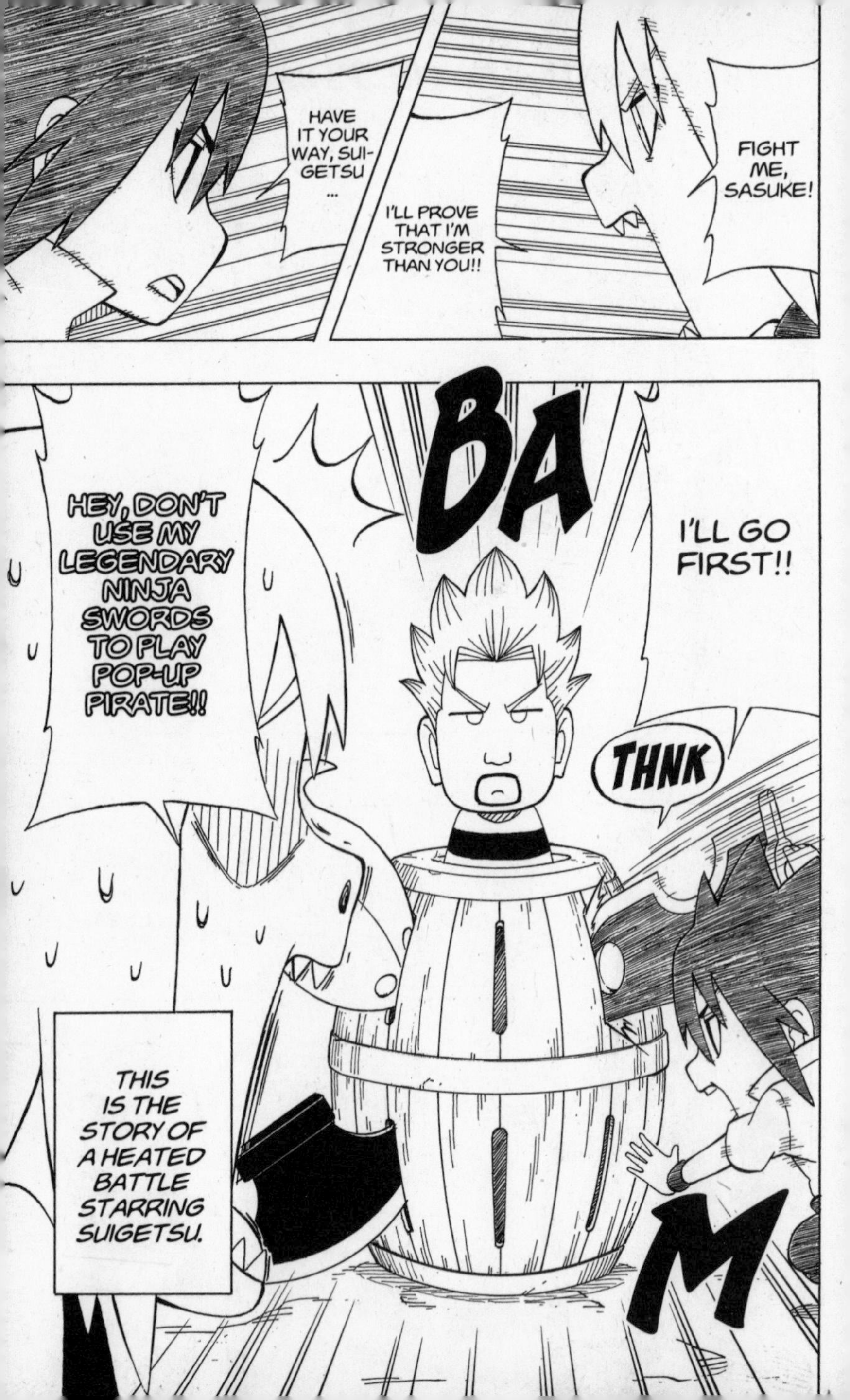
FIGHT ME, SASUKE!
I'LL PROVE THAT I'M STRONGER THAN YOU!!
HAVE IT YOUR WAY, SUI-GETSU ...
I'LL GO FIRST!!
BA
THNK
M
HEY, DON'T USE MY LEGENDARY NINJA SWORDS TO PLAY POP-UP PIRATE!!
THIS IS THE STORY OF A HEATED BATTLE STARRING SUIGETSU.

THE LIGHTNING BLADE, KIBA THE FANG

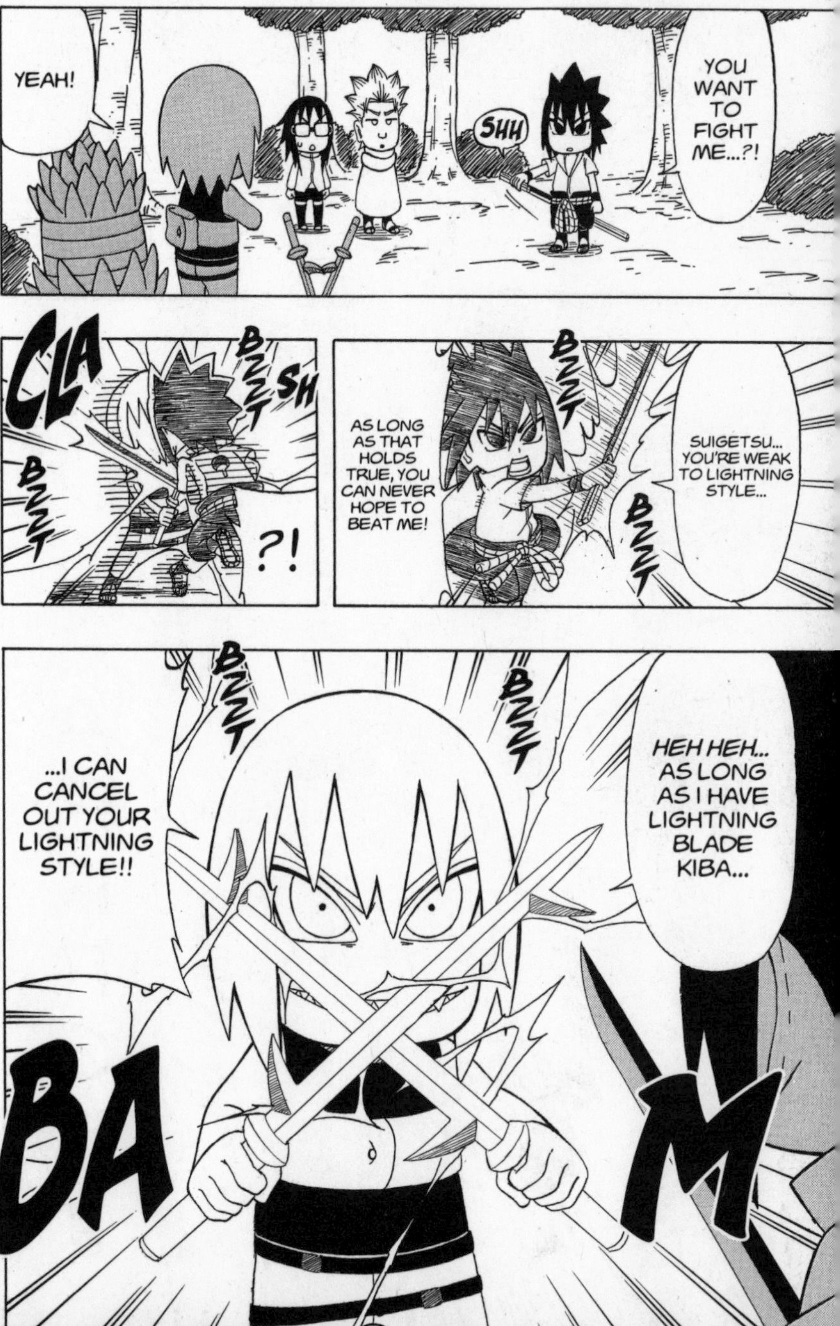

YOU WANT TO FIGHT ME...?!
SHH
YEAH!
SUIGETSU... YOU'RE WEAK TO LIGHTNING STYLE...
BZZZT
BZZZT
AS LONG AS THAT HOLDS TRUE, YOU CAN NEVER HOPE TO BEAT ME!
BZZZT
SH
CLA
BZZZT
?!
HEH HEH... AS LONG AS I HAVE LIGHTNING BLADE KIBA...
BZZZT
BZZZT
...I CAN CANCEL OUT YOUR LIGHTNING STYLE!!
BAM

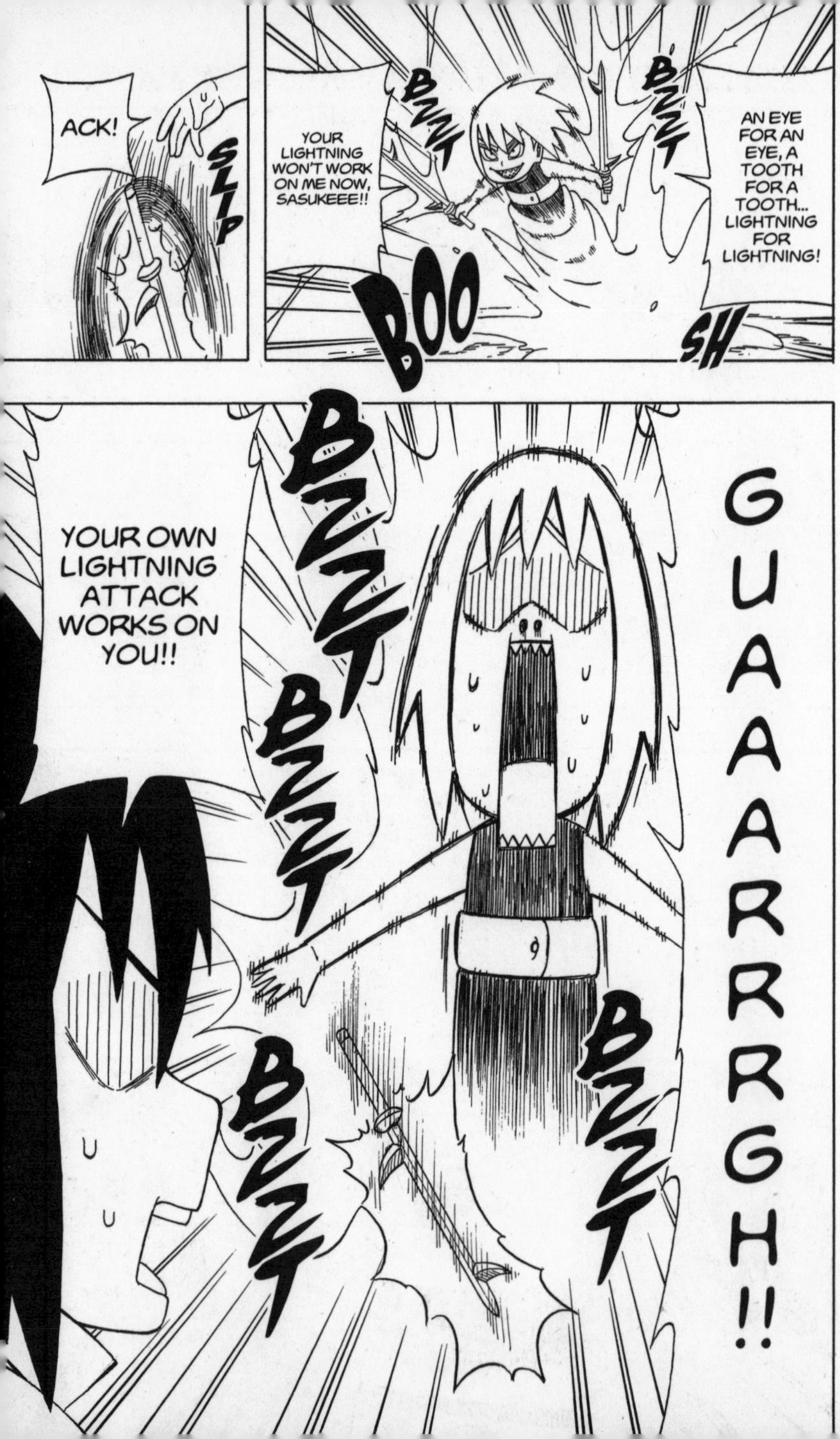
AN EYE FOR AN EYE, A TOOTH FOR A TOOTH... LIGHTNING FOR LIGHTNING!
BZZT
BZZZK
YOUR LIGHTNING WON'T WORK ON ME NOW, SASUKEEE!!
BOO
SH
SLIP
ACK!
GUAARRRGH!!
BZZZT
BZZZT
YOUR OWN LIGHTNING ATTACK WORKS ON YOU!!
BZZZT
BZZZT

SAMEHADA

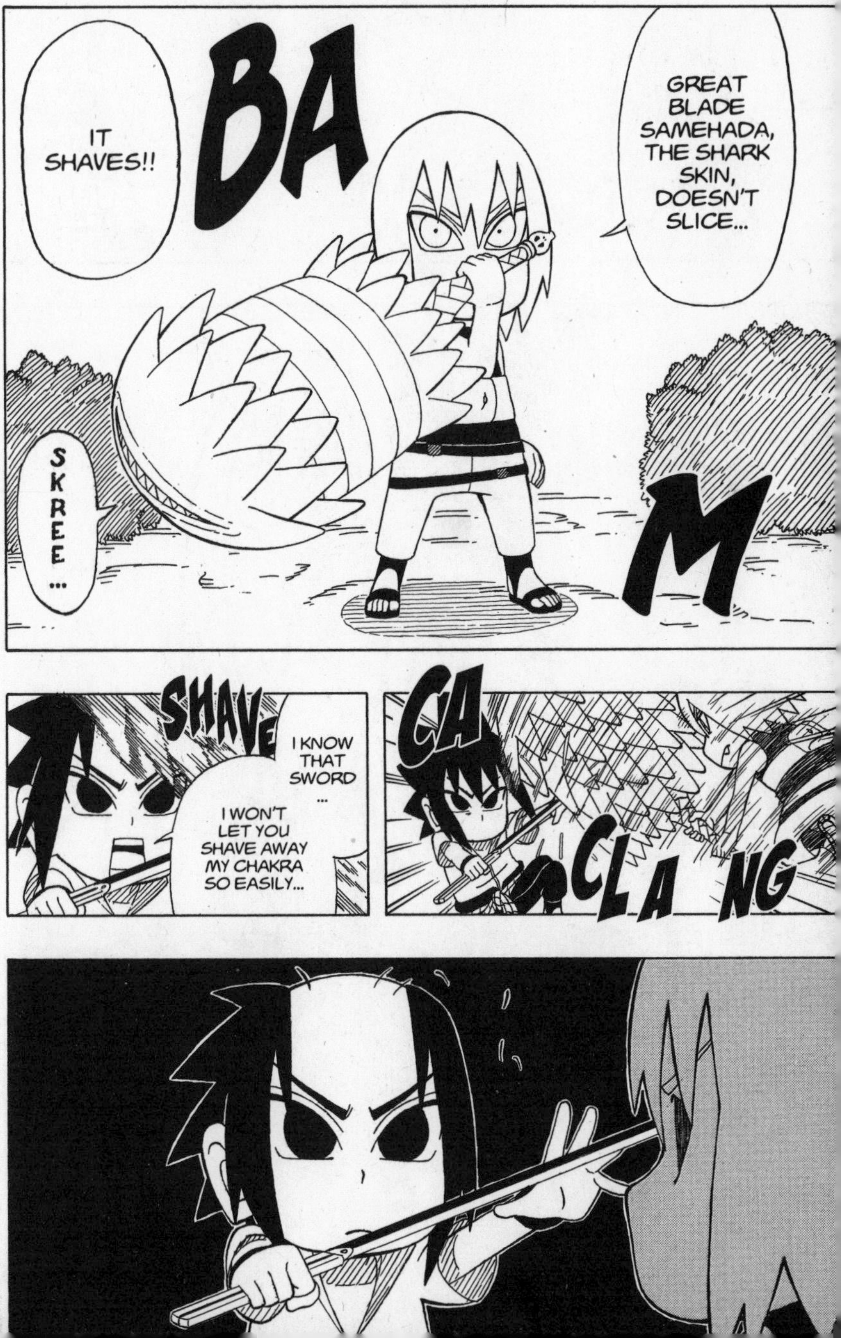

GREAT BLADE SAMEHADA, THE SHARK SKIN, DOESN'T SLICE...
BA
M
IT SHAVES!!
SKREE...
CA
CLANG
SHAVE
I KNOW THAT SWORD...
I WON'T LET YOU SHAVE AWAY MY CHAKRA SO EASILY...

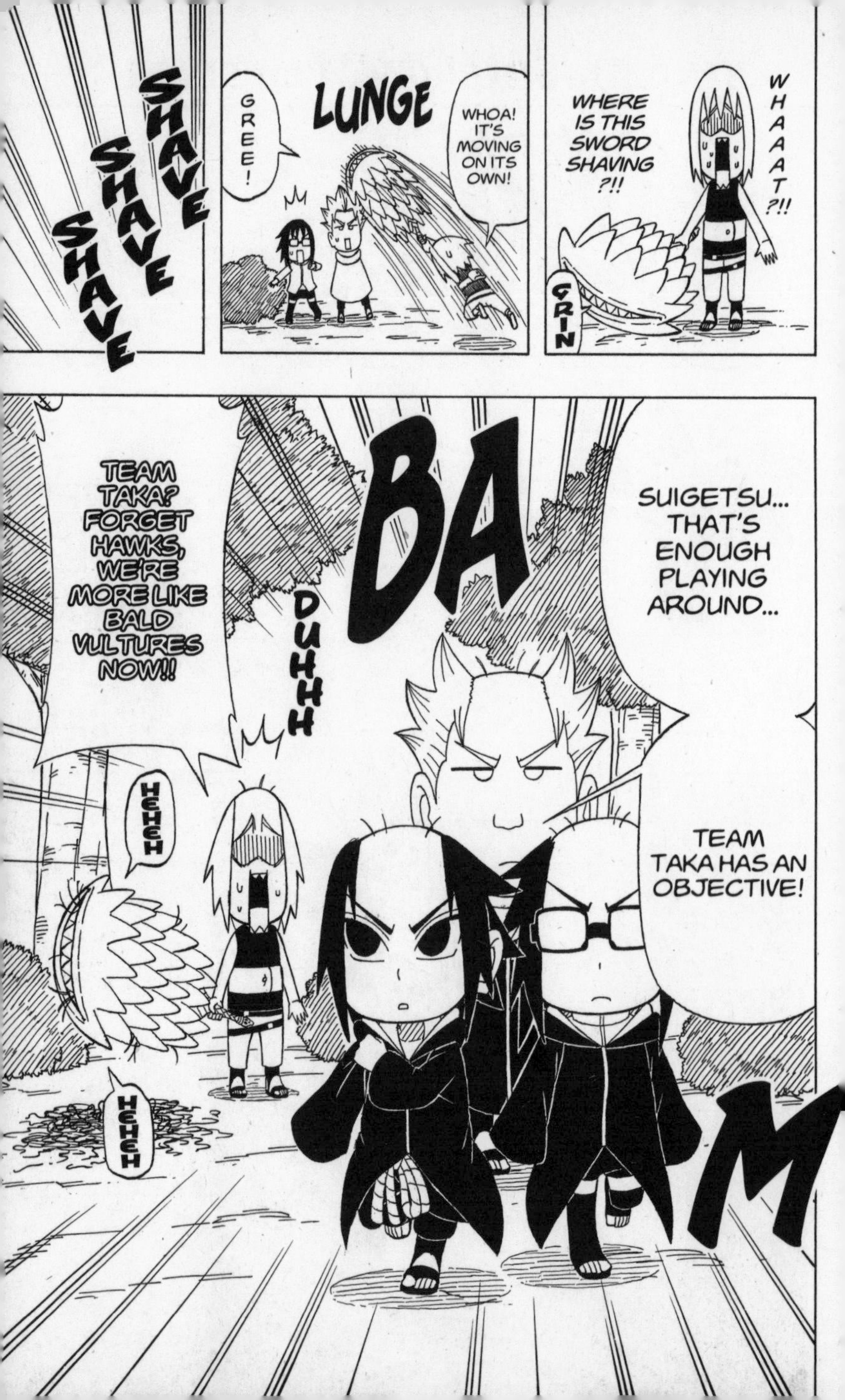
WHAAAAT?!!
WHERE IS THIS SWORD SHAVING?!!
GRIN
WHOA! IT'S MOVING ON ITS OWN!
LUNGE
GREE!
SHAVE SHAVE SHAVE
SUIGETSU... THAT'S ENOUGH PLAYING AROUND...
BA
TEAM TAKA? FORGET HAWKS, WE'RE MORE LIKE BALD VULTURES NOW!!
DUHHH
HEHEH
TEAM TAKA HAS AN OBJECTIVE!
M
HEHEH

HIRAMEKAREI, THE FLATFISH

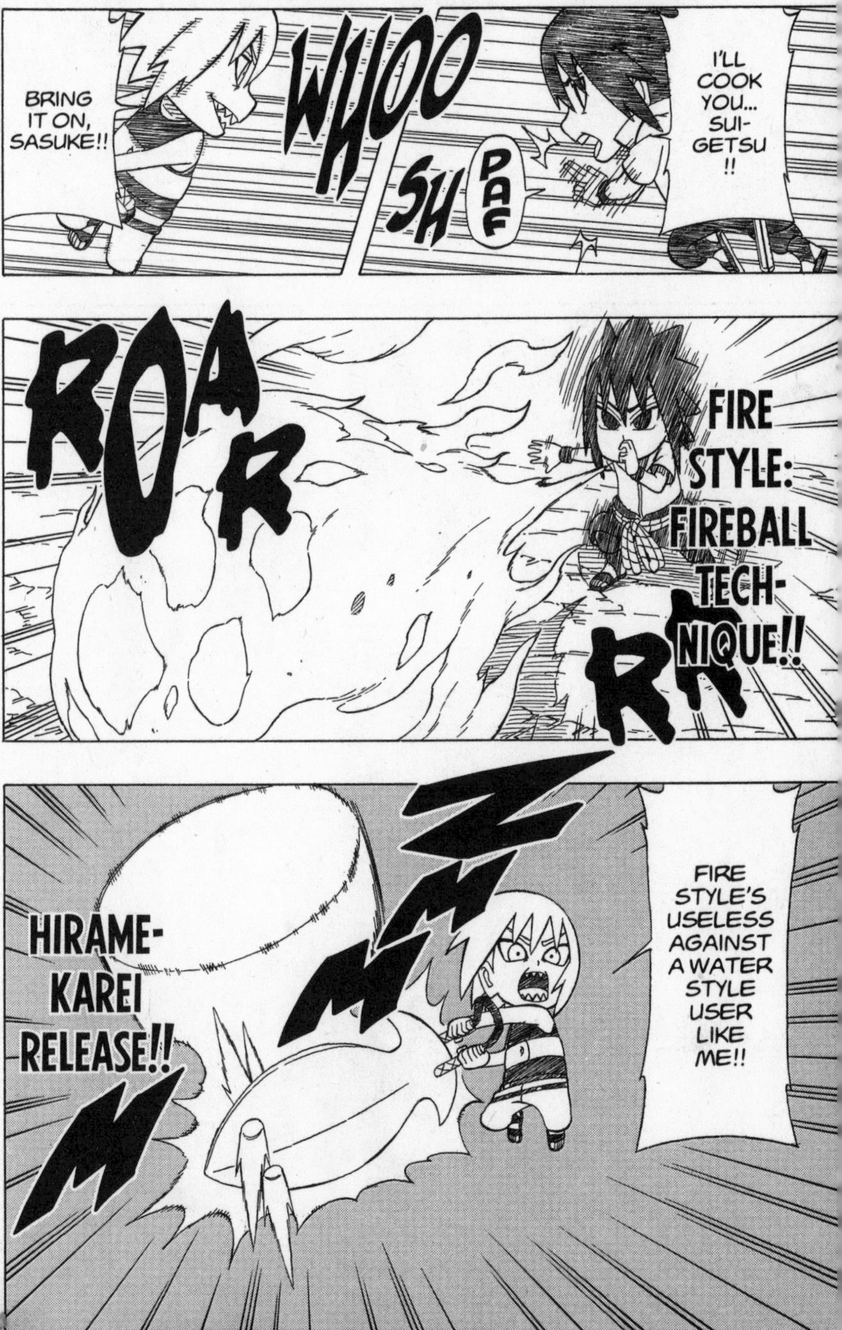
I'LL COOK YOU... SUI-GETSU !!
PAF
WHOOSH
BRING IT ON, SASUKE!!
FIRE STYLE: FIREBALL TECH-NIQUE!!
ROAR
RR
FIRE STYLE'S USELESS AGAINST A WATER STYLE USER LIKE ME!!
HIRAME-KAREI RELEASE!!
ZMMM
M

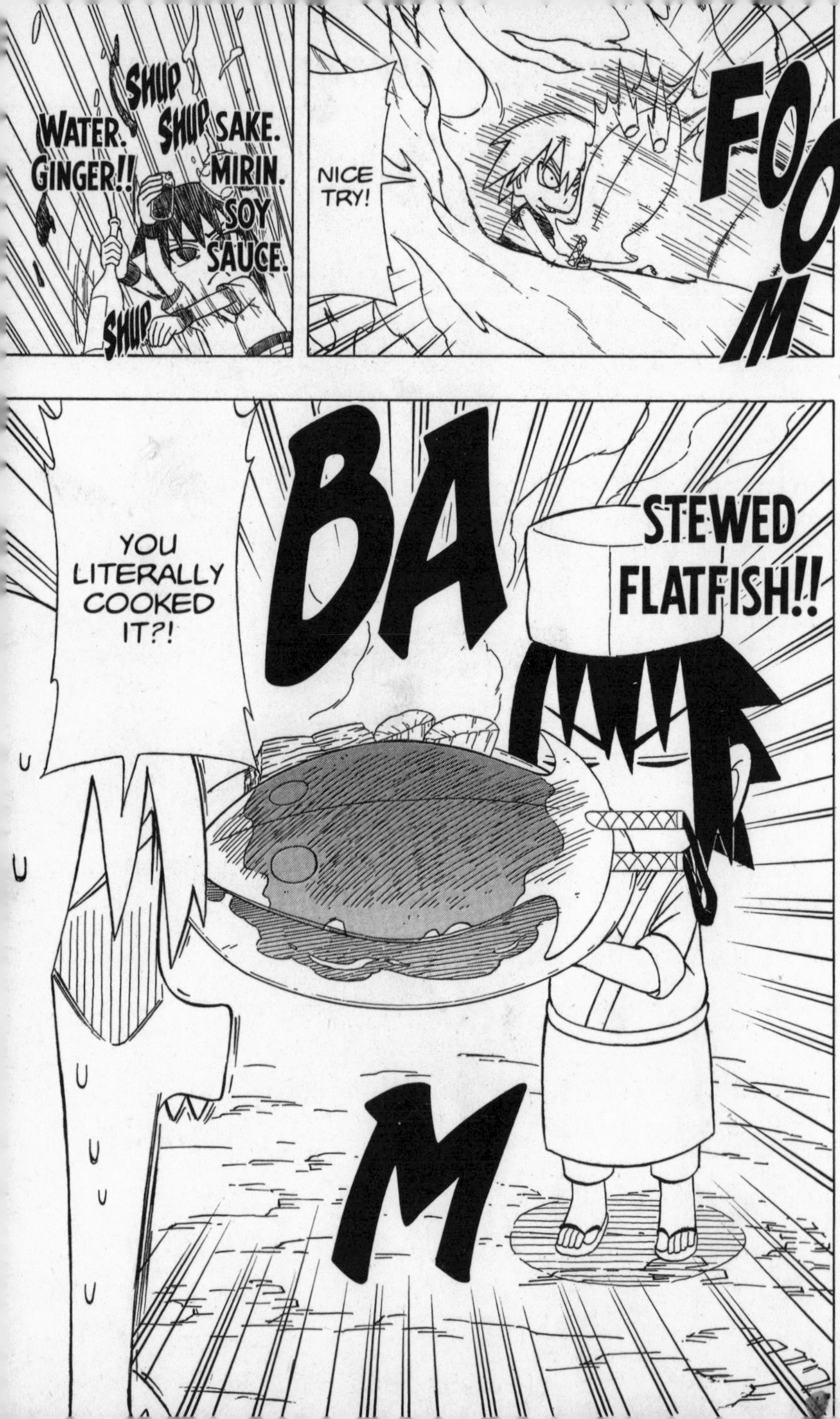
NICE TRY!
FOOM
SHUP
SHUP
SAKE. MIRIN. SOY SAUCE.
WATER. GINGER!!
SHUP
STEWED FLATFISH!!
BAM
YOU LITERALLY COOKED IT?!

SO MANY SWORDS

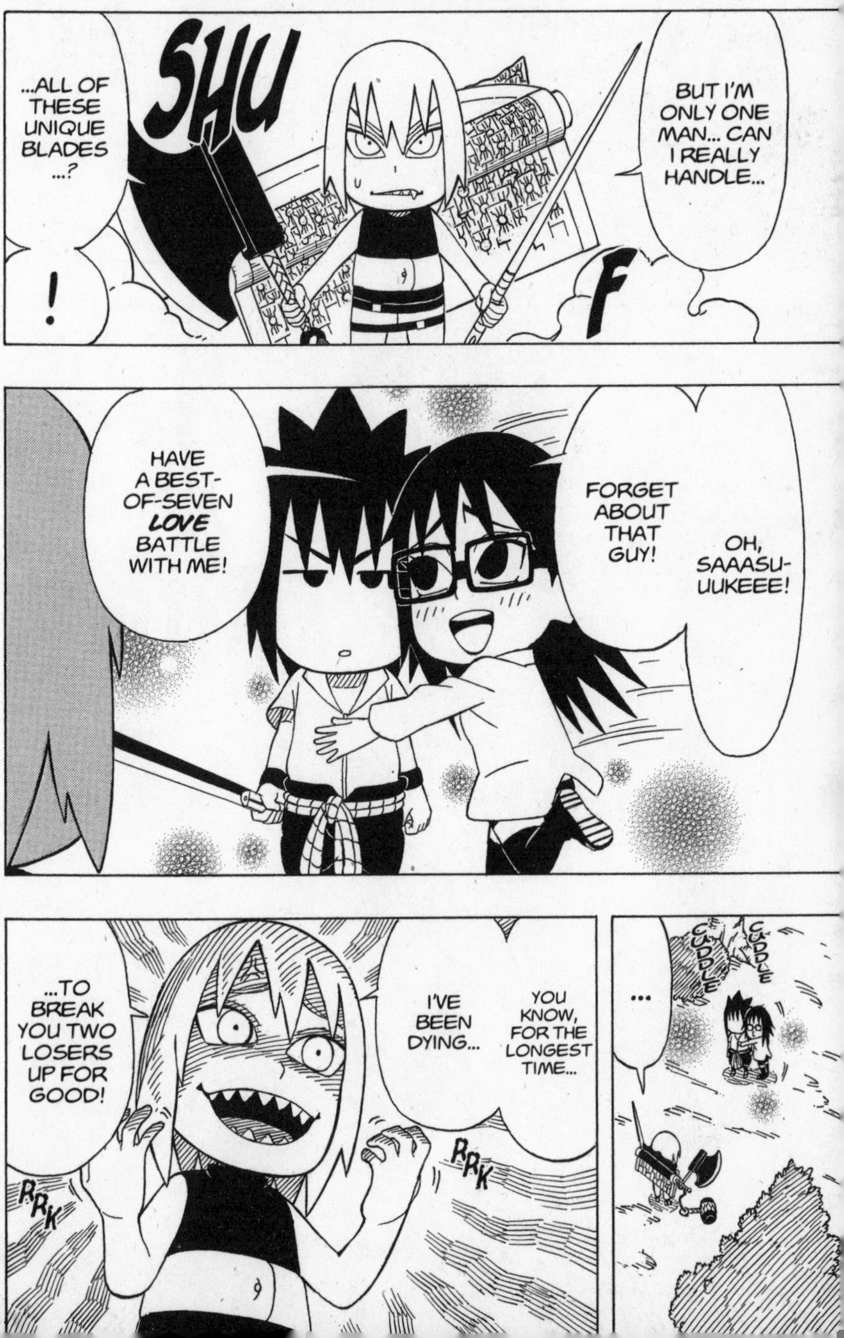
BUT I'M ONLY ONE MAN... CAN I REALLY HANDLE...
SHU
...ALL OF THESE UNIQUE BLADES ...?
F
!
OH, SAAASU-UUKEEE!
FORGET ABOUT THAT GUY!
HAVE A BEST-OF-SEVEN LOVE BATTLE WITH ME!
CUDDLE
CUDDLE
...
YOU KNOW, FOR THE LONGEST TIME...
I'VE BEEN DYING...
...TO BREAK YOU TWO LOSERS UP FOR GOOD!
RRK
RRK

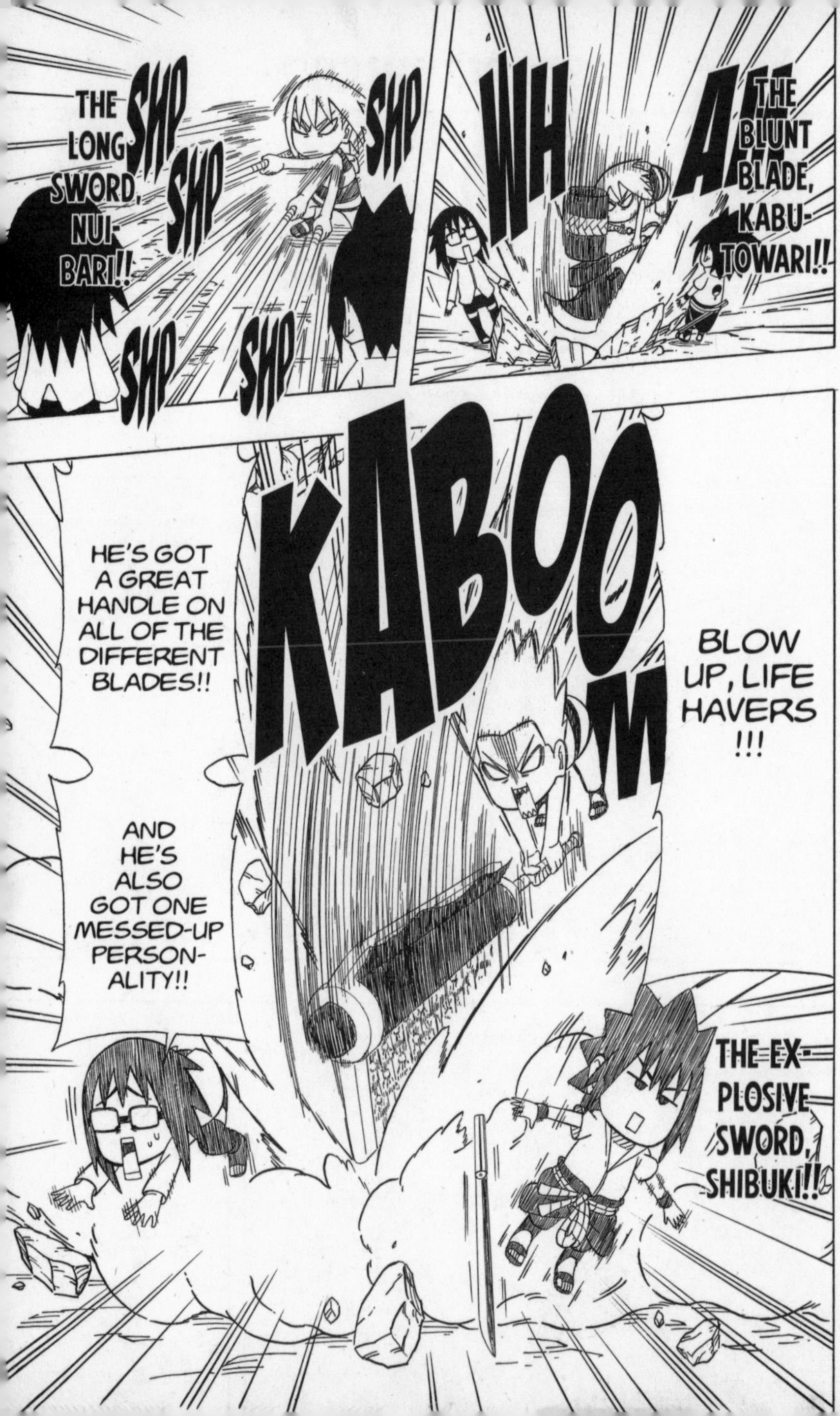
WH
AM
THE BLUNT BLADE, KABU-TOWARI!!
THE LONG SWORD, NUI-BARI!!
SHP
SHP
SHP
SHP
SHP
KABOOM
BLOW UP, LIFE HAVERS!!!
HE'S GOT A GREAT HANDLE ON ALL OF THE DIFFERENT BLADES!!
AND HE'S ALSO GOT ONE MESSED-UP PERSON-ALITY!!
THE EX-PLOSIVE SWORD, SHIBUKI!!

BIG BROTHER

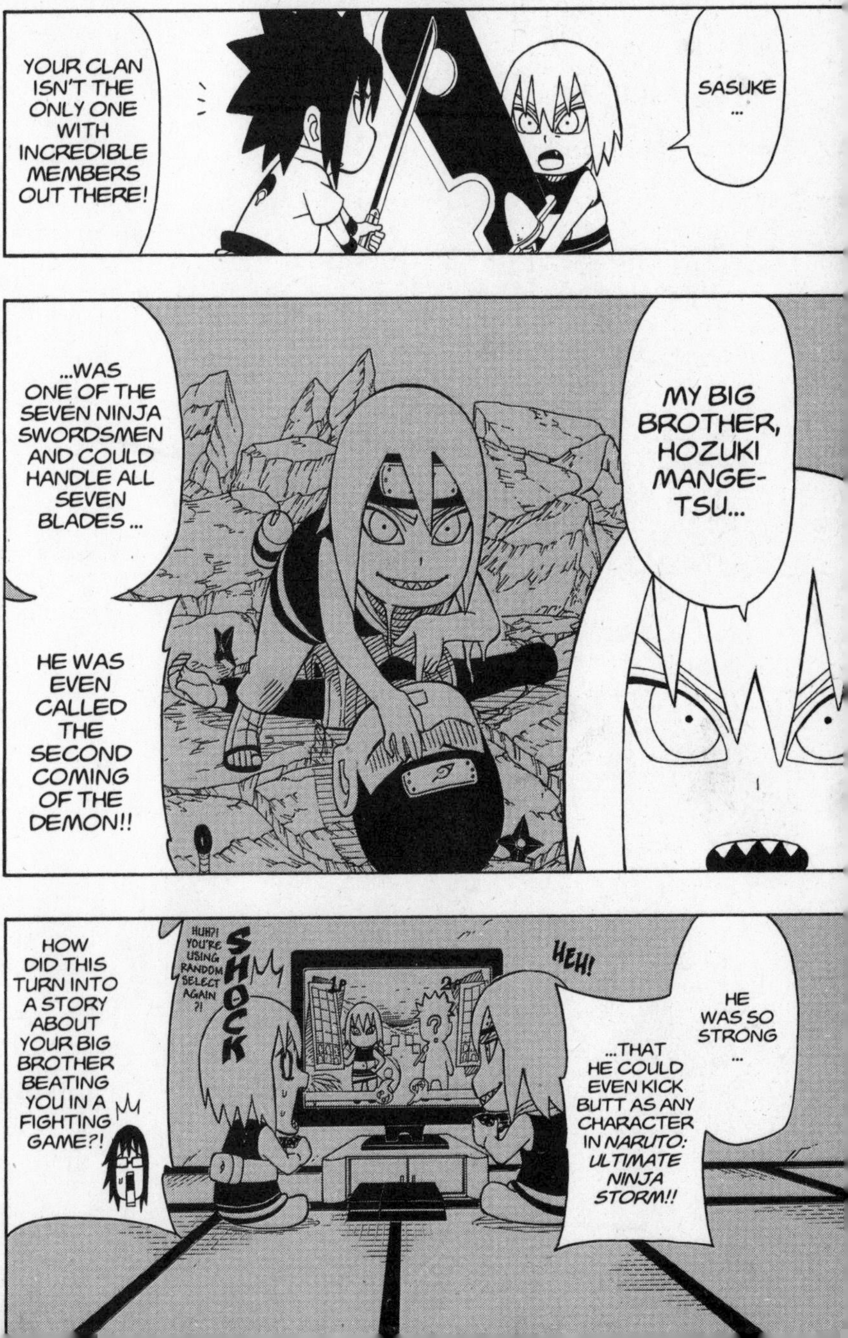
SASUKE ...
YOUR CLAN ISN'T THE ONLY ONE WITH INCREDIBLE MEMBERS OUT THERE!
MY BIG BROTHER, HOZUKI MANGE-TSU...
...WAS ONE OF THE SEVEN NINJA SWORDSMEN AND COULD HANDLE ALL SEVEN BLADES ...
HE WAS EVEN CALLED THE SECOND COMING OF THE DEMON!!
HE WAS SO STRONG ...
...THAT HE COULD EVEN KICK BUTT AS ANY CHARACTER IN NARUTO: ULTIMATE NINJA STORM!!
HEH!
SHOCK
HUH?! YOU'RE USING RANDOM SELECT AGAIN ?!
HOW DID THIS TURN INTO A STORY ABOUT YOUR BIG BROTHER BEATING YOU IN A FIGHTING GAME?!

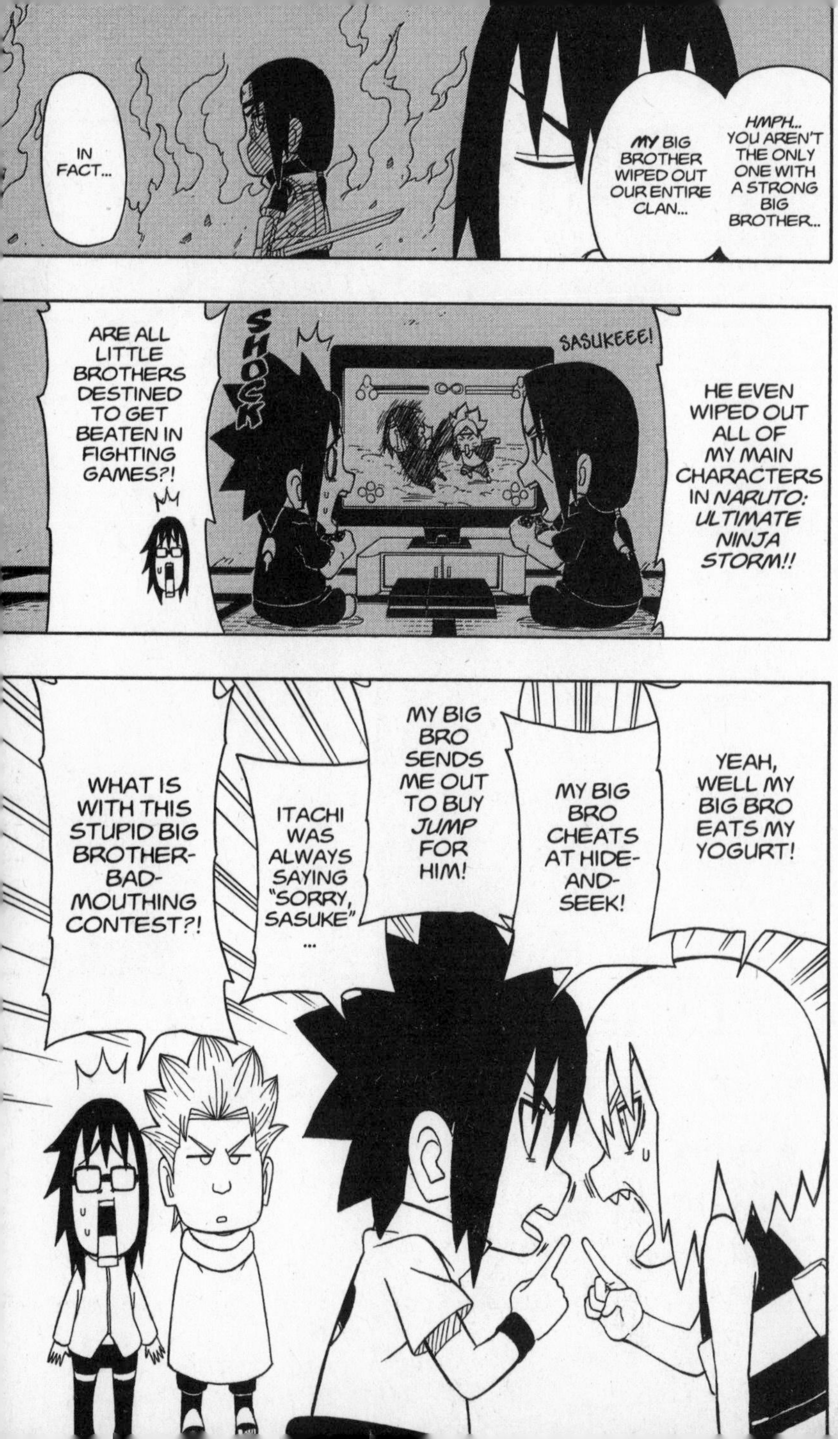
HMPH... YOU AREN'T THE ONLY ONE WITH A STRONG BIG BROTHER...
MY BIG BROTHER WIPED OUT OUR ENTIRE CLAN...
IN FACT...
HE EVEN WIPED OUT ALL OF MY MAIN CHARACTERS IN *NARUTO: ULTIMATE NINJA STORM*!!
SASUKEEE!
SHOCK
ARE ALL LITTLE BROTHERS DESTINED TO GET BEATEN IN FIGHTING GAMES?!
YEAH, WELL MY BIG BRO EATS MY YOGURT!
MY BIG BRO CHEATS AT HIDE-AND-SEEK!
MY BIG BRO SENDS ME OUT TO BUY *JUMP* FOR HIM!
ITACHI WAS ALWAYS SAYING "SORRY, SASUKE"...
WHAT IS WITH THIS STUPID BIG BROTHER-BAD-MOUTHING CONTEST?!

CLASH!!

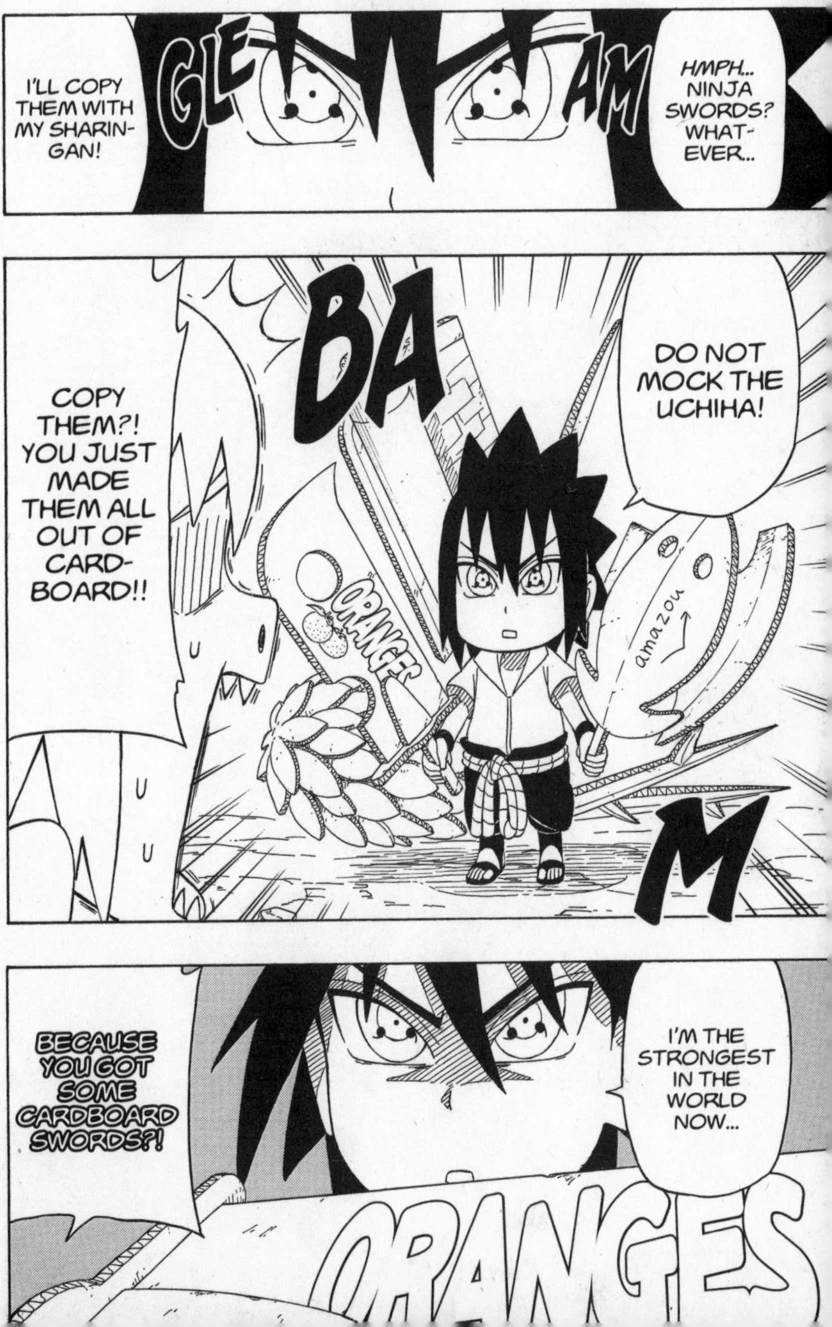
HMPH... NINJA SWORDS? WHATEVER...
GLEAM
I'LL COPY THEM WITH MY SHARINGAN!
DO NOT MOCK THE UCHIHA!
BAM
ORANGES
COPY THEM?! YOU JUST MADE THEM ALL OUT OF CARDBOARD!!
I'M THE STRONGEST IN THE WORLD NOW...
BECAUSE YOU GOT SOME CARDBOARD SWORDS?!
ORANGES

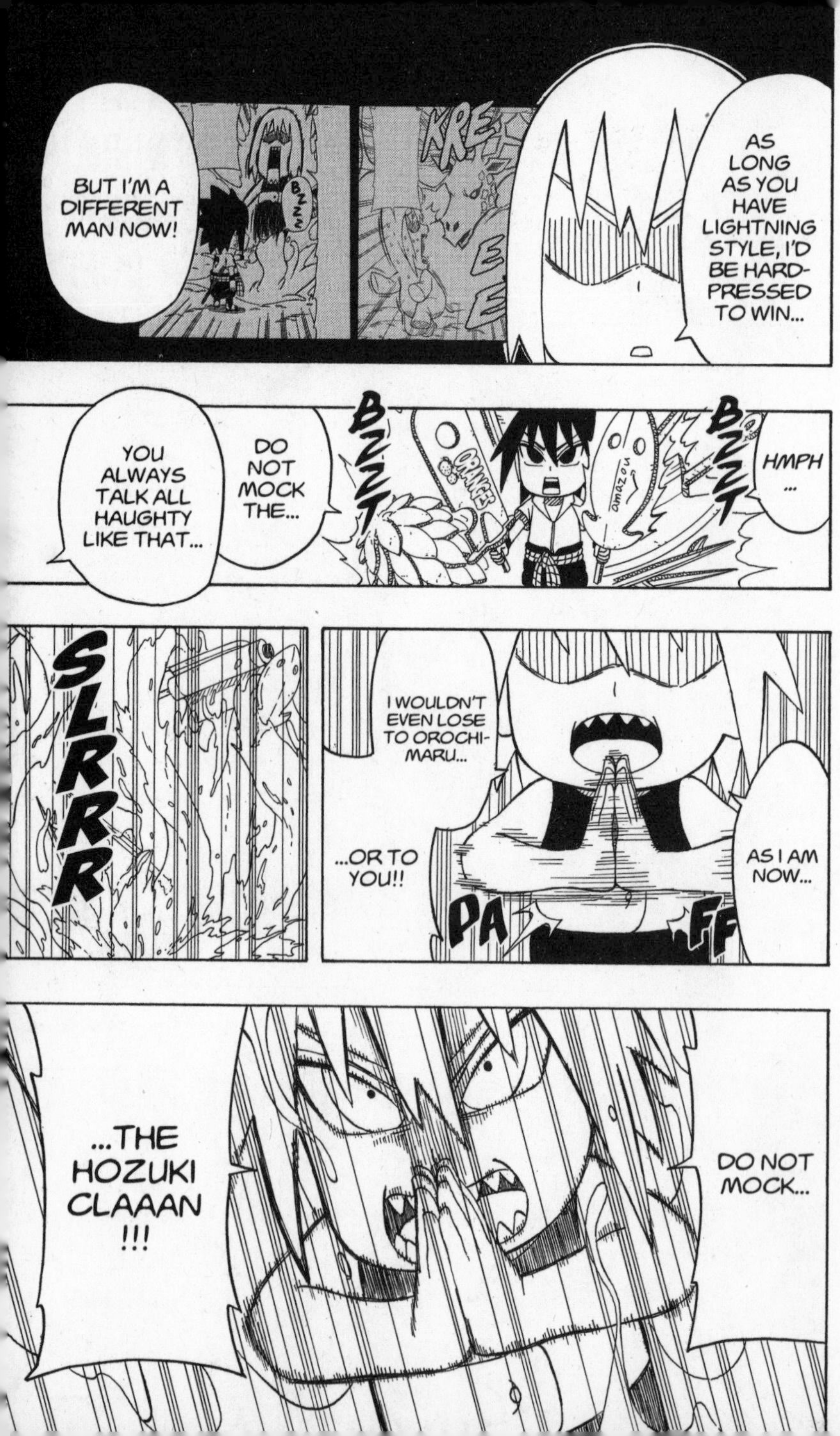
AS LONG AS YOU HAVE LIGHTNING STYLE, I'D BE HARD-PRESSED TO WIN...
KREEE
BZZZ
BUT I'M A DIFFERENT MAN NOW!
HMPH ...
BZZZT
ORANGE
BZZZT
DO NOT MOCK THE...
YOU ALWAYS TALK ALL HAUGHTY LIKE THAT...
I WOULDN'T EVEN LOSE TO OROCHI-MARU...
AS I AM NOW...
...OR TO YOU!!
PAFF
SLRRR
DO NOT MOCK...
...THE HOZUKI CLAAAN !!!

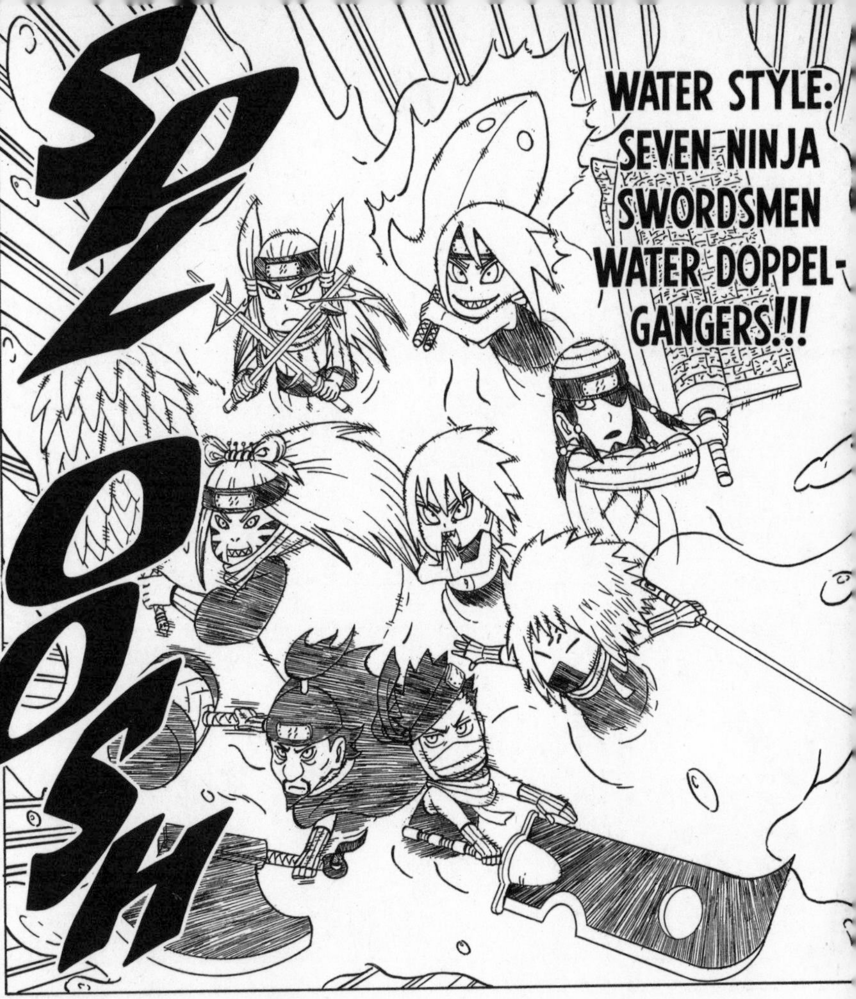
WATER STYLE: SEVEN-NINJA SWORDSMEN WATER DOPPEL-GANGERS!!!
SPLOOSH
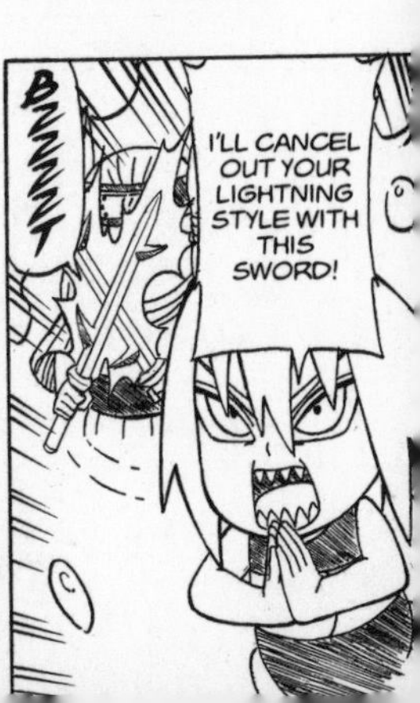
BZZZT
I'LL CANCEL OUT YOUR LIGHTNING STYLE WITH THIS SWORD!
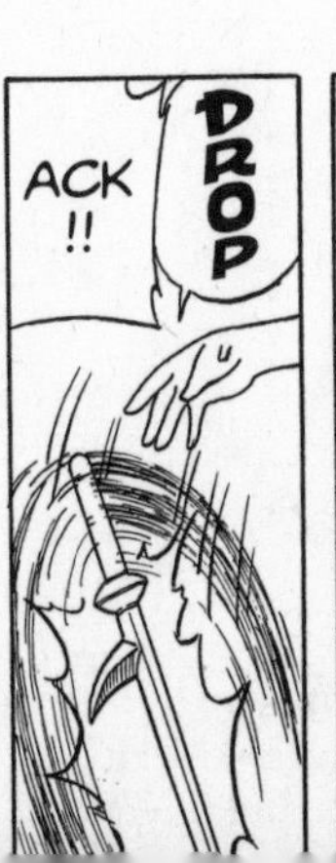
DROP
ACK !!
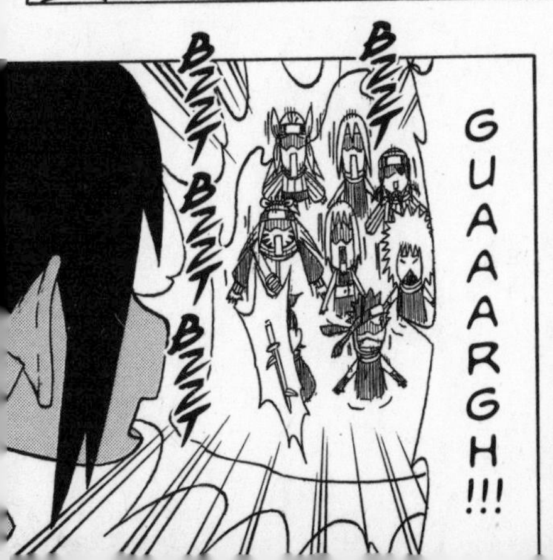
GUAAARGH!!!
BZZZT
BZZZT BZZZT BZZZT

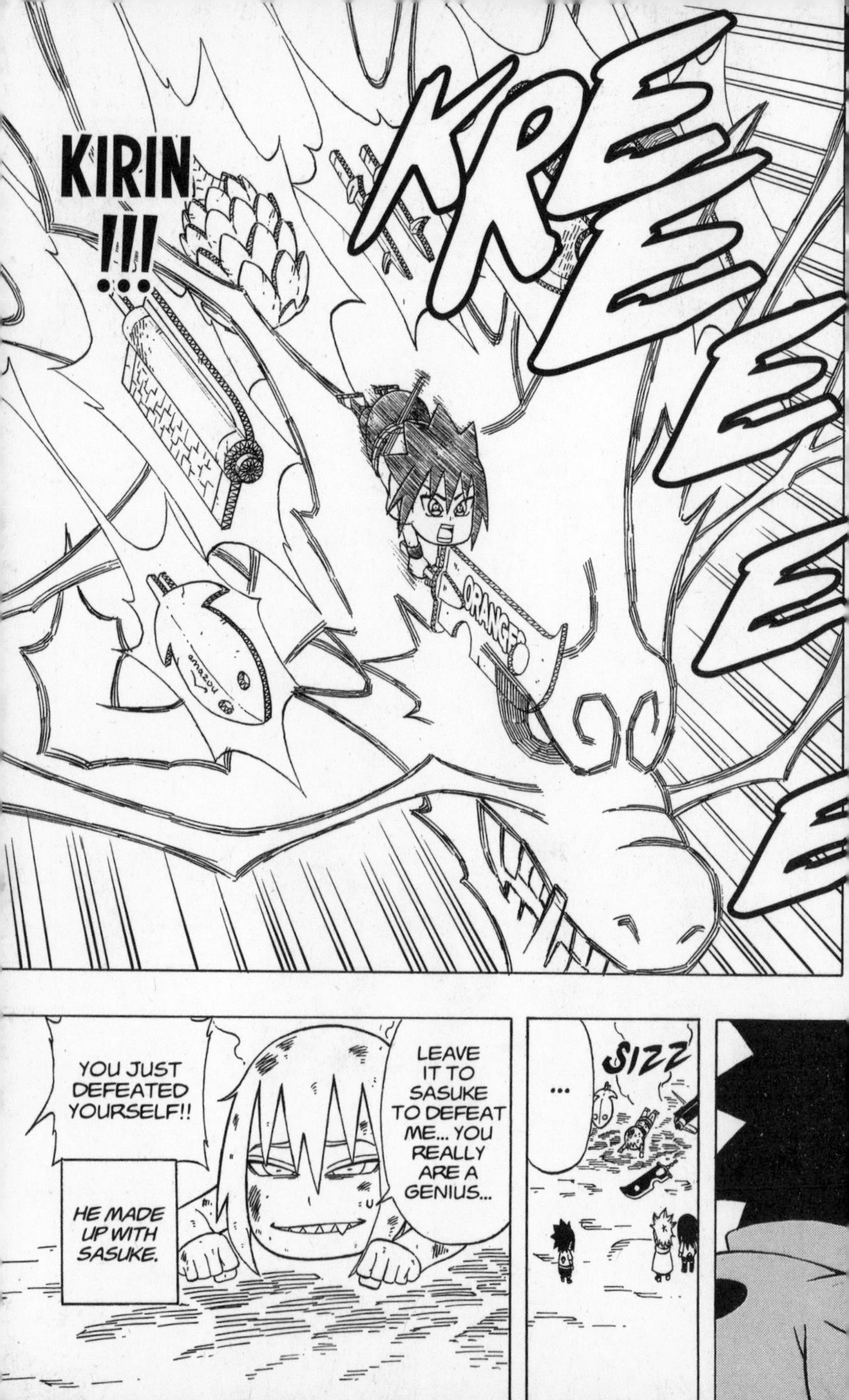
KREEEEEEE
KIRIN!!!...
ORANGE
SIZZ
...
LEAVE IT TO SASUKE TO DEFEAT ME... YOU REALLY ARE A GENIUS...
YOU JUST DEFEATED YOURSELF!!
HE MADE UP WITH SASUKE.

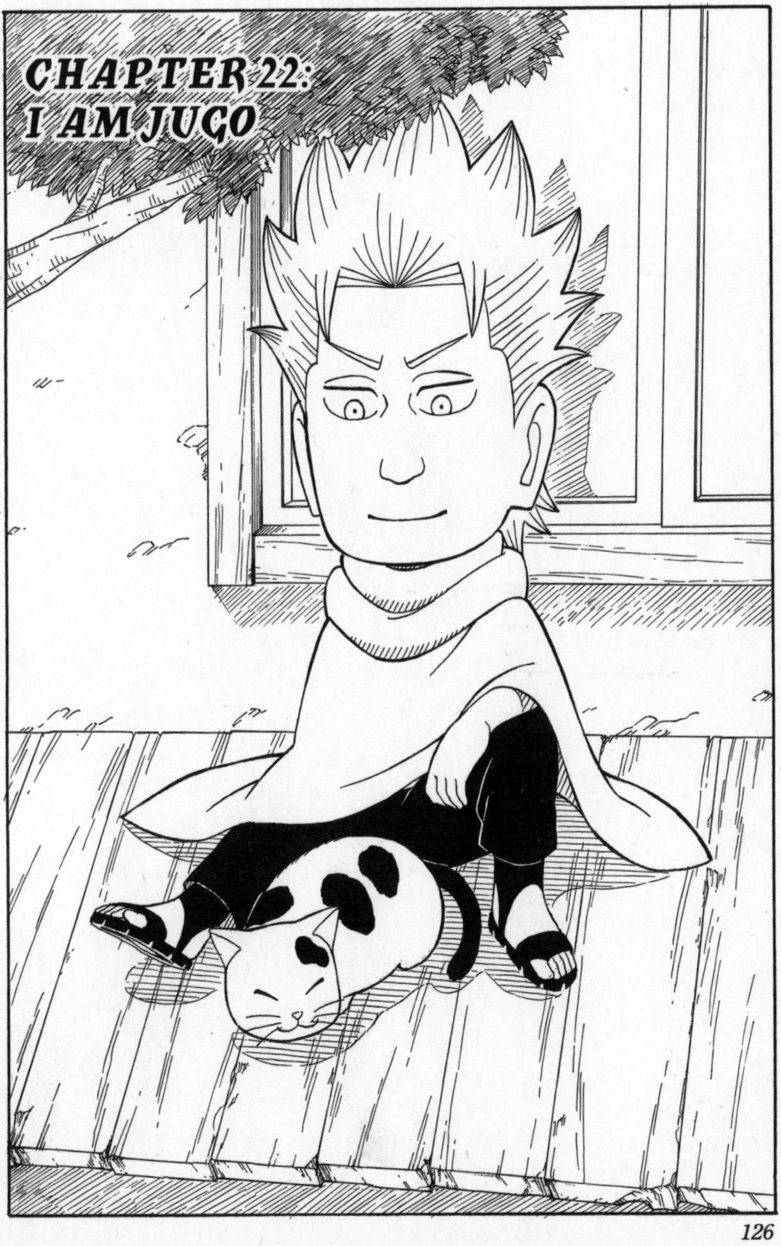
CHAPTER 22:
I AM JUGO

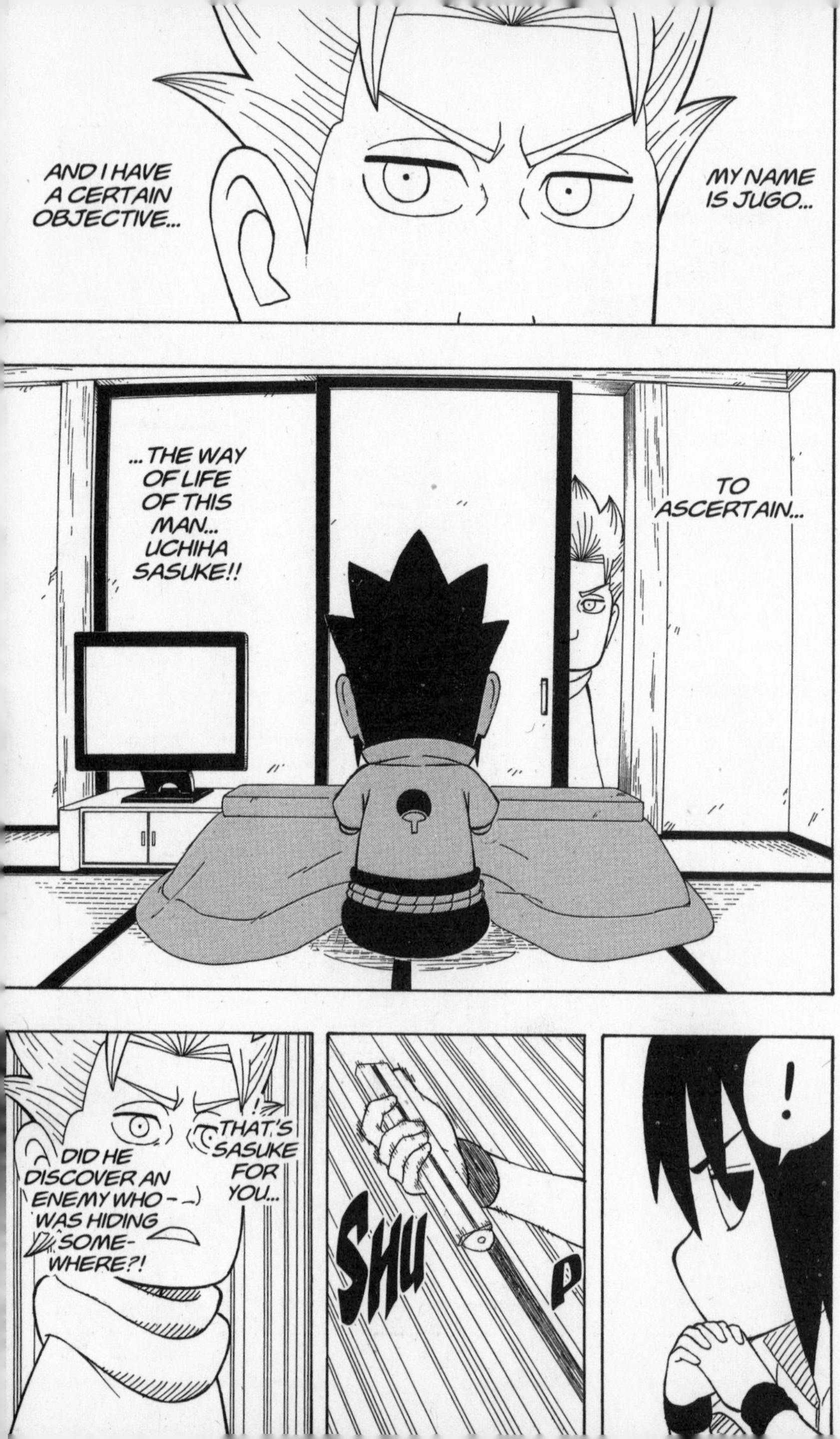
MY NAME IS JUGO...
AND I HAVE A CERTAIN OBJECTIVE...
TO ASCERTAIN...
...THE WAY OF LIFE OF THIS MAN... UCHIHA SASUKE!!
!
SHUP
THAT'S SASUKE FOR YOU...
DID HE DISCOVER AN ENEMY WHO WAS HIDING SOMEWHERE?!

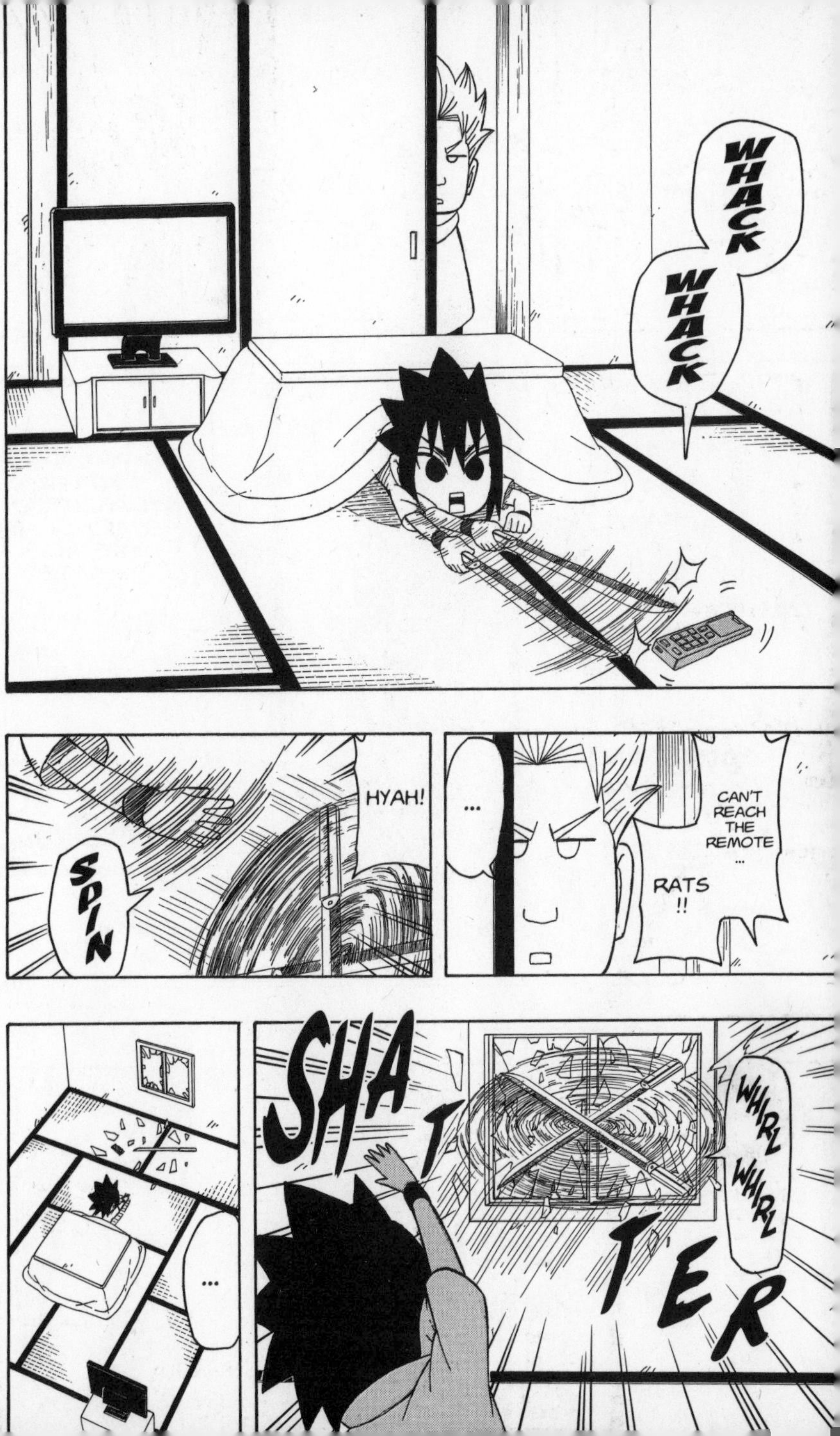
WHACK WHACK
CAN'T REACH THE REMOTE ...
RATS !!
...
HYAH!
SPIN
WHIRL WHIRL
SHATTER
...

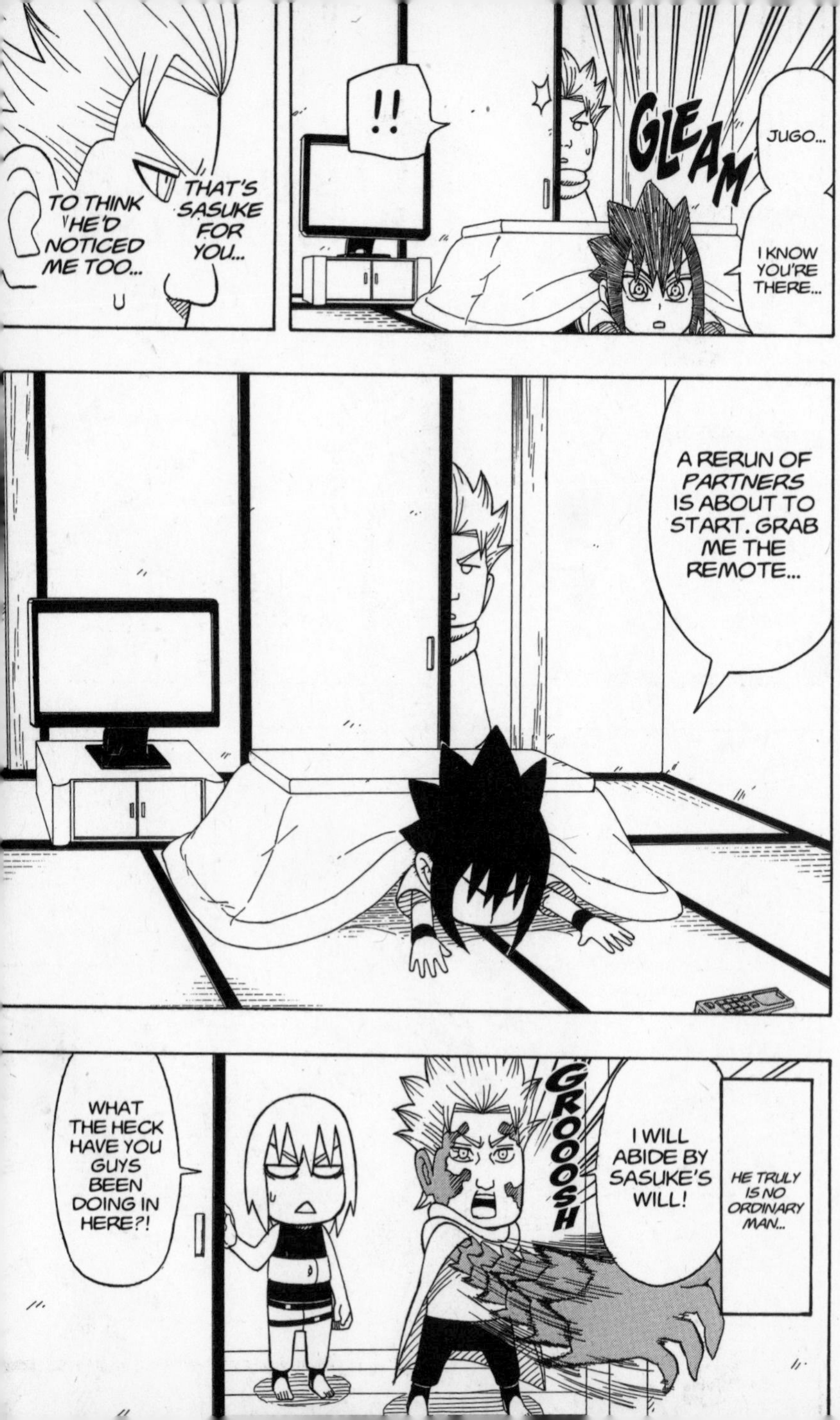
JUGO...
I KNOW YOU'RE THERE...
GLEAM
!!
THAT'S SASUKE FOR YOU...
TO THINK HE'D NOTICED ME TOO...
A RERUN OF PARTNERS IS ABOUT TO START. GRAB ME THE REMOTE...
HE TRULY IS NO ORDINARY MAN...
I WILL ABIDE BY SASUKE'S WILL!
GROOOSH
WHAT THE HECK HAVE YOU GUYS BEEN DOING IN HERE?!

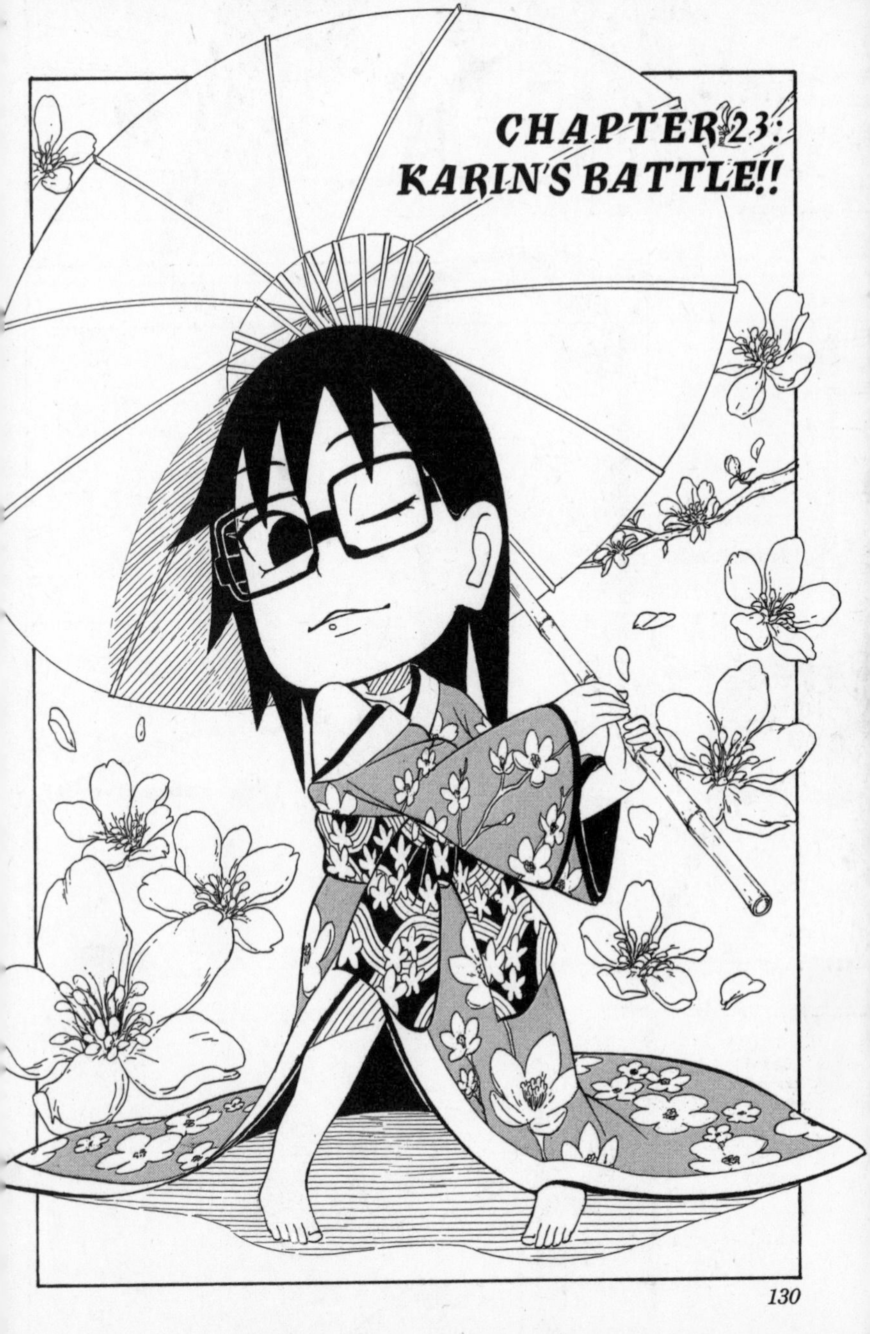
CHAPTER 23:
KARIN'S BATTLE!!

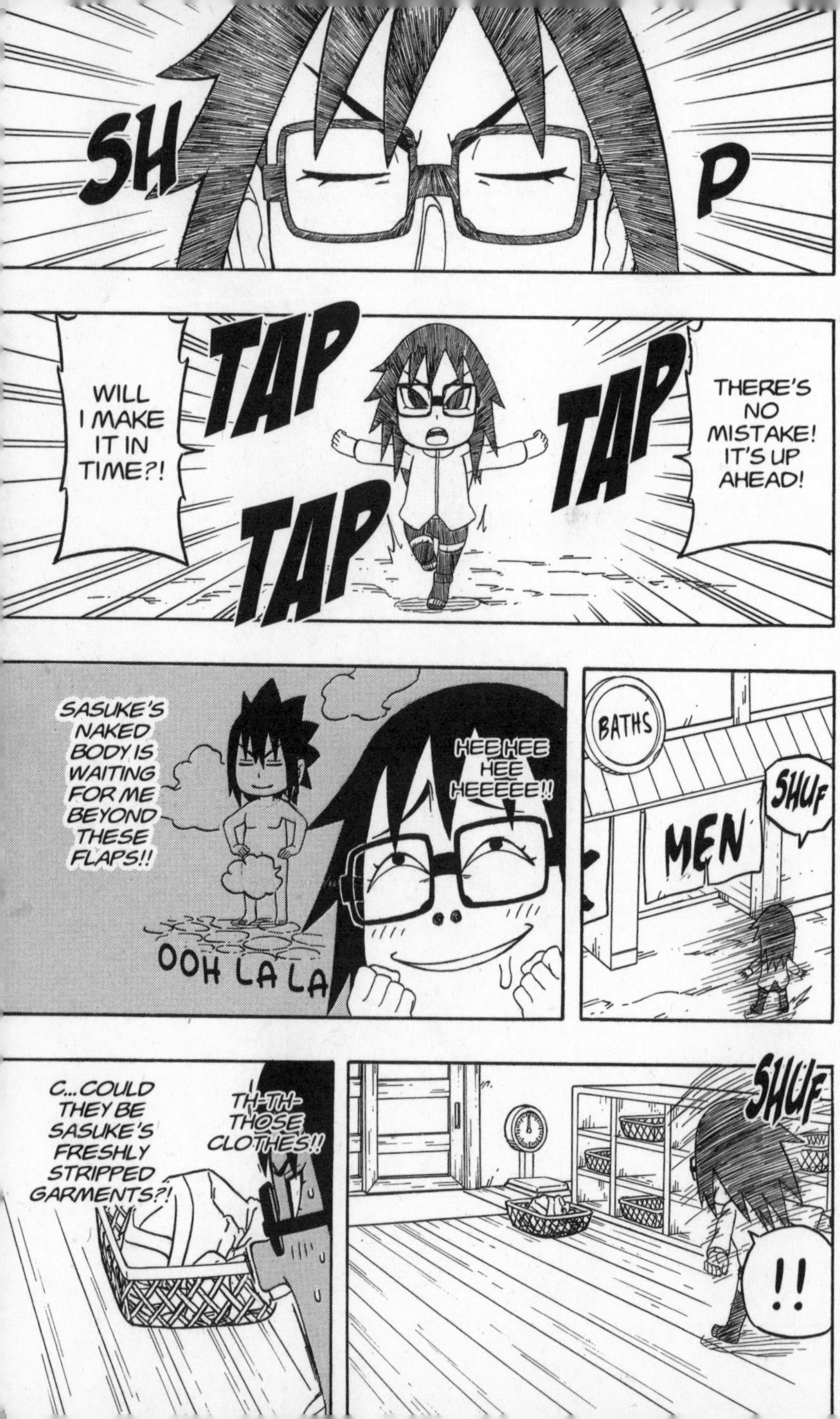
SH P
THERE'S NO MISTAKE! IT'S UP AHEAD!
TAP
TAP
TAP
WILL I MAKE IT IN TIME?!
BATHS
SHUF
MEN
HEE HEE HEE HEEEEEE!!
SASUKE'S NAKED BODY IS WAITING FOR ME BEYOND THESE FLAPS!!
OOH LA LA
SHUF
!!
TH-TH-THOSE CLOTHES!!
C...COULD THEY BE SASUKE'S FRESHLY STRIPPED GARMENTS?!

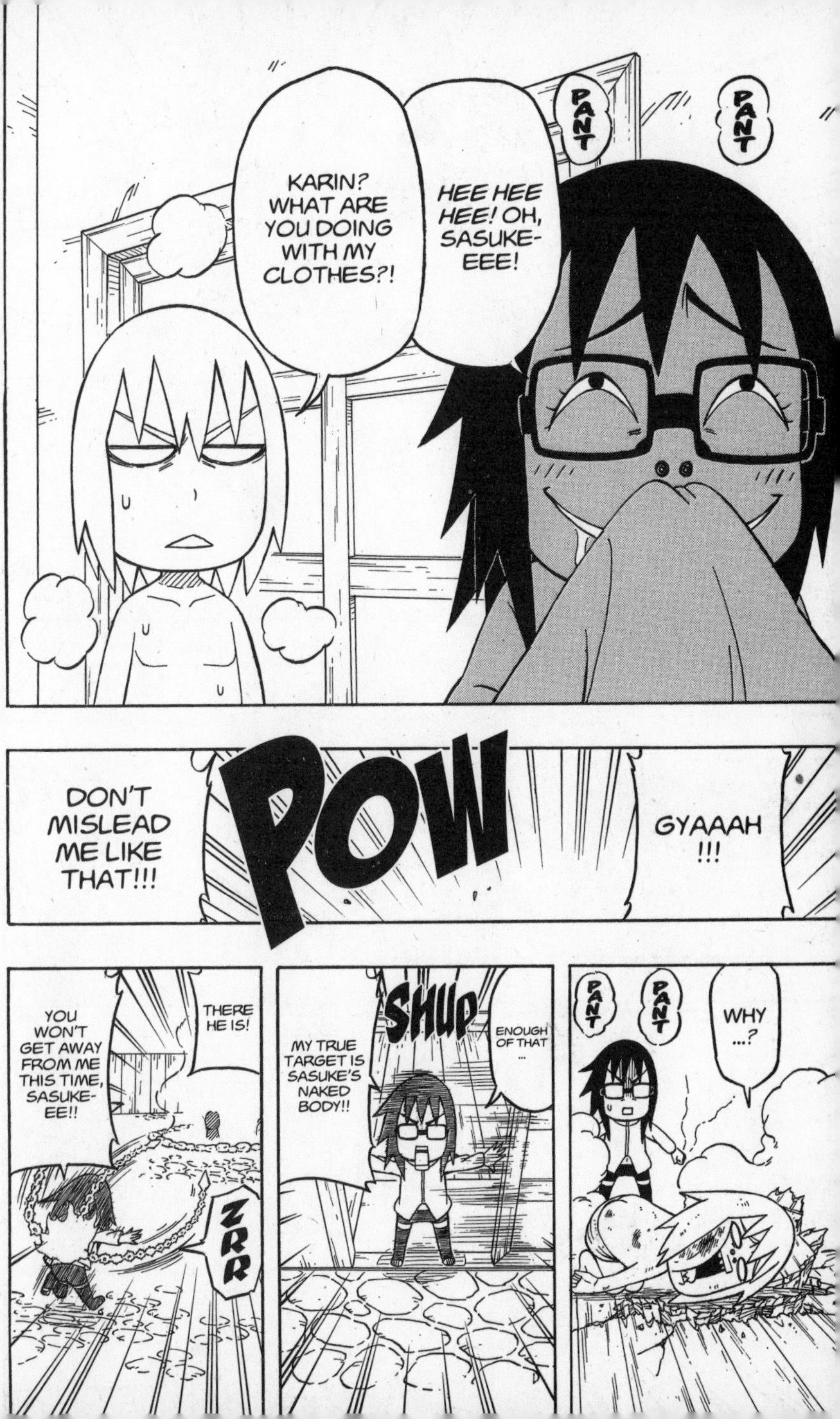
PANT
PANT
HEE HEE HEE! OH, SASUKE-EEE!
KARIN? WHAT ARE YOU DOING WITH MY CLOTHES?!
GYAAAH!!!
POW
DON'T MISLEAD ME LIKE THAT!!!
PANT
PANT
WHY...?
SHUP
ENOUGH OF THAT...
MY TRUE TARGET IS SASUKE'S NAKED BODY!!
THERE HE IS!
YOU WON'T GET AWAY FROM ME THIS TIME, SASUKE-EE!!
ZRR

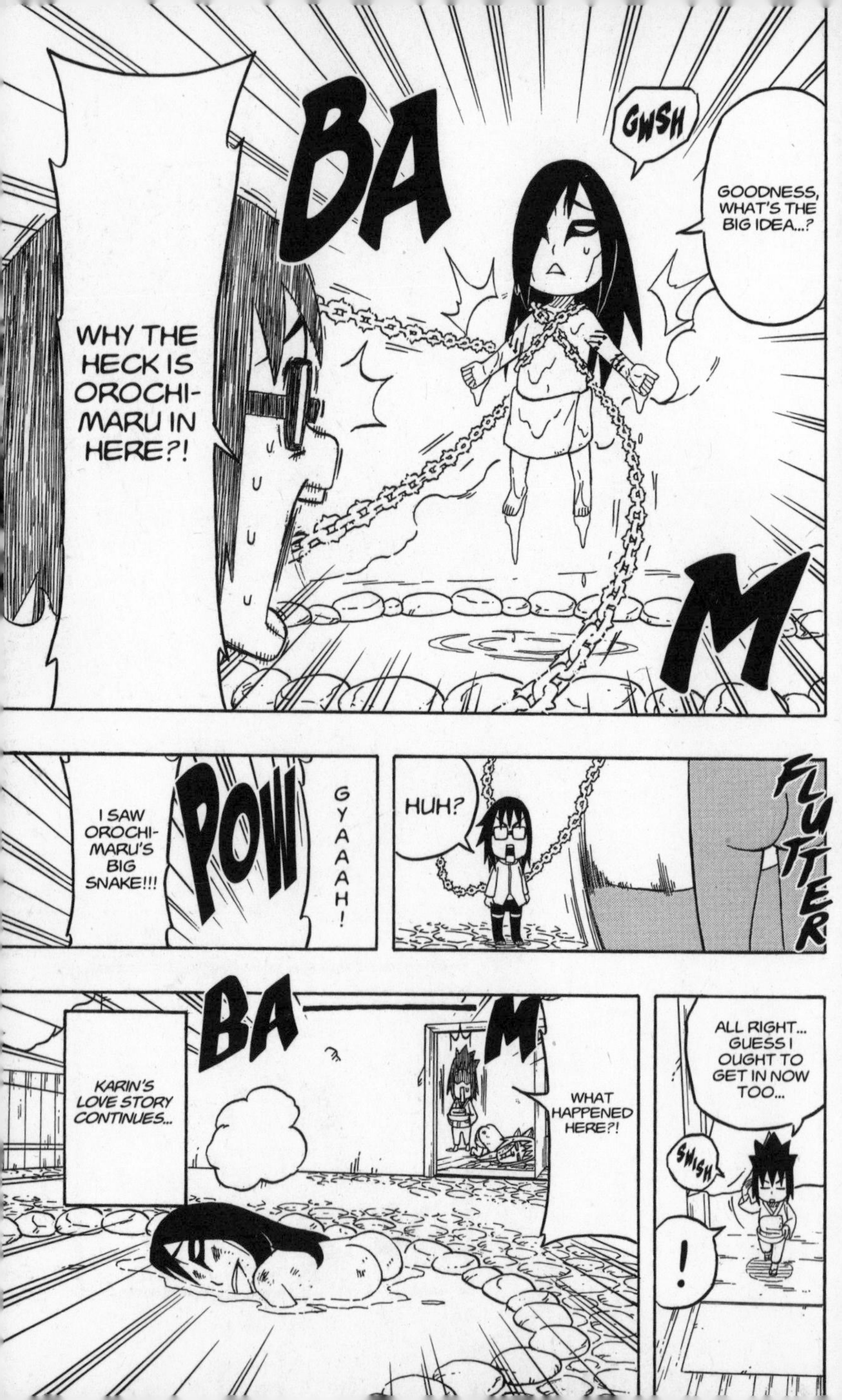
GOODNESS, WHAT'S THE BIG IDEA...?
GWSH
BA
M
WHY THE HECK IS OROCHI-MARU IN HERE?!
FLUTTER
HUH?
GYAAAAH!
POW
I SAW OROCHI-MARU'S BIG SNAKE!!!
ALL RIGHT... GUESS I OUGHT TO GET IN NOW TOO...
SWISH
!
BA—M
WHAT HAPPENED HERE?!
KARIN'S LOVE STORY CONTINUES...

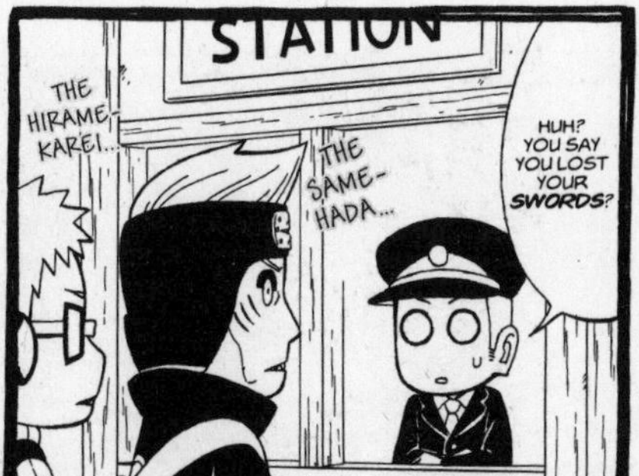
STATION
HUH? YOU SAY YOU LOST YOUR SWORDS?
THE SAME-HADA...
THE HIRAME-KAREI...

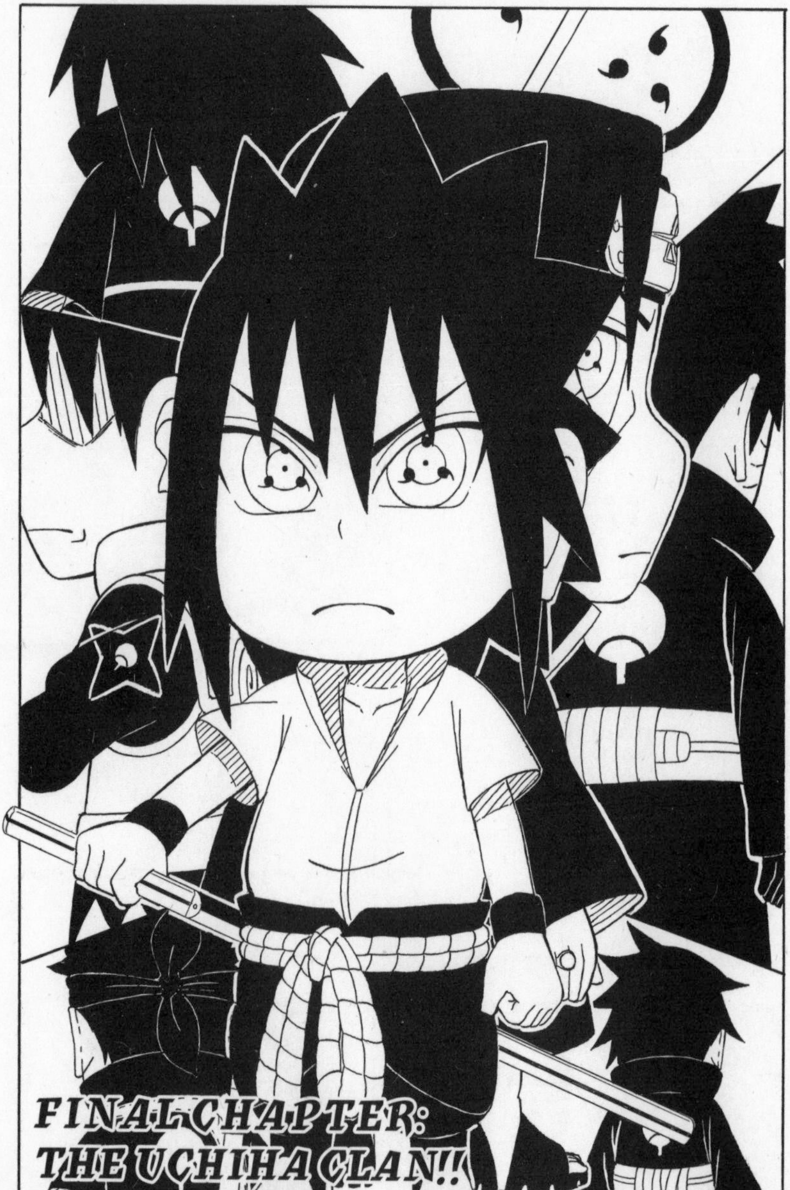
FINAL CHAPTER:
THE UCHIHA CLAN!!

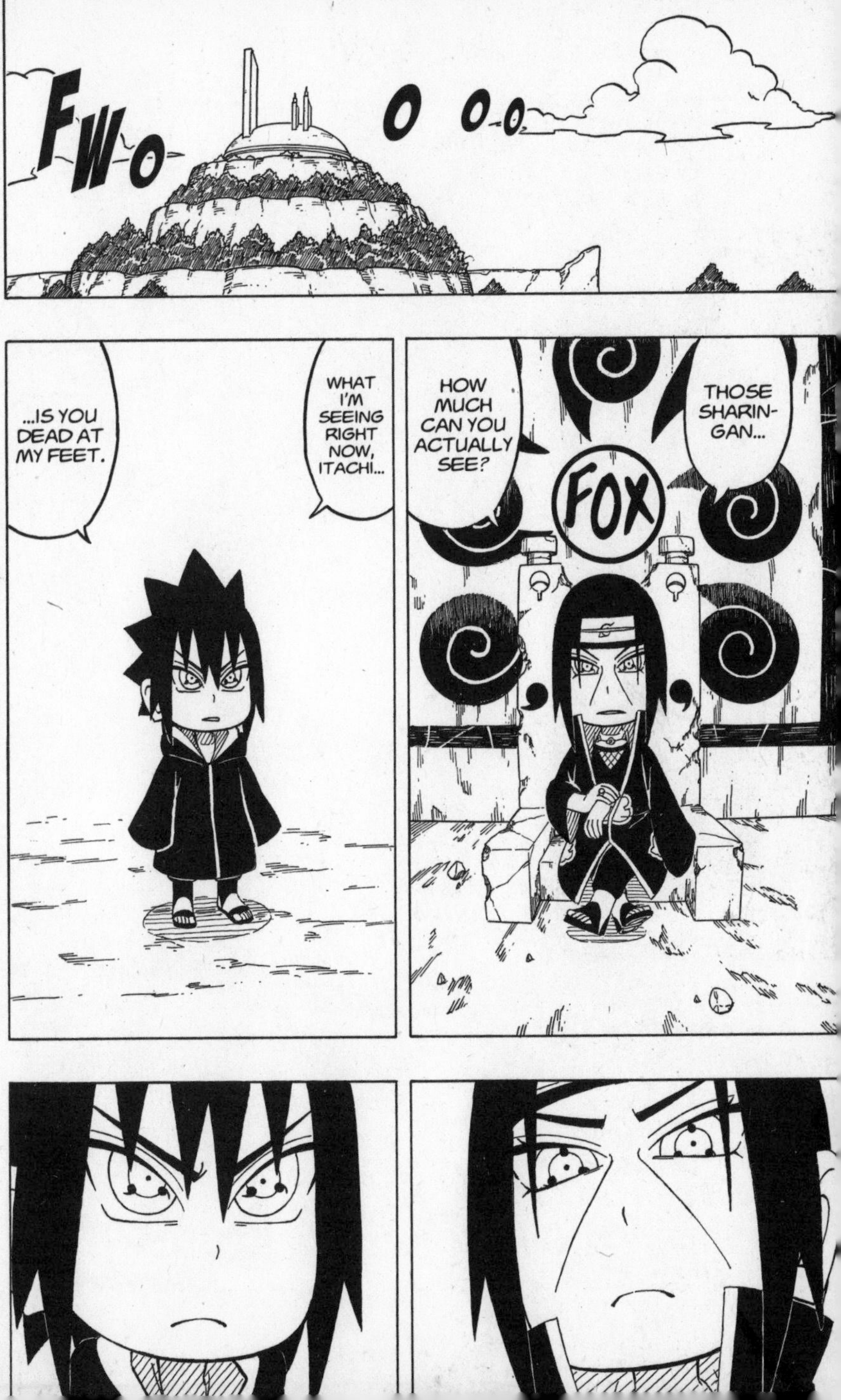
FWO O O-O
THOSE SHARIN-GAN...
HOW MUCH CAN YOU ACTUALLY SEE?
FOX
WHAT I'M SEEING RIGHT NOW, ITACHI...
...IS YOU DEAD AT MY FEET.

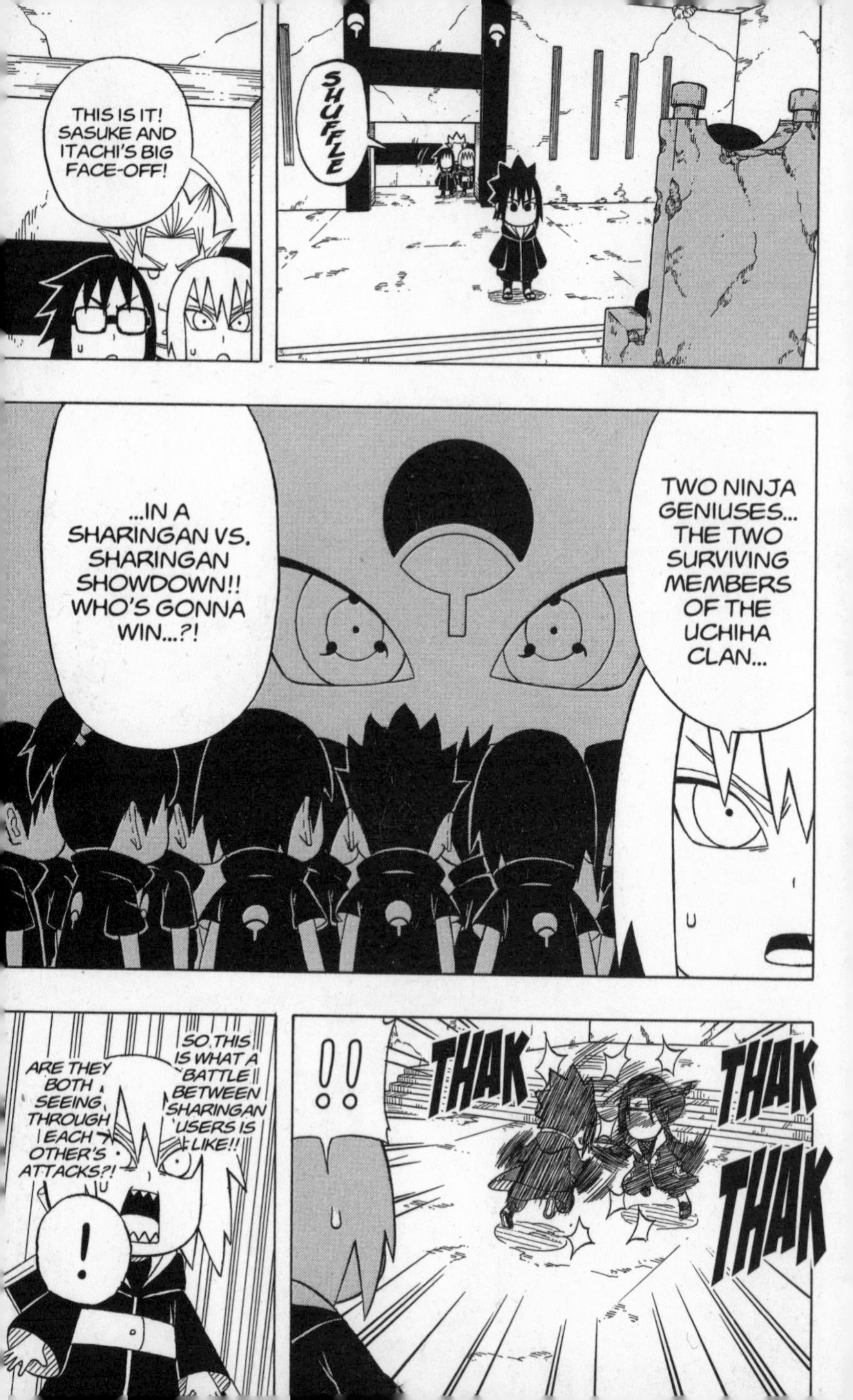
SHUFFLE
THIS IS IT! SASUKE AND ITACHI'S BIG FACE-OFF!
TWO NINJA GENIUSES... THE TWO SURVIVING MEMBERS OF THE UCHIHA CLAN...
...IN A SHARINGAN VS. SHARINGAN SHOWDOWN!! WHO'S GONNA WIN...?!
!!
THAK
THAK
THAK
SO THIS IS WHAT A BATTLE BETWEEN SHARINGAN USERS IS LIKE!!
ARE THEY BOTH SEEING THROUGH EACH OTHER'S ATTACKS?!
!

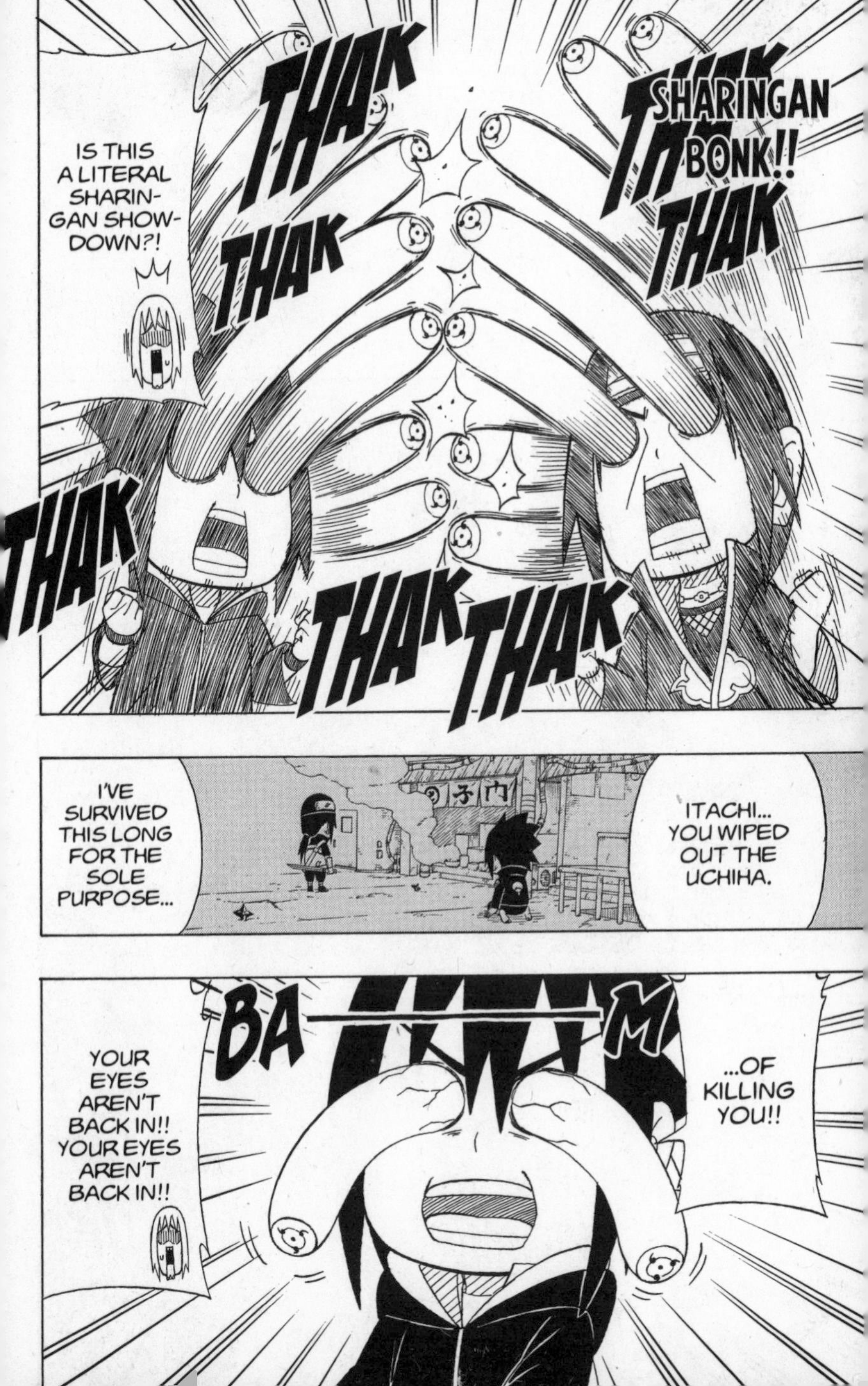
SHARINGAN BONK!!
THAK
THAK
THAK
THAK
THAK THAK
IS THIS A LITERAL SHARIN-GAN SHOW-DOWN?!
ITACHI... YOU WIPED OUT THE UCHIHA.
I'VE SURVIVED THIS LONG FOR THE SOLE PURPOSE...
BA—M
...OF KILLING YOU!!
YOUR EYES AREN'T BACK IN!! YOUR EYES AREN'T BACK IN!!

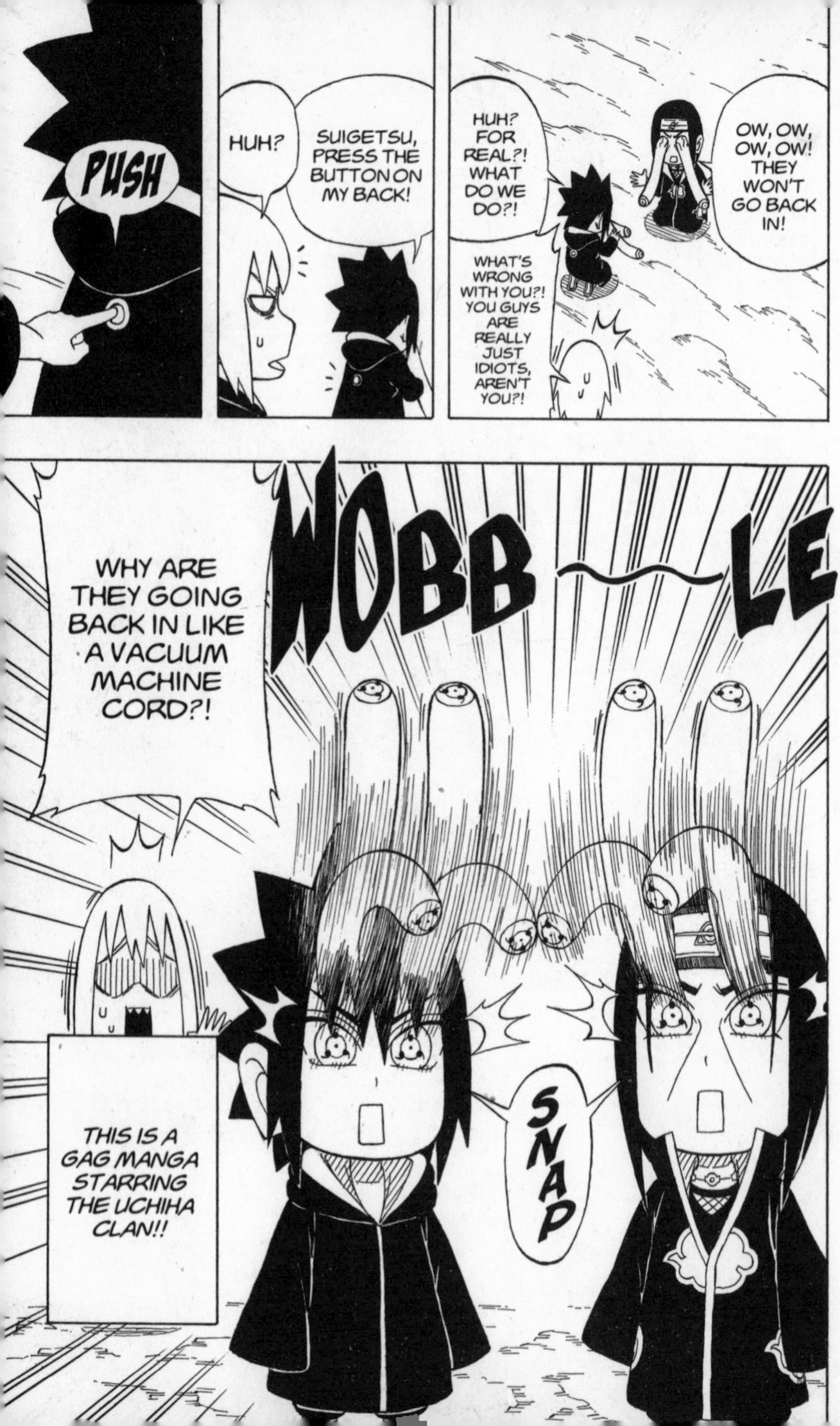
OW, OW, OW, OW! THEY WON'T GO BACK IN!
HUH? FOR REAL?! WHAT DO WE DO?!
WHAT'S WRONG WITH YOU?! YOU GUYS ARE REALLY JUST IDIOTS, AREN'T YOU?!
SUIGETSU, PRESS THE BUTTON ON MY BACK!
HUH?
PUSH
WOBB~~LE
WHY ARE THEY GOING BACK IN LIKE A VACUUM MACHINE CORD?!
SNAP
THIS IS A GAG MANGA STARRING THE UCHIHA CLAN!!

TAIJUTSU BATTLE?!

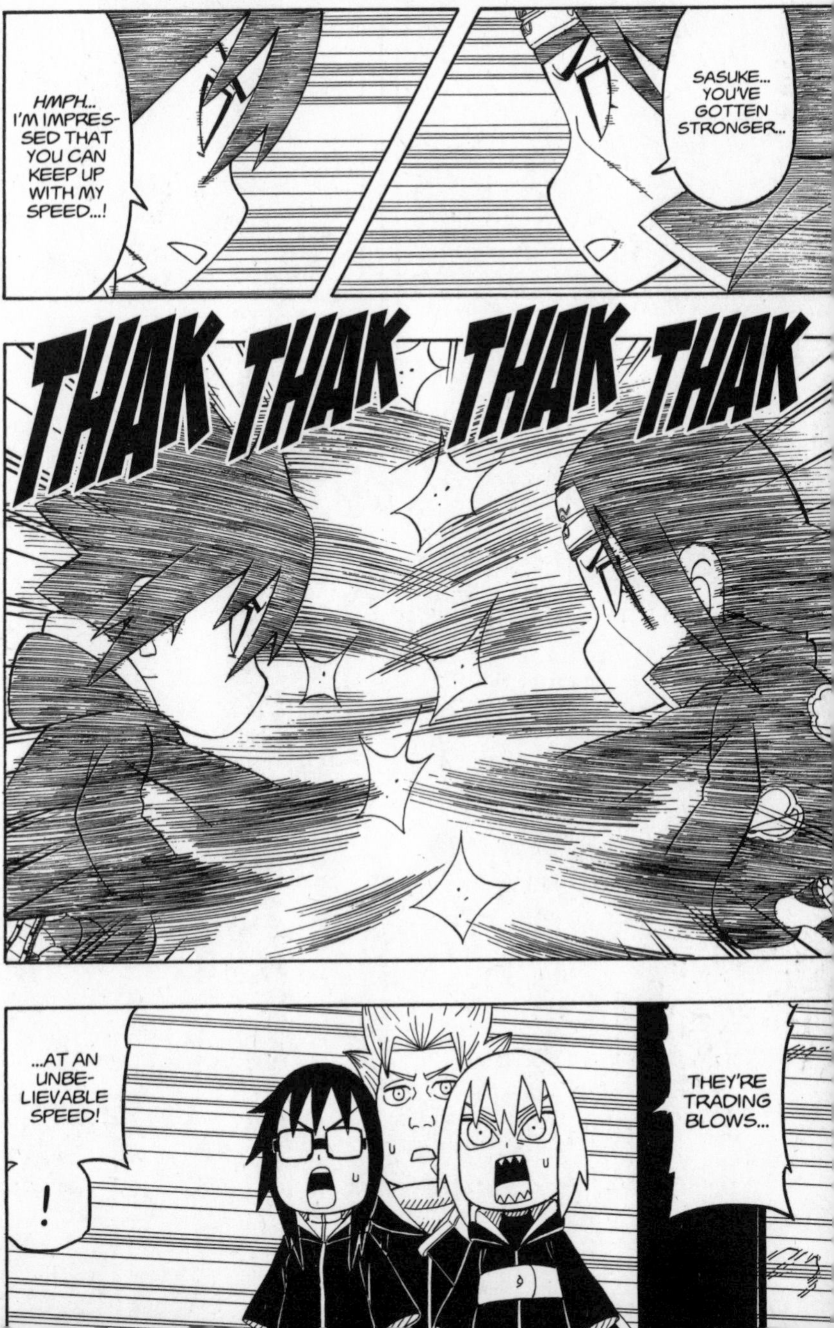
SASUKE... YOU'VE GOTTEN STRONGER...
HMPH... I'M IMPRES-SED THAT YOU CAN KEEP UP WITH MY SPEED...!
THAK THAK THAK THAK
THEY'RE TRADING BLOWS...
...AT AN UNBE-LIEVABLE SPEED!
!

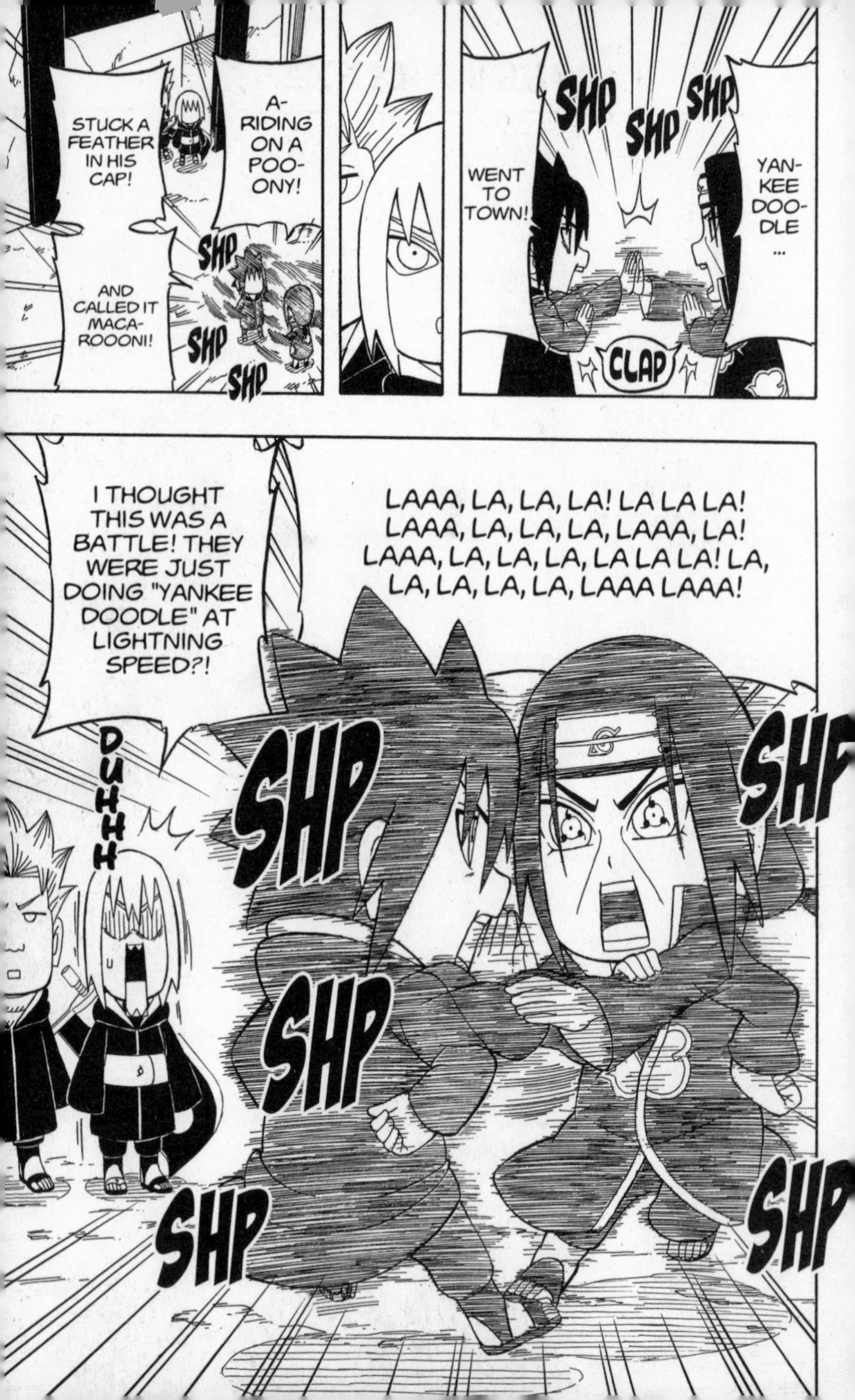
YAN-KEE DOO-DLE...
WENT TO TOWN!
SHP SHP SHP
CLAP
A-RIDING ON A POO-ONY!
STUCK A FEATHER IN HIS CAP!
AND CALLED IT MACA-ROOONI!
SHP
SHP
SHP
LAAA, LA, LA, LA! LA LA LA! LAAA, LA, LA, LA, LAAA, LA! LAAA, LA, LA, LA, LA LA LA! LA, LA, LA, LA, LA, LAAA LAAA!
SHP
SHP
SHP
SHP
SHP
I THOUGHT THIS WAS A BATTLE! THEY WERE JUST DOING "YANKEE DOODLE" AT LIGHTNING SPEED?!
DUHHH

SORRY, SASUKE

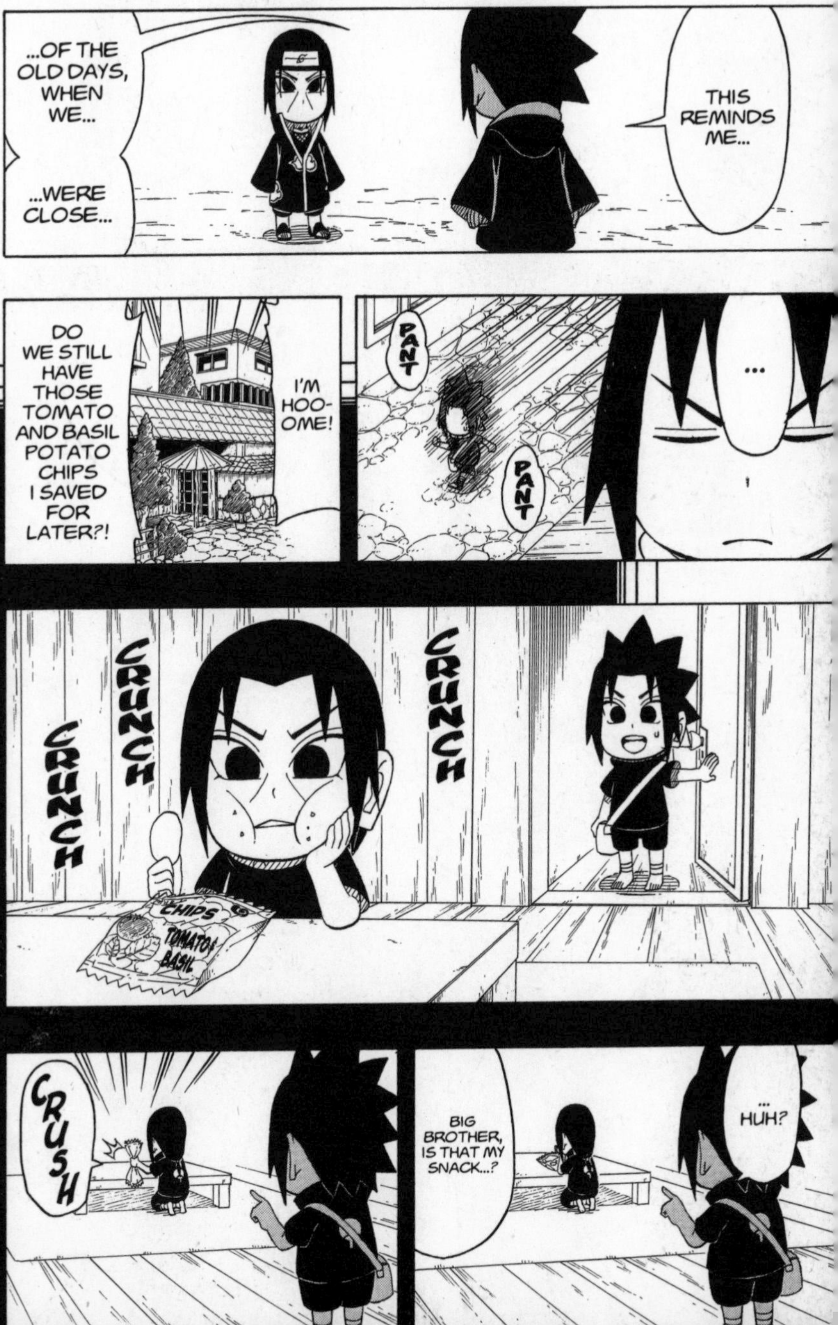
THIS REMINDS ME...
...OF THE OLD DAYS, WHEN WE...
...WERE CLOSE...
...
PANT
PANT
I'M HOO-OME!
DO WE STILL HAVE THOSE TOMATO AND BASIL POTATO CHIPS I SAVED FOR LATER?!
CRUNCH
CRUNCH
CRUNCH
CHIPS
TOMATO & BASIL
... HUH?
BIG BROTHER, IS THAT MY SNACK...?
CRUSH

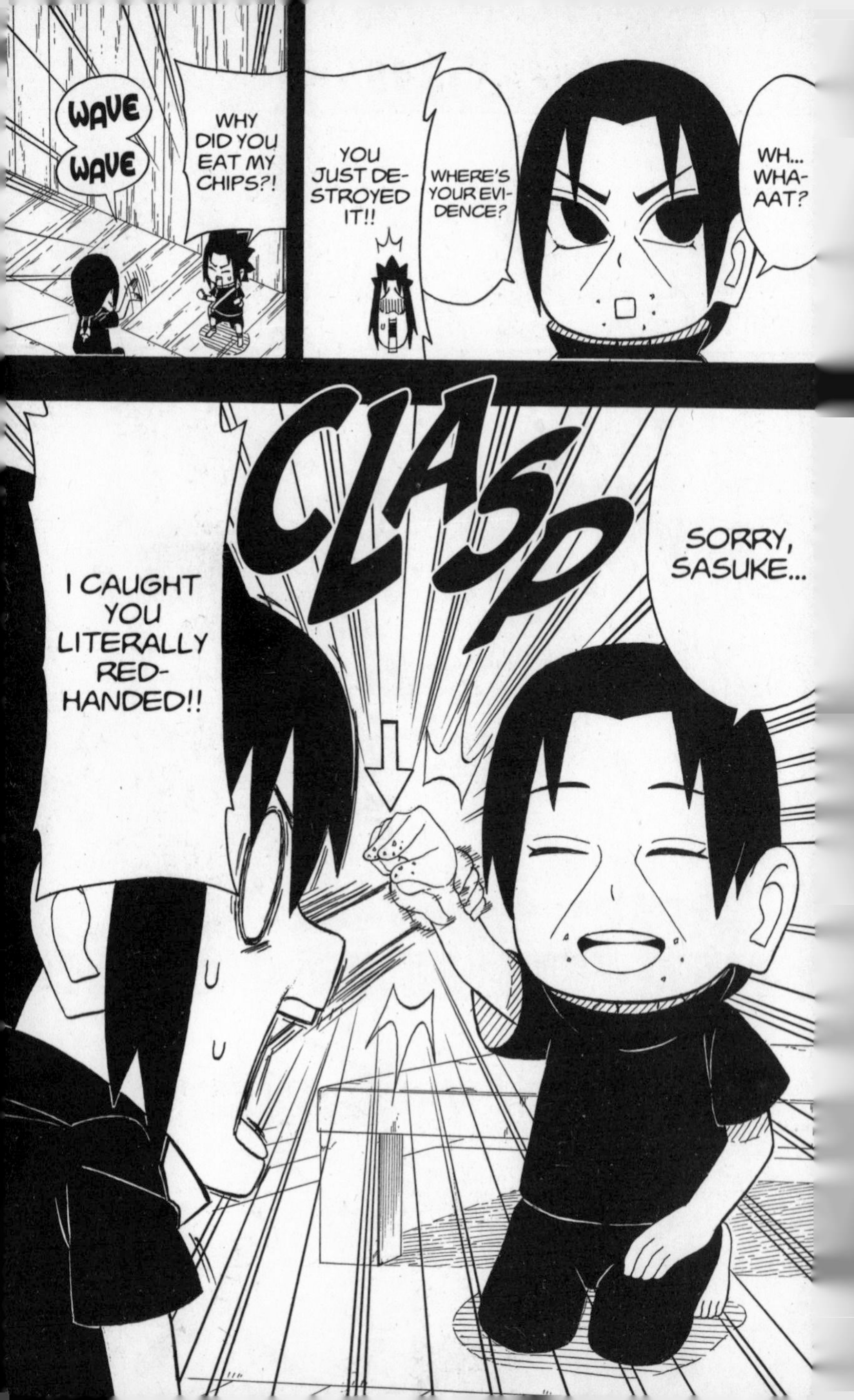
WH... WHA-AAT?
WHERE'S YOUR EVI-DENCE?
YOU JUST DE-STROYED IT!!
WHY DID YOU EAT MY CHIPS?!
WAVE WAVE
SORRY, SASUKE...
CLASP
I CAUGHT YOU LITERALLY RED-HANDED!!

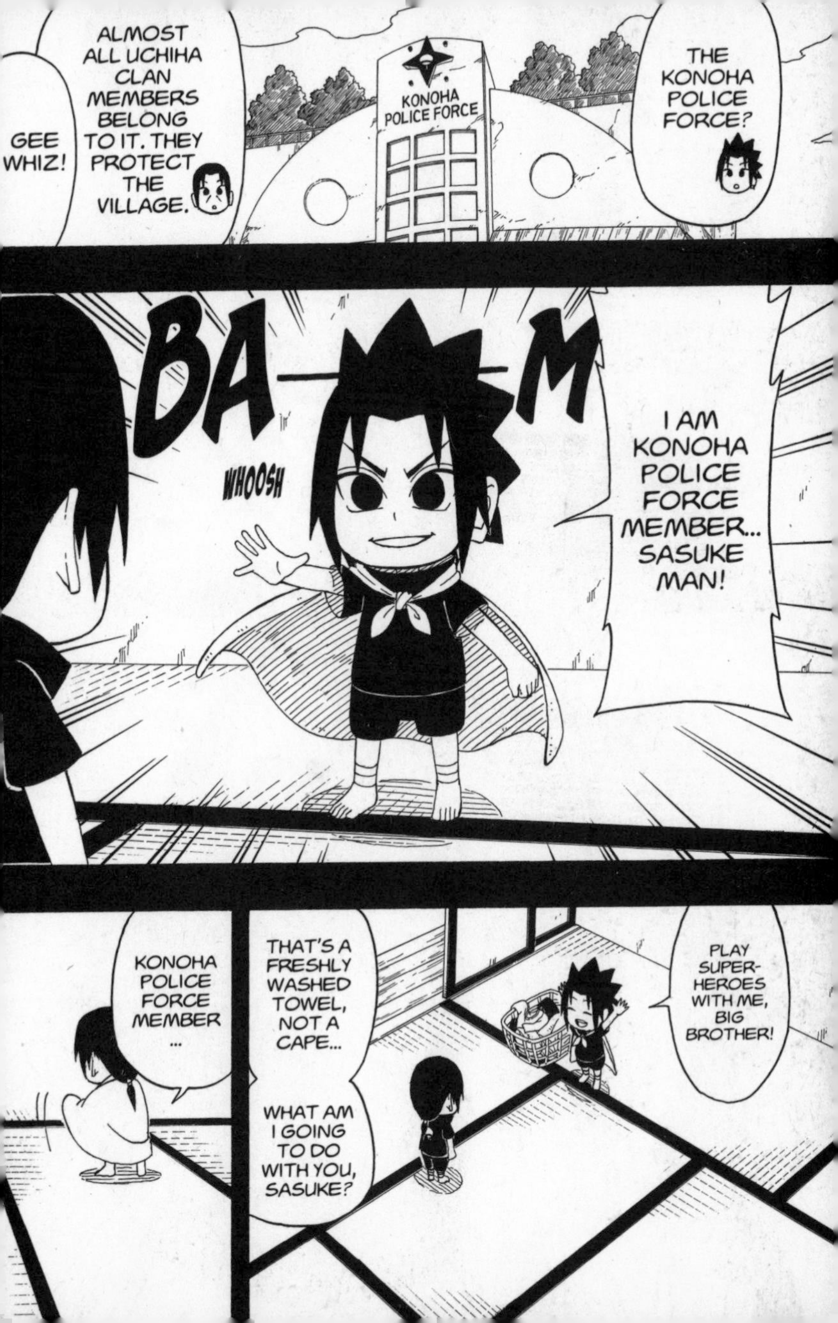
THE KONOHA POLICE FORCE?
KONOHA POLICE FORCE
ALMOST ALL UCHIHA CLAN MEMBERS BELONG TO IT. THEY PROTECT THE VILLAGE.
GEE WHIZ!
I AM KONOHA POLICE FORCE MEMBER... SASUKE MAN!
BA—M
WHOOSH
PLAY SUPER-HEROES WITH ME, BIG BROTHER!
THAT'S A FRESHLY WASHED TOWEL, NOT A CAPE...
WHAT AM I GOING TO DO WITH YOU, SASUKE?
KONOHA POLICE FORCE MEMBER ...

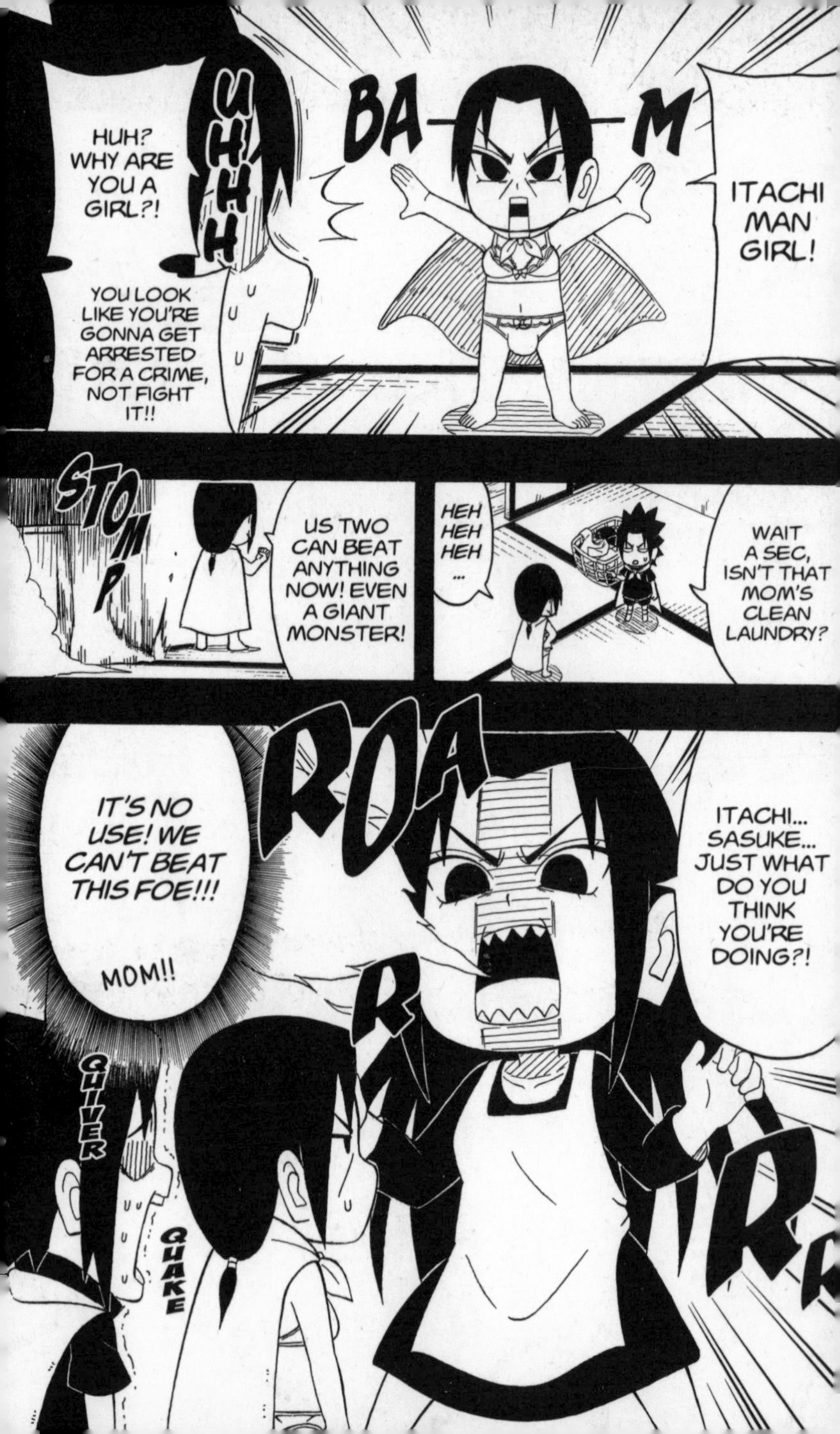
BA—M
ITACHI MAN GIRL!
UHHHH
HUH? WHY ARE YOU A GIRL?!
YOU LOOK LIKE YOU'RE GONNA GET ARRESTED FOR A CRIME, NOT FIGHT IT!!
WAIT A SEC, ISN'T THAT MOM'S CLEAN LAUNDRY?
HEH HEH HEH ...
US TWO CAN BEAT ANYTHING NOW! EVEN A GIANT MONSTER!
STOMP
ITACHI... SASUKE... JUST WHAT DO YOU THINK YOU'RE DOING?!
ROAR
IT'S NO USE! WE CAN'T BEAT THIS FOE!!!
MOM!!
QUIVER
QUAKE

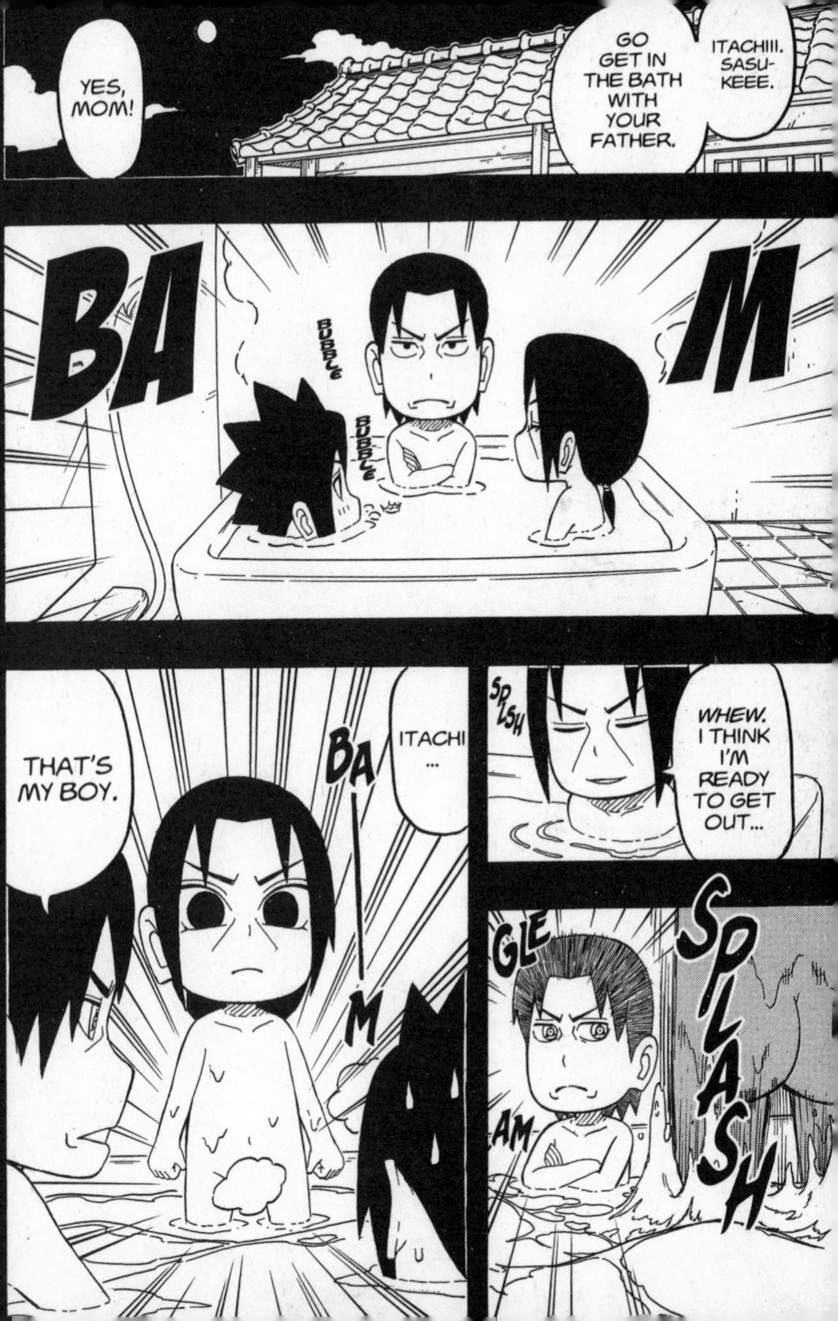
ITACHIII. SASUKEEE.
GO GET IN THE BATH WITH YOUR FATHER.
YES, MOM!
BAM
BUBBLE
BUBBLE
SPLSH
WHEW. I THINK I'M READY TO GET OUT...
GLE
AM
SPLASH
BAM
ITACHI ...
THAT'S MY BOY.

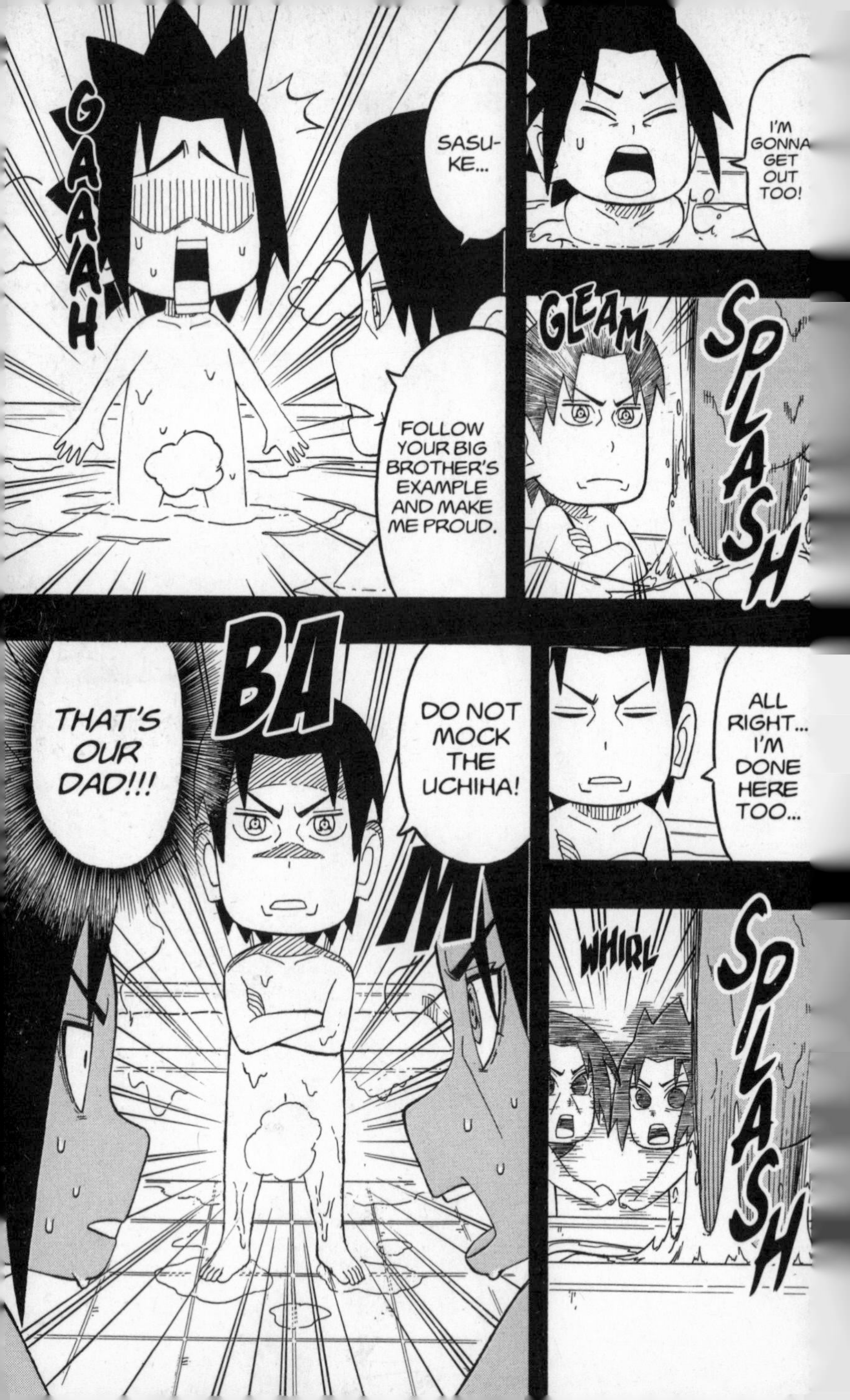
I'M GONNA GET OUT TOO!
GLEAM
SPLASH
SASU-KE...
FOLLOW YOUR BIG BROTHER'S EXAMPLE AND MAKE ME PROUD.
GAAAAH
ALL RIGHT... I'M DONE HERE TOO...
WHIRL
SPLASH
BAM
DO NOT MOCK THE UCHIHA!
THAT'S OUR DAD!!!

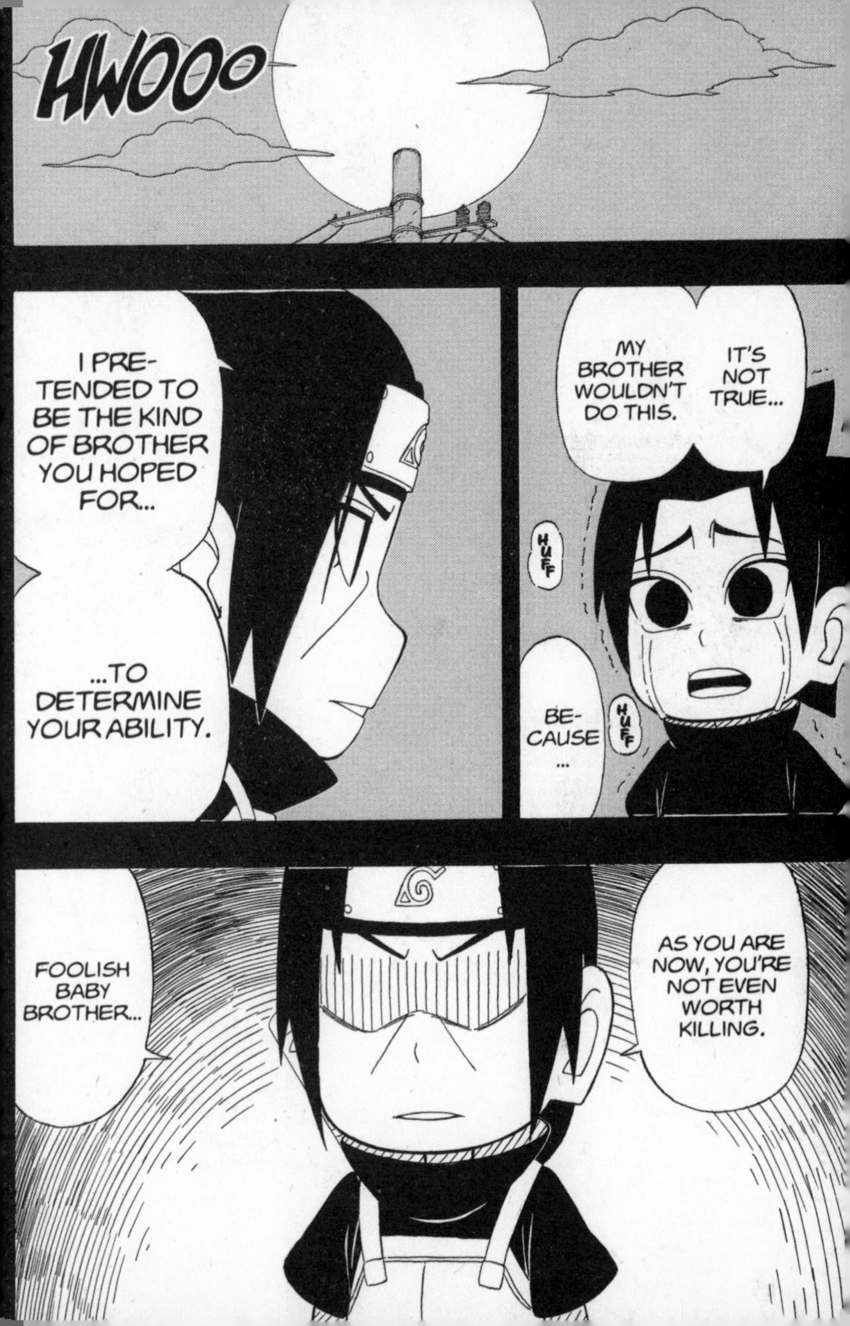

HWOOO
IT'S NOT TRUE...
MY BROTHER WOULDN'T DO THIS.
HUFF
HUFF
BE-CAUSE ...
I PRE-TENDED TO BE THE KIND OF BROTHER YOU HOPED FOR...
...TO DETERMINE YOUR ABILITY.
AS YOU ARE NOW, YOU'RE NOT EVEN WORTH KILLING.
FOOLISH BABY BROTHER...

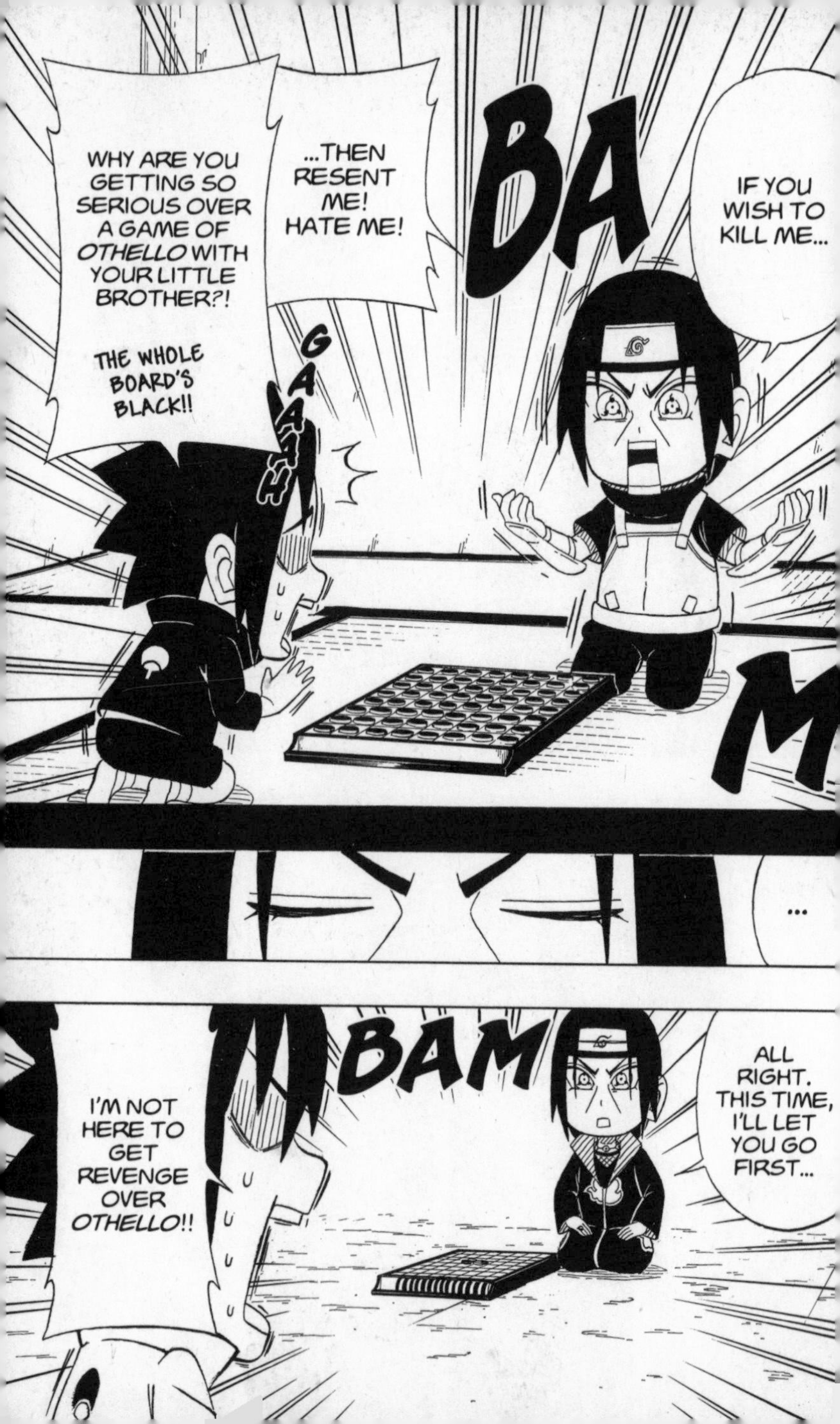
IF YOU WISH TO KILL ME...
BA
M
...THEN RESENT ME! HATE ME!
GAAAH
WHY ARE YOU GETTING SO SERIOUS OVER A GAME OF *OTHELLO* WITH YOUR LITTLE BROTHER?!
THE WHOLE BOARD'S BLACK!!
...
ALL RIGHT. THIS TIME, I'LL LET YOU GO FIRST...
BAM
I'M NOT HERE TO GET REVENGE OVER OTHELLO!!

THE UCHIHA CLAN

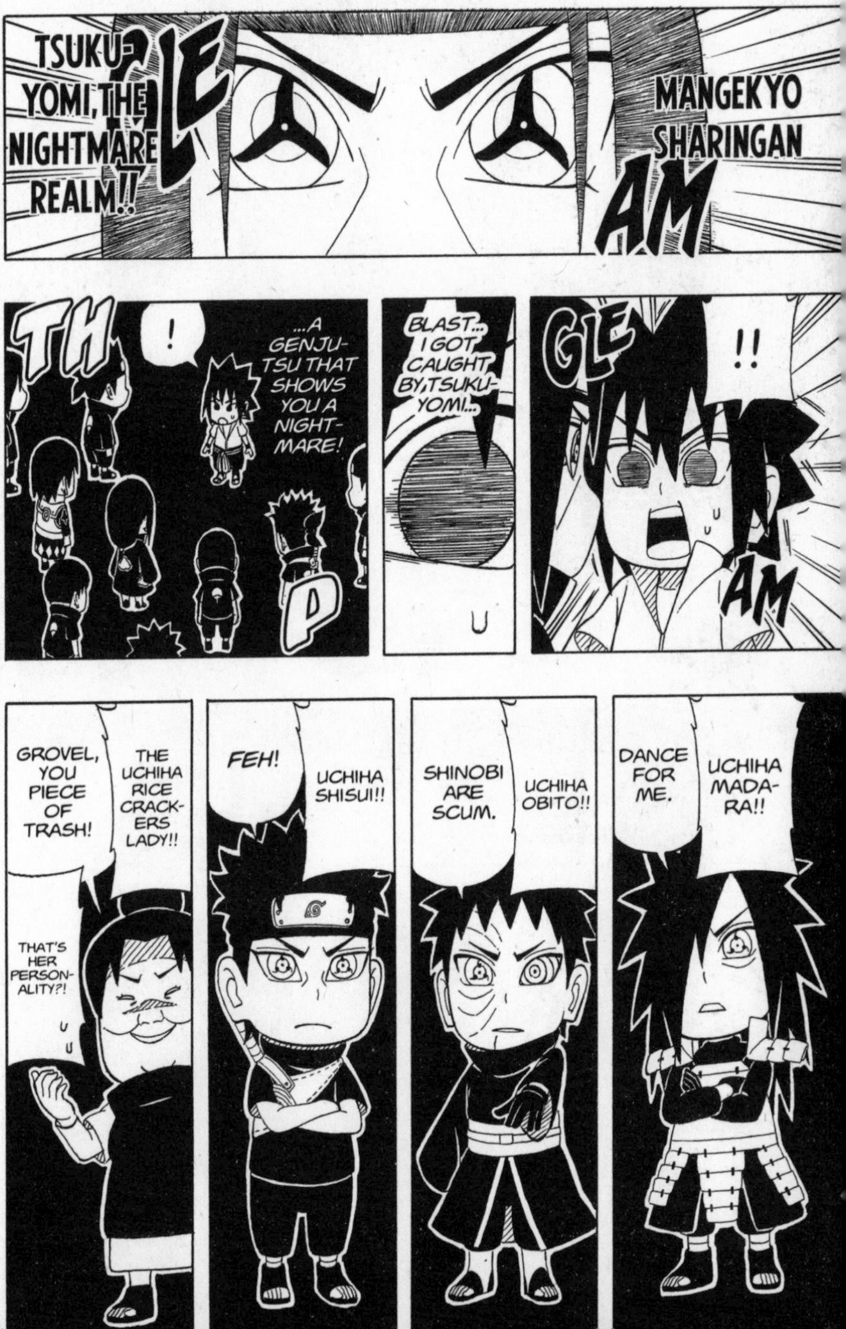
MANGEKYO SHARINGAN
GLE
AM
TSUKUYOMI, THE NIGHTMARE REALM!!
GLE
!!
AM
BLAST... I GOT CAUGHT BY TSUKUYOMI...
...A GENJUTSU THAT SHOWS YOU A NIGHTMARE!
!
TH
P
UCHIHA MADARA!!
DANCE FOR ME.
UCHIHA OBITO!!
SHINOBI ARE SCUM.
UCHIHA SHISUI!!
FEH!
THE UCHIHA RICE CRACKERS LADY!!
GROVEL, YOU PIECE OF TRASH!
THAT'S HER PERSONALITY?!

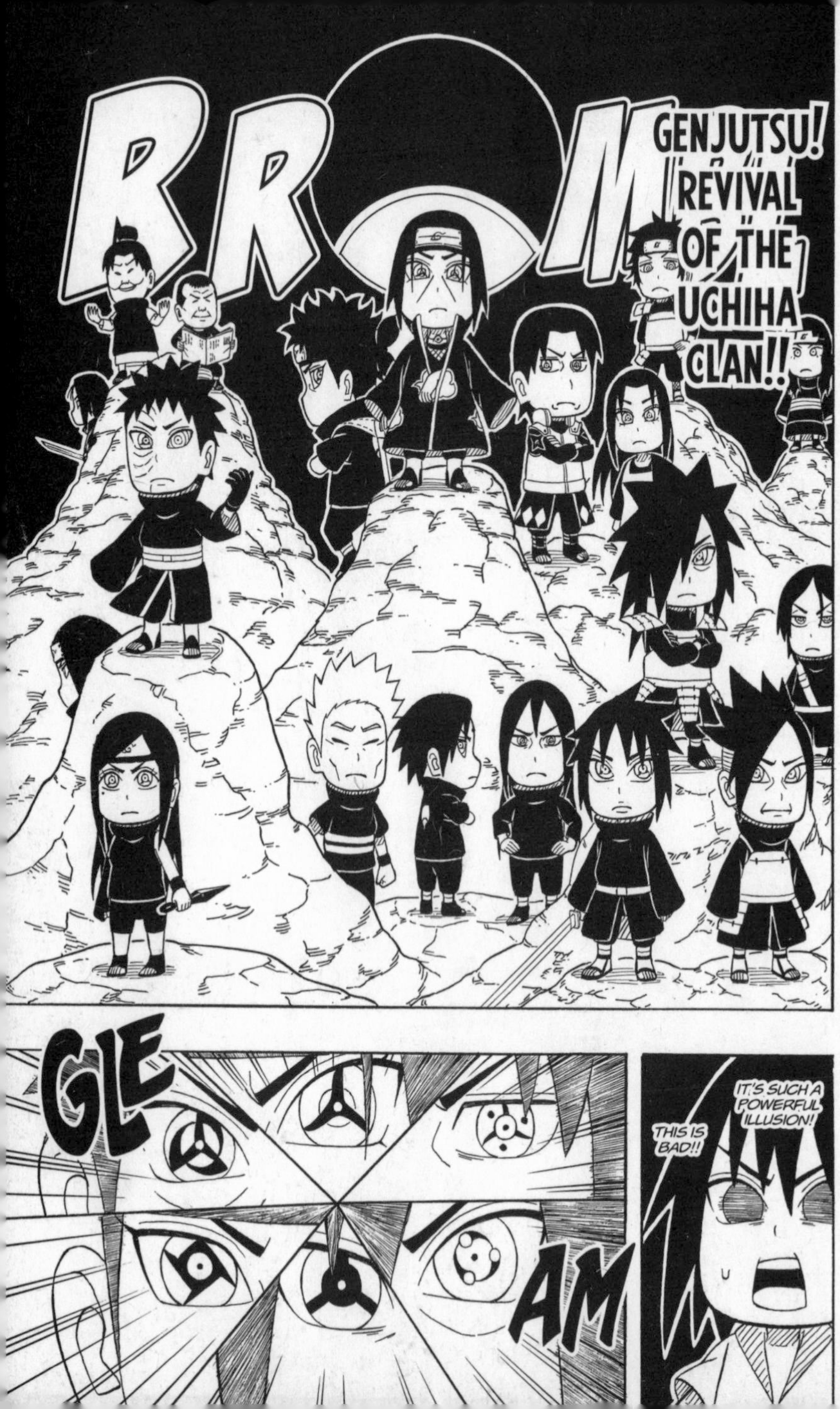
BROM
GENJUTSU! REVIVAL OF THE UCHIHA CLAN!!
IT'S SUCH A POWERFUL ILLUSION!
THIS IS BAD!!
GLE
AM

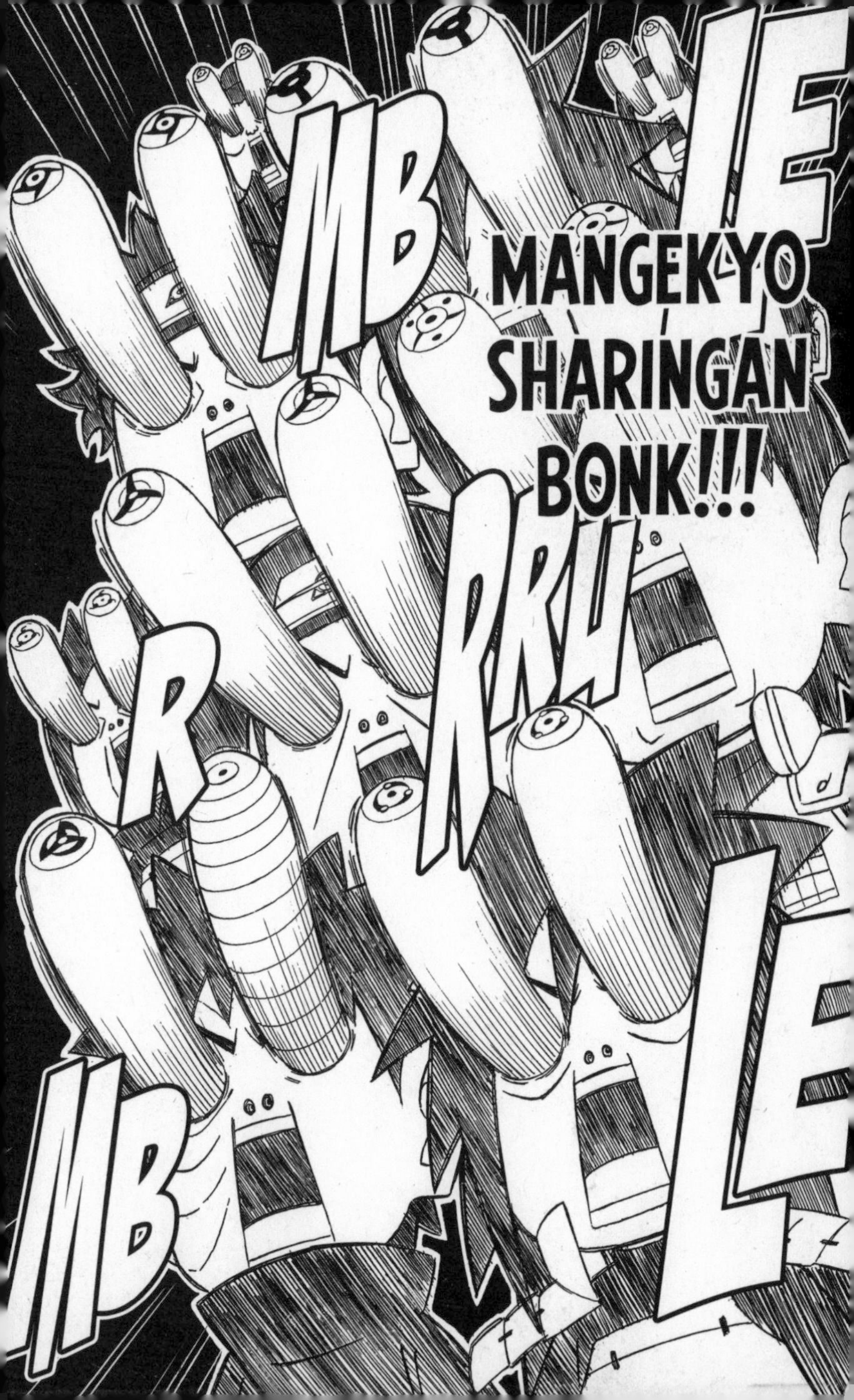
MANGEKYO SHARINGAN BONK!!!

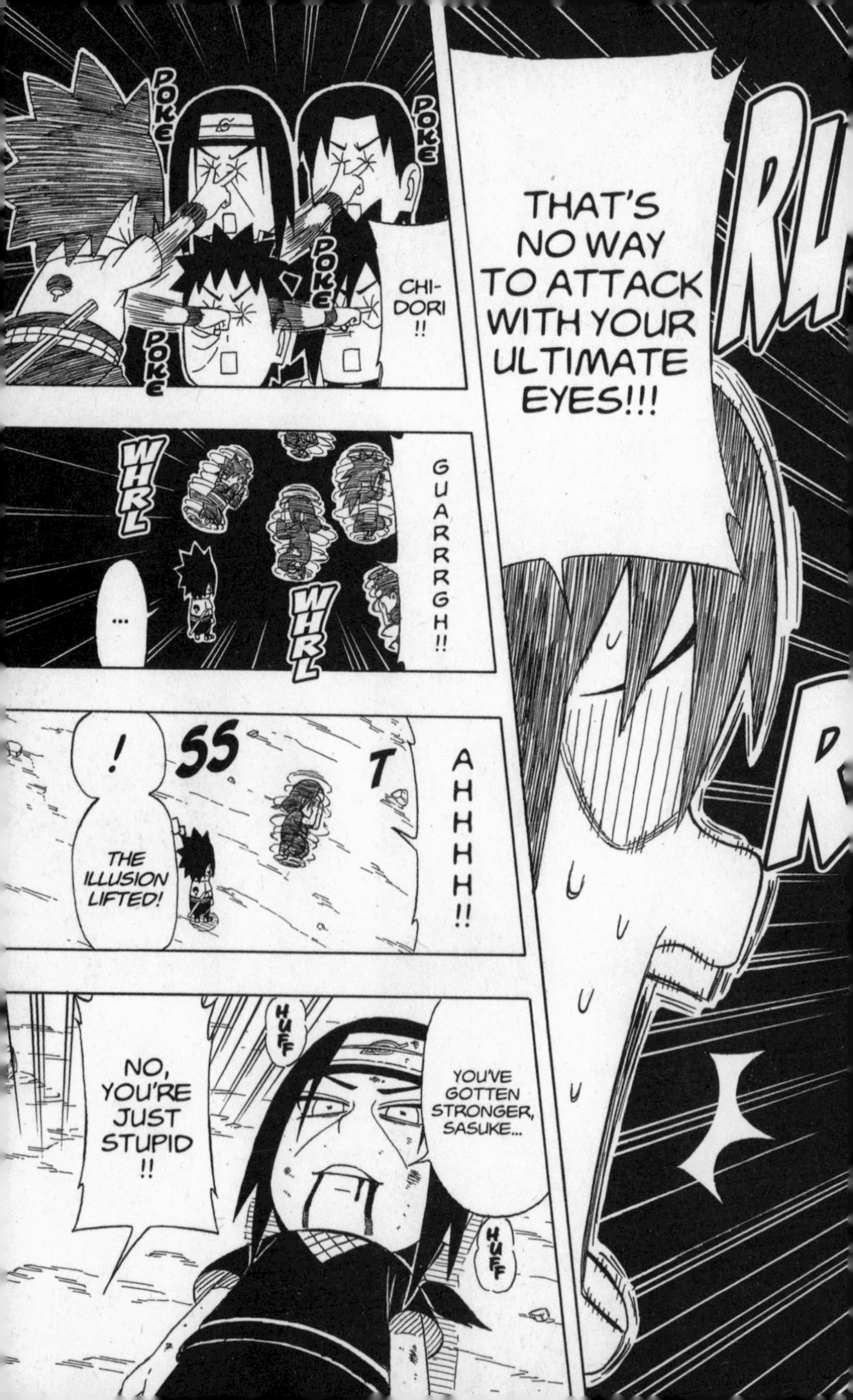
THAT'S NO WAY TO ATTACK WITH YOUR ULTIMATE EYES!!!
CHI-DORI !!
POKE
POKE
POKE
POKE
GUARRRGH!!
WHRL
WHRL
...
AHHHHH!!
T
SS
!
THE ILLUSION LIFTED!
YOU'VE GOTTEN STRONGER, SASUKE...
HUFF
HUFF
NO, YOU'RE JUST STUPID !!

THIS IS IT

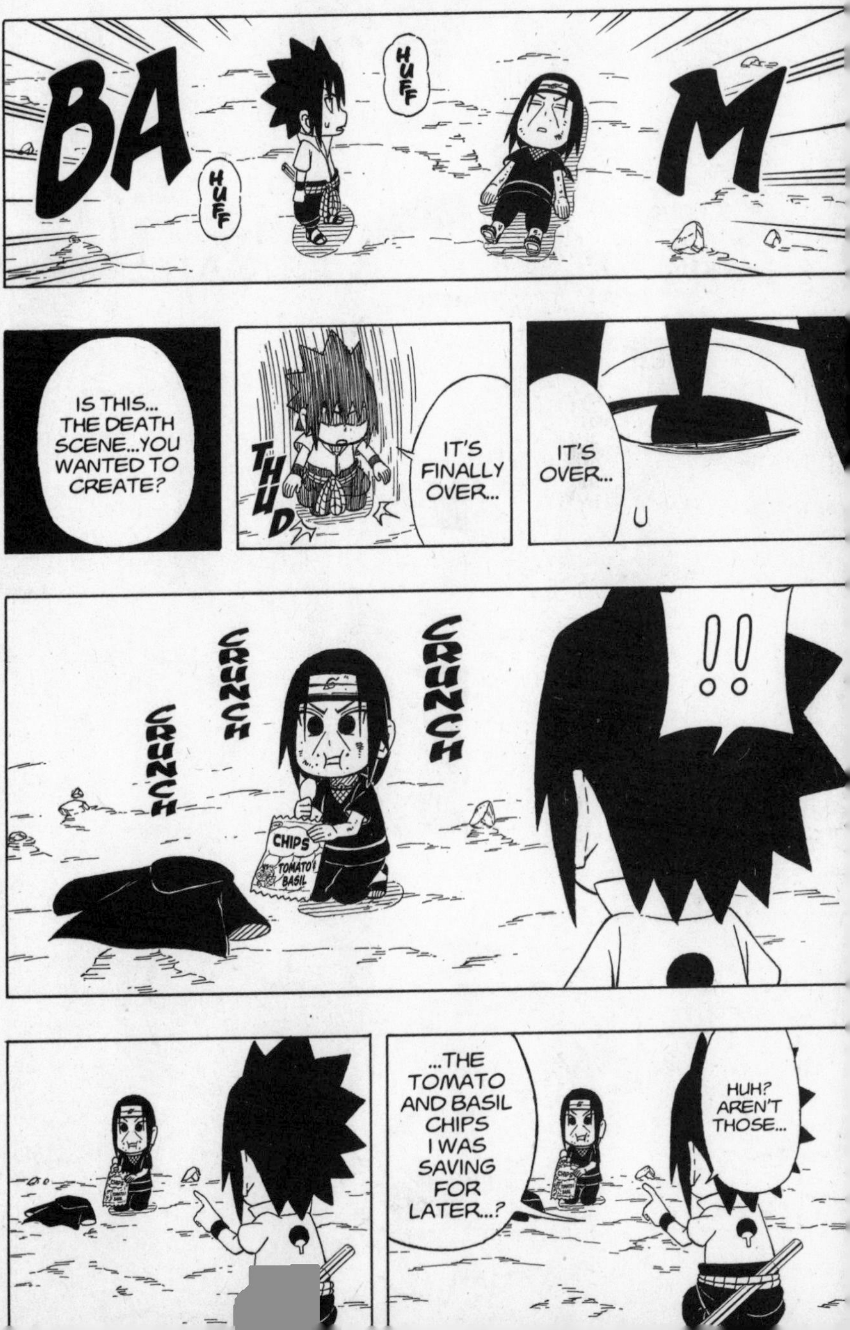
BA
M
HUFF
HUFF
IT'S OVER...
IT'S FINALLY OVER...
THUD
IS THIS... THE DEATH SCENE...YOU WANTED TO CREATE?
!!
CRUNCH
CRUNCH
CRUNCH
CHIPS
TOMATO BASIL
HUH? AREN'T THOSE...
...THE TOMATO AND BASIL CHIPS I WAS SAVING FOR LATER...?

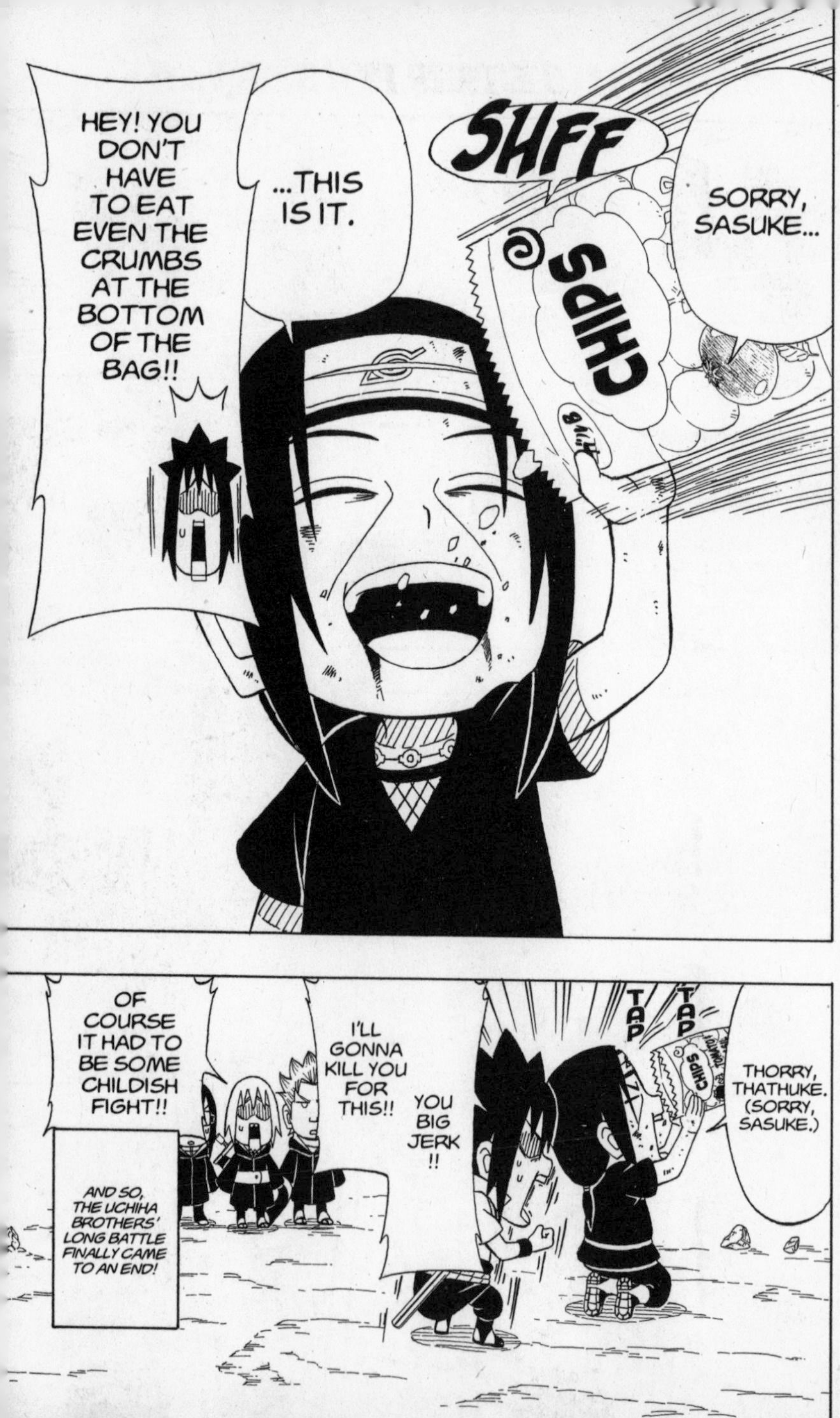
SHFF
SORRY, SASUKE...
CHIPS
...THIS IS IT.
HEY! YOU DON'T HAVE TO EAT EVEN THE CRUMBS AT THE BOTTOM OF THE BAG!!
TAP TAP
CHIPS
THORRY, THATHUKE. (SORRY, SASUKE.)
YOU BIG JERK!!
I'LL GONNA KILL YOU FOR THIS!!
OF COURSE IT HAD TO BE SOME CHILDISH FIGHT!!
AND SO, THE UCHIHA BROTHERS' LONG BATTLE FINALLY CAME TO AN END!

THE END OF THE JOURNEY...?!

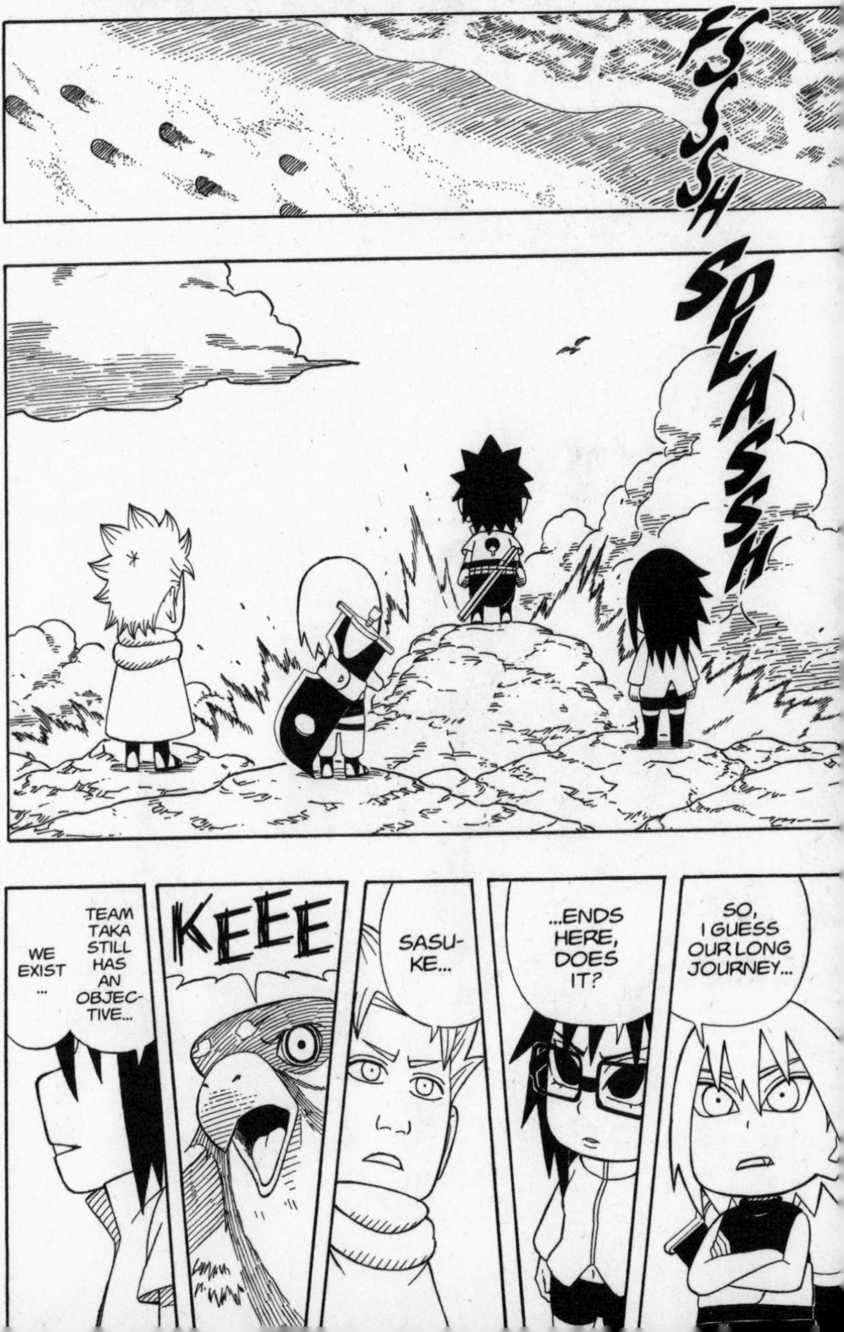
FSSSH
SPLASSH
SO, I GUESS OUR LONG JOURNEY...
...ENDS HERE, DOES IT?
SASUKE...
KEEE
TEAM TAKA STILL HAS AN OBJECTIVE...
WE EXIST...

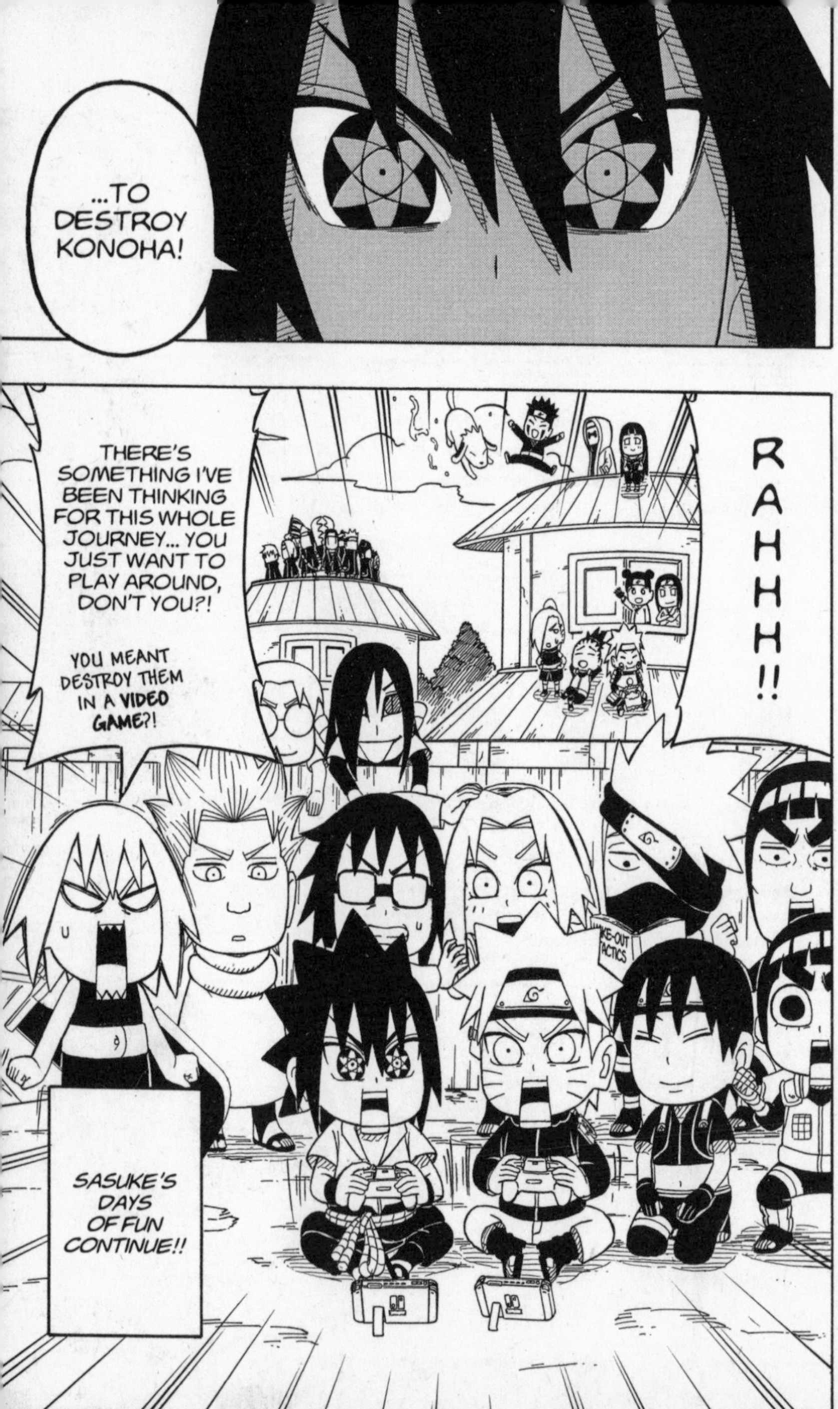

...TO DESTROY KONOHA!
RAHHHH!!
THERE'S SOMETHING I'VE BEEN THINKING FOR THIS WHOLE JOURNEY... YOU JUST WANT TO PLAY AROUND, DON'T YOU?!
YOU MEANT DESTROY THEM IN A **VIDEO GAME**?!
SASUKE'S DAYS OF FUN CONTINUE!!

BONUS MATERIAL MINI MANGA CHAPTERS

MINI MANGA 1: LET'S GO TO THE NARUTO ART EXHIBIT! (ROCK LEE VERSION)

(from *Saikyo Jump* 2015 No. 3)

MINI MANGA 2: LET'S GO TO THE NARUTO ART EXHIBIT! PART 2 (ROCK LEE VERSION)

(from *Saikyo Jump* 2015 No. 5)

A Rock Lee version of the *Naruto Art Exhibit* manga. The content is pretty similar to the Sasuke version that was included in the previous volumes, but since we did it, we included this version for your enjoyment, too.

MINI MANGA 3: ROCK LEE'S YOUTH AT FULL POWER COOKING PART 1: FRENCH TRAINING ARC

MINI MANGA 4: ROCK LEE'S YOUTH AT FULL POWER COOKING PART 2: NARUTO VS. NEJI ARC

I drew these for a collaboration with the gourmet guide website *GURUNAVI*.

MINI MANGA 5: SASUKE VS. THE FOREIGNER!!

MINI MANGA 6: SASUKE VS. THE DENTIST!!

MINI MANGA 7: SASUKE VS. THECOLORED TILES!!

More of Sasuke's ridiculous battles! Personally, I had a ton of fun drawing these silly Sasuke Vs. XXX battles!

(from *Jump Victory Carnival Official Guidebook 2016*)

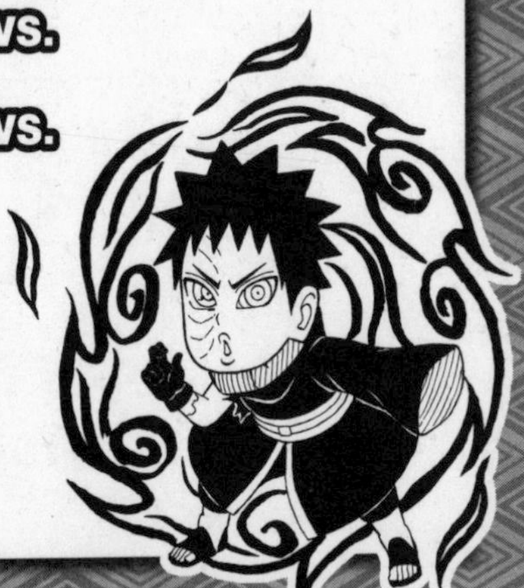

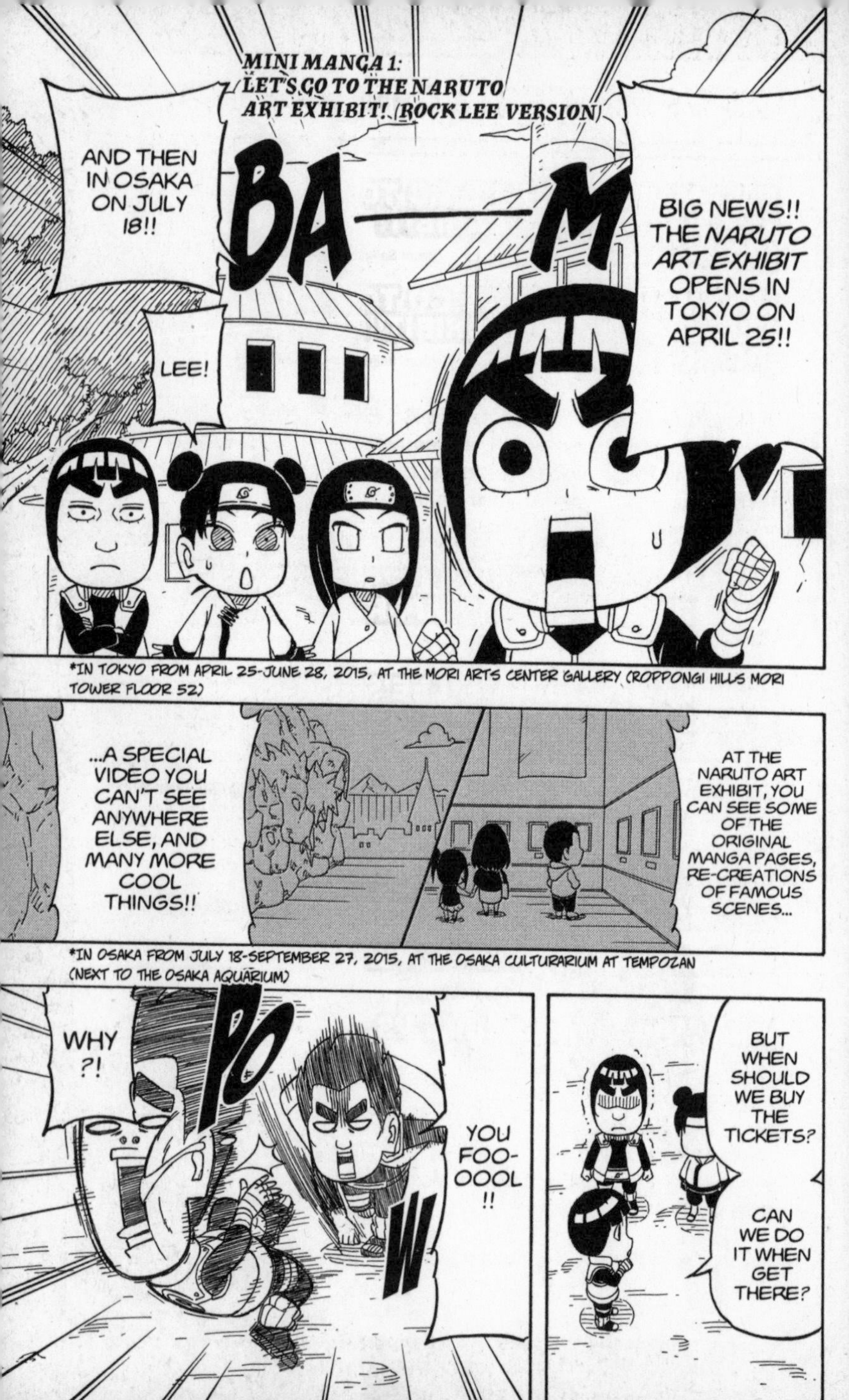
MINI MANGA 1: LET'S GO TO THE NARUTO ART EXHIBIT! (ROCK LEE VERSION)
BIG NEWS!! THE NARUTO ART EXHIBIT OPENS IN TOKYO ON APRIL 25!!
BA—M
AND THEN IN OSAKA ON JULY 18!!
LEE!
*IN TOKYO FROM APRIL 25-JUNE 28, 2015, AT THE MORI ARTS CENTER GALLERY (ROPPONGI HILLS MORI TOWER FLOOR 52)
AT THE NARUTO ART EXHIBIT, YOU CAN SEE SOME OF THE ORIGINAL MANGA PAGES, RE-CREATIONS OF FAMOUS SCENES...
...A SPECIAL VIDEO YOU CAN'T SEE ANYWHERE ELSE, AND MANY MORE COOL THINGS!!
*IN OSAKA FROM JULY 18-SEPTEMBER 27, 2015, AT THE OSAKA CULTURARIUM AT TEMPOZAN (NEXT TO THE OSAKA AQUARIUM)
BUT WHEN SHOULD WE BUY THE TICKETS?
CAN WE DO IT WHEN GET THERE?
YOU FOO-OOOL!!
POW
WHY?!

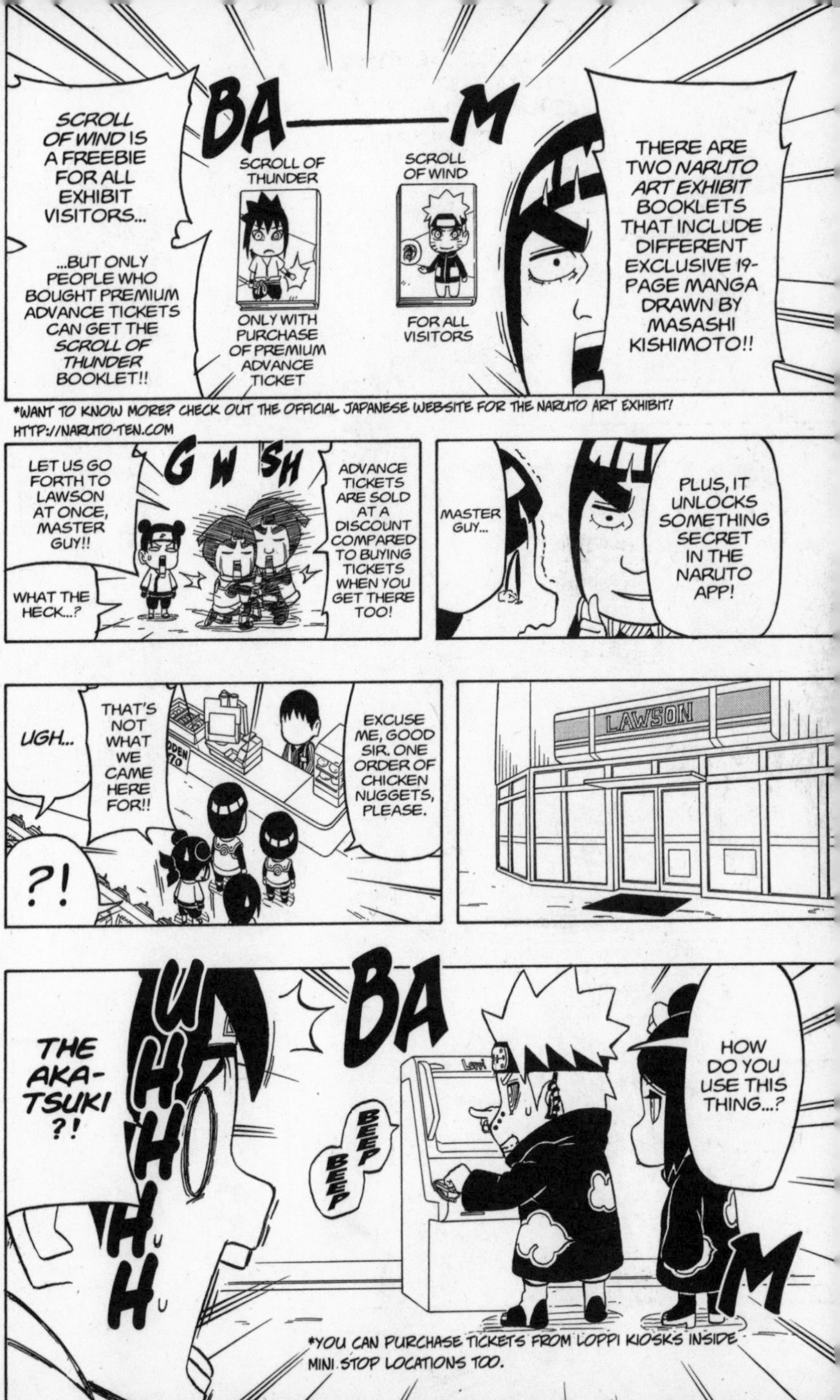
THERE ARE TWO NARUTO ART EXHIBIT BOOKLETS THAT INCLUDE DIFFERENT EXCLUSIVE 19-PAGE MANGA DRAWN BY MASASHI KISHIMOTO!!
BA——M
SCROLL OF WIND
FOR ALL VISITORS
SCROLL OF THUNDER
ONLY WITH PURCHASE OF PREMIUM ADVANCE TICKET
SCROLL OF WIND IS A FREEBIE FOR ALL EXHIBIT VISITORS...
...BUT ONLY PEOPLE WHO BOUGHT PREMIUM ADVANCE TICKETS CAN GET THE SCROLL OF THUNDER BOOKLET!!
*WANT TO KNOW MORE? CHECK OUT THE OFFICIAL JAPANESE WEBSITE FOR THE NARUTO ART EXHIBIT!
HTTP://NARUTO-TEN.COM
PLUS, IT UNLOCKS SOMETHING SECRET IN THE NARUTO APP!
MASTER GUY...
ADVANCE TICKETS ARE SOLD AT A DISCOUNT COMPARED TO BUYING TICKETS WHEN YOU GET THERE TOO!
GWSH
LET US GO FORTH TO LAWSON AT ONCE, MASTER GUY!!
WHAT THE HECK...?
LAWSON
EXCUSE ME, GOOD SIR. ONE ORDER OF CHICKEN NUGGETS, PLEASE.
ODEN 70
THAT'S NOT WHAT WE CAME HERE FOR!!
UGH...
?!
HOW DO YOU USE THIS THING...?
BA
M
Loppi
BEEP BEEP
BEEP
THE AKA-TSUKI?!
UHHHHHH
*YOU CAN PURCHASE TICKETS FROM LOPPI KIOSKS INSIDE MINI STOP LOCATIONS TOO.

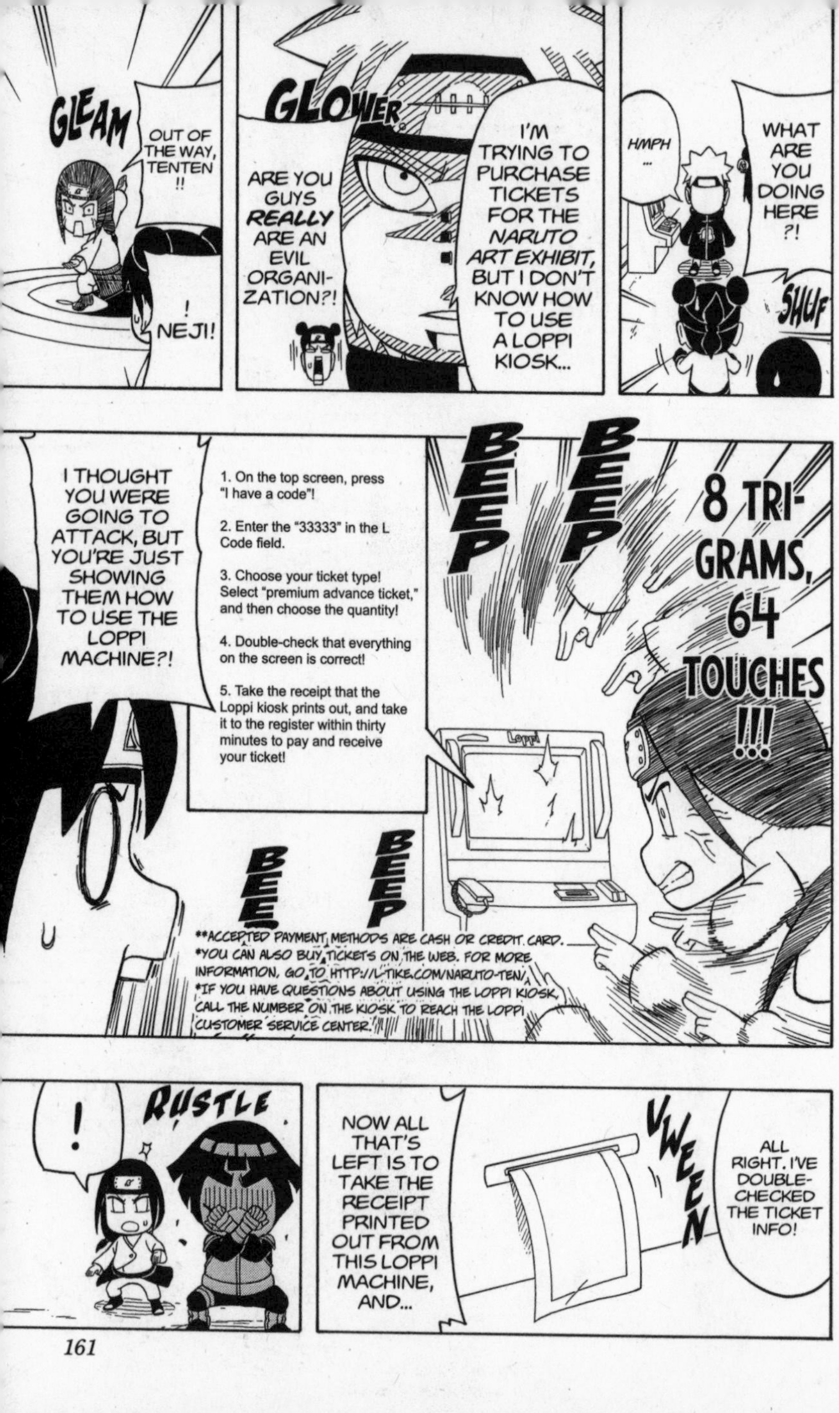
WHAT ARE YOU DOING HERE?!
HMPH ...
SHUF
GLOWER
I'M TRYING TO PURCHASE TICKETS FOR THE NARUTO ART EXHIBIT, BUT I DON'T KNOW HOW TO USE A LOPPI KIOSK...
ARE YOU GUYS REALLY ARE AN EVIL ORGANIZATION?!
GLEAM
OUT OF THE WAY, TENTEN !!
! NEJI!
BEEP
BEEP
8 TRIGRAMS, 64 TOUCHES!!!
Loppi
1. On the top screen, press "I have a code"!
2. Enter the "33333" in the L Code field.
3. Choose your ticket type! Select "premium advance ticket," and then choose the quantity!
4. Double-check that everything on the screen is correct!
5. Take the receipt that the Loppi kiosk prints out, and take it to the register within thirty minutes to pay and receive your ticket!
BEE
BEEP
**ACCEPTED PAYMENT METHODS ARE CASH OR CREDIT CARD.
*YOU CAN ALSO BUY TICKETS ON THE WEB. FOR MORE INFORMATION, GO TO HTTP://L-TIKE.COM/NARUTO-TEN/
*IF YOU HAVE QUESTIONS ABOUT USING THE LOPPI KIOSK, CALL THE NUMBER ON THE KIOSK TO REACH THE LOPPI CUSTOMER SERVICE CENTER.
I THOUGHT YOU WERE GOING TO ATTACK, BUT YOU'RE JUST SHOWING THEM HOW TO USE THE LOPPI MACHINE?!
ALL RIGHT. I'VE DOUBLE-CHECKED THE TICKET INFO!
VWEEN
NOW ALL THAT'S LEFT IS TO TAKE THE RECEIPT PRINTED OUT FROM THIS LOPPI MACHINE, AND...
RUSTLE
!

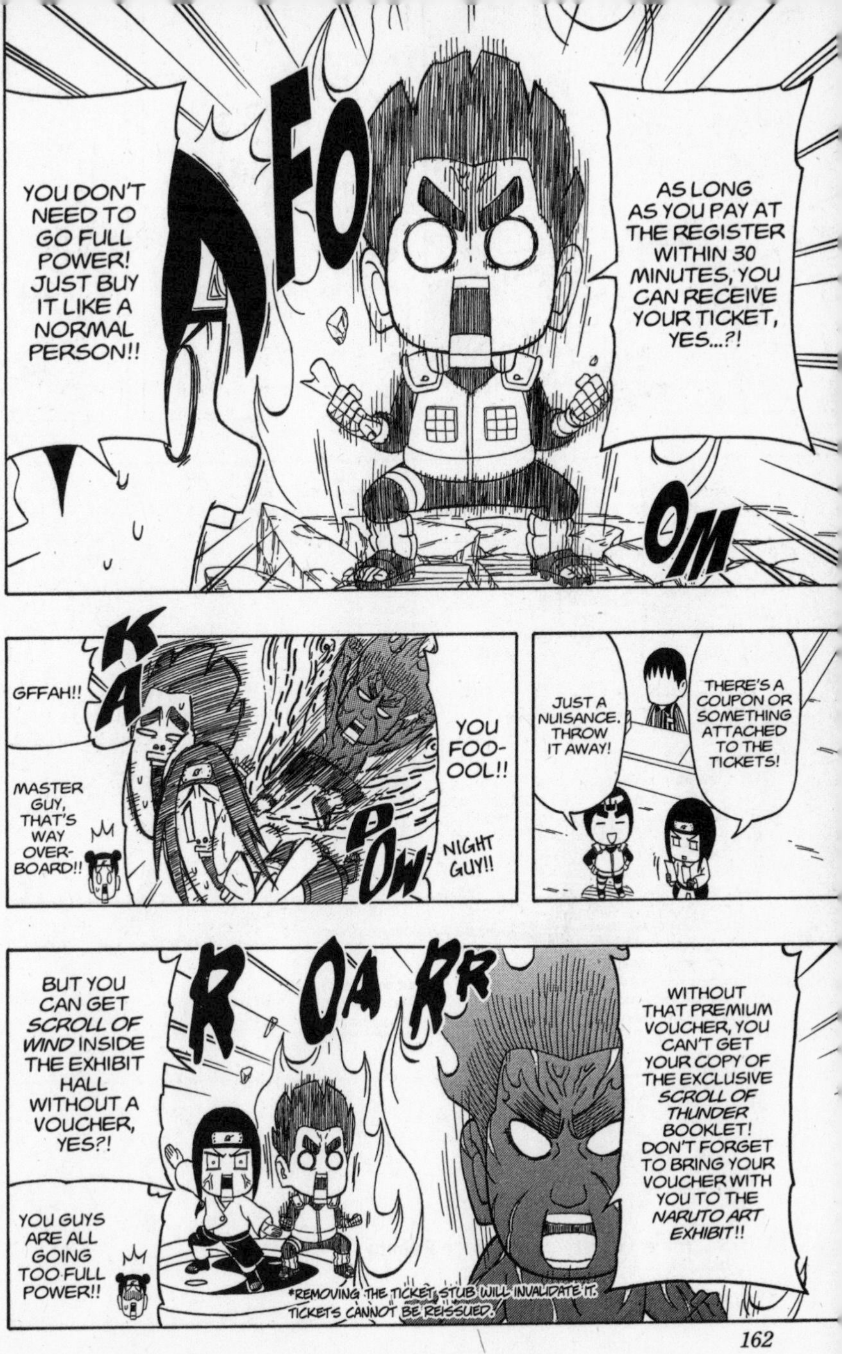
AS LONG AS YOU PAY AT THE REGISTER WITHIN 30 MINUTES, YOU CAN RECEIVE YOUR TICKET, YES...?!
FO
OM
YOU DON'T NEED TO GO FULL POWER! JUST BUY IT LIKE A NORMAL PERSON!!
THERE'S A COUPON OR SOMETHING ATTACHED TO THE TICKETS!
JUST A NUISANCE. THROW IT AWAY!
YOU FOO-OOL!!
NIGHT GUY!!
POW
KA
GFFAH!!
MASTER GUY, THAT'S WAY OVER-BOARD!!
WITHOUT THAT PREMIUM VOUCHER, YOU CAN'T GET YOUR COPY OF THE EXCLUSIVE *SCROLL OF THUNDER* BOOKLET! DON'T FORGET TO BRING YOUR VOUCHER WITH YOU TO THE *NARUTO ART EXHIBIT*!!
R OA RR
BUT YOU CAN GET *SCROLL OF WIND* INSIDE THE EXHIBIT HALL WITHOUT A VOUCHER, YES?!
YOU GUYS ARE ALL GOING TOO FULL POWER!!
*REMOVING THE TICKET STUB WILL INVALIDATE IT. TICKETS CANNOT BE REISSUED.

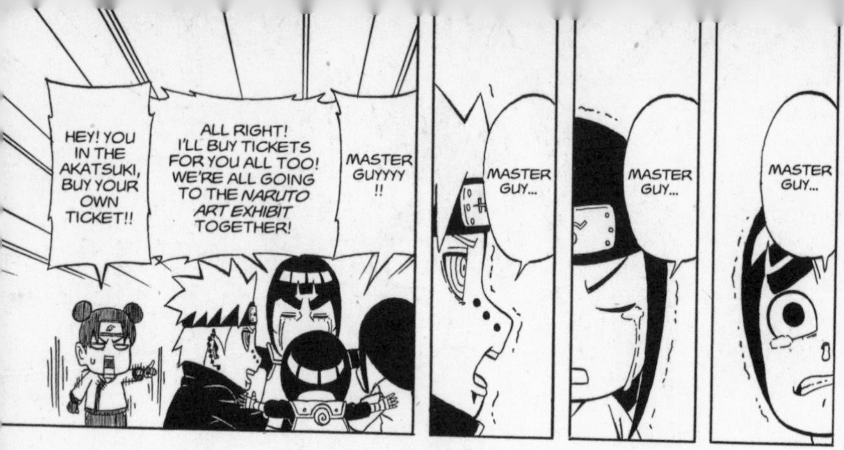

MASTER GUY...
MASTER GUY...
MASTER GUY...
MASTER GUYYYY !!
ALL RIGHT! I'LL BUY TICKETS FOR YOU ALL TOO! WE'RE ALL GOING TO THE *NARUTO ART EXHIBIT* TOGETHER!
HEY! YOU IN THE AKATSUKI, BUY YOUR OWN TICKET!!

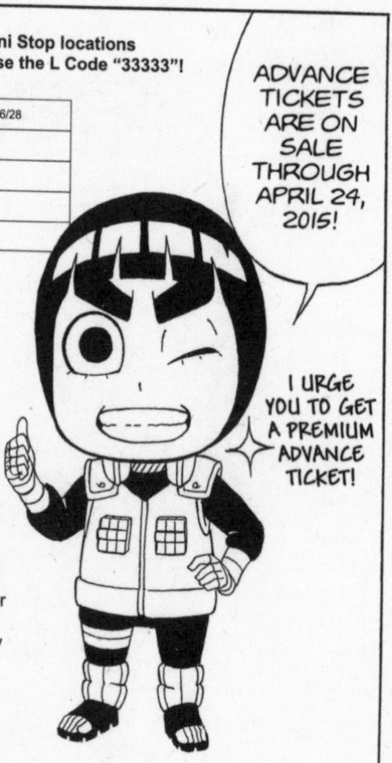

ADVANCE TICKETS ARE ON SALE THROUGH APRIL 24, 2015!
I URGE YOU TO GET A PREMIUM ADVANCE TICKET!

Tickets on sale at Loppi kiosks inside Lawson and Mini Stop locations nationwide, or on the web at http://l-tike.com/naruto-ten/! Use the L Code "33333"!

Sales Period for Tokyo	2/7 through 4/24		4/25 through 6/28
Ticket Type	Premium Advance Tickets	Regular Advance Tickets	At the door
Adults	¥1900	¥1800	¥2000
Middle/High Schoolers	¥1400	¥1300	¥1500
Children over 4	¥600	¥500	¥800

*Dates for the sales period of tickets for the Osaka location will be announced on the *Naruto Art Exhibit* website at a later date.

Caution:
*Taxes included in the price.
*This L Code applies only to the Tokyo location.
*Advance tickets sold only through Lawson Tickets.
*Please be advised that advance tickets are issued only at Loppi kiosks, and will not be delivered.
*At-the-door tickets are also available at the Mori Arts Center Gallery ticket counter.
*Premium booklet not for sale.
*Both the Tokyo and Osaka locations will offer the same premium booklet.
*Booklet design and contents subject to change.
*To receive your premium booklet, please present your voucher at the exhibit location during the duration of the Tokyo exhibit.
*Depending on crowding, there may be a wait time, or you may be unable to enter.

The *Naruto Art Exhibit* brings even Pain to tears!

See you at the super-deluxe exhibit!!

THE END

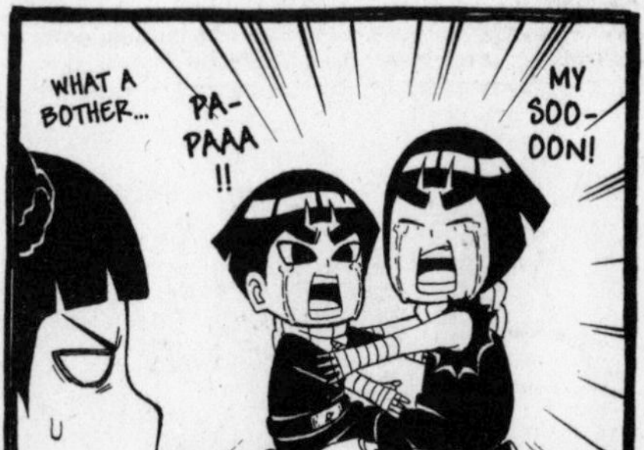
MY SOOO-OON!
PA-PAAA !!
WHAT A BOTHER...

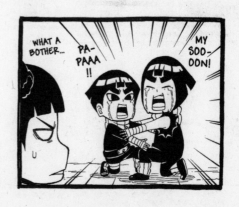

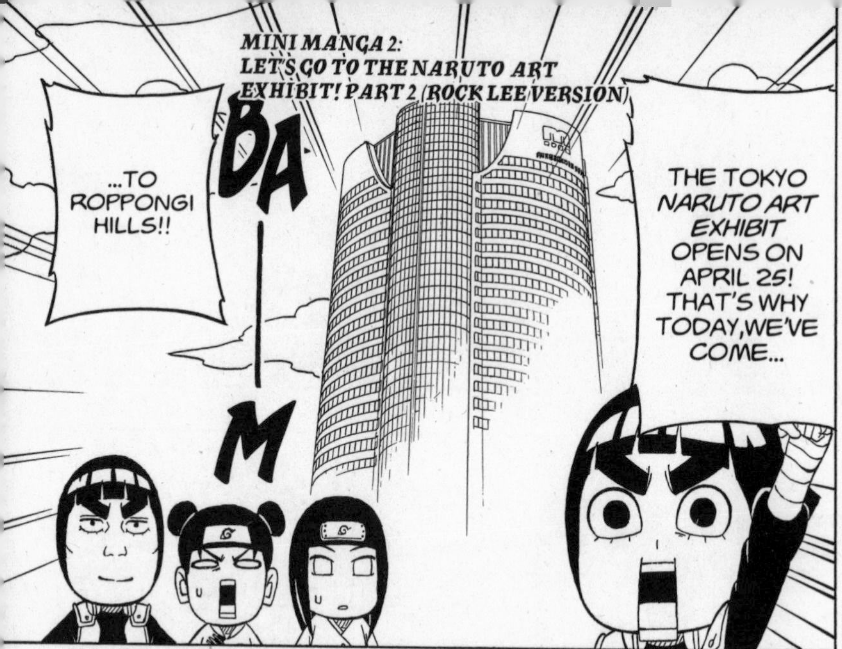
MINI MANGA 2: LET'S GO TO THE NARUTO ART EXHIBIT! PART 2 (ROCK LEE VERSION)
THE TOKYO NARUTO ART EXHIBIT OPENS ON APRIL 25! THAT'S WHY TODAY, WE'VE COME...
BA-M
...TO ROPPONGI HILLS!!

*THE NARUTO ART EXHIBIT TOKYO LOCATION IS OPEN FROM APRIL 25 THROUGH JUNE 28, 2015 IN THE MORI ARTS CENTER GALLERY (ROPPONGI HILLS MORI TOWER FLOOR 25).

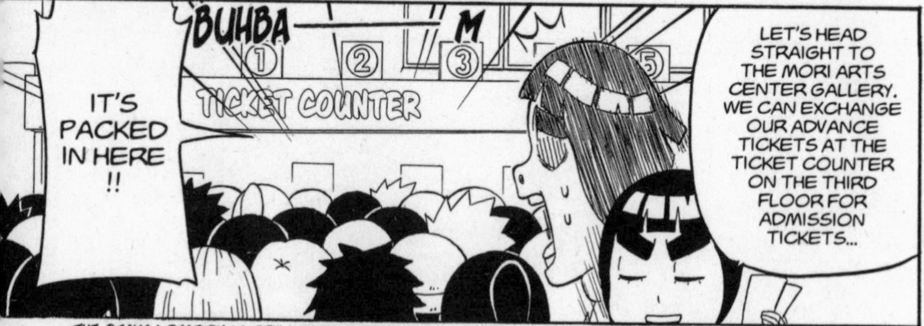
LET'S HEAD STRAIGHT TO THE MORI ARTS CENTER GALLERY. WE CAN EXCHANGE OUR ADVANCE TICKETS AT THE TICKET COUNTER ON THE THIRD FLOOR FOR ADMISSION TICKETS...
BUHBA-M
TICKET COUNTER
IT'S PACKED IN HERE!!

THE OSAKA LOCATION IS OPEN FROM JULY 18 THROUGH SEPTEMBER 27, 2015 AT THE OSAKA CULTURARIUM AT TEMPOZAN (NEXT TO THE OSAKA AQUARIUM).

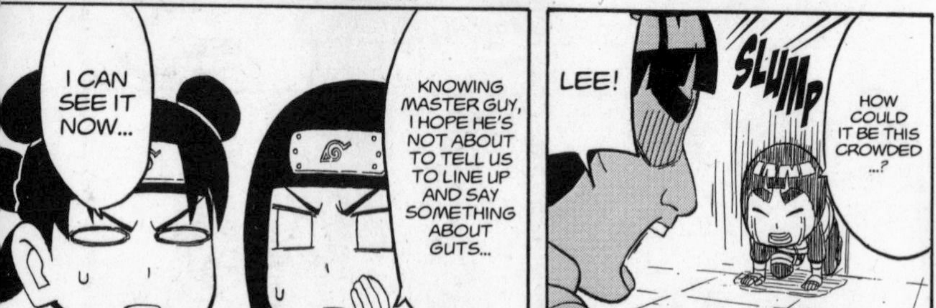
HOW COULD IT BE THIS CROWDED...?
SLUMP
LEE!
KNOWING MASTER GUY, I HOPE HE'S NOT ABOUT TO TELL US TO LINE UP AND SAY SOMETHING ABOUT GUTS...
I CAN SEE IT NOW...

*ADVANCE TICKETS FOR THE TOKYO LOCATION ON SALE THROUGH APRIL 24, 2015. FOR MORE INFORMATION, VISIT THE OFFICIAL WEBSITE.

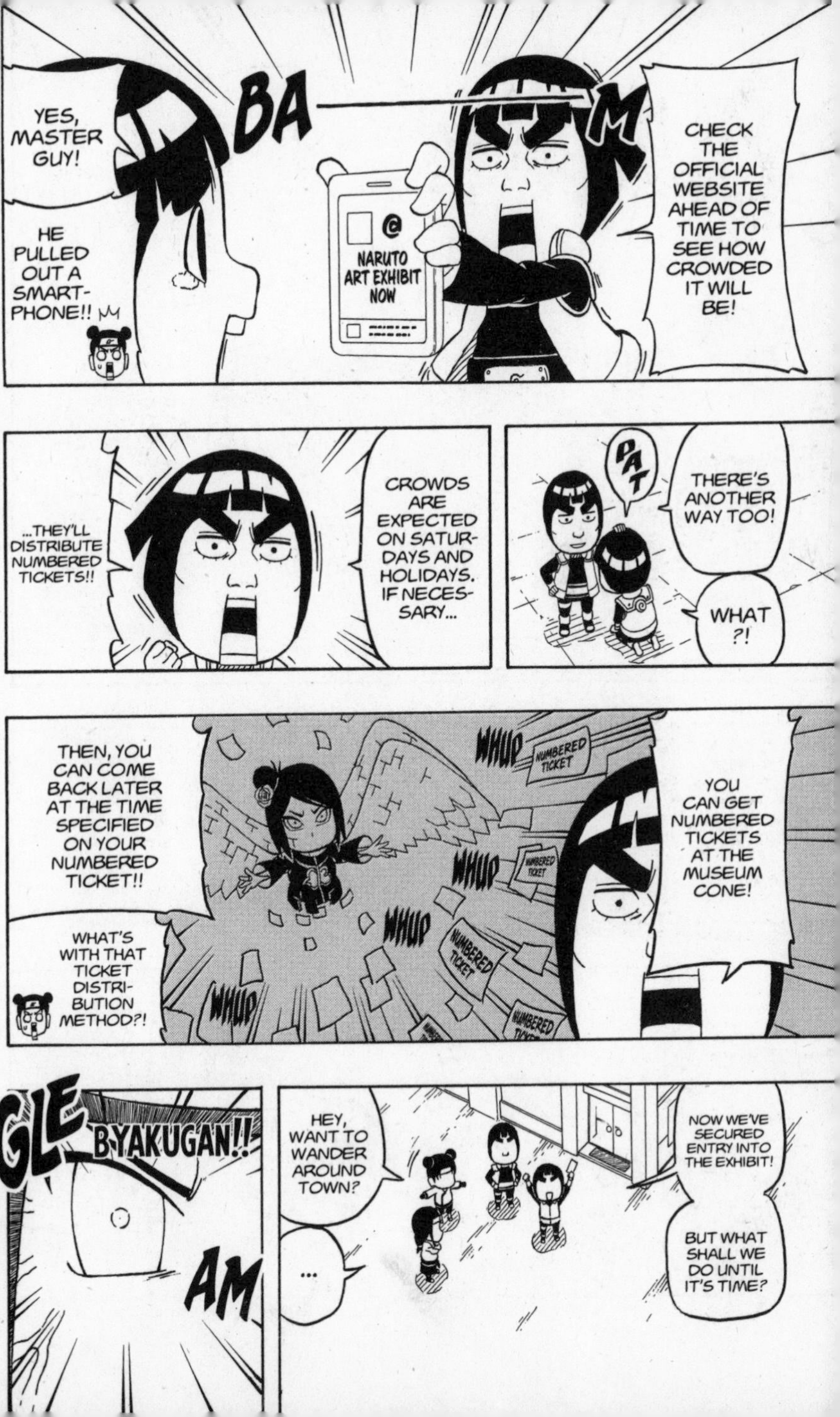
CHECK THE OFFICIAL WEBSITE AHEAD OF TIME TO SEE HOW CROWDED IT WILL BE!
BA—M
@
NARUTO ART EXHIBIT NOW
YES, MASTER GUY!
HE PULLED OUT A SMART-PHONE!!
DAT
THERE'S ANOTHER WAY TOO!
WHAT ?!
CROWDS ARE EXPECTED ON SATUR-DAYS AND HOLIDAYS. IF NECES-SARY...
...THEY'LL DISTRIBUTE NUMBERED TICKETS!!
YOU CAN GET NUMBERED TICKETS AT THE MUSEUM CONE!
WHUP
NUMBERED TICKET
WHUP
NUMBERED TICKET
WHUP
NUMBERED TICKET
WHUP
NUMBERED
THEN, YOU CAN COME BACK LATER AT THE TIME SPECIFIED ON YOUR NUMBERED TICKET!!
WHAT'S WITH THAT TICKET DISTRI-BUTION METHOD?!
NOW WE'VE SECURED ENTRY INTO THE EXHIBIT!
BUT WHAT SHALL WE DO UNTIL IT'S TIME?
HEY, WANT TO WANDER AROUND TOWN?
...
GLE
BYAKUGAN!!
AM

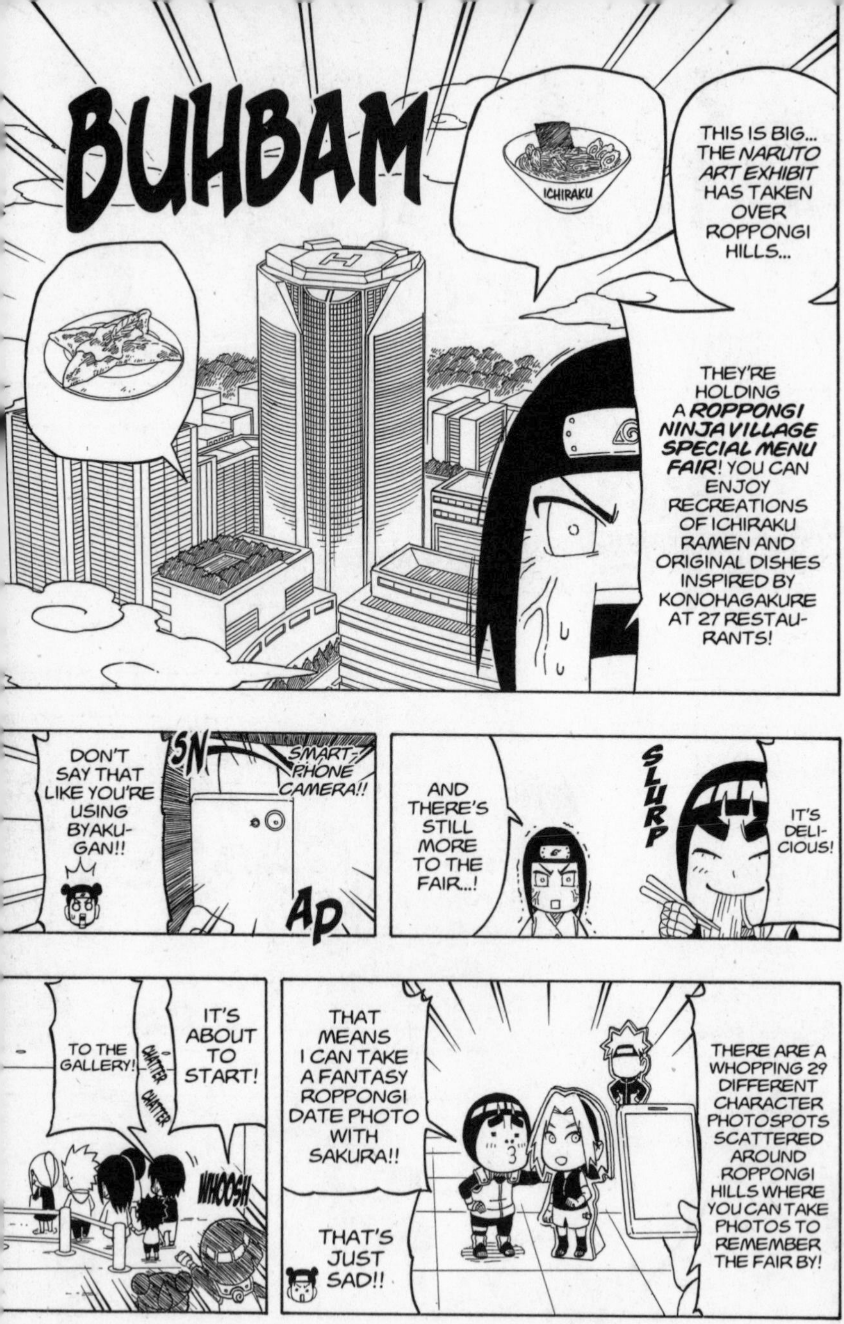

THIS IS BIG... THE NARUTO ART EXHIBIT HAS TAKEN OVER ROPPONGI HILLS...
ICHIRAKU
BUHBAM
THEY'RE HOLDING A ROPPONGI NINJA VILLAGE SPECIAL MENU FAIR! YOU CAN ENJOY RECREATIONS OF ICHIRAKU RAMEN AND ORIGINAL DISHES INSPIRED BY KONOHAGAKURE AT 27 RESTAU-RANTS!
IT'S DELI-CIOUS!
SLURP
AND THERE'S STILL MORE TO THE FAIR...!
SMART-PHONE CAMERA!!
SN
AP
DON'T SAY THAT LIKE YOU'RE USING BYAKU-GAN!!
THERE ARE A WHOPPING 29 DIFFERENT CHARACTER PHOTOSPOTS SCATTERED AROUND ROPPONGI HILLS WHERE YOU CAN TAKE PHOTOS TO REMEMBER THE FAIR BY!
THAT MEANS I CAN TAKE A FANTASY ROPPONGI DATE PHOTO WITH SAKURA!!
THAT'S JUST SAD!!
IT'S ABOUT TO START!
CHATTER CHATTER
TO THE GALLERY!
WHOOSH

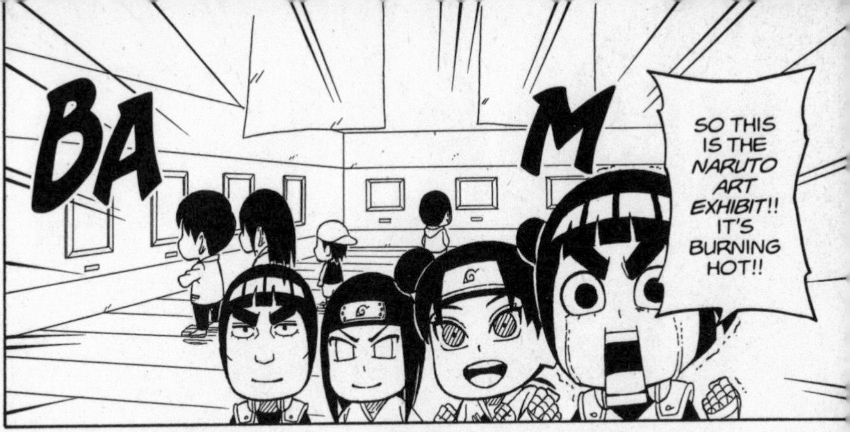

SO THIS IS THE NARUTO ART EXHIBIT!! IT'S BURNING HOT!!
BAM

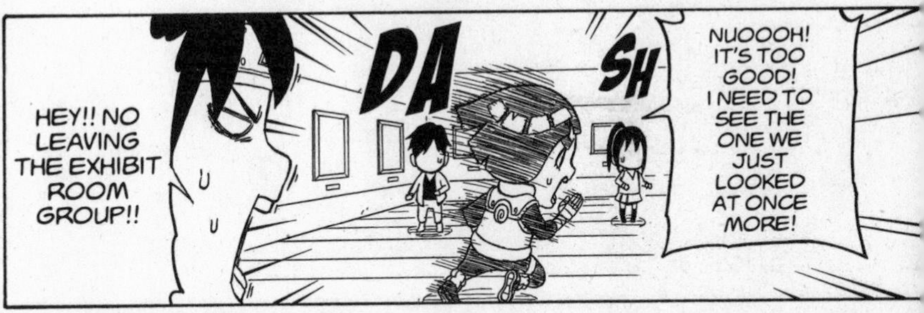

NUOOOH! IT'S TOO GOOD! I NEED TO SEE THE ONE WE JUST LOOKED AT ONCE MORE!
DASH
HEY!! NO LEAVING THE EXHIBIT ROOM GROUP!!

*PLEASE REMAIN ON THE TOUR ROUTE AT ALL TIMES.
*INSIDE THE EXHIBIT, PLEASE FOLLOW THE STAFF'S INSTRUCTIONS. FOR DETAILED GUIDELINES, SEE THE OFFICIAL EXHIBIT WEBSITE.

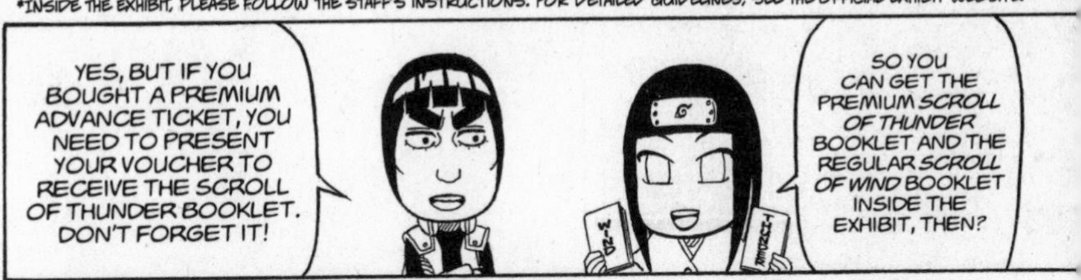

SO YOU CAN GET THE PREMIUM *SCROLL OF THUNDER* BOOKLET AND THE REGULAR *SCROLL OF WIND* BOOKLET INSIDE THE EXHIBIT, THEN?
WIND
YES, BUT IF YOU BOUGHT A PREMIUM ADVANCE TICKET, YOU NEED TO PRESENT YOUR VOUCHER TO RECEIVE THE SCROLL OF THUNDER BOOKLET. DON'T FORGET IT!

*SCROLL OF WIND BOOKLETS LIMITED TO ONE PER PERSON PER VISIT.
*TO GET YOUR PREMIUM SCROLL OF THUNDER BOOKLET, PLEASE EXCHANGE THE VOUCHER THAT COMES WITH THE PREMIUM ADVANCE TICKET FOR IT DURING YOUR VISIT TO THE EXHIBIT.

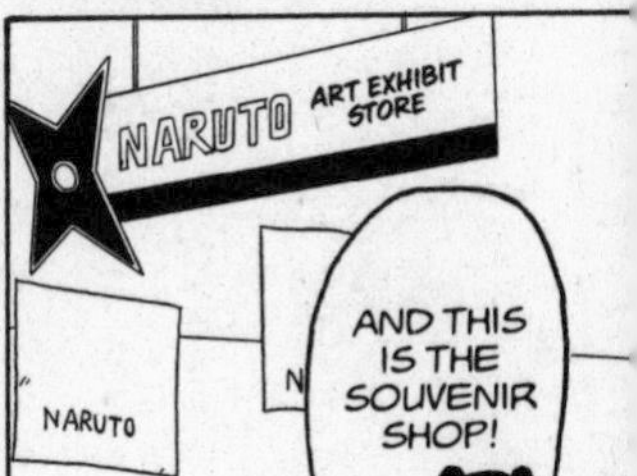

NARUTO ART EXHIBIT STORE
NARUTO
AND THIS IS THE SOUVENIR SHOP!

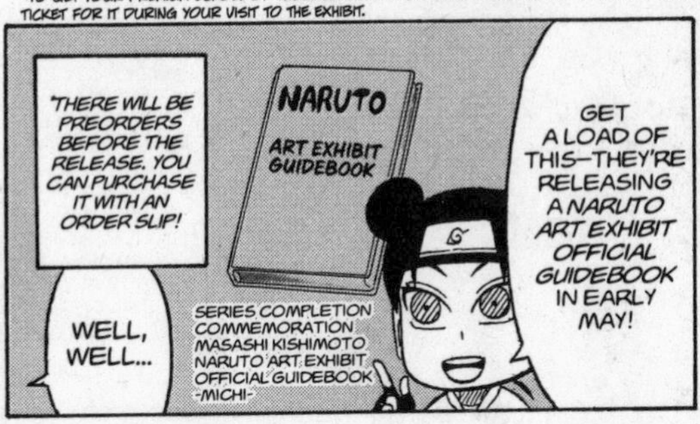

GET A LOAD OF THIS—THEY'RE RELEASING A *NARUTO ART EXHIBIT OFFICIAL GUIDEBOOK* IN EARLY MAY!
NARUTO
ART EXHIBIT GUIDEBOOK
THERE WILL BE PREORDERS BEFORE THE RELEASE. YOU CAN PURCHASE IT WITH AN ORDER SLIP!
SERIES COMPLETION COMMEMORATION MASASHI KISHIMOTO NARUTO ART EXHIBIT OFFICIAL GUIDEBOOK -MICHI-
WELL, WELL...

*FOR SALE ONLY AT THE EXHIBIT.
*PREORDERS SHIPPING WITHIN JAPAN ONLY.

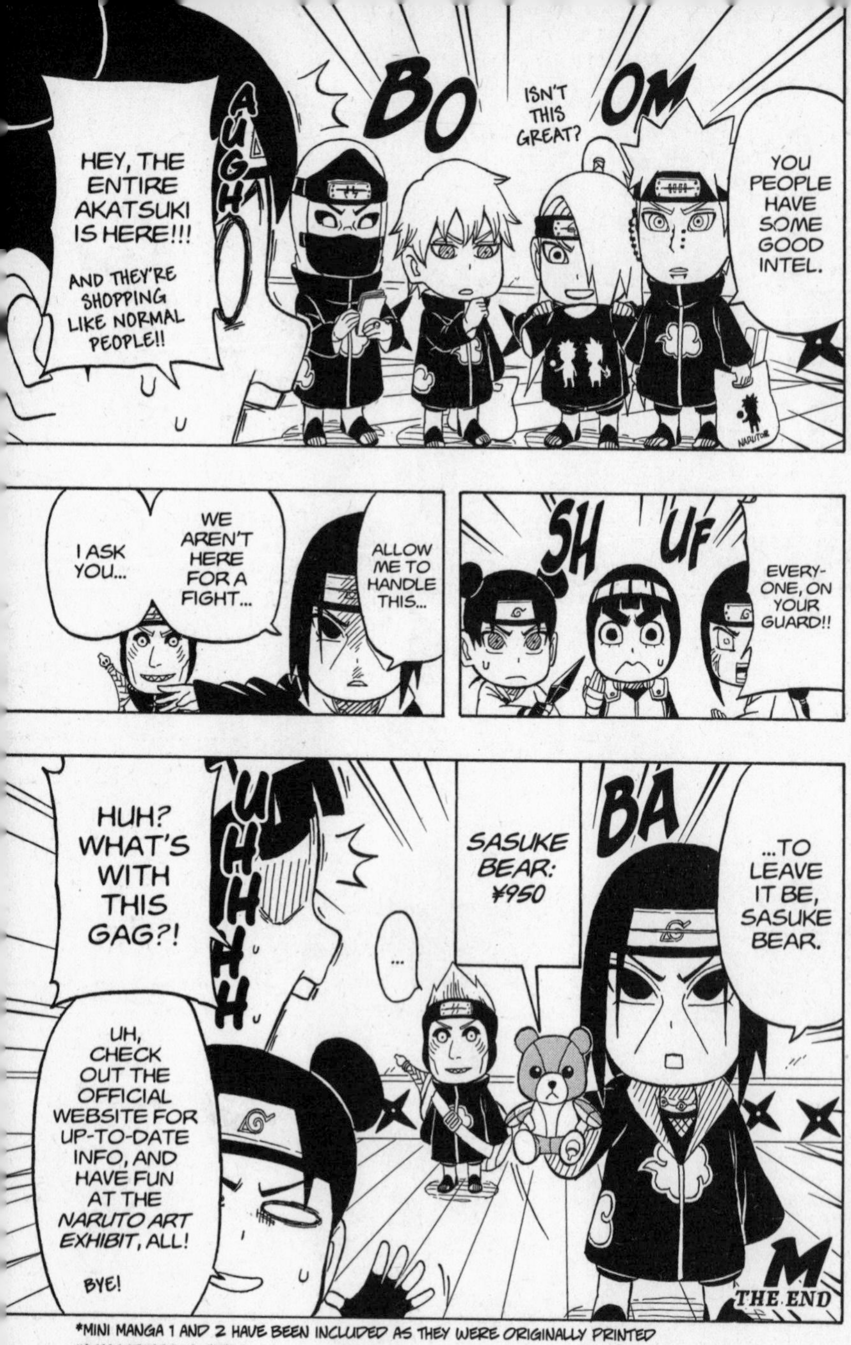
YOU PEOPLE HAVE SOME GOOD INTEL.
OM
ISN'T THIS GREAT?
BO
AUGH
HEY, THE ENTIRE AKATSUKI IS HERE!!!
AND THEY'RE SHOPPING LIKE NORMAL PEOPLE!!
EVERY-ONE, ON YOUR GUARD!!
SH
UF
ALLOW ME TO HANDLE THIS...
WE AREN'T HERE FOR A FIGHT...
I ASK YOU...
...TO LEAVE IT BE, SASUKE BEAR.
BA
SASUKE BEAR: ¥950
...
UHHHHHH
HUH? WHAT'S WITH THIS GAG?!
UH, CHECK OUT THE OFFICIAL WEBSITE FOR UP-TO-DATE INFO, AND HAVE FUN AT THE *NARUTO ART EXHIBIT*, ALL!
BYE!
M
THE END

*MINI MANGA 1 AND 2 HAVE BEEN INCLUDED AS THEY WERE ORIGINALLY PRINTED IN MAGAZINES IN JAPAN.

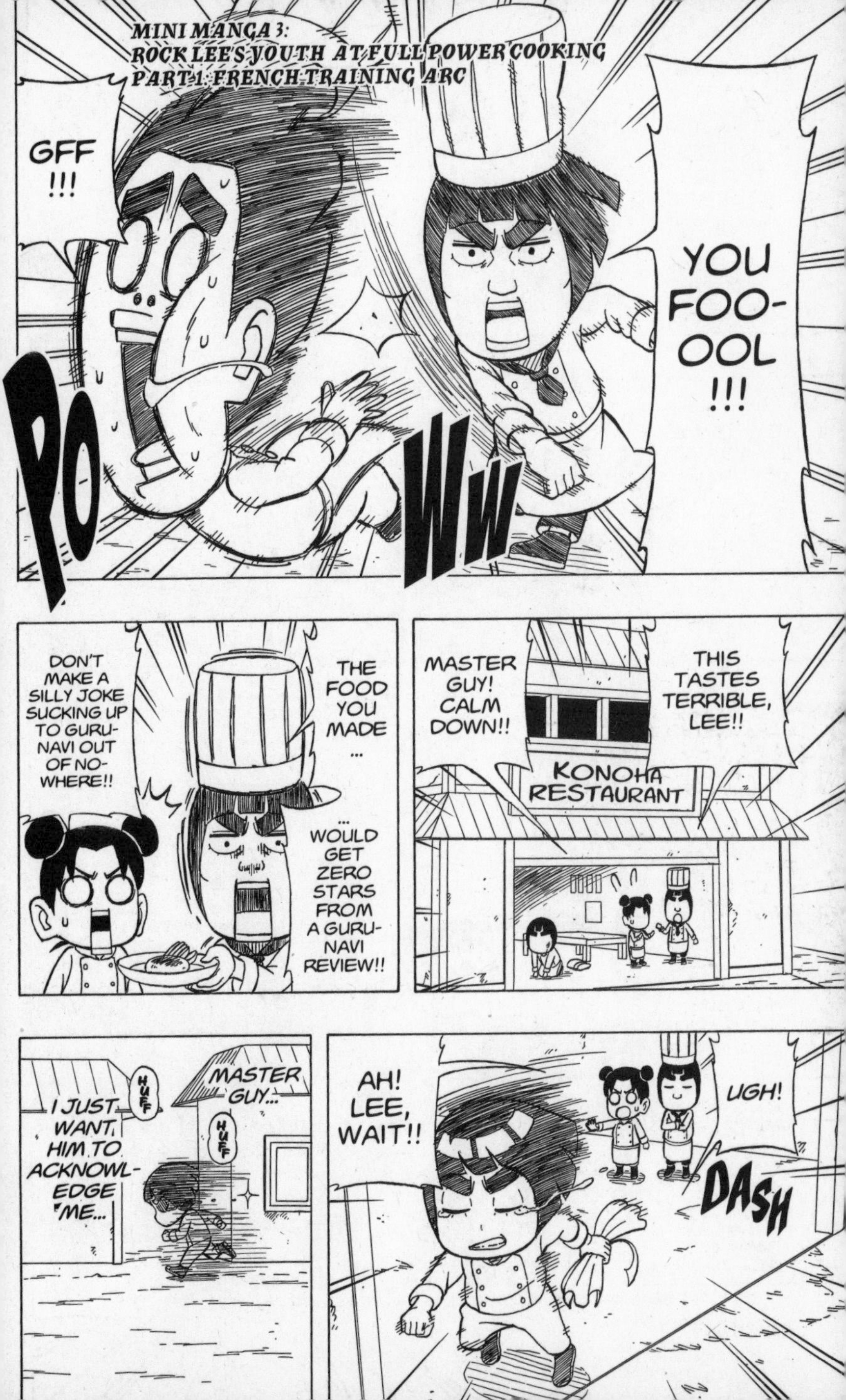
MINI MANGA 3:
ROCK LEE'S YOUTH AT FULL POWER COOKING
PART 1: FRENCH TRAINING ARC
YOU FOO-OOL!!!
POW
GFF!!!
THIS TASTES TERRIBLE, LEE!!
MASTER GUY! CALM DOWN!!
KONOHA RESTAURANT
THE FOOD YOU MADE...
...WOULD GET ZERO STARS FROM A GURU-NAVI REVIEW!!
DON'T MAKE A SILLY JOKE SUCKING UP TO GURU-NAVI OUT OF NO-WHERE!!
UGH!
AH! LEE, WAIT!!
DASH
MASTER GUY...
HUFF
HUFF
I JUST WANT HIM TO ACKNOWL-EDGE ME...

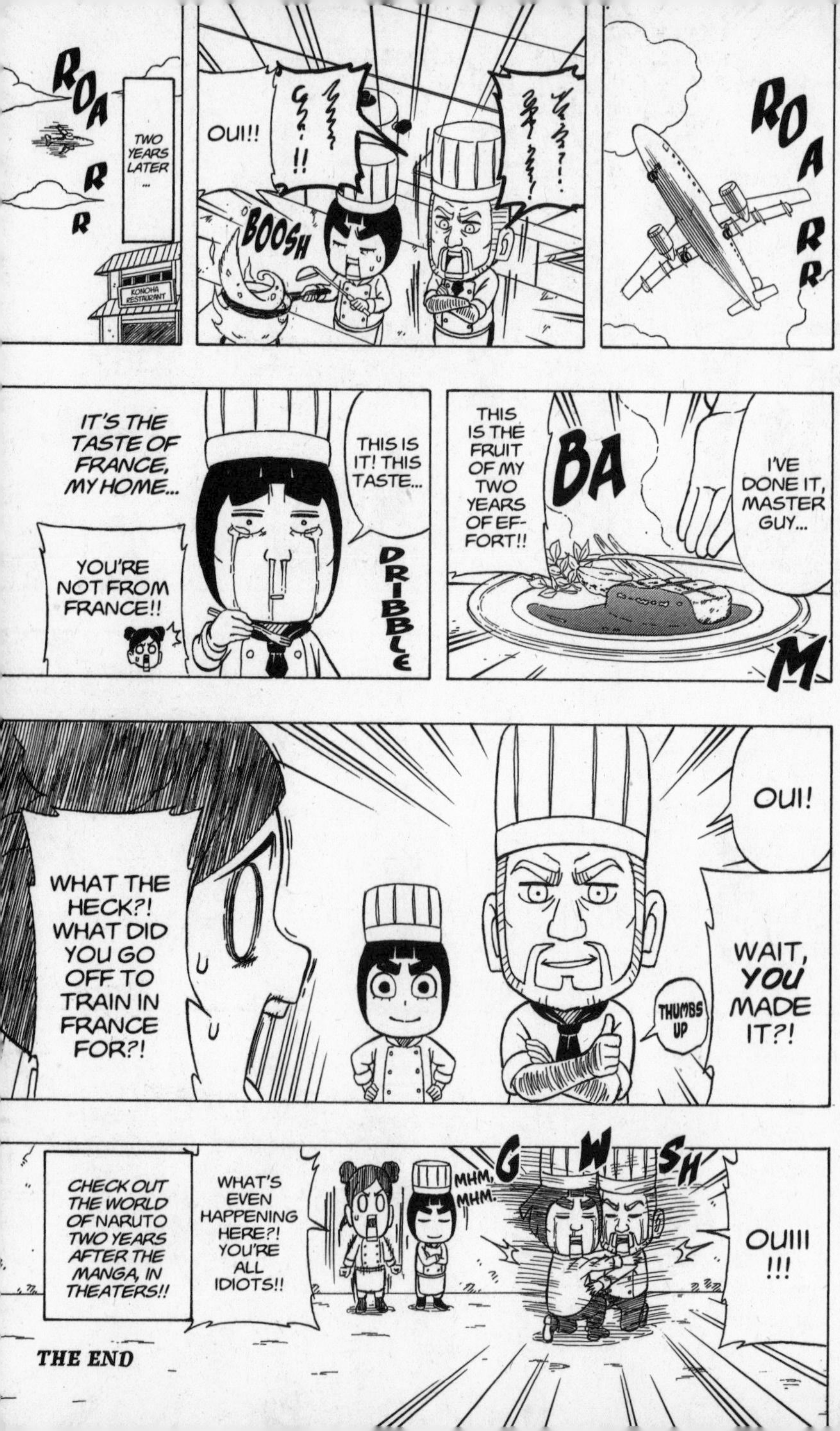
ROARR
OUI!!
BOOSH
TWO YEARS LATER ...
ROARR
KONOHA RESTAURANT
I'VE DONE IT, MASTER GUY...
THIS IS THE FRUIT OF MY TWO YEARS OF EFFORT!!
BAM
THIS IS IT! THIS TASTE...
DRIBBLE
IT'S THE TASTE OF FRANCE, MY HOME...
YOU'RE NOT FROM FRANCE!!
OUI!
WAIT, YOU MADE IT?!
THUMBS UP
WHAT THE HECK?! WHAT DID YOU GO OFF TO TRAIN IN FRANCE FOR?!
OUIII !!!
GWSH
MHM, MHM.
WHAT'S EVEN HAPPENING HERE?! YOU'RE ALL IDIOTS!!
CHECK OUT THE WORLD OF NARUTO TWO YEARS AFTER THE MANGA, IN THEATERS!!
THE END

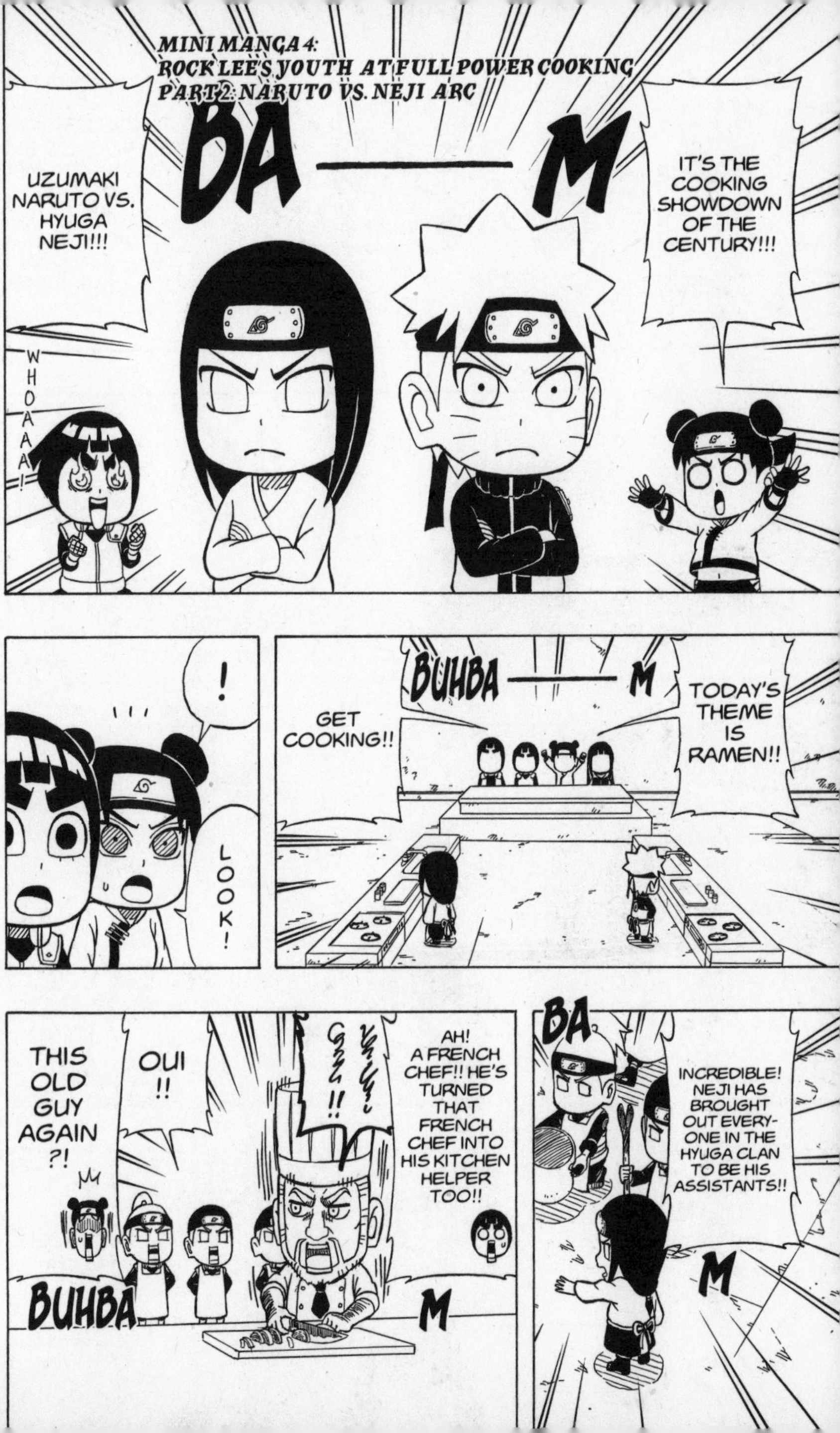
MINI MANGA 4:
ROCK LEE'S YOUTH AT FULL POWER COOKING
PART 2: NARUTO VS. NEJI ARC
BA——M
IT'S THE COOKING SHOWDOWN OF THE CENTURY!!!
UZUMAKI NARUTO VS. HYUGA NEJI!!!
WHOAAAA!
BUHBA——M
TODAY'S THEME IS RAMEN!!
GET COOKING!!
!
LOOK!
BA
INCREDIBLE! NEJI HAS BROUGHT OUT EVERY-ONE IN THE HYUGA CLAN TO BE HIS ASSISTANTS!!
M
AH! A FRENCH CHEF!! HE'S TURNED THAT FRENCH CHEF INTO HIS KITCHEN HELPER TOO!!
OUI !!
THIS OLD GUY AGAIN ?!
BUHBA
M

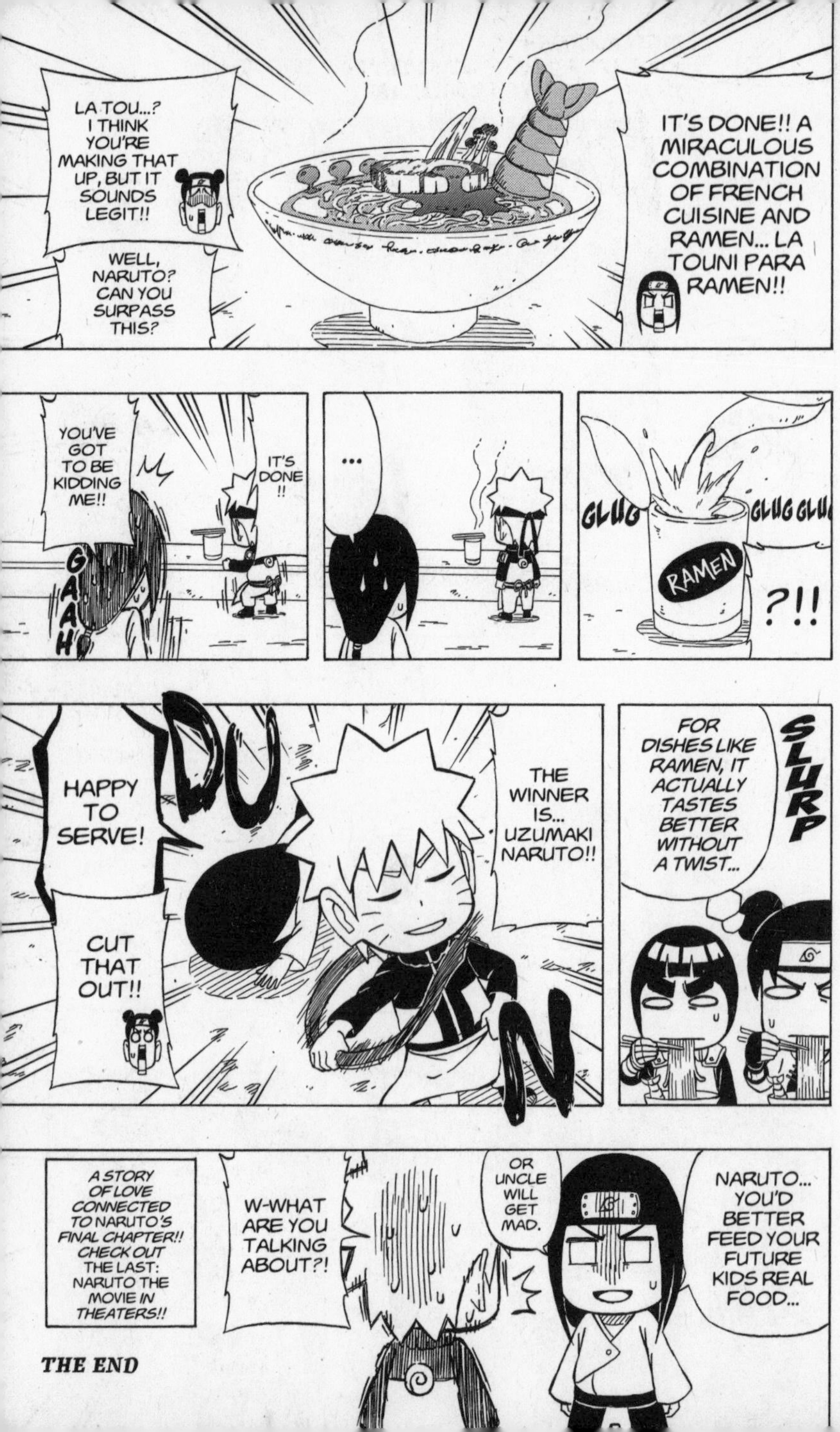
IT'S DONE!! A MIRACULOUS COMBINATION OF FRENCH CUISINE AND RAMEN... LA TOUNI PARA RAMEN!!
LA TOU...? I THINK YOU'RE MAKING THAT UP, BUT IT SOUNDS LEGIT!!
WELL, NARUTO? CAN YOU SURPASS THIS?
GLUG
GLUG GLUG
RAMEN
?!!
...
IT'S DONE!!
YOU'VE GOT TO BE KIDDING ME!!
GAAAH
SLURP
FOR DISHES LIKE RAMEN, IT ACTUALLY TASTES BETTER WITHOUT A TWIST...
THE WINNER IS... UZUMAKI NARUTO!!
DUN
HAPPY TO SERVE!
CUT THAT OUT!!
NARUTO... YOU'D BETTER FEED YOUR FUTURE KIDS REAL FOOD...
OR UNCLE WILL GET MAD.
W-WHAT ARE YOU TALKING ABOUT?!
A STORY OF LOVE CONNECTED TO NARUTO'S FINAL CHAPTER!! CHECK OUT THE LAST: NARUTO THE MOVIE IN THEATERS!!
THE END

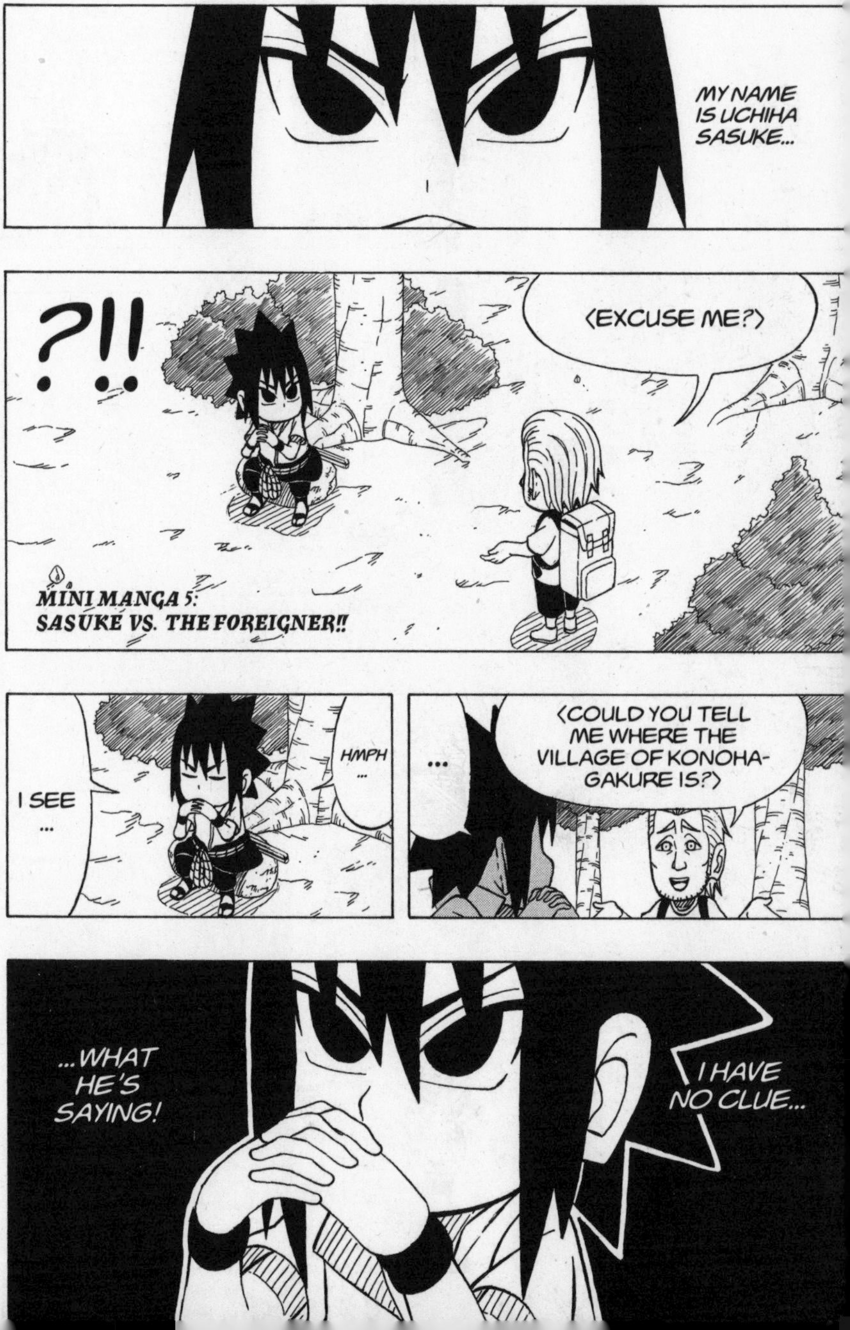
MY NAME IS UCHIHA SASUKE...
⟨EXCUSE ME?⟩
?!!
MINI MANGA 5: SASUKE VS. THE FOREIGNER!!
⟨COULD YOU TELL ME WHERE THE VILLAGE OF KONOHA-GAKURE IS?⟩
...
HMPH ...
I SEE ...
I HAVE NO CLUE...
...WHAT HE'S SAYING!

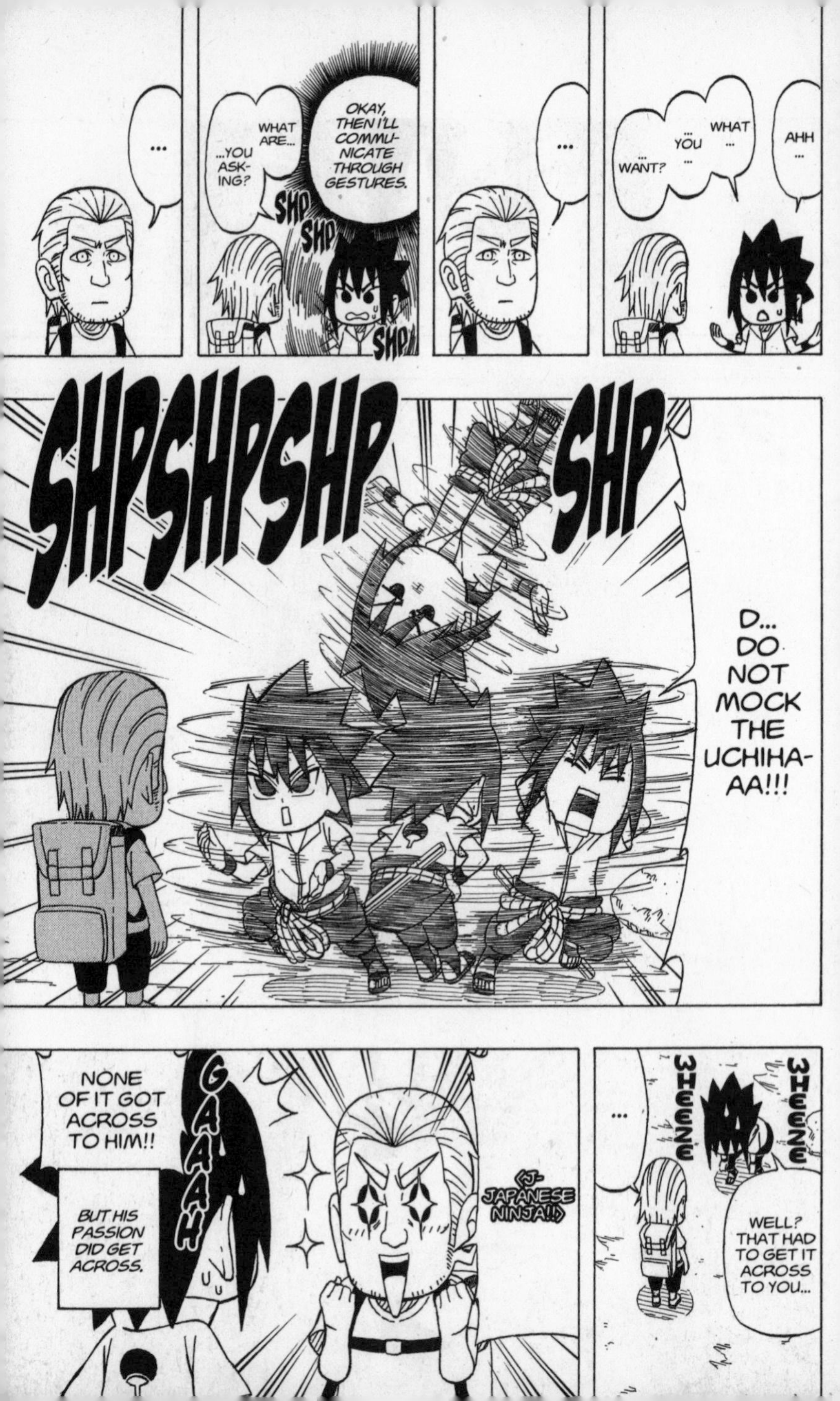
AHH ...
WHAT ... ... YOU ... ... WANT?
...
OKAY, THEN I'LL COMMUNICATE THROUGH GESTURES.
WHAT ARE... ...YOU ASKING?
SHP SHP SHP
...
D... DO NOT MOCK THE UCHIHA-AA!!!
SHP
SHPSHPSHP
WHEEZE WHEEZE
...
WELL? THAT HAD TO GET IT ACROSS TO YOU...
⟨J-JAPANESE NINJA!!⟩
GAAAAH
NONE OF IT GOT ACROSS TO HIM!!
BUT HIS PASSION DID GET ACROSS.

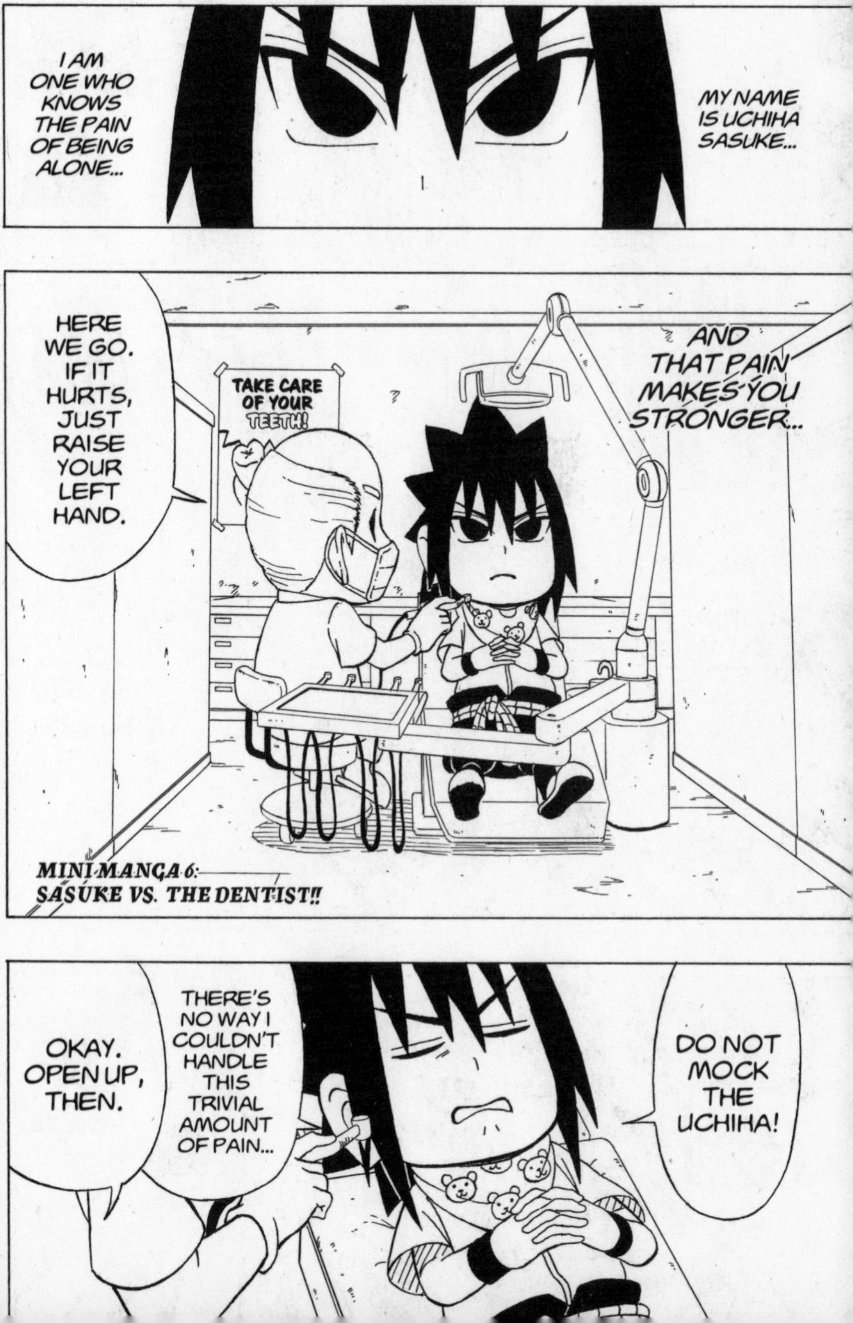
MY NAME IS UCHIHA SASUKE...
I AM ONE WHO KNOWS THE PAIN OF BEING ALONE...
AND THAT PAIN MAKES YOU STRONGER...
TAKE CARE OF YOUR TEETH!
HERE WE GO. IF IT HURTS, JUST RAISE YOUR LEFT HAND.
MINI MANGA 6: SASUKE VS. THE DENTIST!!
DO NOT MOCK THE UCHIHA!
THERE'S NO WAY I COULDN'T HANDLE THIS TRIVIAL AMOUNT OF PAIN...
OKAY. OPEN UP, THEN.

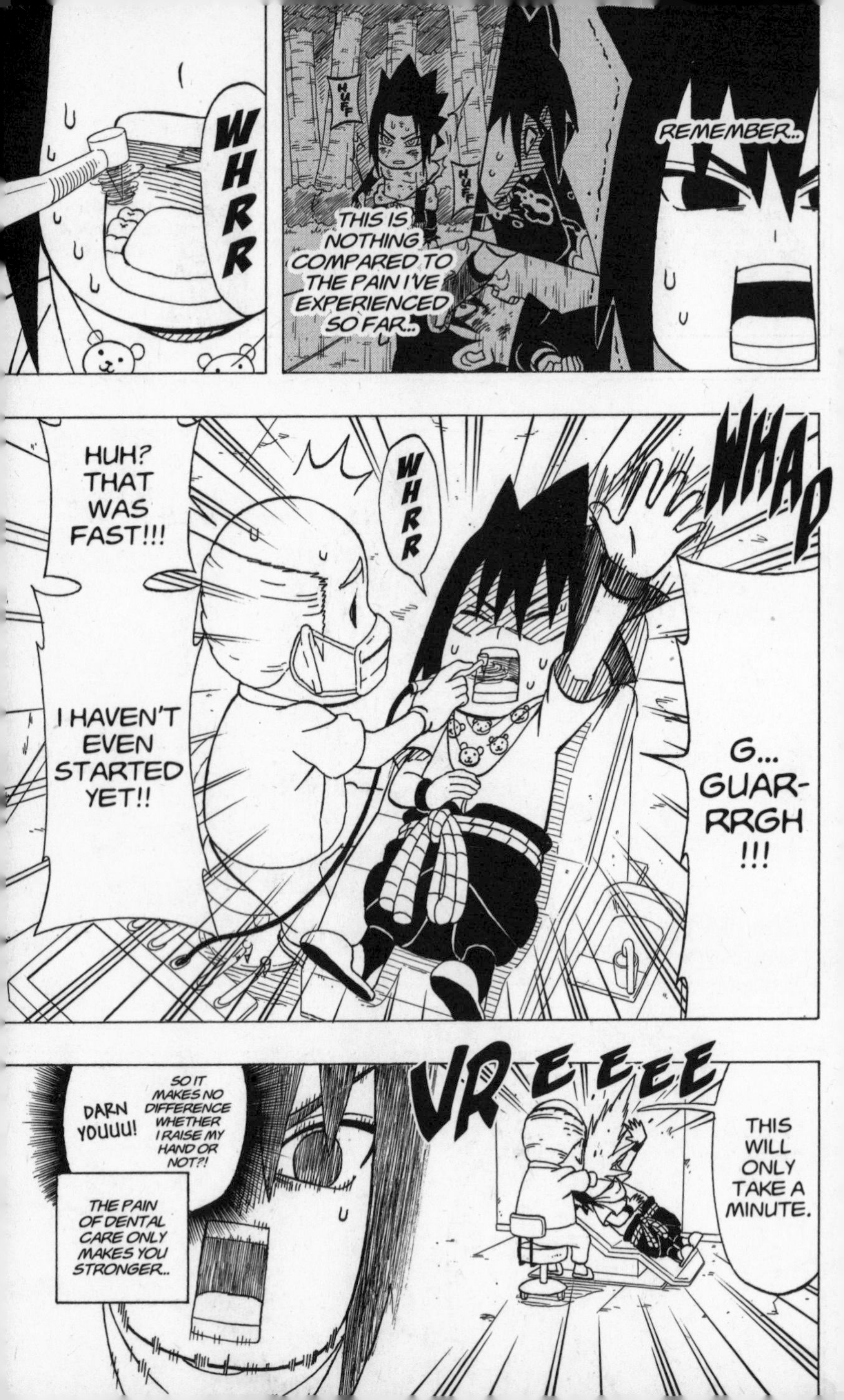
REMEMBER...
HUFF
HUFF
THIS IS NOTHING COMPARED TO THE PAIN I'VE EXPERIENCED SO FAR...
WHRR
WHAP
G... GUAR-RRGH!!!
WHRR
HUH? THAT WAS FAST!!!
I HAVEN'T EVEN STARTED YET!!
VREEEE
THIS WILL ONLY TAKE A MINUTE.
SO IT MAKES NO DIFFERENCE WHETHER I RAISE MY HAND OR NOT?!
DARN YOUUU!
THE PAIN OF DENTAL CARE ONLY MAKES YOU STRONGER...

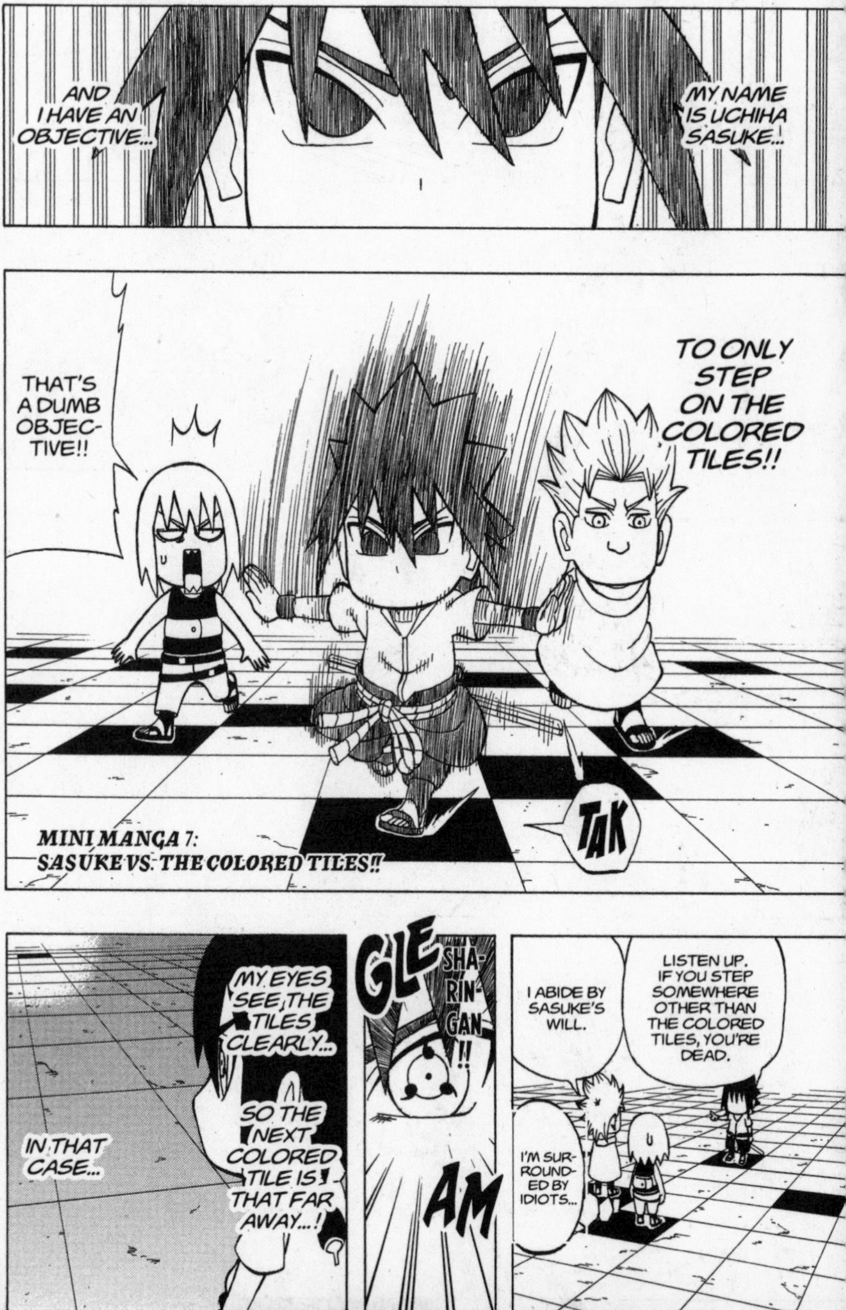
MY NAME IS UCHIHA SASUKE...
AND I HAVE AN OBJECTIVE...
TO ONLY STEP ON THE COLORED TILES!!
TAK
THAT'S A DUMB OBJECTIVE!!
MINI MANGA 7: SASUKE VS. THE COLORED TILES!!
LISTEN UP. IF YOU STEP SOMEWHERE OTHER THAN THE COLORED TILES, YOU'RE DEAD.
I ABIDE BY SASUKE'S WILL.
I'M SURROUNDED BY IDIOTS...
GLE
SHARINGAN!!
AM
MY EYES SEE THE TILES CLEARLY...
SO THE NEXT COLORED TILE IS THAT FAR AWAY...!
IN THAT CASE...

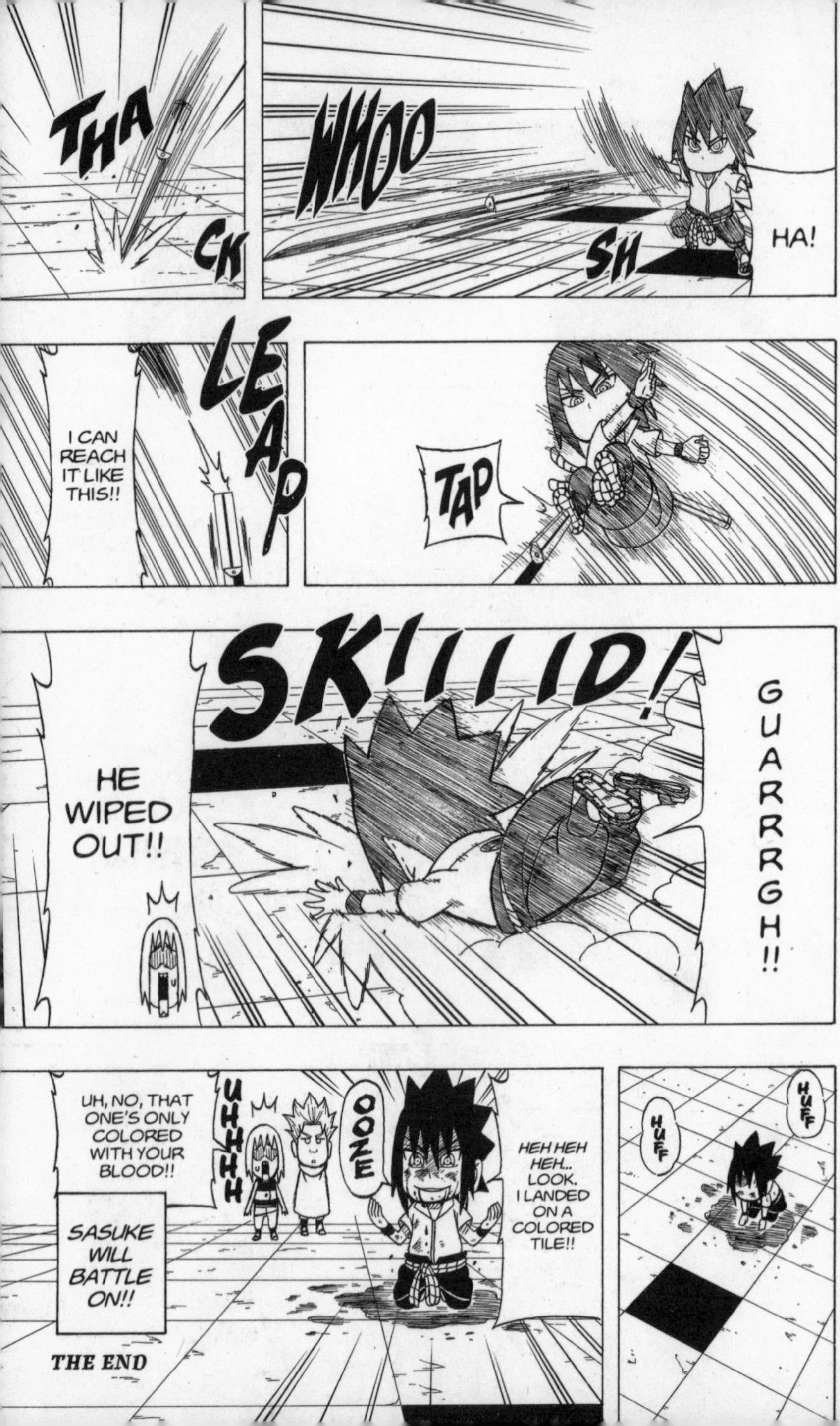
WHOO
HA!
SH
THA
CK
TAP
LEAP
I CAN REACH IT LIKE THIS!!
SKIIID!
GUARRRGH!!
HE WIPED OUT!!
HUFF
HUFF
HEH HEH HEH... LOOK. I LANDED ON A COLORED TILE!!
OOZE
UHHHH
UH, NO, THAT ONE'S ONLY COLORED WITH YOUR BLOOD!!
SASUKE WILL BATTLE ON!!
THE END

BONUS MANGA: MARADA VS. THE LINE!!

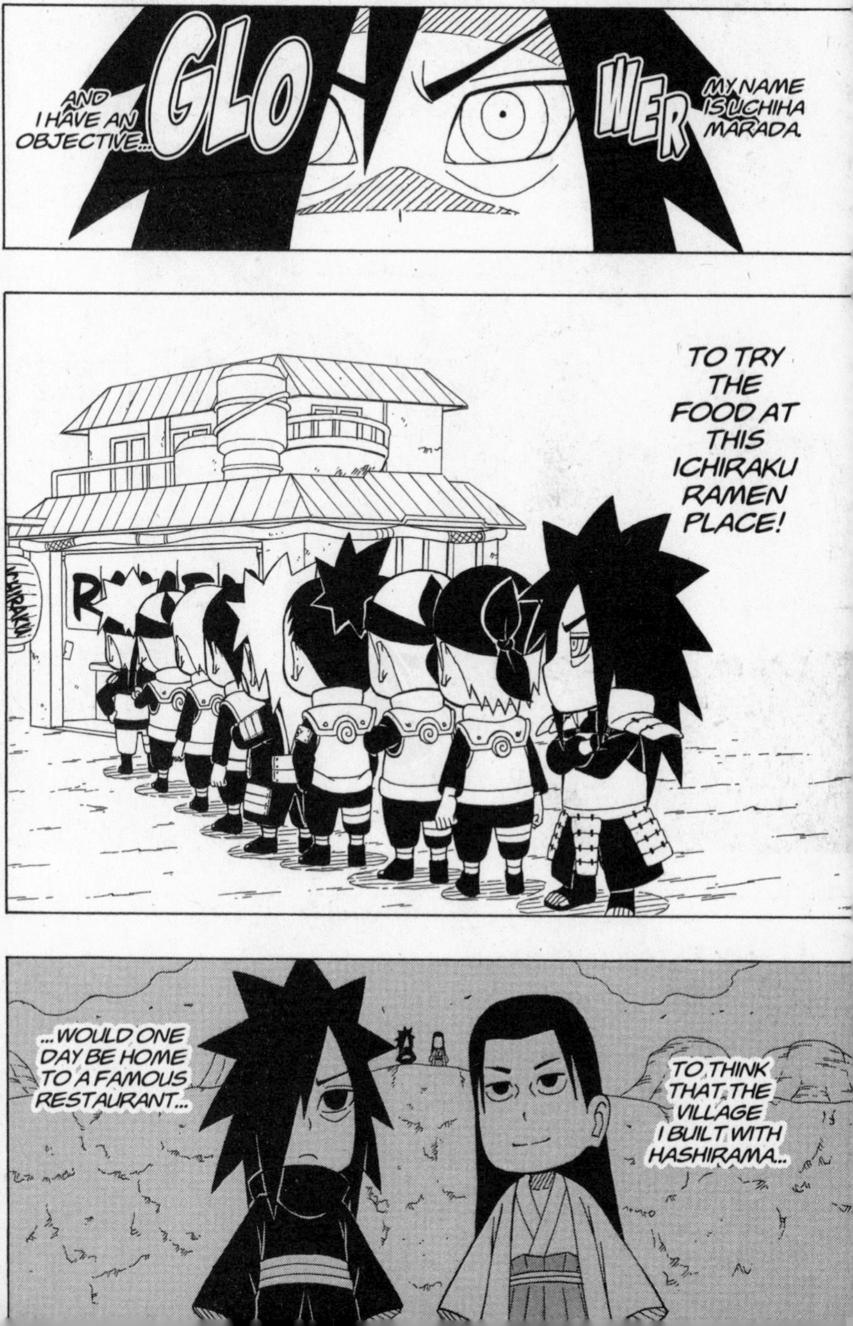
MY NAME IS UCHIHA MARADA.
GLO WER
AND I HAVE AN OBJECTIVE...
TO TRY THE FOOD AT THIS ICHIRAKU RAMEN PLACE!
ICHIRAKU
TO THINK THAT THE VILLAGE I BUILT WITH HASHIRAMA...
...WOULD ONE DAY BE HOME TO A FAMOUS RESTAURANT...

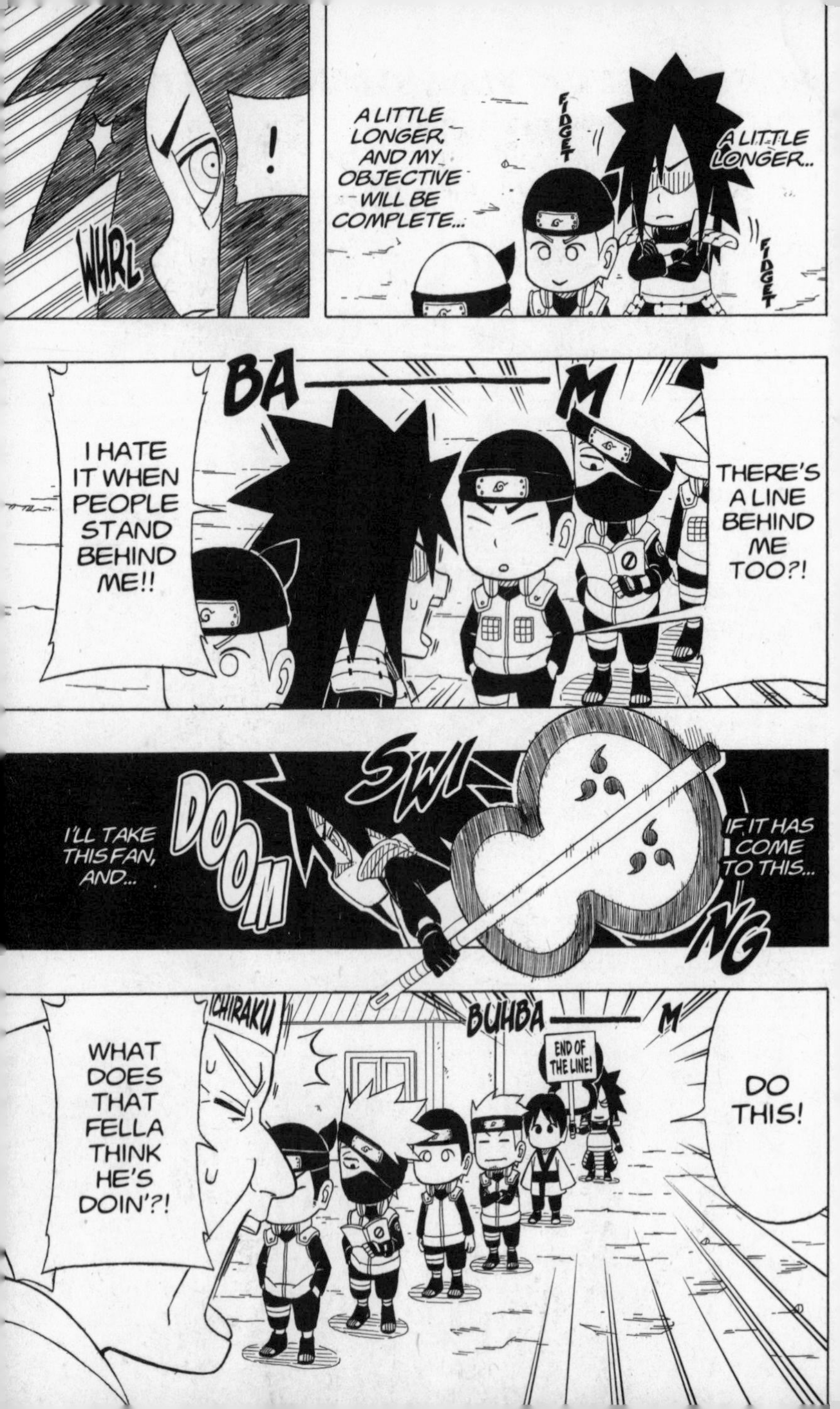

A LITTLE LONGER...
FIDGET
A LITTLE LONGER, AND MY OBJECTIVE WILL BE COMPLETE...
FIDGET
!
WHRL
BA———M
THERE'S A LINE BEHIND ME TOO?!
I HATE IT WHEN PEOPLE STAND BEHIND ME!!
IF IT HAS COME TO THIS...
SWI
NG
DOOM
I'LL TAKE THIS FAN, AND...
DO THIS!
BUHBA———M
END OF THE LINE!
ICHIRAKU
WHAT DOES THAT FELLA THINK HE'S DOIN'?!

BONUS MANGA: GROWN-UP SASUKE VS. THE GAP!!

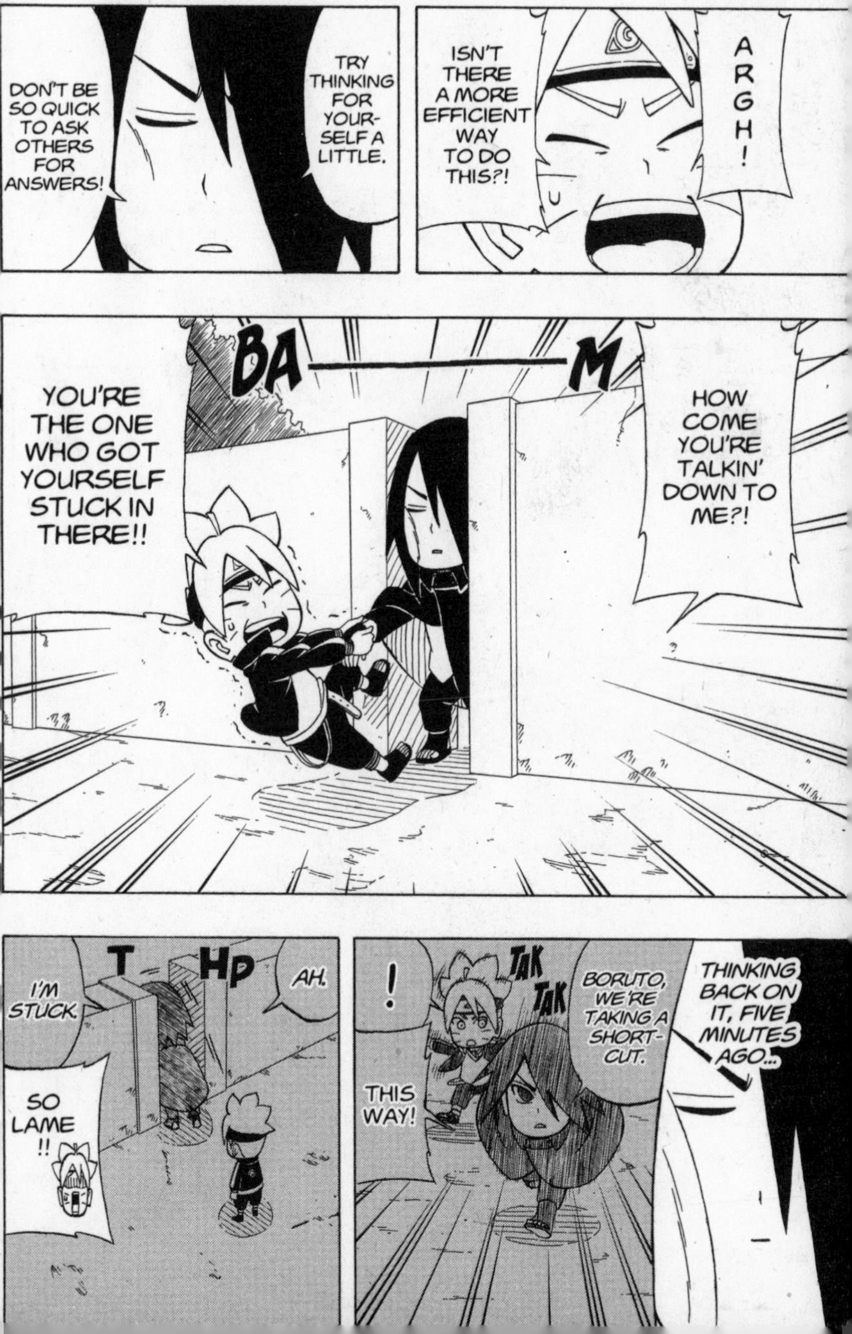
ARGH!
ISN'T THERE A MORE EFFICIENT WAY TO DO THIS?!
TRY THINKING FOR YOURSELF A LITTLE.
DON'T BE SO QUICK TO ASK OTHERS FOR ANSWERS!
BA———M
HOW COME YOU'RE TALKIN' DOWN TO ME?!
YOU'RE THE ONE WHO GOT YOURSELF STUCK IN THERE!!
THINKING BACK ON IT, FIVE MINUTES AGO...
BORUTO, WE'RE TAKING A SHORTCUT.
TAK TAK
!
THIS WAY!
AH.
T HP
I'M STUCK.
SO LAME!!

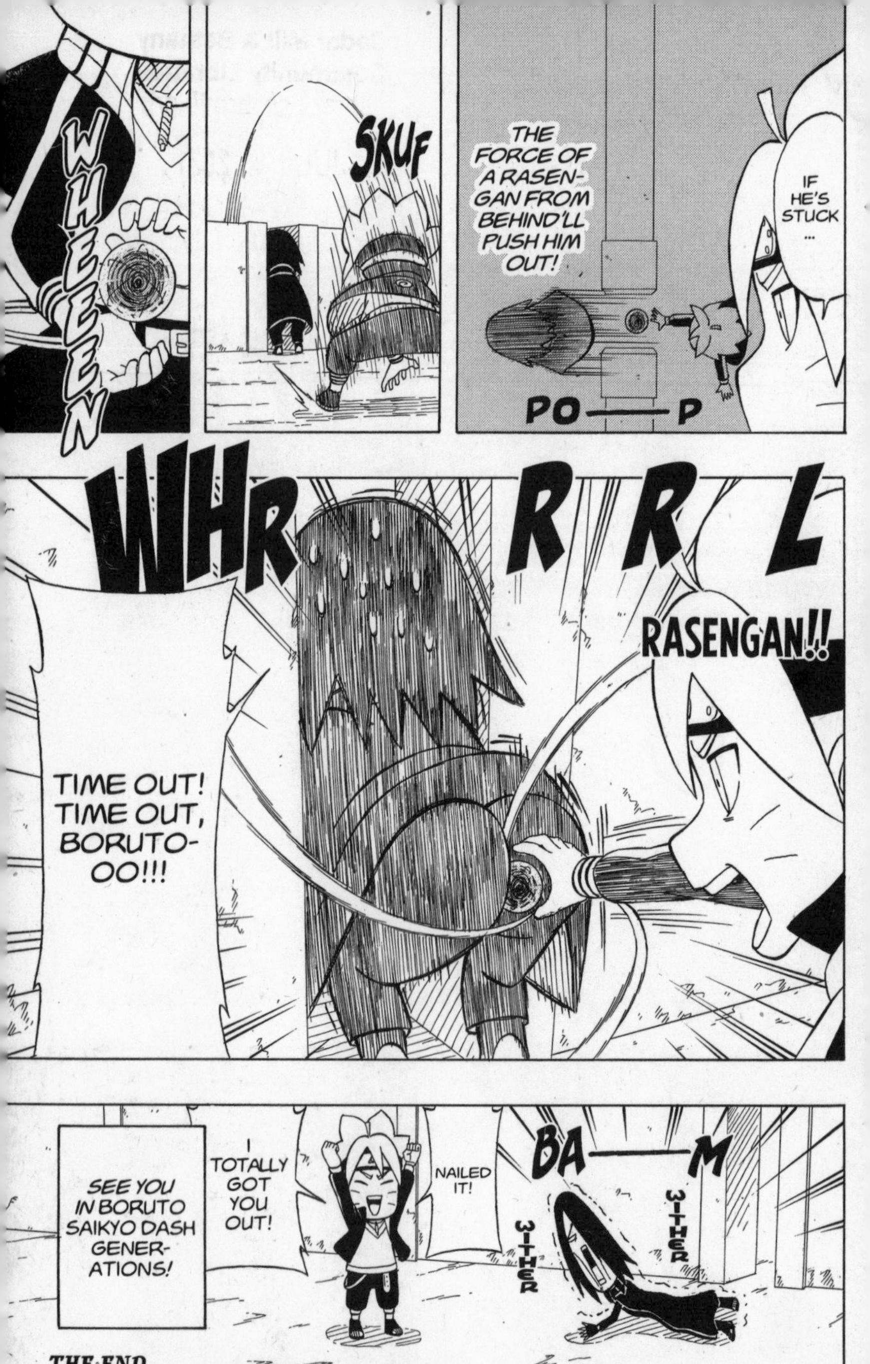
IF HE'S STUCK ...
THE FORCE OF A RASEN-GAN FROM BEHIND'LL PUSH HIM OUT!
PO——P
SKUF
WHEEEEN
WHR R R L
RASENGAN!!
TIME OUT! TIME OUT, BORUTO-OO!!!
BA——M
WITHER
WITHER
NAILED IT!
I TOTALLY GOT YOU OUT!
SEE YOU IN BORUTO SAIKYO DASH GENER-ATIONS!

THE END

You're Reading the WRONG WAY!

NARUTO: CHIBI SASUKE'S SHARINGAN LEGEND reads from right to left, starting in the upper-right corner. Japanese is read from right to left, meaning that action, sound effects and word-balloon order are completely reversed from English order.

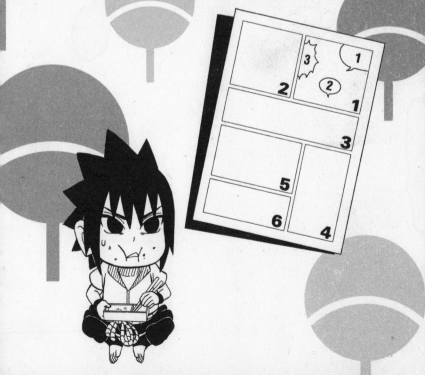